A Frenchman in Search of Franklin

Emile Frédéric de Bray, after his return from the Arctic;
he is wearing the medal of a Chevalier de la Légion d'honneur
and the Arctic Medal

Emile Frédéric de Bray

A Frenchman in Search of Franklin

De Bray's Arctic Journal,
1852–1854

Translated and edited by

WILLIAM BARR

University of Toronto Press
Toronto Buffalo London

© University of Toronto Press Incorporated 1992
Toronto Buffalo London
Printed in Canada
ISBN 0-8020-2813-6

Printed on acid-free paper

Canadian Cataloguing in Publication Data

Bray, Émile-Frédéric de, 1829–1879
A Frenchman in search of Franklin

Includes bibliographical references and index.
ISBN 0-8020-2813-6

1. Bray, Émile-Frédéric de, 1829–1879 – Journeys – Arctic regions.
2. Franklin, John, Sir, 1786–1847.
3. Arctic regions – Discovery and exploration – British.
4. Northwest passage – Description and exploration – British.
5. Resolute (Ship).
6. Great Britain – Exploring expeditions.
I. Barr, William. II. Title.

G662.B73 1992   917.19'5441'092   C92-094064-1

Plates 23, 25, 26, and 28 are reproduced with permission of
Dr Robert Janes and the Archives of the Northwest Territories,
Yellowknife; Plates 14, 15, 16, and 24 are reproduced with permission of
the Archivist, Scott Polar Research Institute, Cambridge; all
other historical illustrations are reproduced with permission of
M. Philippe Henrat, Archives de France and of the late M. Yves Perrussel.

This book has been published with the help of a grant from the
Canadian Federation for the Humanities, using funds provided by
the Social Sciences and Humanities Research Council of Canada.

Contents

Contents

Acknowledgments

The bulk of the work of editing de Bray's journal was completed during a sabbatical leave from the University of Saskatchewan, and I wish to express my thanks to the university for providing this invaluable opportunity for uninterrupted research. I am indebted to the British Council for a travel grant to cover the costs of travel to and from Britain. Most of my sabbatical leave was spent at the Scott Polar Research Institute, Cambridge, England, and I wish to thank the director, Dr Peter Wadhams, the librarian, Mr William Mills, and the archivist, Mr Robert Headland, for their kind hospitality and generous assistance, and all my numerous friends among the staff, students, and visitors at the institute for their kindness and congenial company. I also wish to thank Dr Anthony Lowe, president of Clare Hall, and all the fellows and students of that institution for providing me with a congenial base in Cambridge.

I am also greatly indebted to a number of people in France. Not least of these is the late M. Yves Perrussel, of Quimper, for permission to publish my translation of his grandfather's journal and to reproduce his various maps, paintings, and sketches. I also wish to thank M. Perrussel for his company on a visit to his grandfather's grave in Pont-l'Abbé. Another Frenchman to whom I owe a great debt is M. Philippe Henrat of the Archives de France, Paris, who wrote his master's thesis on de Bray's arctic voyage and who made available to me his thesis, the photo of de Bray which forms the frontispiece, as well as photos of many of de Bray's maps, paintings, and sketches. Another Parisian to whom I am greatly indebted is M. Pierre Waksman of the Service Historique de la Marine, Château de Vincennes, who placed de Bray's dossier at my disposal with courteous efficiency.

I owe a particular debt to Mme Jacqueline Carpine-Lancre, librarian at the Institut Océanographique de Monaco for putting me in contact with M. Perrussel; she has also been extremely helpful with a number of research projects over the years and also acted as a charming and hospitable guide to the attractions of Monaco.

Closer to home, I wish to express my deep gratitude to our departmental technician Mr Keith Bigelow for his usual impeccable workmanship in drafting the maps and copying the photos which form the illustrations.

And finally I wish to acknowledge the enormous contribution of my editors at the University of Toronto Press, Mr Gerald Hallowell and Ms Laura Macleod.

Although it may be rather unusual to acknowledge something borrowed from oneself, it is probably appropriate to point out that some of the information contained in the Translator's Introduction and Postscript is reproduced from the Introduction to my earlier book, *Overland to Starvation Cove.*

Translator's Introduction

On 15 April 1852, as Sir Edward Belcher's Arctic Squadron, consisting of the sailing vessels *Assistance, Resolute,* and *North Star* and the steamships *Pioneer* and *Intrepid,* was dropping down the Thames from Woolwich Basin to Greenhithe, Lieutenant George S. Nares, a young officer on board Captain Henry Kellett's ship *Resolute,* was writing a hurried final note to his father. In the middle of a paragraph containing initial impressions of his fellow officers Nares included the following typically ethnocentric remark: 'The Frenchman does not seem an *Englishman,* but I suppose he will improve on acquaintance' (Nares, 1852). Since the Frenchman was not named in the letter, a casual reader would be left wondering who he was and whether he did indeed improve on acquaintance.

The Frenchman was in fact Enseigne-de-vaisseau Emile Frédéric de Bray. Born in Paris at 37 rue des Martyrs on 9 March 1829, he was the second son of the artist Achille-Hector-Camille de Bray, who died when Emile was only thirteen years old (Henrat, 1982). In the fall of 1844 Emile was enrolled as a cadet at the École Navale and on 1 October he joined the training ship *Borda* at Brest. From the surviving assessments of his performance held at the Service Historique de la Marine, it is evident that the young de Bray must have found the two years he spent aboard *Borda* little to his liking. The comment made on his report sheet by the commanding officer of the school, Capitaine-de-vaisseau Le Presour, on 21 January 1845 is fairly typical: 'The conduct of this student is not as satisfactory as might be desired; he does not work and he is extremely weak in most of his courses. Health good' (Henrat, 1982:92).

During his two years aboard *Borda* de Bray appears to have been something of a rebel: he collected eleven days in the brig, four in the police room, and thirty-five on guard duty. His report sheets reveal a very uneven performance: mediocre or quite deplorable in the exact sciences (except for navigation where he maintained a good average) and in practical subjects; steady progress in English; excellent in literature and geography; and outstanding in artistic drawing. The overall outcome was that throughout his first year he stood at between seventy-first and seventy-fourth in his class. In his second year de Bray seems to have realized the seriousness of the situation; by the end of his second year he had managed to pull up to sixty-first place. On 1 August 1846 he graduated from the École Navale with the rank of Élève-de-2ᵉᵐᵉ classe de la Marine and was posted to Brest.

There he joined the corvette *Galathée* and shortly afterwards sailed for the Pacific on a cruise which would last three years and take him to Valparaiso, Tahiti, and Nuka Hiva in the Marquesas, an archipelago whose inhabitants were still hostile. A note in his dossier reveals that de Bray participated in several expeditions aimed at maintaining order among the rebellious 'kanacks' (Henrat, 1982:94). For almost a year (March 1848 until April 1849) de Bray served on detached service as mate aboard the schooner *Papeete* and even commanded her briefly. On that occasion the voyage from Tahiti to Nuka Hiva took him through poorly charted waters.

His superiors were impressed with his performance, although Capitaine-de-vaisseau Fournier of *Galathée* qualified his remarks when he wrote, in December 1847: 'Very strong constitution. A good boy. Will become a sailor, but laziness will probably prevent him from becoming a good observer' (Henrat, 1982:95). The various captains of *Papeete* had nothing but good to say of him. Thus on 29 July 1848 Enseigne-de-vaisseau Allary wrote: 'In every respect I have nothing but praise for the conduct of this Élève; in all circumstances he has displayed a zeal and an aptitude for the service which cannot but make him a good officer in the future. As captain of the schooner, as he leaves the vessel I am very pleased to give Mr. Debray [*sic*] a strong testimonial with regard to the services which he has rendered on board, along with my particular thanks' (Henrat, 1982:95).

When *Galathée* returned to Lorient on 17 September 1849 even the strict Fournier had the good grace to attest (if somewhat inconsistently) that 'the Élève F.E. de Bray has been posted under my orders for almost three years and I have nothing but praise (!) for his conduct, his zeal for the service and his aptitude' (Henrat, 1982:96). In short, it is clear that the somewhat misfit Élève who had sailed from Brest in the fall of 1846 had matured considerably during his three-year cruise in tropical waters. On the way home de Bray had even shown his mettle by capturing a wanted criminal. In September 1849 the newspaper *Le Constitutionnel* reported that during *Lorient*'s recent visit to Rio de Janeiro de Bray had managed to capture a bandit named Polk. When Polk had fired at him and missed, de Bray had tackled and overpowered him (Henrat, 1982).

Over the next eighteen months de Bray served as 'aspirant' in a sequence of temporary postings aboard the brig *Le Fabert*, the ship *Le Valmy*, the frigates *La Pandore* and *La Capricieuse*, and the despatch vessels *Le Dauphin* and *Scamandre*. During this period he visited Brest, Toulon, Civita Vecchio, and Naples. Then on 3 May 1850 he was given a more permanent posting to *Valmy*, a ship of 120 guns and flagship of Contre-amiral Dubourdieu. When a fire broke out on board, de Bray played a major role in suppressing it and was mentioned in despatches. No doubt partly because of this he received a favourable report from his commander, Capitaine-de-vaisseau Maussion de Candé, who described him as 'intelligent, capable and zealous in the service' (Henrat, 1982:97). Having sat the appropriate examinations at Brest early in 1851, on 2 April 1851 de Bray was promoted to the rank of Enseigne-de-vaisseau, at the extremely early age of twenty-two. At this point he had started a well-merited leave which was to last until the end of the year.

Like the majority of naval officers around the world, and indeed the bulk of the educated public worldwide, de Bray had been closely following the progress of the Royal Navy's search for the missing expedition of Sir John Franklin, dispatched in 1845 to find the Northwest Passage. *Erebus* and *Terror*, barque-rigged bomb vessels of 370 and 340 tons respectively, had sailed from Greenhithe on the morning of 19 May 1845. Their combined crews totalled 134 officers and men, and their objective was to sail north through Baffin Bay, then west through the Northwest Passage; having reached the Pacific via Bering Strait, Franklin was ordered to proceed to the Sandwich Islands (Hawaii) and thence return home via Cape Horn (Cyriax, 1939).

In hindsight these instructions may appear incredibly optimistic, but given the existing knowledge of the geography of the Canadian Arctic Archipelago in 1845, Franklin's task did not seem particularly daunting. In 1819–20 *Hecla* and *Griper*, commanded by Captain William Edward Parry, had penetrated as far west along Parry Channel as the southwest corner of Melville Island and had wintered at Winter Harbour (Parry, 1821). In 1829–33 Sir John Ross had mounted a private expedition with *Victory* and had penetrated south along Prince

Regent Inlet as far as Felix Harbour, to the east of the present settlement of Spence Bay on Boothia Isthmus (Ross, 1835), and had wintered there. In the spring of 1830 his nephew James Clark Ross had sledged west across the isthmus and had explored the north coast of King William Island as far west as Victory Point.

Within a decade another expedition would reach almost the same point from the west. In the summer of 1839 Peter Dease and Thomas Simpson of the Hudson's Bay Company, travelling by canoe, headed east along the mainland coast from the mouth of the Coppermine (Simpson, 1843). Passing through Simpson Strait, they explored the south coast of King William Island and turned back near Cape Selkirk, just south of the mouth of the Murchison River. At Cape John Herschel they were within one hundred kilometres of Victory Point. Hence only this small gap remained to complete the picture of the northern limits of the continent. But it is one thing to travel across the tundra and sea ice on foot, hauling sledges, as James Ross and his men had done, or to sail the coastal waters by canoe during the brief weeks of open water in summer, as Dease and Simpson had done. It is quite another thing to battle the ice and tackle these same waters, uncharted and shoal, in ocean-going vessels.

Erebus and *Terror* probably represented the best possible type of vessel for the task. As bomb vessels they had been designed to carry large mortars capable of hurling large-calibre shells on a high trajectory into coastal towns under siege or into entrenched positions. The mortars were positioned amidships on extremely strongly built wooden beds. To absorb the recoil of these formidable weapons, the ships were unusually well built and hence ideal for withstanding the enormous pressures they were liable to encounter in polar ice. If caught between large floes driven against each other by wind or current, they were much more likely to survive than an ordinary vessel.

Both ships had already seen considerable polar service. In 1836, under the command of Captain George Back, *Terror* had tried to reach Wager Bay in northwestern Hudson Bay, as the intended starting point for an overland attempt at exploring the central section of the Northwest Passage. Beset in the ice off the north coast of Southampton Island, she drifted southeast along the east coast of that island and was eventually released from the ice, badly damaging and leaking, near the west end of Hudson Strait in July 1837 (Back, 1838). Between 1839 and 1843, in company with *Erebus*, *Terror* took part in a major expedition to the Antarctic under the command of James Clark Ross (Ross, 1847). They explored the Ross Sea and discovered the Ross Ice shelf and Mount Erebus, an active volcano overlooking the Ross Sea. Both ships were badly damaged by ice during this epic voyage.

For their attempt on the Northwest Passage special adaptations were made to both vessels. They were given additional ice sheathing and their bows were strengthened to the extent that they represented a mass of timber almost 2.5 m thick. Their bows were then sheathed with sheets of iron. For the first time in the Royal Navy's polar voyages, both ships were provided with steam power for manoeuvring in ice or during calms. Slightly modified railway engines were mounted athwartships in the holds, a drive shaft extending aft from one of the driving wheels to a two-bladed propeller (Cyriax, 1939). The engines were of only 20 horsepower and under even the best conditions could move the ships at only 4 knots. But since with their bluff bows the ships could make a maximum of only 8 knots under sail, this auxiliary power probably proved quite useful. The propellers could be hoisted out of the water via a vertical well if they were in danger of damage by ice. Other innovative adaptations included condensers attached to the galley stoves for producing drinking water from sea water and hot water heating systems throughout the living quarters. The ships also carried provisions for three years.

The leader of the expedition, Sir John Franklin, was fifty-eight years old. He had joined the navy at the age of fourteen and had fought aboard HMS *Polyphemus* at the battle of Copenhagen, and as signal midshipman aboard HMS *Bellerophon* at Trafalgar. His first arctic experience had been as commander of HMS *Trent*, which in company with HMS *Dorothea* (Captain David Buchan) had made an unsuccessful attempt to sail across the Arctic Basin via a route between Svalbard and Greenland in 1818 (Beechey, 1843). This was Franklin's only experience of handling a ship in ice. By contrast, his experience of arctic overland travel and coastal travel by canoe and small boats was practically unparelleled. In 1819–22, Franklin had explored the mainland coast, travelling by canoe from the mouth of the Coppermine River to Point Turnagain on Kent Peninsula. Unfortunately, during the disastrous overland retreat to their base at Fort Enterprise on Winter Lake eleven of his companions died, mainly of starvation (Franklin, 1823; Houston, 1974; 1984). On his second arctic expedition in 1825–7, this time travelling by boat, he explored the mainland coast west from the Mackenzie Delta to Return Reef, west of Prudhoe Bay. Meanwhile another detachment of the expedition, led by Dr John Richardson, travelled eastward by boat from the Mackenzie Delta to the mouth of the Coppermine. Sir John had not been in the Arctic since then and had spent much of the time as an administrator, serving as governor of Tasmania from 1837 until 1843.

The officer commanding *Terror* was Captain Francis Crozier, aged forty-eight; in terms of shipborne polar exploration he was by far the most experienced member of the expedition. He had served as midshipman aboard HMS *Fury* during Parry's second expedition of 1821–3, which had wintered first at Winter Island in Frozen Strait and then at Igloolik (Parry, 1824; Lyon 1824). During both winterings the expedition members had established close and generally harmonious relations with the Inuit of the area, and Crozier had probably acquired a working knowledge of Inuktitut. Then in 1824–5 Crozier had served as midshipman aboard *Hecla* on Parry's third voyage, which had wintered at Port Bowen in Prince Regent Inlet (Parry, 1826). And finally, Crozier had commanded *Terror* on James Ross's epic antarctic voyage, where he gained a wealth of experience in handling a ship in ice.

By contrast Commander James Fitzjames, captain of *Erebus* on the new expedition, had no previous arctic experience, although he had distinguished himself by his exploration of the Euphrates River with a steamer in 1835 and by his handling of a rocket brigade during the hostilities in China in 1841. However, his first officer, Graham Gore, had had previous arctic experience. In 1836–7 he had served as mate under Captain George Back aboard *Terror*, and was only too familiar with the dangers of a winter adrift in the pack. Other officers with arctic experience included Charles Osmer, purser and paymaster of the *Erebus*, who had served under Captain Frederick Beechey on his voyage to the Bering Straits area aboard *Blossom* in 1825–8 (Beechey, 1831). Dr Alexander McDonald, assistant surgeon of the *Terror*, had had previous arctic experience aboard whalers. And finally, each ship carried an ice-master to advise the captain about ship-handling in ice. James Reid served in this capacity aboard *Erebus* and Thomas Blanky on *Terror*; both men had served on whalers.

Most of the officers and men were recruited especially for the expedition, mainly from the north of England, and many of them had probably served previously on whalers sailing out of ports such as Whitby and Hull. Everyone was to receive double pay for the duration of the arctic expedition, in keeping with Admiralty practice.

Franklin's actual route was specified quite narrowly in his orders. He was to head west through Lancaster Sound and Barrow Strait as

far as the longitude of Cape Walker (the northeast tip of Russell
Island, off the north coast of Prince of Wales Island, at about 98°W).
From that point he was to steer southward or westward towards
Bering Strait, maintaining as straight a course as ice and/or unknown
land would permit. If this proposed course were totally impassable,
he was to try heading north via Wellington Channel, between Devon
and Cornwallis islands (Cyriax, 1939).

On 25 July 1845 the whalers *Enterprise* (Captain Robert Martin) of
Peterhead and *Prince of Wales* (Captain Dannett) of Hull encoun-
tered *Erebus* and *Terror* in Melville Bukt in the northern part of
Baffin Bay. The four ships kept company among the ice for several
days, with men and officers exchanging visits. When last seen by
Captain Martin *Erebus* and *Terror* were moored to an iceberg. He
and his crew were the last Europeans to see any members of the
Franklin expedition alive (Jones, 1969).

No particular concern was felt in Britain when there was no word
from Franklin in 1846. But by 1847 some anxiety was developing; the
Admiralty requested that whaling captains keep an eye out for *Erebus*
and *Terror* and Lady Franklin offered a reward to encourage them.
As a result, Captain William Penny, of *St Andrew*, made a deliberate
attempt to look for the missing ships in Lancaster Sound that summer, although he was unable to get farther west than 78°W due to ice.
On his way out of the sound he questioned the Inuit of the Pond Bay
area about the missing vessels, but without success (Holland, 1970).

Plans for the first naval searches were also laid that summer.
Under the auspices of the Admiralty, Sir John Richardson and Dr
John Rae travelled west via the fur trade route, descended the
Mackenzie, and searched the coast east to the mouth of the Cop-
permine by boat in 1848 (Richardson, 1851). After wintering at Fort
Confidence on Great Bear Lake, Rae resumed his search in 1849; he
hoped to search the coasts of Victoria Island but ice prevented him
from crossing Dolphin and Union Strait (Rich and Johnson, 1953). Also
in 1848 HMS *Plover* (Captain Thomas Moore) was dispatched to Bering
Strait; she reached her destination in October and wintered on the
Siberian side of the Strait (Hooper, 1853), the first of many winterings
she would spend in the area. Meanwhile HMS *Herald*, under Captain Henry Kellett, while on a surveying voyage to the Pacific, was
dispatched northward from Panama in the summer of 1848 to make
rendezvous with *Plover* in Kotzebue Sound (Seemann, 1853, vol. 2), but
on failing to meet her returned to Central American waters.

Also in 1848, the Admiralty dispatched an expedition from the

Atlantic to attempt to follow the route specified in Franklin's instructions. Two ships, HMS *Enterprise* and HMS *Investigator* (Captain Sir James Clark Ross and Captain Edward Bird, respectively), sailed in May and wintered at Port Leopold on northeastern Somerset Island. In the spring of 1849 sledging parties explored extensive sections of the coasts of Somerset and adjacent islands (Gilpin, 1850). After a protracted drift, beset in the ice, the ships struggled free of Lancaster Sound in the summer of 1849 and arrived safely back in England that fall.

That spring Captain Kellett again took *Herald* north through Bering Strait, met *Plover* in Kotzebue Sound, and proceeded north along the Alaskan coast, but was blocked by ice off Wainwright Inlet. Following the edge of the pack westward, Kellett discovered Ostrov Geral'da (Herald Island), before heading south to winter again in Mexican waters (Seemann, 1853, vol. 2). In the mean time a party from *Plover*, travelling in two boats commanded by lieutenants William Pullen and William Hooper, travelled east along the arctic coast of Alaska to the mouth of the Mackenzie (Pullen, 1979).

Yet another expedition was active in the Baffin Bay area that summer of 1849. HMS *North Star*, commanded by Captain James Saunders pushed north across Melville Bukt and wintered at the head of Wolstenholme Sound in Northwest Greenland (Saunders, 1851). Getting free of the ice on 1 August 1850, Saunders ran south and into Lancaster Sound, where he established a major depot of provisions at the mouth of Navy Board Inlet before heading for home.

On 10 January 1850 two ships sailed from London, bound for the North Pacific via Cape Horn; they were HMS *Enterprise* (Captain Richard Collinson) and HMS *Investigator* (Captain Robert M'Clure). Their orders were to push north through Bering Strait then attempt to make their way east along the north coast of Alaska searching for any signs of the missing expedition as they went (Osborn, 1856; Collinson, 1889).

The summer of 1850 also saw a great flurry of activity in the eastern Arctic, involving both private and naval search expeditions; it even included an American component. The Admiralty dispatched four ships: *Resolute* (Captain Horatio Austin), *Assistance* (Captain Erasmus Ommanney), *Intrepid* (Captain Bertie Cator), and *Pioneer* (Captain Sherard Osborn). Lady Jane Franklin dispatched a search vessel of her own, *Prince Albert*, under the command of Captain Charles Forsyth (Snow, 1851). The arctic veteran Sir John Ross led another private venture, financed by the Hudson's Bay Company, aboard *Felix* (Dodge, 1973; Wilson, 1973). In addition, the Admiralty sent out two vessels, *Lady Franklin* and *Sophia*, under the leadership of Captain William Penny, this time devoted entirely to searching for Franklin. Finally, the American contribution, consisting of the ships *Advance* (Captain E.J. de Haven) and *Rescue* (Captain Samuel P. Griffin), sailed from New York, northward bound, in May 1850 (Kane, 1854).

All these vessels pushed west into Barrow Strait and congregated in the area of Beechey Island at the southwestern tip of Devon Island in late August 1850. It was here that the first traces of the missing expedition were found. Captain Ommanney of *Assistance*, accompanied by some of his officers, landed on Cape Riley, across Erebus Bay from Beechey Island on 23 August; they found traces of an encampment 'and collected the remains of materials which evidently prove that some party belonging to Her Majesty's ships have been detained on this spot' (Ommanney, 1851:70). Having examined the remains, which included rope, canvas, wood, and animal bones, such experts as Captain William Parry, Dr John Richardson, and Colonel Sabine later deduced that a party from *Erebus* and *Terror* had camped here, probably to carry out magnetic observations (Great Britain. Parliament, 1851).

Captain Penny was the next to discover further traces of the missing expedition; on 26 August, leading a boat party from *Lady Franklin*, he found traces of another camp 10 km north of Cape Spencer on the shores of Wellington Channel. A litter of soup cans, barrel fragments, charred pieces of wood, rope, mittens, rags, and a scrap of newspaper dated 1844 was scattered in and near the remains of a circular stone hut with a neatly paved floor. Sledge tracks were also discovered nearby (Sutherland, 1852:299–301).

The next day *Lady Franklin* and *Sophia* joined *Felix*, *Advance*, and *Rescue*, at anchor in Union Bay between Beechey Island and Cape Spencer. Parties from the various ships went ashore on Beechey Island (then, as now, joined to the mainland of Devon Island by a shingle spit), and immediately realized that this was where *Erebus* and *Terror* had spent the winter of 1845–6 (Sutherland, 1852; Kane, 1854). The most obvious evidence was the headboards of three graves, two of the occupants being from *Erebus* and one from *Terror*; all had been buried in the early months of 1846. There were also clear signs of where a smith's forge had stood and a general litter of tin cans, wood chips, fragments of canvas, rope, and so on. Captain Osborn of *Pioneer*, which arrived a day later, even found a pair of gloves laid out to dry, weighted down with pebbles on their palms to prevent them from blowing away (Osborn, 1852). But a determined search of the area failed to turn up any message as to the expedition's achievements and intentions. The movements of Franklin's ships after they left Beechey Island, presumably in the summer of 1846, were still a total mystery.

Subsequently the Royal Navy vessels (*Resolute, Assistance, Pioneer,* and *Intrepid)* wintered off Griffith Island, while Penny's ships, *Lady Franklin* and *Sophia,* joined Ross's *Felix* in winter quarters in Assistance Harbour on southern Cornwallis Island. The two American vessels (*Advance* and *Rescue)* became beset in the ice and drifted north down Wellington Channel as far as 75° 24′N, then southwards again. Throughout the winter their drift continued eastwards down Lancaster Sound and southwards to Davis Strait, where they were released in June 1851 (Kane, 1854).

In the spring of 1851 sledge parties from Austin's squadron searched the coasts of Cornwallis and Bathurst islands; Lieutenant McClintock pushed west to Winter Harbour and searched the coasts of Dundas Peninsula; and other sledge parties crossed Barrow Strait and searched much of the coastline of Prince of Wales Island. Meanwhile sledge parties from Penny's ships searched the shores of Wellington Channel (Sutherland, 1852), while Commander Charles Phillips, Ross's second-in-command, made a sledge journey from south to north across Cornwallis Island (Wilson, 1973).

News of the discoveries at Beechey Island reached Britain with the return of Forsyth's *Prince Albert* in October 1850 (Snow, 1851). And it was in the light of this information that a further expedition, sponsored by Lady Franklin, sailed from Aberdeen aboard *Prince Albert* in May 1851 (Kennedy, 1853; Bellot, 1855). The leader was William Kennedy, a Hudson's Bay Company man of Métis descent (Kennedy, 1853). The second-in-command was a French naval officer, Joseph-René Bellot, who had volunteered his services to Lady Franklin (Bellot, 1855). His application was strongly supported by the French naval authorities and by the French ambassador in London, but was initially opposed by Lady Franklin's advisers in the Royal Navy; they were afraid that the presence of a foreign officer on a British ship might result in problems of discipline and rank. Kennedy, however, fully supported the appointment, being particularly impressed by Bellot's skills as a navigator (Holland, 1985a). The expedition sailed from Aberdeen on 22 May 1851; its aim was to search

Prince Regent Inlet and the area southwest of Cape Walker at the western entrance to Peel Sound.

It was also in the light of the discoveries at Beechey Island that the next Royal Navy expedition was conceived and organized after the return of Austin's squadron in the autumn of 1851. This sequel, consisting of Austin's four ships plus the depot ship *North Star*, was to sail for the Arctic in the summer of 1852. In command was Sir Edward Belcher. To quote from Belcher's orders:

> Beechey Island is the point indicated as the basis of your operations, and you are to consider it as the grand rendezvous to which you are to push forward, there to establish the 'North Star' as a general depot.
>
> ... Arrived at this point, two great objects will engage your attention: 1st. The endeavouring to pass up Wellington Channel with one sailing-vessel and one steamer. 2nd. The advance of a similar force towards Melville Island.
>
> ... The object of the first of these expeditions will be to endeavour to recover those traces of Sir John Franklin which ceased at Cape Bowden, to the north of Beechey Island; and to follow up such traces if they should be found. The object of the other expedition will be, to deposit, if possible, at Winter Harbour, Melville Island, or failing that at Byam Martin Island, a supply of provisions, fuel and clothing, for any parties that might reach such positions from Captain Collinson's or Commander M'Clure's ships (Belcher, 1855a, vol. 2:2).

There can be little doubt that de Bray's imagination was fired by Bellot's participation in the expedition aboard *Prince Albert*; although the two men had never met, they had corresponded. On learning of the British Admiralty's plans to despatch Sir Edward Belcher's expedition in the summer of 1852 de Bray decided similarly to offer his services. On 20 December 1851 he wrote to the Minister of the Navy and the Colonies:

> Dear Minister,
>
> Since my leave is about to expire and since I have no hope of getting a ship for a long time, I am soliciting your kindness for authorization to offer my humble services to the British Admiralty to take part in the expedition which is now being fitted out to go in search of Sir John Franklin.
>
> I dare to hope, Mr. Minister, that the First Lord of the Admiralty will

receive my request favourably and that this temporary absence will not
prejudice my naval career in any way.

 Please accept, Mr Minister, the assurance
<blockquote>of my deep respect,
E.F. de Bray</blockquote>

(De Bray, 1851)

Although no word of Bellot's major role in the *Prince Albert*
expedition can yet have reached London, it seems likely that Bellot's
precedent must have predisposed their Lordships of the Admiralty
towards the idea of a French officer participating in a Naval (rather
than private) arctic expedition. On 20 January 1852 the British foreign minister, Earl Granville, wrote to Count Walewski, the French
Ambassador:

> Monsieur l'Ambassadeur,
> I did not fail to submit to the Board of the Admiralty Your Excellency's
> request, made in your note of the 7th instant, that Monsr. de Bray, an
> *enseigne-de-vaisseau* in the French Navy, might be allowed to accom-
> pany the next British expedition sent in search of Sir John Franklin; and
> I have now the pleasure of informing Your Excellency that, although
> no ships have yet been put into commission for this expedition, the
> Admiralty will be happy to consider the wishes of the Government of
> France with regard to Monsr. de Bray, when arrangements shall be
> made for despatching ships on this service (Granville 1852a).

Walewski promptly forwarded this letter via the French Foreign
Office to the Minister of the Marine and the Colonies.

A month later, on 23 February, Earl Granville again wrote to
Walewski with more concrete details of the planned expedition;
Captain Sir Edward Belcher had been appointed to its command, and
the expedition would sail around 1 April 1852. More to the point,
perhaps, 'if the French Government is desirous of attaching Mr de
Bray to that expedition the Lords of the Admiralty will be happy to
give orders for his being received on board the Commanding Officer's
ship' (Granville, 1852b). This message was similarly relayed by
Walewski to the Naval Ministry in Paris. In point of fact de Bray
was posted to Captain Kellett's ship *Resolute*, rather than to Belcher's
ship *Assistance*; as events turned out, de Bray would be extremely
grateful for this change of plan.

Over the next few days internal arrangements concerning de Bray's secondment were finalized. In an internal memo to the Naval Minister on 2 March 1852, the Director of Military Personnel and Fleet Movements reported that: 'From today and throughout the forthcoming voyage this officer will enjoy his full salary. He will receive in addition travel expenses to get from Paris to the French port where he will embark for England.' This, the Director further noted, was the way in which Bellot's secondment to the *Prince Albert* expedition had also been handled.

Thus it was that on 13 April 1852 de Bray left Paris, bound for London to join Nares and his fellow officers on board *Resolute* in the search for Franklin.

The whereabouts of de Bray's original journal, written day by day throughout his two winters in the Arctic, are unknown. His grandson, M. Yves Perrussel (who died in August 1990), told me that he could remember handling it as a child, and could picture it clearly. He described it to his brother, Colonel Alain Perrussel, as 'a very thick school notebook. Its covers were marbled and the spine was of grey canvas' (A. Perrussel, quoted in Henrat, 1982:150)

Henrat has suggested one possible location (1982:150). In the late 1930s and 1940s Commandant Jules Rouch, the director of the Institut d'Océanographie de Monaco, took a great interest in Emile de Bray and wrote several articles about him (Rouch, 1938; 1944; 1945); he attempted to promote him as one of France's few polar explorers. With the approval and cooperation of de Bray's son, Lieutenant-colonel Georges de Bray, a number of items pertaining to de Bray's arctic sojourn (including the Arctic medal awarded by Queen Victoria, the flag from his sledge, *Hero*, and perhaps the original journal) were presented to the Musée de la Marine (Henrat, 1982: 149–50), then housed in the Trocadero. Numerous recent attempts to find the journal and the other memorabilia at the Musée de la Marine (now at the Palais de Chaillot) have been unsuccessful. One can only hope that Henrat's suggestion that they may still be buried somewhere in the storage areas of the Palais de Chaillot turns out to be correct.

Given the fact that de Bray is one of only a handful of French polar explorers, it is perhaps surprising that the journal has never previously been published, either in French or any other language. But it is clear that at some point after his return from the Arctic de Bray reworked the journal, presumably with a view to publication. M. Yves Perrussel showed me a manuscript copy of this reworked journal in March 1990. It was neatly written, in a clear regular hand.

Most of it had obviously been written over a fairly short span of time, in the same colour of ink, and in the calm of an office rather than day by day under the cramped conditions of a cabin of a ship wintering in the Arctic.

Although written in the same hand, the section describing events after the expedition's return to England in October 1854 is in a much lighter ink. This is only to be expected since its contents show that it was written considerably later than de Bray's return to Europe.

As Henrat has pointed out (1982:154) evidence exists in the form of a draft of a letter by de Bray, written some time between June 1865 and February 1866, very probably to the explorer Gustave Lambert, as to when he rewrote (and probably polished) his journal. He reports that he had just finished rewriting the journal with a view to recruiting the help of an experienced writer who could help him mould it into a publishable work. There is no record, unfortunately, of what became of these plans.

The typescript from which I worked – now in the archives of the Scott Polar Research Institute in Cambridge, England, where it had been deposited by M. Yves Perrussel – was produced from this 'polished' version of de Bray's journal. This was also the version used by Philippe Henrat in his 1982 thesis. M. Henrat still cherishes the hope that the original day-by-day journal may resurface in due course.

A Frenchman in Search of Franklin

Introduction

Once the Portuguese had discovered the Indies, which provided them with limitless wealth, thoughts soon turned to a means of shortening the route via the Cape of Good Hope, which presented terrifying dangers for the navigators of the period. Corte-Real was the first to have the idea of following the coast of North America in order to find an access route to the Pacific Ocean.

He reached one of the vast embayments with which the American coast is punctuated, and believed that he had reached the object of his dreams. He then returned to Portugal to announce his discovery and outfitted another expedition, which never returned. His brother met the same fate when he went in search of him; at the same period several navigators such as Juan de Fuca, Fanta, Cabot, and Jacques Cartier also made some fruitless attempts.

Barents lost his life after horrible sufferings, while trying to force a passage through the Svalbard ice. In the sixteenth century Hudson attempted a passage in the same direction and penetrated to 62°N latitude but was soon forced to retreat by the terrible ice of the polar basin. Without abandoning the enterprise he rounded Greenland and reached the vast inlet discovered by Corte Real, which was now named Hudson Bay. It was here that he met his death.

Baffin next discovered the bay which bears his name. Bering discovered the strait which also bears his name, and which separates America from Asia.

Hearne in 1771 and Mackenzie in 1789 headed into the inhospitable regions of North America and after innumerable perils reached the shores of the Arctic Ocean, but without finding the long-sought passage. The former traced the course of the Coppermine River and the latter that of the Mackenzie River.

From this point on the objective of discovering the Northwest

Passage seems to have been almost abandoned; it was not until 1817 that the British mounted an expedition which consisted of two separate branches. One, under the command of John Ross, accompanied by Edward Parry, was to enter Baffin Bay; the other, under the command of Franklin and David Buchan, was to enter the Arctic Basin via Svalbard.

Extraordinarily easy ice conditions favoured this expedition. John Ross discovered Lancaster Sound and thus returned to Britain proclaiming the start of the solution to the problem he had been pursuing. After innumerable perils, in the face of which he displayed an energy and courage which presaged the man who later made his name so renowned, Franklin returned after an unsuccessful voyage; he had been stopped by the same polar ice which had stopped his predecessors.[1]

In 1819 another British expedition, commanded By Captain Parry, entered Lancaster Sound, while the indefatigable Franklin, accompanied by Richardson and Back, headed overland towards the Arctic Ocean. At this point a reward of £20,000 (500,000 francs) was voted by the British Parliament to any ship which passed the 108°W meridian (from Paris).

Parry discovered Prince Regent Inlet; soon after he discovered Barrow Strait (named after Sir John Barrow, moving force behind all the arctic expeditions mounted at this time). He then charted the northern shores of this strait and bestowed the names Cornwallis Island, Bathurst Island, Byam Martin Island and Melville Island. He crossed the 108°W meridian [110°W from Greenwich], thus winning the promised reward, and, favoured by an exceptional season, penetrated to Cape Providence. Since that location offered no shelter for his ships, he retraced his steps and established winter quarters at Winter Harbour on the south coast of Melville Island. In October 1820 he returned to England, having reached the 114° meridian, a longitude which no previous explorer had reached. From that point he could make out a coastline which seemed to run east-west and on which he bestowed the name Bank's Land.[2]

Around the same time Franklin set off from York Factory to penetrate into the icy wastes of the Northwest, accompanied by a few Indians. Never has such a terrible journey been accomplished with more courage and perseverance. Fighting the elements, hunger, thirst, and innumerable trials, Franklin refused to be beaten. Assisted by his two brave companions, Richardson and Back, he returned to York Factory in July 1822 having covered a distance of 2,000 leagues, and having given the whole world an example of what human will can do when pushed to the extreme limits.[3]

Parry had scarcely returned to England when he received command of another expedition to explore the area of Hudson Bay and the various straits which branch from it, in the hope that one of these straits would lead to the coasts explored by Franklin. During this expedition he discovered Fury and Hecla Strait, named after his ships, spent the winter of 1821–2 at Winter Island and that of 1822–3 at Igloolik.[4] Realizing that it was impossible to get any farther he decided to return to England, intending to mount a third expedition via Barrow Strait, while another under the command of Captain Beechey would push north via Bering Strait.[5] At the same time a detachment led by Franklin would descend the Mackenzie River and would explore the still unknown coasts of North America.[6] These three expeditions were mounted and it was on the one commanded by Captain Beechey that Sir Edward Belcher, then Lieutenant Belcher, had his first experience of the arctic seas.[7]

More fortunate than Parry, Franklin and Beechey succeeded in reaching the shores of the polar basin. Refusing to be discouraged, Parry again tried to penetrate into Prince Regent Inlet but was blocked by the ice and forced to return to England for the winter. In 1826 he made a further attempt to reach the Pole but returned to England without reaching his goal.[8]

In 1829 Captain [John] Ross again attempted the Passage, penetrating deep into Prince Regent Inlet. He spent four winters in this desolate area, lost his ship, and was picked up by the ship *Isabella*, Captain Humphreys, which took him and his crew back to England. It was during this expedition that [James Clark] Ross discovered the Magnetic Pole.[9]

Between 1833 and 1835 Back, Dease and Simpson, and Rae made several overland attempts. Back discovered the Great Fish River which he descended, thus reaching the shores of the polar sea.[10] Dease and Simpson discovered the strait which bears their names, and also Victoria Island;[11] finally Rae explored Bathurst Inlet.[12]

After these various expeditions there was nothing left to do on the American continent and all eyes now turned to Barrow Strait, which alone perhaps offered a chance of resolving the problem which had been pursued for so long, i.e., that of a shorter route for reaching the Indies.

In 1845 Franklin received command of two ships, *Erebus* and *Terror*, one under the command of Captain Fitzjames, the other under that of Captain Crozier. These two ships were fitted out with the greatest care and set sail on 26 May 1845, with a total complement of 168 men and provisions for four years. The last news from Franklin was dated from Disco, then around early August he was sighted by whalers as he tried to penetrate into Lancaster Sound.[13] From that time on there has been total silence; there has been no information which might suggest that such a skilfully organized expedition has been successful.

In 1847, anxious as to Franklin's fate the British government felt that it should organize a search plan to rescue him. Sir James Ross entered Baffin Bay with two ships, *Enterprise* and *Investigator*, while Captains Kellett and Moore with *Herald* and *Plover* passed through Bering Strait.

Dr Richardson, Franklin's faithful companion, also undertook an expedition which headed overland towards Wollaston Land.[14] But none of these expeditions succeeded in finding any trace as to the fate of the unfortunate explorers, and anxiety became general. Rewards of 500,000 and 250,000 francs [£20,000 and £10,000] were offered by the British government to those who rescued Franklin or could give news of him, and in 1850–1 a major campaign was launched.

Two sailing ships and two steamers under the command of Captain Austin wintered at Griffith Island in Barrow Strait. Captain Penny wintered at Assistance Harbour, almost at the entrance to Wellington Channel. Sir John Ross also took part in the expedition in his yacht, while two American ships, fitted out by Mr Grinnell of New York and under the command of Captain de Haven, joined forces with the British. Finally the *Prince Albert*, fitted out by Lady Franklin and commanded by Mr Kennedy, with Lieutenant-de-vaisseau Bellot of the French Navy as second-in-command, arrived in 1851 to explore Prince Regent Inlet and the northern part of Boothia.[15]

The only traces found by these various expeditions were three graves on Beechey Island; the dates on them proved incontestably that Franklin had spent the winter of 1845–6 at this island. The most active searches produced no further results, and the various ships had to return home to evolve a new search plan. The new expedition was entrusted to Captain Sir Edward Belcher who was to enter the arctic regions via Baffin Bay and attempt to join the expedition which had left Plymouth on 20 January, had passed through Bering Strait in 1850, and consisted of *Enterprise*, Commander Collinson, and *Investigator*, Commander M'Clure.

Britain's noble perseverance had aroused the keenest sympathies in France; for my own part I admired and envied the fate of these men, as generous as they were bold, again exposing themselves to new perils in the hope of snatching from death equally glorious beings.

Luck served me better than I could have hoped; through the benevolent support of Maréchal de St-Arnaud, to whom I had expressed my hopes, I obtained support and authorization from the Naval Minister to request permission from the British Admiralty to take part in this last expedition. The reply with which the Admiralty honoured me represented the full realization of my wishes; I was accepted with an alacrity which went straight to my heart, and on 13 April 1852 I left France, bound for London.

If chance had favoured me, surely providence must also have guided me. Luckier than my brave, unfortunate compatriot and friend Bellot, I was able to embrace my mother and see my family again.

CHAPTER 1

The Outward Voyage

The British expedition sent in search of Franklin consisted of five ships:

Assistance. Commander Sir Edward Belcher, C.-in-C., 424 tons, sixty–one men.[1]

Resolute. Captain Henry Kellett, 424 tons, sixty-one men.

Pioneer. Captain Osborn. Attached to *Assistance*, steamer, 60 hp, thirty men.

Intrepid. Captain McClintock. Attached to *Resolute*, steamer, 60 hp, thirty men.

North Star. Captain Pullen. Transport, 600 tons, thirty men.[2]

On 16 April 1852 all the ships being ready for sea, we left Woolwich Basin[3] to run down to Greenhithe,[4] a small, very picturesque community about eight leagues from London; here I went aboard *Resolute*.

On 21 April, after the ships had been inspected by the First Lord of the Admiralty, the Duke of Northumberland,[5] we left Greenhithe. The three sailing vessels were towed by the steamers *Monkey*, *African*, and *Lightning*; *Pioneer* and *Intrepid* proceeded under their own steam.[6]

At 3.00 p.m. we dropped anchor at the mouth of the Thames off the Arsenal to take aboard some replacements; soon afterwards we were taken in tow by two other steamers, *Basilisk* and *Desperate* [screw-steam frigates], which were to accompany us through the North Sea. We now headed for Longhope Bay in the Orkneys.[7] But on reaching those islands the C.-in-C. changed course and headed for Stromness Bay where we dropped anchor on 26 April [25 April] at 2.00 p.m.

The officers on board *Resolute* were:

Mr Mecham, Lieutenant;

Mr Pim, Lieutenant;

Mr Hamilton, Lieutenant;

McDougall, Master;
Domville, Surgeon;
Roche, Mate;
Nares, Mate.[8]

I fairly quickly made the acquaintance of my future companions who, moreover, showed themselves to be full of regard for me, and at the same time very obliging, since I had only an imperfect command of English, and understanding me required a great deal of good will. I hope that in time I shall be able to express myself more easily in order to be of some use.

27 April 1852. Messrs Pim, Hamilton, Nares, and I hired a carriage to go to Kirkwall, capital of the Orkneys, some eighteen miles from Stromness.[9] This little town has about 3,700 inhabitants and an ancient cathedral which features in Walter Scott's *The Pirate*. I tried in vain to decipher some of the inscriptions; after a rather meagre dinner we set off back at 10.00 p.m., reaching Stromness at midnight.

28 April 1852. The weather, which had been fine, has become foggy; the wind blew violently during the night. Hence I stayed aboard despite some kind invitations which we received in several of the houses we had visited ashore.

29 April 1852. We left Stromness at 2.00 p.m. today, although the weather was quite bad and we had to fight against a strong westerly wind. *Basilisk* took *Assistance* in tow; *Desperate* towed *Resolute* and we left the port of Stromness amidst the cheers of the crowds which covered the surrounding heights.

To our great surprise we found the wind much less fresh outside, and the sea very fine; by about 5 o'clock the wind had dropped completely and *North Star*, which did not have a tug, fell astern. *Basilisk* cast off *Assistance*'s towline and went in search of her, then brought her up astern of *Resolute*, which passed her a towline. We now proceeded in the following order: *Desperate* towing *Resolute* and *North Star*, *Basilisk* towing *Assistance*, *Pioneer*, and *Intrepid* in order to save the last ships' coal.

At 10.00 p.m. the wind strengthened greatly; *Intrepid* broke one of her lines and we were obliged to stop.[10]

30 April 1852. The night was very bad; towards morning rain began to fall and to reduce the wind, but the weather remained foggy. The commander has just warned us that the tugs must soon leave us and that I should hold my letters in readiness. In the evening the weather turned fair.

1 May 1852. This morning as I came on deck I noticed a mannequin, decorated with ribbons, hanging from the topgallant stay.[11] It appears that this is a custom among whalemen, for whom 1 May is a holiday; since we have several of them on board they thought they should bring the fact to the commander's attention, so that he might double their rations.

Around 3 o'clock the weather became superb, after some very heavy rain; the wind has dropped and we are becalmed.

2 May 1852. It is Sunday today and the morning was very quiet on board; the commander conducted a service from 10 to 11,[12] then everyone retired to his cabin until noon. An invitation to dinner was passed by semaphore to the officers of our tug, *Desperate,* and at 2 we hove-to and two of those gentlemen came aboard.

We sat down at table at 3 o'clock and it was not until 8 o'clock that we noticed that the wind had freshened to the point that it was prudent for these gentlemen to rejoin their ship very quickly. While launching their boat a sailor injured his hand in a block.

In the evening the wind was very fresh, and although the steamers are about to leave us we can expect to soon have Kap Farvel in sight.

3 May 1852. During the night *Assistance* parted her towline and since the wind was too strong, was unable to pass a new one. Soon afterwards one of *North Star*'s hawsers also broke; we cast off the other immediately, as well as that of the steamer.

During the morning the weather strengthened again and the sea is very high. *Resolute* appears to be a good ship, behaving well in the heavy seas, and rolling much less than our neighbour, *Assistance,* although carrying a deck cargo of two rows of barrels along the entire length of the ship.

4 May 1852. The sea is still very high; the men are occupied with repairing the ice anchors.

The commander has communicated to all officers an order-of-the-day from the C.-in-C., the tenor of which is as follows:

The Lords Commissioners of the Admiralty having ordered me to take command of the ships comprising the Arctic Expedition, and having authorized me to communicate my instructions to the commanders of the various ships placed under my orders, I wish to impress on the minds of those officers the conviction that these instructions are confidential and that they are not to become the subject of discussion among the officers, especially in front of servants, who might communicate them to the crew. However, although there is nothing in the orders which demands secrecy, I have found that such matters should not be known to the crews, and since there may be circumstances where necessity obliges that they be changed completely, more ample explanations are pointless.

I wish it to be perfectly understood throughout the squadron that I shall be at all times open to unreserved communication with all the officers, upon matters which are not already defined by their naval instructions to be transmitted through the commanding officer; and that upon any ideas which may occur to them upon scientific, theoretical or other interesting matters, their remarks will find a place in the general journal of the voyage, which will be kept confidentially by myself.

It is, I hope, from what I have seen (and from the feeling which I know brought the majority of officers together to support me in this arduous undertaking), unnecessary to say more, than that each will strive to maintain the general happiness of our community – that they will see the necessity of avoiding any subjects which may cause irritation or difference of opinion; and that if any exciting discussions should arise between others, they will use their utmost endeavours to turn the conversation, or to soften irritable remarks, which may unfortunately have escaped.

To carry out the important service in which we are all engaged, we should remember that *all must pull together*; that the success of the expedition is the *success of all*, and that according to the importance of the general result, so will they be entitled to ask for reward.

One failure, one dark spot on the record, may not at the moment be thought important – but remember that the eyes of the whole civilized world are upon us! As those who preceded us have done well, let us strive to exhibit what can be achieved by discipline, good feeling and that untiring zeal which is ever conspicuous in our noble profession.

The weather is now quite fair all day, but towards evening the wind strengthened considerably and we are tacking so that we can heave-to if necessary, and we are reefing the topsails.

5 May 1852. A terrible night and I was unable to sleep for a moment; since my bunk is athwart ship it was untenable and I had to stay up all night.

Towards noon the gale was at its height and poor *Resolute* was labouring terribly, hove-to under main topsail and fore-topmast staysail.[13] Water was coming aboard from every side and the sea was dull. Towards evening the squalls began to be less violent and I hope that we will be able to go about and get under way.

6 May 1852. The bad weather continues, with very violent squalls and intermittent calm spells. Towards noon the wind swung into the northwest and flattened the sea, although there were still hail squalls.

We have taken advantage of this opportunity to get rid of the weight on deck; some of the barrels have been sent below.[14]

7 May 1852. The weather remained squally all day; this evening we were almost becalmed, with baffling breezes; the swell is still heavy. The two steamers are still in company despite the bad weather and are waiting for a favourable moment to transship their complement of coal to *Pioneer* and *Intrepid*.

The ship is labouring much less, thanks to the precaution yesterday of removing the barrels which were encumbering our decks.

8 May 1852. Weather fair all night and the wind has decided to swing into the south. The C.-in-C. made a signal to the two steamers accompanying us to prepare to leave us. All the ships hove-to and their captains came aboard *Assistance* to receive their final orders. The mail bags, which were filled in an instant, were carried aboard *Basilisk* which, followed by *Desperate*, has just passed ahead of each ship. The crews manning the rigging saluted us with three cheers and each of us replied with all his heart, since in truth one feels a keen emotion in saying goodbye to his friends, for a long time and perhaps for ever. We do not know where we are going; we certainly have a goal but we cannot say that we will go to a specific place, or that we will return. I watched the two ships until I lost sight of them over the horizon, and I had a lump in my throat as I thought of all those I had left behind, and hence I have been sad all day.

Around midnight we got under way with a fine quartering wind but at 6.00 p.m. we were becalmed again. The barometer is very low and we might again have bad weather which would drive us away from Kap Farvel, which seems to be receding ahead of us, and which we want so much to reach.

9 May 1852. Not until 2 o'clock did a breeze suddenly get up from the SW, developing into a squall, a true whiplash.[15] During a very violent squall *Pioneer* was unable to hold her course and was obliged to bear away. In the last squall *North Star* lost a boat, washed overboard, and before leaving us *Desperate* had to give her one of her boats. Captain Kellett has been indisposed since yesterday.[16]

Towards evening we were obliged to send down the t'gallant masts and to heave-to under main topsail and fore topmast staysail.

10 May 1852. The wind had slackened greatly during the night and this morning we were able to make sail with a fine southerly wind, hauling into the SW and E. It is a long time since we had a fair wind and we are taking advantage of it by crowding on sail.

Time passes very slowly for me since I do not know enough English yet to mix in the conversation, and although I am not naturally talkative, I realize that this is an absolute necessity.

11 May 1852. We have magnificent weather which, I believe, promises to last. Everyone has been taking advantage of it, staying on deck until 1.00 a.m. to admire a fine *aurora borealis* which extended from east to west.

12 May 1852. Today's weather the same as yesterday, but almost calm; we exercised all morning at shooting at sea birds.

13 May 1852. Captain Kellett is still indisposed and *Assistant's* surgeon, Mr Lyall, came aboard to see him, accompanied by the C.-in-C., Sir Ed. Belcher. These gentlemen dined aboard and did not leave until 9.00 p.m.

14 May 1852. The weather is completely foggy; the wind began to freshen around 4.00 and in the evening it was blowing strongly from the NE; the sea became very rough and water was coming aboard with every wave. Around 9.00 p.m., since the main hatch was open and since my cabin is in the orlop deck immediately opposite, an enormous wave came in and I was completely inundated.

15 May 1852. Last night was one of the worst we have had so far; I was unable to rest for an instant and our messing arrangements felt the effects of the rolling. This morning the wind has dropped and we are becalmed.

Assistance's surgeon came aboard again and he is to spend the night, since our captain is seriously indisposed.

16 May 1852. Today we sensed the proximity of ice; I believe that we will soon encounter it.[17] In the evening it was very fresh and so humid that if one ran one's hand over one's clothing it came away wet.

17 May 1852. This morning the movement of the ship woke me; on going on deck I experienced great delight on seeing that we were being pushed along by a fine wind abeam.

In the afternoon the surgeons from *Assistance* and *North Star* came aboard; the latter stayed to help our surgeon watch over our captain whose condition does not improve. In the evening a little before sunset we spotted an ice-blink or a yellowish brightness on the horizon to the north and the cold wind coming from that direction seemed to confirm the presence of ice, perhaps some fifty miles from the ship.

I believe we will not raise Kap Farvel since at this point there is too much ice in that vicinity and it is pointless to get into it at this point, especially since we have no time to waste in getting into Baffin Bay.

18 May 1852. Nothing worthy of note.

19 May 1852. Same weather and nothing to report.

20 May 1852. This morning we saw drift ice for the first time, but only in small quantities of limited extent; we are about eight miles off Cape Desolation, and the wind is swinging into the south with a little fog.

This evening a yellowish line which rose above the horizon indicated a certain amount of ice in this area.

21 May 1852. We still have ice in sight and the wind has strengthened considerably; it has brought snow which covers the deck and the rigging.[18] The thermometer is dropping rapidly and has stopped at 0.5° above zero.

Many small birds are following the ship and have landed in the rigging. These poor little creatures, which have no doubt been driven offshore by a strong wind, are so exhausted that one can take them in one's hand.

22 May 1852. The wind is rising and the snow is still falling very heavily; the cold is very penetrating. We thought we could see land, but the weather is so thick that it has been impossible to be certain.[19]

23 May 1852. We are making little headway; weather still the same and very cold.[20]

24 May 1852. We have been running in to the land all night and around 1.00 this morning we sighted a fairly high coast with snow-covered mountains, which we estimate to be about thirty miles away. We are approaching to within five to six miles of the coast to identify it better; our plotted position on the chart puts us somewhere in the interior of the land, since this part of Greenland has never been carefully surveyed.

We were then able to recognize Godthåb on the west coast of Greenland and we headed along the coast with a fine easterly wind. The sea had been quite quiet but then a short, choppy sea developed, heralding the approach of a shoal bottom. Indeed, on sounding we got 60 fathoms.

Captain Kellett is much better today and I hope that he will soon be completely recovered.

25 May 1852. We were becalmed all day; it was not until 2.00 p.m. that a wind arose, preceded by a violent squall with heavy snow. The weather was very grey and quite a strange phenomenon caught my attention. At the height of the squall I and everybody else thought we could see a long line of breakers about a mile from the ship. We were already preparing to bear away since we had the wind on the quarter, when we noticed that the setting sun had made the breakers disappear; they were simply the effect of a mirage.

For two days now our position on the chart has been quite strange; for the past two days our calculations put us inland, which makes us suppose that there is quite a major error in the alignment of the west coast of Greenland. The chart of this country has never been made with much care, especially the west coast, which was not discovered until long after the east coast.

It was a Norwegian named Gunbioris [Gunnbjorn] who was the first to discover signs of land in this area around the beginning of the tenth century. He was driven to it by a violent gale, and gave his name to the lands he discovered. Shortly afterwards Eric the Red, condemned to banishment [in 982], fitted out a ship and announced to his friends that he was going to explore the land which Gunbioris had discovered.

In fact he headed west and having sighted land he coasted south, rounded a cape which he named Hvarf and reached an island which was named Kerikvey, where he spent his first winter. After three years of exploration he returned to his country and gave such a favourable report on the lands that twenty-eight ships were fitted out immediately and loaded with emigrants.[21] Only half reached their destination; the other half perished due to bad weather. This was how Greenland began to be colonized; several bishops were named for the new colony.

One of the first exploits of these colonists was the discovery of America by Eric the Red's son Lief in 1001; this land was named Helluland, Markland, and Vinland.[22] One may assume that Christopher Columbus was aware of this fact, and hence persevered in his enterprise, certain of succeeding.

By the fourteenth century there was no further word of the colony, which had been ravaged by the plague shortly before.[23] Since then several expeditions have been sent to find some trace of this colony; the last one was commanded by Captain Graah of the Danish navy in 1828, who wrote a very interesting account of his voyage.[24]

26 May 1852. Nothing noteworthy. The wind has been foul all day and we have been on the landward tack; in the evening we tacked. I have been spending the evening writing letters since we are soon to arrive at one of the Danish establishments in Greenland.[25]

27 May 1852. It has been very cold all day; the weather is foggy

and there has been a sort of hoar-frost falling which ices up one's face.

In the morning we tacked with a fairly fresh north wind which slackened greatly, however, so that we are almost becalmed. My correspondence is finished and if the Danish mail has not left it will soon reach its destination.

CHAPTER 2

Greenland and Melville Bukt

*28 May 1852.*We dropped anchor at 2.00 p.m. today off one of the Whalefish Islands, Kron, in a bay where we are obliged to lie almost side-by-side.[1] It is an excellent anchorage, perfectly sheltered from the wind, and since there are two entrances one could always get out if one were obliged to weigh.

We reached the anchorage towed by our boats, since there is generally little wind in this group of islands, whose mountains are very high, or else it is very variable. Moreover it is noteworthy that when there is ice near the land, it cuts the wind, and it is not uncommon to see a very fresh wind on one side of a belt of pack and almost calm or baffling winds on the other.

About twenty Eskimos live on Kron Prins[2] and are governed by a Dane who is charged with collecting, on behalf of the government, seal oil and furs which they sell at very moderate prices. This man is a subordinate to the governor at Lievely on Disko.[3]

This evening I went hunting but although we had been told that there were lots of ducks, I returned on board at 2.00 a.m. very tired and without any game.

During my walk I saw the sun set at 11.30 and at 1.30 I saw it re-appear above the horizon. There is now almost no night and it is as bright as in full day during the time the sun remains below the horizon.[4]

30 May 1852. This evening I went to visit the huts of the Eskimo, and it is impossible to think without shuddering that a human being could live in such hovels. These huts are holes excavated in the ground and covered with turf, forming a slightly flattened dome; the walls are 3 to 4 feet thick. The door is so low that one is obliged to enter by crawling and before reaching what one might call the communal chamber one is obliged to pass along a corridor just as low as the door and generally forming two sides of a right angle for the

Plate 1 De Bray's sketch of a Greenlandic woman wearing sealskin clothing and with her hair in a typical 'top-knot'

purpose, I suppose, of preventing the cold from penetrating directly into the hut.

A few planks, when they can procure them, or failing that the bare ground on which some seal or reindeer skins are spread, represents the bed on which the entire family sleeps pell-mell.

When one enters one of these huts one is seized by an insurmountable repugnance and a stench grips one's throat[5] since the outer air never penetrates here, except by a very small hole in the roof, up which the stove-pipe runs. Since the Eskimo of this area are in contact with Europeans they enjoy some minor conveniences. The clothing of both men and women is almost the same, made entirely of sealskin. It consists of a blouse with openings for the head and arms, trousers reaching a little below the knee and mocassins, all with the hair outside except for the footgear.

In winter one pulls on over this garment another of the same style made of reindeer skin with the hair side inside, and inside the boots or mocassins one wears a second pair made of dog skin. A hood of reindeer skin is attached to the blouse and completely covers the head; only the oval of the face is visible.

When the women have young children at breast the blouse has a large pocket at the back, opening into the hood, and they place the child there; in this manner they can work and still have their movements free. The women dress their hair in Chinese style, forming a top-knot of hair on top of the head [Plate 1], and they are delighted when they can procure a pretty ribbon to tie their hair with.

The Eskimo have a copper hue and very round faces; they have little facial hair and are generally dirty, especially the men, whose hair is always in disorder and full of seal oil. Only unmarried women can wear red clothes; this reminds me of a similar custom in the Marquesas where the colour red is tabu, i.e., sacred to certain tribes.

The Eskimo live on seal meat which they dry to preserve it, since they are often short of food, and they are obliged to eat their dogs, although this is a great sacrifice since these animals form their main wealth. During the winter they harness them to sledges, and with three or four dogs they cover up to fifty miles a day across the ice. Dog skins are also used for making camp beds which are totally impenetrable to cold.

These dogs are very wild and are almost unapproachable by strangers; they strongly resemble our wolf hounds but they are a bit bigger and fawn-coloured.

During the severe winters the Eskimos stay in their huts and since the dogs do not go out either they give rise to a stench so that it is very difficult for a European to enter their dwellings. However the resident Dane also lives in one of these huts in winter with his wife, who is an Eskimo. He receives from the government 1,000 francs per year for leading this terrible existence and seems to be very satisfied with his position.

31 May 1852. Today was the birthday of Mrs Domville, the wife of our doctor, and we set off to go hunting, carrying all kinds of provisions. After eating supper on the top of a mountain amidst the snow we started off to return aboard; we did not get back until 3.00 a.m., very satisfied with the manner in which we had spent the night.[6]

1 June 1852.[7] Since we have been at Kron Prins the weather has been superb, true summer weather, and were it not for a little snow which covers the mountains, and the floating ice which one can see drifting past from time to time, one would never believe that one was on the coast of Greenland at 60°N latitude. The Eskimos came today to display their skill at throwing the harpoon, which they handle with great vigour. Then they demonstrated to us how their canoes were unsinkable by rolling over in them several times in the water without leaving their craft. One man sits in each, his legs stretched out [Plates 2 and 3]. A piece of sealskin which is placed around the hole which accommodates the man's body and which is secured below his arms, prevents the water from entering the canoe.

The canoes themselves are made of sealskin; only the keel and some ribs are made of light wood, or failing that of reindeer or whale bone. Each canoe is equipped with a double paddle, a harpoon and a line for fishing or making fast the harpoon. This line is always kept in front of the Eskimo on a little stand and is attached to an inflated

Plates 2 and 3 De Bray's sketches of Greenlanders in their kayaks, showing the inflated sealskin float behind the kayaker and the stand for his harpoon line in front

bladder which acts as a buoy for retrieving the harpoon once it has been thrown.

Women may not use these canoes, which are called *kayaks*; for their own use they have much larger boats, like flat-bottomed river boats, which are called *umiaks*.

2 June 1852. We were again hunting for recreation but in general our efforts have not been very productive; but the exercise is beneficial and we need to temper ourselves to fatigue.[8]

3 June 1852. Nothing noteworthy.

4 June 1852.[9] This evening some Eskimos from Disko came aboard with their wives and we organized a little dance; the ladies were so delighted that it was very difficult to get them to leave at midnight.

I distributed to the women some dolls with which each officer has been supplied, having taken care to write on the white petticoat the name of our ship and the date. This is a very ingenious idea of the

English ladies who thought that this might serve to locate Franklin
or at least give him hope that somebody was looking for him if one
of these dolls happened by chance to come into his hands.

5 June 1852. We weighed at 7 this morning to proceed to Lievely
on Disko, in superb weather and a very light breeze; as a result we
did not reach the anchorage until 4.00 p.m. *Assistance* signalled to
Pioneer to take the lead to look for the channel while we hove-to. A
little later we got under way, with *Assistance* in the lead.

Once the latter had anchored the wind freshened and she dragged
her anchor and was obliged to reset her topsails and stand out to sea.
Pioneer joined us at this point and having made five tacks, *Resolute*
entered the bay; seeing that we could not weather a rock lying in the
middle of the entrance to Godhavn harbour we decided to anchor in
16 fathoms with a rocky bottom. Our anchor began to drag, too, and
it was only by paying out a great length of cable that we managed to
hold.

Pioneer, which had found herself somewhat blanketed, was attempting to luff as much as possible to weather a large ice mass, but
was unable to do so and we watched her drive briskly onto the ice.
Her mizzen shrouds hooked on some ice projections and the mizzen
mast broke halfway up. *Assistance* entered shortly afterwards and
tried to anchor in the harbour itself, since she had the governor of
Lievely on board as a pilot, but having made about fifteen tacks and
having lost part of her false keel on the rock in the middle of the
bay, the captain decided to anchor beside us.

North Star and *Intrepid* arrived soon afterwards and also anchored
near us. Each ship then sent her boats to *Pioneer*, which was soon
rescued from her unfortunate position and was able to drop anchor.

6 June 1852. First thing this morning all the ships began to shift
their anchorage and by 9 o'clock we were all anchored safely in
Godhavn harbour, opposite the Danish establishment. During this
manoeuvre *North Star* shaved too close to the coast and since the
tide was ebbing very fast, the ship ran aground and was obliged to
wait for the flood tide to get off.

7 June 1852. This morning at 8 I set off with two officers to climb
a mountain and after about six hours of strenuous gymnastics we
arrived at the summit, which was still snow-covered. We marked
our victory by a general discharge of our guns, which was heard
perfectly on board, as we learned later.[10] I estimate the height of this
mountain at about 2,500 feet above sea level.

Having recuperated a little and built a small pyramidal cairn we set off to find a descent route on the other side of the mountain. For most of the route we were waist-deep in snow and were greatly encumbered by our guns; in fact they were of little use to us since the only game we encountered was a fox which we were unable to get a shot at, and two or three white partridges which flew off out of range.

Finally at 10.00 p.m. I found a descent route which seemed less hazardous, but it still appeared so treacherous that my two companions refused to follow me. A few moments after I had started down I found myself greatly embarrassed, being unable either to descend or to climb back up. Finally, taking my courage in both hands, I slid down the snow on my back and was lucky enough to encounter a projecting rock which I grabbed, since my descent was becoming too rapid. I had successfully negotiated the bad pitch and now there was only soft, shallow snow, which I descended in thirty minutes. My two companions ultimately found a route that was slightly better, and reached the bottom three hours after me.

While they were descending I had walked to the houses where I was very pleased to find the officers from *Assistance* dancing with the beauties of Lievely; they offered me some stimulants, of which I was in great need, since I had been walking for fifteen hours and had had only a piece of biscuit and cheese to maintain my strength.

Since we had agreed on the houses as our rendezvous, my two companions rejoined me there and we returned on board. After a fine supper we headed for our bunks, for my part, with very great pleasure.

8 June 1852. Nothing noteworthy today. I did not go ashore, still feeling a little fatigued after my climb yesterday.

9 June 1852. We have taken four Eskimo dogs aboard each ship for use with our sledges.

10 June 1852. At 8 o'clock this morning *Assistance* made the signal to weigh and we left Godhavn Bukt, heading for Waigat Strait where we have heard one can pick up coal along the shore.

Before leaving Disko, which is the last point where we will find any vestige of civilization, a few notes on this island naturally find a place here. Disko is an island of fairly large extent, inhabited by about three hundred Eskimos, who are subjects of Denmark and obey a governor who lives at Lievely with his wife and children. An inspector constantly makes the rounds during the summer to watch over the various little settlements scattered on the mainland or on the islands.

At Lievely the inhabitants are almost all Danes or are of mixed blood, and were it not for their dress one might mistake them for Europeans. They do not live in Eskimo huts as at Kron Prins, but in very comfortable wooden houses, and they never lack for anything since in the event of scarcity the governor must provide for their needs.

Disko is very rich in minerals, but extracting them entails great difficulties. I observed large amounts of volcanic materials and in some places the same lava as near Vesuvius, although in the various parts of the island which I visited I found no signs of a crater.

There are few animals on Disko: a few foxes, a few reindeer and sometimes a polar bear, but only rarely since they prefer to live on the mainland and only stay on the island when the ice break-up cuts off their return route. One also finds some white partridges [rock ptarmigan] which are delicious to eat, ducks of various species, and a great variety of sea birds.

11 June 1852. The wind has freshened a little but it is foul and we are tacking amongst drift ice in Waigat Strait.

12 June 1852. In the evening it fell almost calm and the C.-in-C. signalled every ship to send a boat ashore to look for coal; but all our searches were in vain, except for *Assistance*'s boat which found a few scattered pieces.[11]

13 June 1852. Towards noon the ice became closer and we could no longer tack; we decided to bear away and pass to the west of Disko. In the evening the wind dropped and we made only slow progress.

14 June 1852. Still little wind and it is foul again. We are running along the coast in short tacks in order to take advantage of the changes of wind produced by the high mountains and the deep valleys which characterize this land.

15 June 1852. We have finally managed to get to windward of Lievely and now the wind is favourable to head north. The weather has been very unpleasant all day due to the snow which did not cease until midnight. The ice is becoming more common and I have noticed some black floes. I presume that in descending from the mountains the snow carries with it earth and rocks which are bound together by frost and thus form these black masses which one might easily mistake for little islands.

16 June 1852. A magnificent following wind all day. Around 3.00 p.m. we entered a true sea of ice, broken into pieces 5 to 6 feet thick. Thanks to *Resolute*'s iron-shod bow we quickly passed through this bad area and by 5 o'clock we were in a completely ice-free sea, heading for Upernavik. The sea is as smooth as a mirror despite quite a fresh wind.

17 June 1852. A light breeze all day and quite calm in the evening. We are following the land five or six miles off without encountering much ice.

Around 11.00 p.m. we were abeam of Svartenhuk three miles off the lowest point and having to struggle against a strong tidal current; we were almost stationary, yet the log recorded 3 knots. The weather has become very foggy and there is a sort of snow pellets and melted snow falling.

18 June 1852. We have been hugging the coast all day to reach Upernavik, but night fell before we could reach the anchorage and we are heaving-to to wait for daylight.

19 June 1852. This morning, without making any signal *Assistance* went to anchor off the settlement of Upernavik. Not knowing if we were to anchor also we moored to a grounded iceberg with three heavy cables;[12] *Pioneer* came and moored astern of us. *North Star* and *Intrepid*, which were a little to leeward, did not arive until 11 o'clock and anchored with two anchors since the weather had become squally and the wind was strengthening rapidly.

After dinner I went ashore with two of the officers to purchase some garments and boots from the Eskimos; the wind was still strengthening and the snow becoming heavier and the captain specified a rendez-vous of 8 o'clock sharp at the boat. Having finished all our purchases in short order and having visited the governor, around 7 o'clock we were thinking of returning on board. Great was our surprise on reaching the summit of a little hill which hid the ships from view to see *Resolute* and *Pioneer* under sail and running before the wind. We then made some signals to *Assistance* to come for us since the weather was terrible, but they probably did not see us and we sat for two hours against a rock trying to shelter as well as possible from the wind and snow.[13]

Finally, to our great joy, one of *Intrepid*'s boats came for us and when we got aboard that ship they plied us with hot drinks, of which we were in great need. We rolled up in two blankets on the deck of the main cabin and were soon fast asleep.

20 June 1852. This morning after a good breakfast I set off with *Intrepid*'s captain and some officers to visit a graphite mine which is now completey abandoned. By 2 o'clock we were back aboard *Intrepid* where we found a boat from *Resolute* waiting for us. After an excellent dinner we thanked the captain and officers of *Intrepid* for their warm hospitality and returned to our own ship, which we reached at 6 o'clock. On our arrival the incident of the previous night was explained to us. Around 7 p.m., almost at the time when we were heading for the boat and when the wind was strongest, *Resolute*'s cables were still holding although she was working heavily; but then the iceberg to which she was moored could not hold any longer and began rotating. The ice anchors tore out and the ship began drifting at a terrifying speed.

Pioneer, lying a ship's length astern of *Resolute*, did not have time to slip her cable and as a result the outer end of *Resolute*'s jib-boom fouled the rigging of *Pioneer*'s fore topmast and both these masts carried away at the same time.

Resolute now set her topsails with four reefs and her foresail to try to get off the coast which was very close but which could barely be distinguished, the snow was falling so heavily. Around 10 o'clock the wind began to drop and the ship was able to place herself in a good position and make a series of short tacks off the bay. Only then was it possible to assess the full extent of the danger which *Resolute* had run since she might have been wrecked a thousand times on the numerous rocks scattered around the bay, barely awash and of whose existence we had absolutely no knowledge. Moreover, the fog and snow were so thick that it would have been impossible to see them.

At 8 o'clock the other ships weighed and we set a course to pass to windward of the Woman Islands. Around 10 o'clock *Assistance* fired three guns; the weather was foggy and we could not tell what they meant. We thought she might be ashore and we immediately sent several boats but they soon returned to inform us that the signal had been in response to *North Star*, which had already fired several shots. The C.-in-C. at the same time gave us a northeasterly course to run through a channel through the middle of the islands, thus avoiding the west coast of the archipelago which is strewn with reefs.

21 June 1852. The fog is a little less thick today but a lot of snow has fallen and at 10 a.m. the drift ice blocked our progress. Crowding on sail with a fairly fresh wind we bravely entered the ice and by 2 o'clock the sea ahead was completely ice-free and we were heading along the coast, eight miles off. In the evening the wind dropped and we were becalmed. The settlement of Upernavik which we have just left is the best of all the Danish settlements on the coast of Greenland; it provides fine furs and since last winter's hunting was very good, we were able to outfit ourselves with boots and clothing which we had not found in the other settlements.

The governor is a Dane, born in Upernavik, and he was very obliging to us. The Eskimos are the same as those I had seen before, possessing a certain degree of civilization from their constant contact with Europeans.

22 June 1852. Yesterday's calm continued all day and we took advantage of it to shoot some sea birds which we fed to the dogs. The C.-in-C. then made a signal for the two steamers to raise steam and at 5 o'clock they passed us towlines, all our sails having been furled.

Ice appears only rarely and the season seems quite favourable since we are fifteen days ahead of the last expedition, which was forced to wait for several days in this same area without making any progress.

23 June 1852. Around 2.00 a.m. we cast off the towlines and set sail with a light west wind which brought a very thick fog. We are constantly encountering floes which force us to deviate from our course and hence we are making slow progress.

At daybreak we were trying to check our position when all of a sudden, through a break in the fog, we spotted land only about 200 m away; the lead gave 5 fathoms and a rock bottom. We immediately moored to a berg and *Intrepid* passed us a towline so that we could close with *Assistance*, which lay only a short distance from us in 4.5 fathoms.

The fog has been thickening but so as to not waste time we took towlines from the steamers and ventured to get under way, avoiding impacts with the ice as much as possible, although one cannot see the floes until one hits them. At midnight the ice became so close that we abandoned our progress and moored to wait for the fog to clear and let us find a passage.

24 June 1852. Around 3 a.m. we got under way, heading northeast, towed by the steamers, in superb weather and through floes 2 feet thick. At 8 p.m. we moored again.[14] Shortly afterwards the wind got up from the west and a vast berg near us began to move in our direction; this awkward neighbour made us hurriedly cast off our lines. The Eskimo dogs had been put out onto the ice to get a bit of exercise and at the point of our hurried departure a boat was sent to pick them up. One of them refused to let anyone approach, however. Having tried every means possible to make him come back we were forced to leave him to his sad fate, since it is certain that he will die of hunger or fall prey to a polar bear.[15]

25 June 1852. Very fine weather with a good wind abeam. We are

Plate 4 De Bray's sketch of the situation on 26 June 1852 when *Resolute* (centre) was nipped. The other vessels are (left to right) *Intrepid*, *North Star, Assistance,* and *Pioneer.*

approaching the coast of Greenland where we find the sea encumbered with drift ice, but we are encountering enormous icebergs the whole time, which force us to deviate from our course.[16]

26 June 1852. This morning *North Star* came so close to us that her bowsprit fouled our mizzen shrouds but without causing any dam-age.[17] The sea is still almost free of ice but rain is falling constantly.

Around 8.00 p.m., since the weather did not look promising and the ice was becoming closer, we moored. A little later the wind rose and drove the ice down on us. Soon *Resolute's* rudder, which we had not been able to unship quickly enough, was unable to resist the pressures and was smashed. The ship was lifted two feet and heeled 35° to port [Plate 4].[18]

There was nothing to do but wait for the ice to slacken, allowing the ship to right herself. While waiting for this event all the crews were set to work cutting docks in the floe to place at least the others ships in some shelter.

The method used for cutting these docks involves first outlining on the floe the dimensions required [Plate 5]; the shape is a trapezium whose length is a little greater than the total length of the ship; thus in the figure AB is the edge of the floe and ABCD the trapezium. Then, using a saw (Figure 1), one cuts along the three sides AC, CD, and DB, then the diagonal AD, and in the middle of each of the triangles ACD and ADB one chops a hole with the instruments shown in Figures 2, 3 and 4, penetrating right through the ice. One

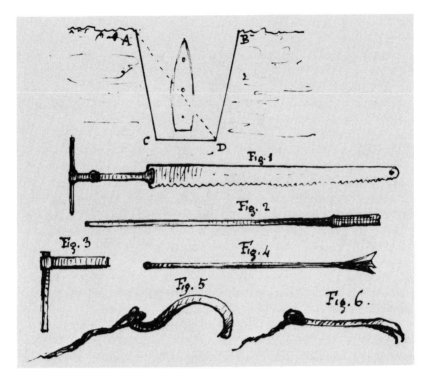

Plate 5 Diagram of the shape and dimensions of an ice dock (top).
Figure 1: an ice saw; Figures 2–4: assorted ice chisels and picks;
Figures 5 and 6: ice anchors

lowers into each hole a charge of 5 or 6 lbs of powder enclosed in a tin can, which one sinks a little below the lower surface of the floe. A fuse encased in gutta percha communicates the fire to the powder; on exploding the latter blasts the ice into pieces. One then clears the ice from the dock by way of side AB and the ship is placed in it stern-first, the stern against CD; the bow, which is the strongest part of the ship, faces any pressures the ice may exert if it closes up again.

With three saws, each handled by ten men, we cut such a dock in ice 4 to 5 feet thick in less than an hour. Each of the saws is handled with a tripod, one and a half times the length of the saw in height [Plate 6]; the saws are generally 10 feet long. A chain fixed to the handle of the saw passes through an iron pulley fixed to the top of the tripod and six ropes running from the end of the chain, each handled by one man, provide an upwards movement, while four

Plate 6 A party sawing ice using a tripod and ice saw.

men using wooden staffs passing through the handle of the saw produce a downwards movement helped by the weight of a pig or ball attached to the lower end of the saw.

In order to moor in the dock one uses ice-anchors (Figures 5 and 6) but especially those (Figure 6) designed in an S-shape. Cables are led ahead and astern to these so that the ship cannot move at all, thus avoiding damage to the sides of the dock. The stern is always at the back of the dock and one eases up the rudder, which is hung athwartships at the stern, ready to be reshipped.[19]

Once the crews of *Resolute* and *Assistance* had cut a dock for those two ships, and once *Resolute* had got free from her unfortunate position, we moored solidly, for the moment sheltered from the pressure of the ice which is in motion in all directions.

27 June 1852. We are still in the same position in our dock off Allison Bay. Since the ice pressure had damaged the entrance to our dock we were obliged to enlarge it to get the ship's bow farther in.[20]

Last night a bear came prowling around the ship; we were able to get only one shot at it at long range; the only result was to put it to flight.

28 June 1852. Since the ice had opened to the NE, in the morning

North Star and *Pioneer*, which were moored some distance from us, came to join us.

When the ice slackened a little all the ships cast off their moorings to take advantage of this opportunity, the crews hauling on towlines along the ice edge. At 4.00 we moored again for the night since the fog was starting to thicken.

29 June 1852. The fog cleared this morning, allowing us to see two ships to the north, probably two whalemen, stopped by the ice like ourselves. Since our position did not seem very secure the steamers passed us towlines to haul us to the other side of the floe; at the same time we sent a work party with a saw to cut away a little mass of ice which might have caused trouble. The C.-in-C. has just issued an order concerning hunting, which reads as follows: 'It is forbidden to fire a gun aboard the ships, and no hunter can go out on the floe without the official permission of the captains of the ships. Any animal killed will be considered as the property of the Crown, and will contribute to the general food supply and will be distributed by a Committee appointed for the purpose.'

30 June 1852. We cast off our moorings around 1.00 a.m. to take advantage of a channel which had opened during the night. At 8.00 a.m. we spotted a ship along the ice edge, only her bow section still being afloat. We moored immediately and identified the abandoned vessel as the whaleman *Regalia* of Kirkcaldy in Scotland. We removed from this vessel everything which might be of use to us,[21] and blew up the floating part to attempt to empty the hold, but the powder charge probably not being large enough, when the ship sank it released only a few empty barrels and three or four casks of oil.[22]

Soon afterwards we sighted a ship to the southeast which was heading towards us, towed by her boats [*St Andrew*, of Aberdeen]; then, as the fog lifted we saw fourteen other whaling ships moored to the floe to the north. The steamers passed us towlines and eighteen hours later we were busy cutting a dock near the fourteen whalemen, whose crews welcomed us with the customary three cheers, accompanied by some quite unharmonious music.[23] This time, guided by experience, the dock was cut, the ship hauled in, and the rudder protected within the space of an hour and ten minutes, using only 10 lbs of powder.

Captain Parker of *Truelove* and three other captains, one of them American, [Captain William Quayle of *McLellan*], came aboard to spend the evening and we learned from them about the wreck of *Regalia*.

On 19 June the gale we had experienced off Upernavik had been experienced here too; *Regalia* had cut a dock in one of the corners of the floe but both sides of the dock gave way and, as they closed, crushed the unfortunate ship. But her crew had time to escape and, following their fatal custom, set fire to the ship[24] and took refuge via their boats aboard the first whaling ship we had encountered that morning.

The whalemen lying near us are all British except for a single American vessel,[25] and they are waiting for a favourable occasion to cross Baffin Bay and head west into Pond's Inlet where the fishing is usually very productive.

1 July 1852. I went hunting today and while pursuing a bird which I had wounded, the ice broke under me and I took a detestable bath; I quickly returned aboard badly chilled and far from happy with my outing.

The whalemen tried to make some progress but after an hour of work they were obliged to cut new docks to shelter from the pack which was starting to move.

2 July 1852. Today I was feeling the effects of my accidental bath of yesterday and I was suffering a little. The C.-in-C. inspected all the ships, despite the fact that it was snowing heavily and there was quite a biting cold.

3 July 1852. The wind is very fresh and we have reason to fear a gale from the southwest which could be quite hazardous; the sea is still completely ice-covered and there are no openings visible from our mastheads.

4 July 1852. We can see land quite distinctly: Cape Walker and Melville Monument, elevated considerably by strong refraction, which presents very extraordinary sights to the eye. One might think one was seeing cities with palaces and domes, all marvellously lit by splendid sunshine.

At 2.00 a.m. we made an attempt to proceed but at 4.00 we were stopped and forced to cut another dock.

Towards evening a bear was sighted, busy devouring a narwhal carcass; a boat was launched and was able to approach to about[25] paces. The first shot did not kill it and it was after only five shots that it fell dead.[26] The bear meat was shared among the ships and provided a meal for our poor dogs, who have not had such a feast for a long time.

5 July 1852. The wind has dropped completely and we have not had such fine weather for a long time. At 4.00 p.m. the ice began moving and the whalemen left their docks, setting sail to take advantage of a small lead which had opened. We, for our part, had made our preparations and accepted towlines from the steamers, but we arrived too late to take advantage of the narrow lead. The ice closed up and after a few fruitless efforts by *Pioneer* to ram it, we were obliged to return to our original position.

6 July 1852. Same weather as yesterday but colder. An officer from *North Star* [the ship's mate, Alfred Alston] set off to walk to Cape Walker, which is about three miles on our beam. Around 3.00 we unmoored to join the whalemen, but when we had cut a dock in the point of the floe the ice split. Seeing the ice on the move, the whalemen hurriedly abandoned their positions; we were obliged to copy their manoeuvre and after two long hours of work we managed to get free. It was now a real steeplechase, each ship trying to take advantage of the least little lead; the steamers passed us towlines and some time afterwards we were quietly moored in another, more solid dock.

7 July 1852. Around 4.00 this morning the wind began to freshen from the southeast and the ice began to move. The American whaleman *McLellan*,[27] which had not cut a dock, was caught between two floes and so badly nipped that she was soon reported leaking in several places. Every ship sent a work party on board her; once the hold had been partly cleared and after the pumps had been manned for two hours they managed to stop the leaks.[28] Carpenters and caulkers set to work and by 10.00 p.m., while still not in perfect condition, the ship could at least put to sea again safely.

8 July 1852. The wind is still blowing extremely violently, and this morning the American whaleman had no chance of escaping. The ice pressure has been so great that she has been lifted by the two floes which have come together. Her stern has been pushed against *North Star*'s bow, having first broken the outer end of the bowsprit of another whaleman, *Alexander*, and her crew were obliged to cut away her mizzen mast to prevent it fouling *North Star*'s bowsprit.[29] Lying on her side and her hull cracking everywhere, the poor ship soon filled and was clearly doomed [Plate 7].

Throughout the day our men were engaged in salvaging from *McLellan* anything that might be of use, her captain having consented to this. Afraid that the crews of the other whalemen would come to loot her in their usual fashion, sentries were posted around the ship.[30]

This evening the ice is moving in every direction and all the

Plate 7 The American whaleman *McLellan* nipped in the ice; she has fouled the bowsprits of the *North Star* and *Alexander* (left). Provisions and equipment are being salvaged from the wreck.

whalemen are in a very tricky position, especially the brig *Orion*, which is making 2 feet of water per hour, despite all our efforts to free her. *Truelove* is also very badly placed and one can only hope that the wind does not strengthen, since it is almost inevitable that one of the whalemen would be wrecked.

As for all our ships, they are perfectly secure although the sides of our docks have been broken, since we always have the option of cutting away the ice astern and of thus retreating from the ice.

The American captain and the crews of two of his whaleboats have been given hospitality aboard *Truelove*; as for the other men, who are Russians, Portuguese or Irish, they have gone aboard various of the whalemen, where they have signed on.

Alexander, which is probably experiencing the greatest pressure, is resisting it totally and is making no water. *North Star* is no longer moving and will probably get away with the loss of a cathead and the outer end of her jib-boom.

This evening a bear was prowling near the ships; I set off in pursuit immediately, along with the doctor, but some of the whalers had spotted it and began running towards it; the animal took fright and ran off at top speed before we could get a shot.

9 July 1852. The wind has slackened but it is still blowing from the southwest, and there is no sign of openings in the ice. We are continuing to salvage what we can from *McLellan* and *North Star* is taking everything we can get out of her.

10 July 1852. The weather is quite fine and the wind is swinging into the east. Towards evening the wind freshened out of the southeast and the barometer is dropping fast.

11 July 1852. The wind has freshened again this evening, with the same foul weather.[31]

12 July 1852. The wind has been fresh all day, and the ice pressures so strong that poor *Resolute* was cracking all over. We can still see land and by taking bearings we can see that we are being slowly carried north with the ice in which we are jammed. The two steamers have been obliged to cut the ice astern of them, since the pack ice was threatening them.

13 July 1852. Foggy weather and that eternal southeast wind which refuses to quit.

14 July 1852. The wind has finally swung into the southwest after several days and I think we can get under way, although we will have to give the ice time to open up. Everything around us promises well; numerous cracks have appeared in the floe.[32]

15 July 1852. The weather is superb but very cold. Today for the first time we lit the stove in the hold to dry the ship which is very damp.[33] In my cabin there is water running in all directions and the 47° temperature which the stove has produced has been very beneficial.

16 July 1852. Still very fine weather but impossible to proceed.

17 July 1852. I have been awaiting today with some anxiety because of the change of the moon, but it is not very favourable for us.[34] The wind is back in the southeast, all the ice is on the move and the edges of our dock are breaking up as we retreat. The steamers have steam up to be ready at the first signal.

In three days the ice has carried us fifteen miles south, which makes a total of four miles northward in nineteen days. Unfortunately the season is passing and if a lucky chance does not present itself we may perhaps spend the winter in the middle of the pack.

18 July 1852. The wind, which had been very fresh all night, dropped at dawn and we had the pleasure of seeing the sea clear along the land. Hence we are making all preparations to try to reach this lead.

19 July 1852. The weather is very foggy and one can hear from every direction the subterranean noises which signal the breakup of the ice. In the afternoon we set to work and cut about 100 m of ice to reach a channel which had opened astern of us. Around 9 o'clock we began moving and having expended quite a large quantity of powder, we have moored to the floe about half a mile from our former position but minus *North Star* and the steamers which were unable to get out of their docks.

We are now ready to get under way and I hope that tomorrow morning we can get completely free by standing in for the land.

20 July 1852. Weather very fine but the barometer dropping very quickly, which would indicate northerly winds in the opinion of our captain, who is very expert in arctic navigation. In the evening the weather was very calm and one could distinctly hear the sound of ice breaking; during the night it nipped us, but without doing any damage.

21 July 1852. At 3 o'clock we began warping using the ice anchors, and the whalemen set sail, heading south, all excepting *Alexander* which has joined us and which we have taken in tow.

We are progressing with difficulty but the least progress made is always for the better, in terms of trying to get out of the impasse in which we have been held for so long.

The barometer has risen again and all day I have noticed strong refraction which is always the precursor of winds from a southern quarter. I had written several letters which I put aboard one of the whalemen[35] which we left today and I think these will be the last from here for a long time, since it is not very likely that we will encounter any more ships.

22 July 1852. The weather foggy all day, and at noon we lost sight of *Assistance* and *Pioneer*. *Intrepid*, which was towing us, has left us to go in search of *North Star* and *Alexander*, which were a mile astern.

The thin ice has broken up, allowing us to advance quite easily all day. In the evening we fired some cannon shots to signal our position to *Assistance* but got no reply.

23 July 1852. We are still advancing slowly through very thick fog, firing signal shots for *Assistance*, which finally replied. From the direction of the sound we can judge that she is a little west of us. This evening we were stopped by ice which is becoming thicker and we are surrounded by enormous bergs; hence we moored for the night, ready to take advantage of the slightest channel.

24 July 1852. The fog has cleared and we have sighted *Assistance* and *Pioneer* about four miles to the northwest. We have tried cutting through the ice to make a passage but the ice closes up, forcing us to abandon our efforts and wait for the ice to stop moving.

25 July 1852. Weather fine all day; a little fog towards evening. At 8 o'clock we recommenced our task of yesterday and by midnight we were free, proceeding in tow of *Intrepid* in a fairly ice-free sea as far as the eye can see.[36]

26 July 1852. We are still advancing but slowly, and by dint of great effort. We stayed moored to the floe for some hours to give the crew a rest, and during this time I went off hunting with other officers.[37] This time we brought back three hundred birds; we've never been so happy.

27 July 1852. All our efforts ended in naught; we are closely beset, so that as we cut away the ice, more ice moves in and we have to start again.

This evening I feared for a moment that the ship would be lifted out of the water, as happened to us once before, but we got off with a scare, and by midnight we were almost in safety. The weather is so foggy that we cannot see the course to follow, even if a passage existed.

28 July 1852. Since the ice astern of us is thin and already shattered in several places the steamers tried to push it apart by running up on it at full speed, but we have been unable to proceed and are now moored to a berg; a lake on top of it gave us some fresh water.

In the evening the weather was magnificent; the men were given permission to play various games such as tennis, rounders, leap-frog, etc.[38] A bear came prowling near the ships; it received a ball but fled before anybody could hit him again.[39]

29 July 1852. Finally, after six hours of strenuous work we managed to break up the ice and we are sailing freely, with a long stretch ahead of us without obstacles.

30 July 1852. The weather remains foggy and very cold, with the thermometer below zero. Today the ice again brought us to a halt and we are moored to a floe. However, in these regions fog is a good sign, especially in spring, since when an opening appears in the ice a dense vapour escapes from it, and as a result one can be almost certain that when one encounters fog there is a certain expanse of water in the vicinity. We are surrounded by enormous bergs which are low, but of great extent.

Towards evening the mate of *Alexander* which is still in company, took a boat to reconnoitre and came rushing back to report that two enormous bergs ahead of us were moving. We immediately accepted towlines from *Intrepid* to get out of the way of these awkward neighbours. As we reached the other side of them the fog cleared and we had the satisfaction of seeing a totally ice-free sea ahead of us as far as the eye could see.[40]

31 July 1852. Superb weather and we advanced all day in tow of the steamers without encountering any obstacles.

CHAPTER 3

West to Winter Harbour

1 August 1852. Today we were under full canvas, sailing freely, something we have not done for thirty days. At 11 o'clock we hove-to off Kap York [Plate 8]. We can see the inhabitants making signals for us to land.[1] We immediately went ashore and made for their tents which lay about three miles from the floe edge to which we are moored.[2]

Six men, six women, and some children live in this inhospitable spot; one cannot imagine the misery of these unfortunates who do not even have wood to build their canoes and who use seal or walrus bones for making their sledges.

Captain Kellett made them a gift of a saw, some knives, and a few pieces of wood which they received with demonstrations of joy. These Eskimos are in every way similar as to type to those we have seen before, only they are more wretched and dirty. One of them, called Kalli-oo-Ruah, who has been nicknamed York, was taken to England by the last expedition and is now completely civilized.[3] We showed his portrait to his compatriots who did not recognize him. Only his mother seemed quite satisfied, but did not ask if he were dead or alive.

I climbed to the top of Kap York to try to spot *Assistance* but despite very clear weather I could not see any sign of her. The Eskimos have not seen her either; it is probable that she passed by here two days ago during the fog.[4]

For the first time I saw red snow, whose colour derives from some microscopic plant.[5]

This evening the whaler *Alexander* left us, taking our last letters, and headed southwest.[6] Soon afterwards we cast off our moorings and headed west with a light northeast wind.

2 August 1852. Weather foggy all day and a fresh easterly wind; we encountered some ice. At 8 in the evening there was no ice in sight

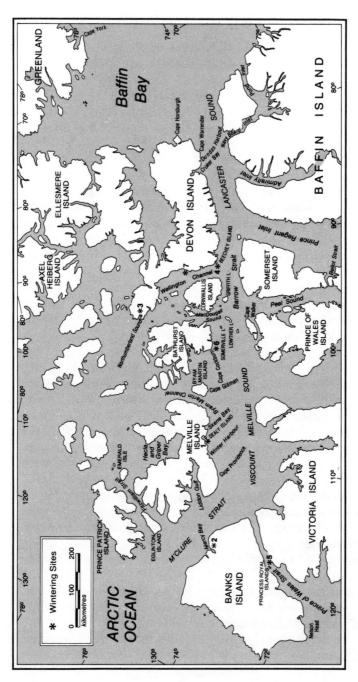

Plate 8 The central part of the Canadian Arctic Archipelago showing the areas of operations of Belcher's, Kellett's, Pullen's, M'Clure's, and Collinson's ships. Wintering sites are as follows: 1. *Resolute and Intrepid*, 1852–3; 2. *Investigator*, 1851–3; 3. *Assistance and Pioneer*, 1852–3; 4. *North Star*, 1852–4; 5. *Investigator*, 1850–1; 6. *Resolute and Intrepid*, 1853–4; 7. *Assistance and Pioneer*, 1853–4.

and we began to feel a heavy swell which definitely proves that we are now in a large expanse of water.[7] The wind is still pushing us vigorously and we are obliged to reduce sail to let *North Star* keep up. There is heavy snow falling, covering the deck.

3 August 1852. The wind still continues and this evening we sighted land, which I presume is Cape Horsburgh.

4 August 1852. The wind has swung into the west and we have been tacking all day, but since *Resolute* often missed stays, we have made little progress; hence Captain Kellett has made *North Star* independent. She immediately set off for Beechey Island, which is our rendezvous.

In the evening the wind was easterly again but the heavy swell and a 2-knot current against us are preventing us from making progress.

5 August 1852. The wind, which is very irregular in strength and varying in direction from N to SW, forces us to tack and we are making slow progress due to the swell from the west, which is still very heavy.

A few isolated floes appeared in the vicinity of Cape Warrender and Dundas Harbour. This latter inlet may serve as a refuge for a ship, the bottom being very good and there being no hazards to fear on entering.

6 August 1852. Calm all day or a light head-wind. In the evening the weather became foggy and the wind got up from the south-east.

7 August 1852. Wind very light all day with very clear weather. This allowed us to observe the land, which is quite close. This part of the strait, which is named Croker Bay, is very remarkable; the summits of the mountains are all in the same horizontal plane, cut here and there by deep gullies. The slopes of these mountains drop almost sheer into the sea and from a certain distance have quite a strong resemblance to the bastions of a fortress.[8] I suppose the gullies are caused by water deriving from snowmelt and flowing down the same furrows for centuries.

8 August 1852. The wind is a little stronger today but still out of the north and west. This is the warmest month of the year but the thermometer reads only -1°C. *Intrepid*, which is to windward of us, is signalling two ships in sight, probably *Assistance* and *Pioneer*. As for *North Star*, which is a better sailer than us, she is scarcely in sight.

9 August 1852. The wind has dropped completely; the signal was

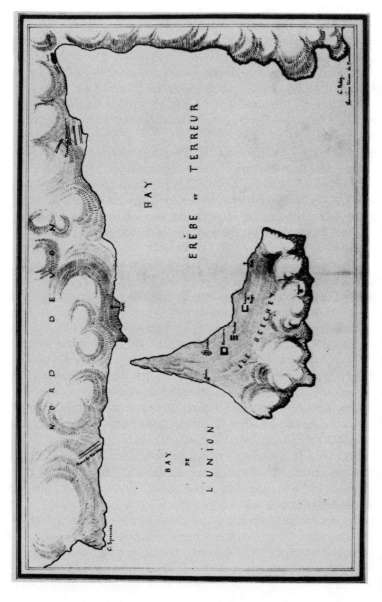

Plate 9 De Bray's manuscript map of Beechey Island and area showing the location of various features associated with the wintering of Franklin's expedition in 1845–6. These include the three graves on Beechey Island.

made to *Intrepid* to raise steam and one hour later we accepted a towline; at 10.00 p.m. we sighted a ship moored to the floe off Beechey Island.

10 August 1852. At 2.00 a.m. we were moored near *North Star* between Beechey Island and Cape Riley.

I set off at 9 this morning to take a little trip and to visit a little cutter, *Mary,* left near Cape Spencer by Captain Ross;[9] she is about 12 tons burden and Captain Ross brought her from the coast of Sweden with the assistance of only one man. She is still in good condition, and apart from some minor repairs one could use her immediately. It was on Beechey Island that the first traces of the Franklin expedition were found, proving that it had spent a winter in this bay, which has since been named Erebus and Terror Bay [Plate 9].

One can still see the graves of three men, one of whom belonged to *Terror* and the other two to *Erebus.*[10] The following inscriptions are carved on the wooden headboards as one faces east:

Sacred to the memory	Sacred to the memory	Sacred to the memory
of John Torrington	of John Hartnell	of W. Braine
who departed this	of HMS *Erebus,*	of HMS *Erebus*
life 1 January 1846	died 4 January 1846,	died 3 April 1846,
on board HMS *Terror,*	aged 25 years.	aged 32 years.
aged 20 years.		

A large number of objects which had belonged to *Erebus* and *Terror* were found scattered in all directions, pieces of sail, tin cans which had contained food, fragments of clothing and bags on which one could clearly read 'Terror.'

Shortly before reaching *Mary* I saw distinctly on the ground the tracks of several sledges, which had been observed earlier by Captain Ommanney's expedition in September 1850. These tracks headed north and ended at a little cairn built on the continuation of the mountain which forms Cape Spencer. Returning from the bay where *Mary* is beached and which is still called Union Bay because the British and American expeditions spent some time there together, I climbed to the top of Beechey Island, whose height is approximately 642 feet.

On the plateau forming the summit I found two ruined cairns, and another a bit farther away, where we found intact notes left by captains Austin and Ommanney in 1850.

The terrain of Beechey Island and Cape Spencer consists of fossils and madrepores[11] of all kinds; I collected some curious specimens.

The captain, worried at not having encountered *Assistance*, sent *Intrepid* to visit Admiralty Inlet, the last rendezvous point given by the C.-in-C.

11 August 1852. Today I climbed to the summit of Cape Riley to build a cairn consisting of a pole buttressed by a pyramid of rocks: a wooden board was nailed to the pole and I carved with my knife 'H.M.S. Résolue 11 août 1852' on one side, and my initials 'E.D.B.' on the other.

At the foot of Cape Riley I found a cairn containing documents signed by captains Austin, de Haven and Griffith, the latter being the captains of *Advance* and *Rescue* which comprised the American expedition. A little farther on was a red-painted cross with the inscription 'Prince Albert 25 August 1851.' I carefully scanned the horizon, which was very clear, but saw no sign of any vessel.

Around 7.00 p.m. *Assistance* suddenly appeared, rounding Cape Riley, towed by a steamer which we recognized as *Intrepid*; soon afterwards the two ships were moored to the floe near us.

12 August 1852. As soon as he arrived, the C.-in-C. organized several four-man parties, commanded by an officer, to conscientiously search the entire surrounding area, but nothing was discovered beyond the traces found in 1850.

The weather is magnificent and everything promises a fine start to our campaign, since it is really only now that we are almost entering the unknown.

Assistance and *Pioneer*, under the command of Sir Edward Belcher, will proceed up Wellington Channel, which at this moment appears free of ice as far as the eye can see from the summit of Beechey Island, while *Resolute*, accompanied by *Intrepid*, under the command of Captain Kellett, will head southwest down Barrow Strait, which at this point is as ice-free as we could wish.

North Star, which has handed over our provisions and replacements, has been cutting the ice in order to warp to the head of the bay and prepare to go into winter quarters. *Assistance* is also taking on her stores, while *Pioneer* is coaling from *North Star*, since we are all in a hurry to start; moreover the ice is giving us trouble, forcing us to shift our moorings constantly.

13 August 1852. *Intrepid* has been sent to examine Wellington Channel.[12] In the evening there was a major gathering aboard *Assistance*, and more than one bottle of champagne was drunk to the success of the expedition and to the health of each of its members;[13] then we separated, each to return to his ship and prepare to depart.

14 August 1852. This morning *Intrepid* returned from her expedition with the good news that Wellington Channel is completely free of ice to a distance of twenty-five miles from Beechey Island, and that from there they sighted a channel running northeast as far as they could see.

This evening all the crews were assembled on the ice at the foot of the British flag and Sir Edward Belcher spoke a few words to express his entire satisfaction at the conduct displayed since we had sailed.[14]

We again bade farewell to the officers of *Assistance* and *Pioneer* and if ever warm handshakes were exchanged it was now; under such circumstances there are lumps in every throat and the bonds of friendship are awakened in all their strength. There is no longer any reserve, and no more quarrels; everything is forgotten and disappears in the face of what may be a permanent separation.

An hour later *Assistance*, towed by *Intrepid*, cast off her moorings and the two ships soon disappeared behind Beechey Island, saluted by the cheers from *Resolute*, *Intrepid*, and *North Star*.

All night *Intrepid* was working to coal from *North Star*, in order to replace what she had consumed the day before, and to stow all she could on deck.

The last orders were given by the C.-in-C. before his departure and we are now left to our own devices, since everything is unpredictable in the circumstances under which we will find ourselves, and we must be able to take advantage of the slightest opportunities which chance provides.

As we had suspected, *Assistance* and *Pioneer* are going up Wellington Channel, *North Star* is staying at Beechey Island as a depot and as a place of refuge if necessary, in case an accident happens to one of the ships, while *Resolute* and *Intrepid* are to try to reach Melville Island. If possible they are to reach Winter Harbour where Parry wintered in 1819–20 and which is also identified as a rendezvous point for *Enterprise* and *Investigator*, both of which had set out via Bering Strait.[15]

Making the best possible course towards that point, we were to leave depots of provisions at points which were easy to recognize, in order to establish the means to get back to Beechey Island in case we had to abandon the ships. If we cannot reach Winter Harbour we are to winter at the site most convenient to our position and send sledges to western Melville Island to meet *Investigator*, as well as northeastwards to meet the sledges from *Assistance*.

In any case, if we are forced by the ice to spend a second winter before reaching Beechey Island, and if we have no news of Sir Edward Belcher, our captain is then to act according to his own devices and either continue the search or return to England according to the state of his crew at the time. As for provisions, we are sure to find them at Beechey Island.

Thus we are completely organized and are all delighted at the part we have been given in the search plan, since if we find nothing of Franklin and his companions we at least have the chance of meeting *Enterprise* or *Investigator*, in whose direction we will be heading.

15 August 1852. At noon, since *Intrepid* was ready and our last arrangements had been made, we cast off our moorings and she passed a towline to us, in order to head straight for Cape Hotham.

Shortly afterwards we rounded Beechey Island, saluted by the cheers of *North Star*, and found the sea ice-free and a fine north wind blowing; the latter allowed us to reach the cape [Cape Hotham] around 10.00 p.m. There the ice forced us to moor to wait until it allowed us to proceed.

16 August 1852. Around 1.00 a.m., the ice having opened, we continued our route in tow of the steamer, in order to round Cape Hotham. We approached to within a mile of it and the captain sent two boats to examine a cairn and the depot left by the last expedition. They found two casks of biscuit which were brought aboard, and left a new depot of provisions with a whaleboat which we could use to cross Wellington Channel and reach Beechey Island in case we had to abandon the ship.

We continued our progress along the land; around 8.00 the ship rammed a large piece of ice; the recoil threw her to starboard and her bow hit bottom in 2¹/₄ fathoms.

We braced her aback immediately but without success since the wind was very light, and *Intrepid* was obliged to pass us a cable over the port quarter to try to pull us off. She succeeded, the sails were furled, and taking a towline from the steamer we entered the ice, which had broken for us and moved offshore. We headed for Assistance Harbour on the east coast of Griffith Island where the 1850 expedition had wintered.[16]

Around 11.30, just as we were rounding the north point of that bay, the ship experienced a violent shock and we were aground for the second time today. This time the accident threatened to be more serious; the steamer could not haul us off, being herself in a bad position, although not aground. The tide was rising very rapidly, producing a very violent current as it rushed through the narrow channel formed by the ice.[17] A kedge anchor was dropped and the warp led aboard over the stern; at the same time *Intrepid*, which had managed to get free, was trying to haul us in the same direction, but all was in vain and poor *Resolute* would not move an inch, although she was creaking in every timber. Soon the ice driving in with the current took us on the starboard side, and pushing us farther inshore, laid us over to port. *Intrepid* was now obliged to leave us to seek safety herself. The ship was moored on all sides with warps and cables to ice anchors. Soon the tide began dropping, clearing us by 5 feet; the boats were now launched and we unloaded all the casks and other objects encumbering the deck and sent them aboard *Intrepid*; we thus lightened the ship by about 30 tons. The rudder was unshipped, the topgallant masts sent down, and then we could only await events. Around 6.30 the ebb current became very violent from the east-southeast and a very thick floe about two miles across, lying on our port side, began to move. Reaching the ship, it threw her violently to starboard at the same time exerting enormous pressure on her sides.[18]

Soon the ice had piled up to the height of the chains and *Resolute* began creaking in every timber. The danger was imminent; there was nothing we could do against such a force; we could only wait, counting on providence which had protected us thus far.

Fortunately the ship was not making any water and withstood the pressures valiantly. After an hour of cruel anxiety we were delighted to see the ice sliding slowly past our stern; a few charges of powder were exploded under the ice and helped in the movement. Finally around 10 o'clock the floe which had threatened to overwhelm us had passed and the ship's stern was afloat.

Intrepid had taken up her station astern of us, having dropped a bower anchor; we passed her a warp which was led to the capstan and the topsails were set and braced aback. But *Intrepid*'s anchor would not hold and we were forced to abandon this strategy. She weighed anchor and then, since the sea was quite high, a strong warp was passed to the steamer via the starboard bower; steaming at full pressure she gave us a jerk which for a moment laid the ship on her beam ends, but she soon righted herself and we were delighted to see her moving ahead under the sails which we had set.

The loss of half of our false keel was the only result of this accident, which might have had the gravest consequences for us. A depot of provisions was placed on the north point of Assistance Harbour and we took advantage of the fine weather to trim the ship and put everything in order.

17 August 1852. This morning the boats were hoisted aboard and the rudder shipped,[19] and taking a towline from *Intrepid* we set a course for the southern point of Griffith Island where, soon afterwards, we moored to the floe. A boat was sent ashore to erect a cairn and leave documents on the hill in the southwest of the island.

I went ashore in this boat[20] and was able to determine that the formation of Griffith Island is like that of Beechey Island, consisting of madrepore fossils with a few granitic rocks. We found intact the cairns built by the 1850 expedition on Cape Martyr on Cornwallis Island, as well as the four left on Griffith Island.

In the evening, with the wind freshening and with very violent squalls from the west, we weighed and with two reefs in our topsails set a course for Lowther Island; the sea ahead of us was clear but seemed completely icebound to the north.

The compass is becoming practically useless due to the sluggishness of its movements; the variation is 140°.

18 August 1852. At 8.00 a.m. we moored to the floe at the southwest point of Lowther Island. The wind, still very fresh from the west, is pushing the ice, which extends solidly to the north and east, preventing us from proceeding. The only route open to us at the moment is towards Cape Walker, completely opposite to the one we want. During the day, since the ice anchors had torn out, we moved towards the north end of Lowther Island.

19 August 1852. The ice did not allow us to reach the north end of the island and we were obliged to come back to the south end.[21]

20 August 1852. We are hugging the east coast of Lowther Island, sometimes tacking, sometimes moored to the floe, the wind blowing from west and southwest.

An officer was sent to the top of the island to examine the state of the ice, and came back to report that it was thin to the north and broken by large areas of water. We got under way immediately, heading in this direction, but were soon stopped again by ice extending from the north point of Lowther Island towards the east as far as the eye could see. To add to our difficulties the wind, which had slackened a little, has regained its strength from the west and the weather is becoming very foggy.

21 August 1852. We have been tacking all day to try to take advantage of the slightest opening in the ice but without success, and we are obliged to moor to the floe, which soon began moving, forcing us to withdraw to a little bay on the east coast of this miserable Lowther Island, which will not let us get away. The ice is pressing close and we have unshipped the rudder.

22 August 1852. Wind still from the west with heart-breaking persistence and the lookout indicates no change in the ice; it is simply piling up around us, blocking us in completely.[22] The temperature is starting to drop; the thermometer reads 5°.

23 August 1852. Captain Kellett gave orders to *Intrepid* to raise steam in order to go and check if we can continue our voyage at all.[23]

24 August 1852. Intrepid did not come back until very late and the news is not good. There is a large expanse of water to the southeast of Lowther Island towards Cape Walker and very little ice between Griffith Island and Garrett Island but between us and this open water our passage is barred by a very thick floe which we cannot tackle at present.

A leading seaman and four men, with a tent and two days' supplies were immediately sent to the north point of Lowther to watch the ice movements and to come and inform us of the least favourable change so that we can get under way, since often the slightest delay can cause a considerable loss of time where the ice is concerned.[24]

25 August 1852. The leading seaman who was on watch has come back aboard, reporting that the ice to the west is beginning to move east and that there is open water off Bathurst Island, but that there is still no passage to get out of our present position.[25] Weather squally; the wind was fresh all day but fell calm towards evening.

At 7 o'clock we released our first balloon, which carries with it about a thousand little squares of paper spaced along an iron wire with a slow match.[26] Assorted information on the present state of the crew and on *Resolute*'s position is printed on each piece of paper. As the balloon was released the match was lit so that the pieces of paper would fall at well-spaced distances; thus distributed at various points in the arctic landscape they may fall into the hands of some travellers and thus give Franklin or his companions news of us. This first balloon rose very high, heading north-northeast.

26 August 1852. Still in the same position, but the wind has swung into the north, shifting to northeast, and I hope that this will lead to a change in the ice. In anticipation of this the lookouts have been recalled.

27 August 1852. I went ashore today to climb to the top of a peak

500 to 600 feet high; from here I could see all around Lowther Island. For two days now the ice has seemed to be moving to the southeast, but still does not allow us any passage. The barometer is dropping and the wind is slackening; perhaps the calm will have more effect on the ice than the wind.

The nights are now lengthening quite quickly and before long we will see the stars again. I am certainly not looking forward to the long winter night but I do like the lamplight in the evening. I have barely got to bed before the sun is again high above the horizon.

28 August 1852. This morning a light wind from the west allowed us to weigh, heading for Griffith Island. Having got through two quite thick floes we found ourselves in a magnificent expanse of water; when it fell calm we received a towline from *Intrepid*.

Around 4.00 p.m. the wind became very fresh out of the north and the weather became foggy. Having rounded Somerville Island, we set a course through the channel between that island and Browne Island, heading for Cape Capel, the western point of McDougall Sound.

The signs are good; the lookout reports no ice ahead and I hope that we have finally seen the last of Lowther Island. However, I should not speak too ill of it since it provided us with an excellent shelter from the wind and ice for a week.

29 August 1852. Throughout the night we proceeded in tow of *Intrepid*. The clear weather allows us to see the land which we are following four to five miles off; around noon we clearly sighted Cape Cockburn surrounded by heavy ice which probably will not allow us to leave a depot there. The captain then decided to land this depot on the point nearest us, which turned out to be a very low point of land. This substantial depot consists of fifteen days' rations for ninety men.[27] Once the boat had returned we immediately headed along a channel between Cape Cockburn and a very heavy floe.

Towards evening the wind freshened from the west with foggy weather and heavy ice appeared to be about to block our route.

30 August 1852. The wind held very fresh throughout the night; we cast off the towline and having made two tacks along the floe we had the satisfaction of being able to proceed without obstruction. Soon afterwards a calm forced us to resume towing and we headed for Byam Martin Island.

We can see some ice to north and south but not a single piece in our path; quite extraordinary is the fact that none of the ships which have penetrated these waters has ever encountered ice here. We have noted a very violent westerly current which might suggest the existence of a channel linking the Arctic Ocean and the Pacific via Bering Strait.

This evening we are ten miles from Cape Gillman (the southern point of Byam Martin); the very clear weather allows us to see the north point of Graham Moore Bay.

The compasses are no longer of any use and we are obliged to use tables of true bearings of the sun calculated every six hours for each day.[28] We are seeing few sea birds and for two days we have seen only one walrus.

31 August 1852. We have been blocked by ice blockading the southern point of Byam Martin Island. When it began moving we were obliged to let ourselves be carried along the land. Having thus progressed about ten miles, we moored to the floe for the night to wait for the ice to let us pass. It is almost calm and the cold weather would make one expect a change of wind to the north.

1 September 1852. We have been kept awake all night by the floe to which we are moored; it kept breaking off the whole time, forcing us to shift our anchors.

This morning, as I had foreseen, the wind got up from the north and at 8 we weighed, heading through the midst of broken ice, and by noon we were free of all impediments and had a very fresh wind; starting to see Melville Island[29] [Plate 10].

2 September 1852. During the night the wind shifted to the northeast and we were able to approach Griffith Point and to send the boats ashore to establish a depot of nineteen days' provisions for twenty men. As soon as the boats were back aboard we headed along the lead, the wind slackening greatly.

Around 11 o'clock the wind had swung into the NW; since we were in a hurry to cover as much distance as possible the signal was made to *Intrepid* to raise steam immediately. An hour later we were under way with trysails set and under tow, heading around Skene Bay. About two miles south of Beverley Bay we were forced by the ice to moor to the floe.

3 September 1852. This morning Lieutenant Mecham and Dr Domville went ashore to hunt muskoxen and caribou which we had spotted yesterday as we coasted along, and were lucky enough to kill four muskoxen.

A work party was sent to bring back the meat;[30] in the meantime Captain Kellett set off with *Intrepid* to examine the entrance to Beverley Bay and to establish whether this harbour could, if necessary, accommodate the ships for the winter. The result of his obser-

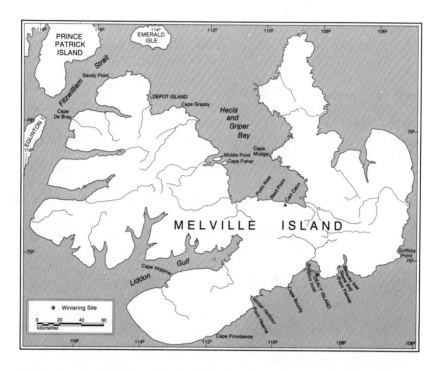

Plate 10 Map of Melville Island showing the wintering site of *Resolute* and *Intrepid* off Dealy Island and the areas of De Bray's sledging trips

vations was not very satisfactory since on approaching the land *Intrepid* grounded forward and was only able to get off by running out a heavy anchor aft.[31]

In the evening a party from *Intrepid* killed eight muskoxen.[32] The ice is on the move towards us, leaving behind it an immense area of open water around Cape Bounty.

4 September 1852. Another three muskoxen were killed yesterday, which makes a total of fifteen in two days; this result allows us to hope that Melville Island will provide us with some food in case of necessity.[33]

The wind was easterly for a moment but then swung to the SW and W, freshened greatly, then swung into the north and began to drive the ice towards the southeast. The gusts are extremely violent and there is heavy snow falling.

6 September 1852.[34] During the night the wind dropped and it was not until this morning that it began blowing violently from the north again. As a result of this wind the ice loosened rapidly; since

Cape Bounty appeared to be free, we cast off our moorings and set off under double-reefed topsails and the foresail.[35]

The ice seems very heavy about four miles off Cape Bounty and Bridport Bay is completely blocked. In the evening we were in Hecla and Griper Bay,[36] tacking between the pack and the fast ice, to try to reach Fife Harbour.

7 September 1852. The wind is still very fresh and we are making little progress to windward. The weather was very foggy this morning; when it cleared we could see the ice stretching from Wakeham Point to Hearne Point, completely blocking the entrance to Winter Harbour.

We approached as close as possible to the west point of Fife Harbour and, having moored to the floe, we actively engaged in loading three sledges to transport provisions for *Investigator* ashore and to resupply our sledges on the autumn journeys.

This depot was placed on the west point of Fife Harbour near Sir Edward Parry's cairn which we could see, despite the fog, at the entrance to Winter Harbour.

This landmark is formed by a block of granite 10 feet high, 22 feet long and 7 to 8 feet wide, and bears a carved inscription as follows: 'His Britannic Majesty's ships, *Hecla* and *Griper*, commanded by W.E. Parry and M. Liddon wintered in the adjacent harbour, 1819–1820.' A. Fisher, Sculp.[37]

When Parry wintered here in 1819 he talked of a hare which lived under this rock and seemed not to be afraid at the sight of men. In 1851 Captain McClintock, who now commands *Intrepid*, found a resident in every way identical at the same spot; it almost allowed itself to be touched and was not afraid of the discharge of a gun.

8 September 1852. Since the ice would not permit us to enter Winter Harbour to take up winter quarters, and since we knew from Parry that west of that bay there was no suitable site to accommodate a ship, we cast off our moorings and headed back east to find a suitable spot. The wind is still very fresh from the north quarter and is driving us vigorously. The temperature is dropping considerably and the surface of the sea is covered with a skin of ice an inch thick which hinders us greatly. Unfortunately the wind has dropped completely and we are obliged to take a towline from *Intrepid*. By 9.00 p.m. we were moored to the fast ice in Fife Harbour.

CHAPTER 4

Fall Sledge Trips and Preparations for Wintering

9 September 1852. At 3.00 a.m. we unmoored and, towed by *Intrepid*, set a course for Point Palmer. Pack ice of very great extent occupies almost the whole of Skene Bay and we are following its edge, sounding constantly, since the water depth is decreasing as we proceed.

For greater safety a boat is sent ahead to show us the way but soon we are forced to moor to the floe in about 3¹/₂ fathoms. An hour later we unmoored to avoid the pack which closed in on us against a fresh north wind and we lay under light canvas while Captain Kellett, who had gone aboard *Intrepid*, went to examine the ice near Dealy Island.

The captain was back by noon having found a suitable location: we are now tracking along the floe to about half a mile from the east point of Dealy Island, in 13 fathoms [Plate 11]. Immediately work was begun to cut a dock and put the ship in a safe position. The wind is still northerly but has slackened greatly; there is very strong refraction over Cape Bounty.

10 September 1852. We are continuing to cut our dock, aligned NNW-SSE, into which the ship will be towed with her bow to the NNW, since the prevailing wind in this area, according to Parry, varies between N and NW.

By evening the dock was completely finished; it was 150 feet long, 20 feet wide at the stern, and 35 feet wide at the bow. The ship was hauled into position and moored with a chain and a strong cable, while we waited for the ice to form around her sides to give her support.[1]

To prevent the drift ice from entering the dock and disturbing the ship a jib-boom was placed across the entrance.[2]

11 September 1852. Since one of our officers, Mr Hamilton, and Mr Purchase, *Intrepid*'s engineer, had killed three muskoxen, a work party was sent to dress the meat and bring it back. We are starting

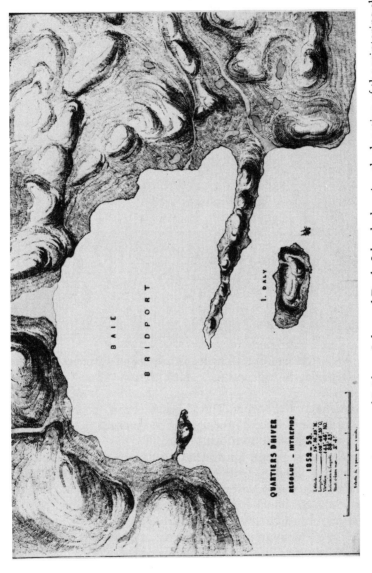

Plate 11 De Bray's manuscript map of Bridport Inlet and Dealy Island, showing the location of the wintering ships and the depot on the south coast of the island

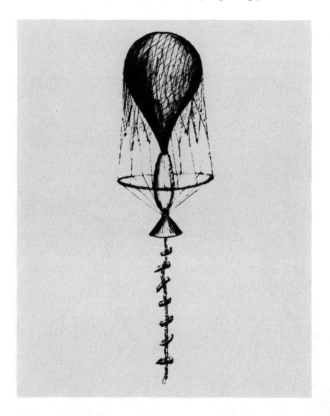

Plate 12 Sketch of one of the balloons released to distribute messages
(attached to the balloon's tail, which consists of a slow-match)

arrangements for the winter. The sails have been unbent and stowed
in the sail locker with the exception of the topsails, and some of the
running rigging has been unrove.

12–13 September 1852. On the 12th a balloon was released [Plate
12], with eight hundred little pieces of paper on which was printed
information as to our position and the state of the crew. Having risen
vertically to a considerable height it headed off to the northwest.[3]

14 September 1852. Captain McClintock, captain of *Intrepid*, decided to set off today to establish a depot of provisions on Hecla and
Griper Bay, despite the poor appearance of the weather. He started
out this morning accompanied by Dr Scott as second-in-command
and thirteen men. The depot, and twelve days' provisions, were
stowed on two carts and a sledge.[4]

In the evening we were very surprised to see Dr Scott coming back with ten men. He reported the annoying news that the two carts, heavily laden, had broken through the ice at the head of Bridport Inlet and that almost all the provisions which were to form the depot were spoiled by sea water.[5]

15 September 1852. A second depot was immediately prepared during the night and at 4.00 a.m. Dr Scott set off again with the new provisions to rejoin Captain McClintock as quickly as possible.

Resolute's boats have been landed and hauled up on Dealy Island, as well as various objects which might get in our way. Since three muskoxen had been killed by Captain McClintock, a sledge commanded by Mr Pim was sent to bring them in.

16 September 1852. Since the captain has announced that the departure of the sledges would take place next week, everyone is busy getting his things ready. The crews of the sledges have been picked and we are weighing provisions and equipment so that the loads will be properly distributed.

Everyone is eager to set off in order to get back before the severe cold, which will not be long in arriving and would prevent us from establishing our depots of provisions which will sustain us on our spring trips. The orlop deck and the hold have been cleared and almost everything has been moved ashore to Dealy Island.

The wind is blowing violently from the south, drifting a large amount of snow around the ship. The sea is congealing around us in the docks and there is already ice 6 inches thick aft.

Mr Pim came aboard this evening having killed four muskoxen and having left behind his sledge which had broken.

17 September 1852. Mr Nares went off with a sledge this morning to bring in the muskoxen killed yesterday; this evening he returned bringing only three, since the fourth had been almost totally devoured by wolves.

The preparations for wintering continued today. We have sent down the topgallant masts and all unnecessary spars such as the jib-boom, the trysail gaff, and the boom. A spar whose length had first been calculated was rigged between the main mast and the fore mast and lashed securely at about 15 feet above the deck. A jib-boom running from the foremast to the fo'c's'lehead and a boom running from the mizzen mast to the taffrail produced a framework the shape of a house roof. Over it was stretched a woollen tent whose sides were firmly secured to eye-bolts outside the bulwarks.

18–19–20 September 1852. Throughout this period a light wind from a southerly quarter or calm; considerable refraction of all surrounding objects.[6]

The sledges are ready to depart and we are waiting only for the weather to show its hand, since everything indicates a change of wind, which probably will be accompanied by a storm.

21 September 1852. As I had foreseen yesterday, the wind has changed and has suddenly swung into the north, blowing with great violence. Despite this, the order has been given to hold ourselves ready to start tomorrow morning and the sledges have been placed on the ice alongside, stowed and lashed.

22 September 1852. At 7.20 a.m. the officers and crew assembled on the ice around Captain Kellett, who delivered a little speech fully appropriate to the circumstances. Then the five sledges, manned by thirty-six men and under the command of Messrs Mecham, Nares, Pim, Hamilton, and myself, set off, saluting the captain with three mighty cheers which were amply returned by those we are leaving behind.

The goal of this autumn trip is to establish depots of provisions which will help us in the spring campaigns. Here are the directions given to each of the officers. Mr Mecham and Mr Nares are to cross Melville Island to Winter Harbour and place their depot on the south coast of the island. Messrs Pim, Hamilton, and myself are to try to establish a depot around Cape Providence in order to explore Bank's Land in the spring.

As I was departing I received from Captain Kellett my orders, which I shall quote here:

Having placed under your command the sledge *Marie,* manned with six men [7] and provisioned for 25 days, you will place yourself under the command of Lieutenant Pim, and follow his orders for your future proceedings.

You will be careful that your men are not unnecessarily exposed; that you examine and inquire every night before getting into your bags, whether any of your crew are suffering from frostbite, particularly in the feet.

That you caution them against eating snow whilst travelling, receiving and inquiring from the experience of Lieutenants Pim and Hamilton, any information you require.

You will keep a record of your proceedings, to be transmitted to me on your return.

Signed H. Kellett KCB
HMS *Resolute*

Journal of the Sledge *Marie*

22 September 1852.	Marched 9 hrs. 45 min
	Lunch 15 min
	Distance covered 16 miles
	Rest 14 hours
	Temp. -7°C

We left the ship at 7.30, heading for the western point of Bridport Bay across quite good ice, although strewn with numerous hummocks. Reaching land we set off across the snow which covered it since the ice did not seem very solid. Stopped 15 minutes for lunch. Immediately afterwards set a course for the two islands near Cape Bounty. At 5 pitched the tent on land and by 7 o'clock everyone sleeping soundly.

Since the spirit lamp in my large cooking apparatus had come unsoldered I lost quite a large quantity of alcohol and found myself reduced to a single lamp.

23 September 1852.	Marched 9 hrs.
	Lunch 15 min
	Distance covered 9 miles
	Rest 14 hrs 45 min
	Temp. -9°C

Breakfast at 6 o'clock; stowed the sledge and got under way by 7.30, heading through the channel between the two islands and the coast across quite smooth ice. At noon stopped for lunch. Weather very clear; wind freshening from the east, set the sail on the sledge.[8]

The ice strewn with vast hummocks; when the ice became so thin as to be dangerous we were obliged to take to the land which fortunately was snow-covered. Pitched the tent at 4.30 in very foggy weather and snow. Dinner at 6 o'clock.

I had occasion to take a bath today, which was far from pleasant under the circumstances. We were on quite thin ice and Mr Hamilton, who was walking ahead, called to me to ask my opinion on a spot which we had noticed ahead and which did not seem safe to him. I walked forward a few paces trying the ice with a pike, when suddenly I disappeared from Hamilton's sight. He just had time to throw himself backwards to avoid following me in my submarine excursion. Fortunately I had the presence of mind to place my pike crossways; this saved me from taking a total bath and they managed to haul me out shaking with cold. The sun had not yet set and it allowed me to dry myself a little; I changed my clothes in the open air and we continued our journey, taking precautions, the necessity for which my accident had clearly demonstrated.[9]

24 September 1852.

Marched	8 hrs 30 min
Lunch	15 min
Distance covered	7 miles
Rest	14 hrs 15 min
Temp.	-13°C

Breakfast at 6:30. Stowed the sledge and got under way at 7:30.

Wind very fresh from the north accompanied by snow mixed with fine gravel blown from the land was blowing in our faces and made forward progress very difficult. The new ice being thin and flexing under the sledge we were obliged to take to the land again and to abandon the heaviest objects which were loaded on Mr Mecham's cart.

At 4 o'clock officers and men being too tired we were obliged to camp. Dinner at 6.30.

25 September 1852.

Marched	5 hrs
Lunch	15 min
Distance	8 miles
Rest	18 hrs
Temp.	-13°C

Breakfast at 7.30. The wind is blowing violently, preventing us from getting under way. But around 11 o'clock, taking advantage of a slight break, we decided to get under way along the fast ice since the young ice had disappeared completely during the night. An hour after my start I joined Mr Pim who had camped a mile ahead, and we headed for Winter Harbour. Around 2.00 p.m., on sighting a herd of muskoxen, Mr Pim and I gave chase and fired three or four shots without success. Camped at 7.00 at the depot at Winter Harbour and fired a rocket in reply to another fired by Mr Mecham, who had found himself slowed down and had fallen behind.

Weather very overcast with a light westerly breeze.

26 September 1852.

Marched	10 hrs
Lunch	15 min
Distance	16 miles
Rest	14 hrs
Temp.	-12°C

Breakfast at 6.30. Cleared off my depot[10] and that of Mr. Hamilton who arrived at 10.00 with Messrs Mecham and Nares.

Completed my load with the depot originating from the ship, lashed the sledge and set off for Cape Hearne while Messrs Mecham and Nares headed for the head of the bay at Winter Harbour.

Around Cape Hearne we found the ice very bad, strewn with numerous hummocks, the hollows between being filled with vast quantities of snow.

Wind quite fresh from the NNE with snow all day. We pitched our tent on the ice for the first time, amidst the hummocks. Dinner at 7.30.

27 September 1852.   Marched   10 hrs
                                Lunch   15 min
                                Distance   15 miles
                                Rest   14 hrs.
                                Temp.   -13°C

Breakfast at 6.30. Stowed the sledge and set off at 7.30. North wind with foggy weather. Since the ice was better and smooth, around 8 o'clock I hoisted my sail to catch up with Mr Pim who was ahead.

A violent blizzard with blowing snow.

At 11 o'clock I caught up with Mr Pim and spotted Mr Hamilton heading along the land under sail.

At 4 o'clock, during a clearing we sighted land and headed in that direction to pitch the tent there since the ice did not seem very safe. Camped at 5.45 p.m. Dined at 7.00.

28 September 1852. During the night the wind had risen and in the morning it was blowing a real blizzard from the NNE (temperature 11°C). I was obliged to stay in the tent all day and there is nothing worse than this constraint, since in such a little space it is impossible to move much to maintain one's circulation; also one is obliged to cook inside the tent and the steam, along with our breath, condenses and forms a fine snow which clings to the walls of the tent.[11]

As our poor dwelling flaps in every direction with the fury of the wind, it shakes the snow down on us and wets us disagreeably. The only thing to do in these circumstances is to bury one's head in one's sleeping bag and try to sleep.

Since the wind had dropped a little and it had become clearer, at 4 o'clock I got all the men up to clean the interior of the tent and give them some exercise, of which we were all in great need.

On examining our surroundings I spotted ahead of us a great expanse of water as far as I could see, and an enormous block of ice drifting west at a speed of at least 2 knots. Once the tent had been well shaken, as well as the sleeping bags, and dinner being ready, everyone got into his bag and received a good ration of preserved meat with a good measure of boiling tea. The pipes were lit and soon after everyone was sleeping soundly.

29 September 1852.   Marched   9 hrs
                             Lunch   15 min
                             Distance   10 miles
                             Rest   14 hrs
                             Temp.   -8°C

Breakfast at 6.30. Stowed the sledge and set off at 7.30 in violent drifting snow.

Since the ice was quite level I set the sail to relieve the sledge a little as it was sinking deeply into the snow. At 2 o'clock the weather cleared and I spotted Mr Hamilton about a mile along the coast. Suddenly, around 3 o'clock this figure disappeared and I had a presentiment of an accident; then I saw Mr Hamilton running towards me. I then learned that the sledge had indeed broken through, the ice giving way under its weight, but that he had hopes of retrieving it.

I immediately sent my men and Mr Pim sent his crew to lend a hand, and at 6 o'clock we had the pleasure of seeing the sledge safely on shore. Camped immediately and dinner at 7.30.

Since Mr Hamilton and his men had no dry bedding I lent him my rubber blanket and everything I could spare without prejudicing my men's comfort.

30 September 1852.   Marched   9 hrs 30 min
                             Lunch   15 min
                             Distance   7 miles
                             Rest   14 hrs
                             Temp.   -7°C

Breakfast at 7.00; stowed the sledge and set off at 8.00, having given Mr Hamilton 30 lbs of biscuit to replace what he had lost, and the rigging from my sail for his tent. I found the ice very bad between the land and a line of hummocks which runs parallel to it about 100 m off. But we must absolutely follow this route since outside the hummocks new ice extends, broken in several places, while on the horizon we can see a dark line indicating the existence of a large expanse of water.

Camped at 3.30. Dinner at 7.30.

1 October 1852.   Marched   9 hrs
                             Lunch   15 min
                             Distance   4 miles
                             Rest   15 hrs
                             Temp.   -13°C
                             Temp. at noon   -7°C

Breakfast at 6. Stowed the sledge and set off at 7 with a light northeast wind and a little snow.

Very bad ice forced me to take to the land several times which made the going much more difficult. At noon the weather became very clear and the cold intense; I spotted several muskoxen far off in the interior. At 4 o'clock since the men were tired I pitched the tent. Dined at 6.

Since Mr Hamilton's equipment was still wet and he did not want to risk the health of his men, he decided to establish his depot near our camp and made arrangements to return to the ship tomorrow morning. All day we have been crossing numerous tracks of foxes and hares.

2 October 1852.

Marched   8 hrs 30 min
Lunch   15 min
Distance   7 miles
Rest   14 hrs
Temp.   -14°C

Breakfast at 6.30. Stowed the sledge and set off at 7.30 across the land, separated from a great expanse of water by a heavy line of hummocks. Mr Hamilton took his leave of us and is returning to the ship.

The going has become so bad that we are forced to relay the sledges;[12] despite all these difficulties by noon we were at the tip of Cape Providence.

Having assured myself that we could not go any farther since the coast was steep-to and the waves breaking on the rocks I established my depot, adding some provisions which I had saved (forty lbs of biscuit and ten cans of preserves).[13]

About a mile from Cape Providence I found an empty tin can which must have contained pemmican and which seemed to have been used for cooking something.

My depot having been carefully stowed and covered with rocks and snow to protect it from animals as much as possible,[14] I had the sledge stowed and immediately started back for the ship. Camped at 5.30 and dinner at 6.30.

3 October 1852.

Marched   8 hrs 45 min
Lunch   15 min
Distance   12 miles
Rest   14 hrs
Temp.   -17°C

Breakfast at 6.30; stowed the sledge and set off northeast.

Since there was a fresh breeze from the northwest I set my sail which now becomes more useful since the sledge is lighter. Camped at 4.30; dinner at 5.30. I observed numerous fox tracks

along the coast and spotted several herds of muskoxen but the
marching conditions were too favourable and I took advantage of
them to get back aboard as fast as possible since, moreover, the
season is advancing rapidly.

4 October 1852.		
	Marched	9 hrs
	Lunch	15 min
	Distance	10 miles
	Rest	15 hrs
	Temp.	-14°C

Breakfast at 5.30; stowed the sledge and set off at 6.30 with the sail
set, pushed by a fresh NW wind.

Spotting a herd of muskoxen quite near the coast around 8
o'clock I headed towards them with Mr Pim. Getting to within
about 30 metres we fired together, having chosen a calf as our
target, but although the animal had a leg broken it escaped with the
herd. I fired another rifle bullet at the mass of the fleeing herd at
about 200 metres, and I was lucky enough to hit a bull which first
stopped dead, then began galloping again when he saw us approaching. Pim then fired two shots at him; they hit him but did not kill
him outright, although he appeared to be reluctant to run any
farther. We then approached to finish him off but we had not
counted with the strength of this animal, which now prepared to
charge us. Fortunately Mr Pim had had time to reload his rifle and
fired two shots point-blank. I fired another bullet in his ear and he
finally expired.

We dressed the animal immediately, selecting the best parts.
Three of our men, who had seen our success, soon arrived and
helped us to carry our booty. We found eight bullets in the body of
this enormous bull.

In the meantime Mr Pim's sledge had continued on its way and
at 4 o'clock we caught up with it and camped. Dinner at 5.30 with
muskox steaks which seemed to me the most delicious meat I had
ever eaten, although a little tough. But we were not very fussy and
any fresh meat would have seemed exquisite to us.

5 October 1852.		
	Marched	8 hours
	Lunch	15 min
	Distance	12 miles
	Rest	16 hrs
	Temp.	-13°C

Breakfast at 6.30; stowed the sledge and set off under sail at 7.30.

Camped at 3.30 at the Winter Harbour depot; dinner at 6.30 and
by 7 o'clock everybody was getting into their sleeping bags, tired
from the past few days.

6 October 1852.   Marched   10 hrs 30 min
                                     Lunch   15 min
                                     Distance   14 miles
                                     Rest   13 hrs 30 min
                                     Temp.   -13°C

Breakfast at 6.30; set off under sail at 7.30 with a good NW wind
which has favoured us since our departure from Cape Providence.
Around noon I was forced to furl the sail; the poor state of the ice
was obliging us to change course the whole time.

Seeing that we could not camp on the floe, which did not seem
very safe, at 5.30 I headed for land where I pitched the tent at 6
o'clock. Dinner at 7.30.[15]

Since my sledge had upset several times during the day, one of
my men's knapsacks was lost.[16] When the loss was noticed it was
too late to go back for it; moreover the darkness would have made
such a search useless and even dangerous.

7 October 1852.   Marched   8 hrs
                                     Lunch   15 min.
                                     Distance   12 miles
                                     Rest   15 hrs
                                     Temp.   -12 to -15°C

Breakfast at 6.30; stowed the sledge and set off at 7.30.

A fresh north wind with heavy snow. Despite the bad state of the
ice we were able to make progress since the sledge was now greatly
lightened. Camped on land at 4; dinner at 5.30.

8 October 1852. Breakfast 6.30; under way at 7.30. Light northerly
breeze freshening around 10 o'clock, allowing us to set the sail.

At noon the captain and the officers who had stayed aboard,
appeared ahead of us and by 1 o'clock we were back aboard, a little
tired from our excursion but all in good health, thank God.[17]

9–10–11 October 1852. I was happy to get back to my little cabin on
board ship and it was with real pleasure that I was able to make my
toilet, since on these sledge trips one has to give up this comfortable
habit.

Despite a great desire to groom oneself it is difficult to do so and it
is totally impossible to think of taking changes of clothing, since
they would simply increase the weight to be hauled.

During my absence *Resolute* had suffered some ice pressure during
the gale of the 24th which had confined us to our tent; at one moment the captain was even afraid that the ship would be set adrift, a
prospect which worried him greatly since we were away from the
ship.[18]

Captain McClintock and Dr Scott had returned aboard on 2 October and on the 7th had set off again with sixteen men, two sledges and nineteen days' provisions to lay depots on Hecla and Griper Bay.[19] Mr Hamilton had also arrived on board in good health despite his accident.

We are finally now all aboard having achieved our goal, which was to place forward provisions depots which will allow us to extend our investigations farther next spring.

During the three days following our return the sledge crews had a complete rest and their food was more select; there were frequent issues of beer.

The men who stayed on board are continuing to put the ship in order;[20] the hold and orlop deck have been cleared as far as possible. All the items which we do not need have been put ashore on Dealy Island and they have completed a snow house which is to serve as an observatory, about 100 metres from the ship.

A flagstaff has been placed on top of Dealy Island so that we can signal the arrival of the sledges; at the same time it will serve as a landmark when one is hunting some distance from the ship.

The stove has been lit in the hold; at the moment it serves especially to dry our camping equipment and the belongings of the sledge crews.[21]

Everyone is busy and everyone is making his own little arrangements for spending the winter which will not be long in bringing its hardships and tedium.

12 October 1852. Messrs Pim, Hamilton, and Domville, taking advantage of the fine weather, have taken three days' provisions on the little sledge with five dogs, and have set off to go hunting to the head of Bridport Inlet, about ten miles from the ship.

13 October 1852. Released a balloon which headed west after rising to a considerable height.

14 October 1852. This morning, while taking a walk on Dealy Island I spotted a sledge in the direction of Cape Bounty; I immediately hoisted the flag and several officers set off, accompanied by some men, to assist the sledge which could only be Mr Mecham's, although we have some doubts and even some anxiety at seeing him returning alone. But our uncertainty was of short duration and was dissipated by Mr Mecham himself when he soon arrived amongst us and announced some important news.

The captain soon arrived and we learned that Mr Mecham had found documents from Captain M'Clure of *Investigator*; he had then made double marches, leaving Mr Nares behind in good health.

While returning to the ship after having established his depot Mr Mecham had passed within two to three miles of the remarkable rock at the head of Winter Harbour, inscribed by Parry. Impelled perhaps by some presentiment, he made a detour to visit the spot and on top of the rock found a tin cylinder which he thought at first had been deposited by Captain McClintock; but on opening it he was greatly surprised to find a paper with M'Clure's signature. He avidly read what was in fact a journal and immediately returned to the ship by forced marches to bring us the news.

I shall transcribe here Captain M'Clure's document as it was found on 12 October 1852 on the rock at Winter Harbour [Plate 13].

Journal of *Investigator* [22] from her separation from *Herald* on 31 July 1850, off Cape Lisburne

2 August. At 5.50 on the morning of 2 August, having met ice at latitude 72° 1′N, longitude 166° 12′W (Gr.) it did not appear very heavy but on entering it our hopes were disappointed and we were forced to get out of it again.

5 August. While running along the pack searching for an opening we exchanged signals with *Plover* [23] and at 11 o'clock we encountered a low point east of Wainwright Inlet; at midnight we rounded Point Barrow in 3 fathoms and a third, without seeing the point due to fog.

8 August. At 1.45 a.m., abeam of Point Drew, sent Mr Court, second master and Mr Miertsching, [24] interpreter, ashore to deposit a message about our passage. They met some Eskimos who had arrived three days before. These Eskimos trade with the Russians and were very sociable; a letter was entrusted to them in the hope that it would reach the Admiralty.

We learned from them that the previous year three boats had passed to the east with Whites and Indians, probably Lieutenant Pullen. In the evening built a cairn and buried a notice on Point Pitt.

9 August. Passed abeam of the Colville River about forty miles off the river mouth in 3.5 fathoms.

11 August. Left a message on Jones Island which was scattered with driftwood.

In the afternoon two baidars containing twenty-four natives came alongside. The leader had a gun with the inscription 'Barnet 1840,' given him by the Russians. Bought some salmon and ducks for tobacco. In the afternoon we met more natives who seemed to us excessively intelli-

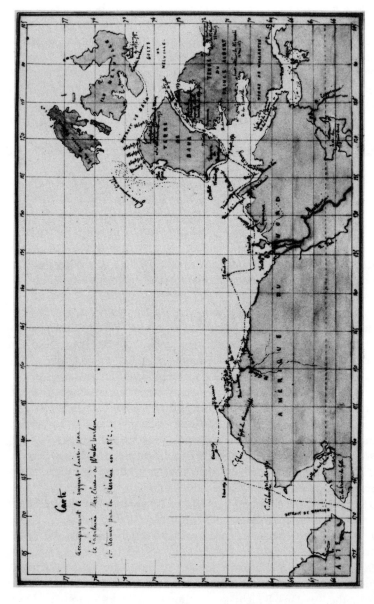

Plate 13 De Bray's copy of the map to accompany the message left by Captain Robert M'Clure at Winter Harbour in the spring of 1852 and showing the route followed by *Investigator* up until that time

gent and clean. Sent dispatches to the Admiralty by way of the Colville River and, according to our interpreter, we certainly believe that they will arrive.

13 August. Several baidars came alongside the ship. Bartered fish and ducks for beads and tobacco. The natives are skillful pilferers.

14 August. Ran onto a shoal seven miles north of the Gulf of Yarborough, having escaped several of these hazards by a miracle during the past two days; they are barely above water level and hidden by the ice.

Led out a kedge anchor but a whaleboat unfortunately capsized and we lost eleven casks of beef, having been obliged to crowd on sail to avoid being driven ashore again.

15 August. We found ourselves unable to move more than two miles in any direction; the ice is pushing in from the north and resting on the shoals to the north; to the south lie the shoals on which we grounded yesterday. Anchored to wait for a change for the better.

16 August. The ice north of the shoals has slackened a little, leaving a channel about 150 metres wide. Weighed and towed the ship a distance of two cables through the ice to reach the spot, which gave us six hours of strenuous work due to the heaviness of the ice.

17 August. At noon the weather, which had been foggy, cleared with a NE wind; set sail through heavy drift ice, experiencing violent jolts every minute. Navigation along this coast is very dangerous, since the sandbanks are very low and numerous. Latitude 70° 30'N, longitude 148° 4'W.

21 August. Recognized the Pelly Islands off the mouth of the Mackenzie. Since the 17th we've encountered vast ice floes; we ran ninety miles along a lead and reached solid pack ice. Fortunately we were able to get out of it before it closed.

24 August. Spotted some huts a little west of Point Warren; sent ashore dispatches for the Admiralty in the hope that they may be forwarded by the Hudson's Bay Company. However this tribe does not trade with the company but with other tribes to the west, who themselves trade with those of the Colville River. They give as the reason the fact that the Hudson's Bay Company gave the Indians water which killed them, and which they do not wish to have.

They appear wild and warlike, and are at war with their neighbours. The dispatches were brought back aboard.

30 August. Spotted a mast erected on the beach near Maitland Point in Liverpool Bay; sent a boat to examine it and leave a note with details of our passage.

It was realized that it was an Eskimo marker; they had recently left the spot, where we found several caches containing birds and fish. In the afternoon spotted some Eskimos as we approached Cape Bathurst. On communicating with them we learned that they belonged to a tribe then camped at Cape Bathurst, and engaged in whaling, and that they had seen Sir John Richardson last year. In the evening the weather was foggy; depth 3.5 fathoms; anchored between Baillie Islands and the mainland.

31 August. Set a course for Cape Bathurst. Met a tribe of three hundred very sociable natives; they are to go south in three weeks. Gave them dispatches for the Admiralty; gave a rifle and ammunition to the chief and distributed presents to others, judging from their intelligence and good appearance that the dispatches will arrive.

1 September. Abeam of Cape Bathurst a large number of natives came aboard and, taking advantage of the calm, stayed until evening; but once the wind rose we said our last farewells to the Eskimos of the American coast, fully convinced that no ship nor any of the crews of Sir John Franklin's expedition had visited these coasts. These Eskimos appear completely inoffensive (with the exception of those at Warren Point with whom they do not communicate) and would certainly lend assistance to any Whites who landed among them.

All this coast is flat, but with the aid of the lead one can navigate safely, the bottom being very regular. Shoals extend for about thirty miles east of Yarborough Bay; with the passage varying from one to forty miles in width, it is always reliable along this coast from early August to 10 September. It is more or less invaded by ice, depending on the wind, but the natives state that the ice leaves the coast every year.

The prevailing winds are from the ESE and NE.

6 September. At 11.30 a.m., being north of Cape Parry, sighted a high land lying from N1/4NE to ENE.

7 September. At 9.30 a.m. landed and took possession of this new discovery which we named Baring Island.

The land is sheer in its southern part, about 1,000 feet high; in the north this is Banks Land.

Erected a signal mast surmounted by a black ball and left a note in latitude 71° 7′N, longitude 122° 48′W.

9 September. Observed land to the NNE. Named this land Prince Albert Land; it is continuous with Victoria and Wollaston lands and extends north to latitude 73° 21′N, longitude 122° 48′W.

11 September. The ship beset by ice at latitude 72° 52′N, longitude 117° 3′W but the ice is moving.

8 October. Since the 11th of last month we have been drifting with the ice, escaping several times from certain destruction; finally today after frightful pressure which lifted the ship and gave her a list of 34°, we find ourselves firmly jammed in the ice, where we would spend nine months, at latitude 72° 47'N, longitude 117° 34'W.

10 October. Took possession of Prince Albert Land which lies four miles from us.

13 October. Took possession of the Princess Royal Islands, in the middle of Prince of Wales Strait, about four miles from the ship. Built a large cairn on these islands, surmounted by a mast and a ball, at latitude 72° 46'N, longitude 117° 44' 10''W. Deposited three months' provisions for forty-six men, plus a boat and some ammunition.

21 October. Discovered the entrance of the strait into Barrow Strait in latitude 73° 30'N, longitude 114° 14'W, thus establishing the existence of the Northwest Passage.

30 October. Five muskoxen killed on Prince Albert Land, thus ending our operations for 1850.

18 April 1851. Today sent three sledges to trace the coast: Lieutenant Haswell to the SE towards Wollaston Land; Lieutenant Cresswell towards Banks Land, and Mr Wynniatt, mate, to the NE. These various sledges traced the coast as it is laid down on the attached chart.

2 June. The captain and the interpreter, Mr Miertsching, communicated with the Eskimos of Prince Albert Land, about six miles south of our position, and who had previously been encountered by Lieutenant Haswell. They traced the coastlines as marked on the chart and said that several of their tribes inhabited the land to the south but that they did not know any to the north. They appear to be good and simple, and were alarmed at the sight of White men, whom they had never seen before.

14 July. The ice opened without any pressure, and the ship finds herself afloat again but so surrounded by pack ice that we can only drift with it, having been able to set sails only twice and then only for a few hours, until 14 August, at which point we reached our most northerly position in Prince of Wales Strait, in latitude 73° 14' 19''N, longitude 115° 32' 30''W.

16 August. Finding the passage closed in Barrow Strait by northeasterly winds pushing large masses of ice towards the south and making us drift fifteen miles in that direction in twelve hours, we bore up to run south of Baring Island.

20 August. Latitude 74° 27'N, longitude 122° 32' 15''W; until today the sea free of ice; running along the coast a mile offshore, but the ice soon stopped us. Moored the ship to a grounded floe piece in 12 fathoms. The ice appears to have only recently been detached from the coast.

29 August. The ship in great danger of being crushed or carried ashore by the great pressure of the ice coming from the Polar Sea. It drove us along for half a mile about 100 yards off shore, heeled to 15° and lifted bodily by 1 foot 8 inches; fortunately we stopped and the ice became stationary.

10 September. The ice in motion again and the ship carried into the main pack by a terrible SE squall.

11 September. We succeeded in getting out of the pack and moored to a large grounded floe. Latitude 74° 29'N, longitude 122° 32' 20''W.

19 September. An open sea along the coast to the east; cast off our moorings and towed the ship in that direction, being frequently stopped and escaping miraculously from the vast polar ice. Until the evening of the 23rd when we grounded on a mud bank, leaving us with 5 feet of water beneath our bow and 5 fathoms aft. We got off without accident.

24 September. At daybreak sighted Barrow Strait full of ice; with large masses entering this bay we decided to establish our winter quarters here; finding a well-sheltered spot south of the bank where we grounded last night we anchored in 4 fathoms, latitude 74° 6'N, longitude 117° 54'W.

Ice formed during the night and we have not moved since. Our position is excellent, being protected against the ice by the reef, which diverts it 600 metres clear of us. The currents along the coasts of the Polar Sea seem to be more or less influenced in their direction by the winds, but along the west coast of Baring Island there is certainly a permanent current towards the east. On one occasion, under calm conditions, we found it to be about 2 knots. The flood tide certainly comes from the west, as was amply proven to us during our detention off the west coast of this island.

The prevailing winds along the American coast and in Prince of Wales Strait are northeasterly, but on this coast they vary from SSE to NW. A ship has no chance of getting west by entering the Polar Sea, the channel along the land being very narrow, the winds contrary, and the ice impenetrable, but I believe the Passage to be very feasible via Prince of Wales Strait and by hugging the American coast.

Driftwood occurs in abundance on the E coast of Prince of Wales Strait and on the American coast; there is also plenty of game. In this vicinity the hills abound with reindeer and hares which stay all winter; we were lucky enough to procure about 4,000 lbs of meat.

The health of the crew has been and continues to be excellent, without any losses or any attacks of scurvy.

My intention, if possible, is to return to England this year, calling at

Melville Island and Port Leopold; but if we are not heard of again it is probably because we have been carried into the polar pack or west of Melville Island, and in either case no help should be sent for us, so as not to increase the losses, since any ship which enters the polar pack must inevitably be crushed; hence a depot of provisions or a ship at Winter Harbour would be the best and only guarantee of safety to save the rest of the crew.

No trace has been encountered, and no information from the Eskimos, which might lead to the supposition that Sir John Franklin's expedition, or part of his crews, has visited the coasts we have covered; nor have we been any more fortunate as to the *Enterprise* which we have not seen since we separated in the Strait of Magellan on 20 April 1850.

This document was deposited in April 1852 by the crew of a sledge consisting of Captain M'Clure, Mr Court, second master, John Calder, captain of the forecastle, Sergeant Woon, Royal Marines, George Gibbs, A.B., George Bounsell, A.B., John Davis, A.B., and Peter Thompson, captain of the foretop.

Whoever finds this paper is asked to forward it to the Secretary of the Admiralty.

Dated aboard HBM discovery ship *Investigator*, beset in the ice in Mercy Bay, latitude 74°N, longitude 117° 54'W.

12 April 1852
Robert M'Clure, Commander

Unless there is a ship at Melville Island now, I have no intention to visit it again; I shall make the best way possible via the straits.

This journal gives a wonderfully exact idea of the miracles achieved by *Investigator*; the most complete success had crowned the efforts and the perseverance of the good Captain M'Clure, who has had the honour of discovering the famous Northwest Passage which has been sought for so long. And although he had snatched one of the greatest prizes from our grasp, since we were to explore the area which he has conquered, I cannot help admiring and envying him, and I am longing to shake his hand, since it is clear that we will be seeking the means to communicate with him.

Unfortunately the great expanse of water which we sighted west of Cape Providence prevents us from sending a sledge now; moreover the season is too far advanced, the nights are too long, and we would be seriously endangering the men whom we sent. It has hence been decided that a sledge will be sent next spring, as early as possible, so as to still find *Investigator* at Mercy Bay. Moreover, according to our calculations she should still have a year's provisions in her hold, and as Captain M'Clure reported himself, there is abundant game on that coast and also ample driftwood which will ensure a fuel supply. According to *Investigator*'s journal we have noticed a bizarre coincidence in terms of date: on 14 May 1851 Lieutenant Haswell of that ship reached his farthest and started back and on the 24th of the same month Dr Rae,[25] travelling that same coast, also started back, thus leaving only a very short stretch of coast unexplored. At the same time Mr Sherard Osborn and Mr Wynniatt of *Investigator* were only thirty miles from each other. These two coincidences occurred in 1851, i.e., almost a year before we sailed, and if a meeting had taken place we could have located *Investigator* without fail at Mercy Bay, either with *Resolute* or at least with boats and sledges.

Everybody is back aboard with the exception of Mr Nares, who is barely a day's march away and all in good health, thank God. There are a few cases of frozen fingers but they do not present any danger.

15 October 1852. Messrs Pim, Hamilton, and Domville came aboard, having killed two reindeer. Since the weather was quite bad in the evening we fired several rockets and Bengal flares to indicate our position to Mr Nares, since we are starting to worry that he has not arrived, and yet he cannot be very far away.

16 October 1852. First thing in the morning a man was sent to the summit of Dealy Island to watch for Mr Nares and soon afterwards we had the pleasure of seeing the flag hoisted to announce his arrival. We headed out to meet him and we soon found him and his men in good health, although they had suffered greatly from the bad weather which has prevailed this past two days.[26]

Resolute finally has her full complement again; the only party still absent is that of Captain McClintock of *Intrepid*.

17–18–19 October 1852. On the 17th I went out hunting with five men and a sledge, accompanied by Messrs Pim and Ibbet, one of *Intrepid*'s engineers, who took with them the little sledge hauled by dogs.[27] At 3 o'clock we camped on a lake about 1.5 miles from the head of Bridport Inlet and after a good dinner we retired to our sleeping bags to rest and regather our strength for the next day.

With daylight we went hunting but the entire day was spent in pursuing a herd of reindeer, at which I fired at long range, but without success.

During the night the wind rose and blew with such fury that we could not get a wink of sleep; we were repeatedly wakened by a subterranean rumbling in the lake which I attributed to cracks in the ice produced by the considerable drop in temperature. To crown our misfortune, around 4.00 a.m. the tent collapsed on top of us when the dogs, who had not ceased to howl in a fearful fashion, pulled away the rear tent pole to which they were tied.

I immediately leaped out, my knife in one hand and a lantern in the other, convinced that the dogs were being attacked by wolves. Fortunately this was not the case and having repitched the tent we went back to bed, half dead with cold.

Next day we tried hunting again but the weather was so bad that I decided to return aboard.

With a northerly wind pushing us rapidly along, we reached the ship at 7 o'clock, only to learn some sad news: a few hours after we left the wardroom steward, named Thomas Mobley, had died sudenly of a heart attack.[28] Our expedition's hunting season is now closed for the year and may be summarized as follows, both in terms of parties working from the ship and of the autumn travelling parties.

Type of game	September	October	Total
Muskoxen	27	–	27
Wolves	1	–	1
Foxes	1	–	1
Hares	22	1	23
Partridges	35	4	39
Bears	–	1 (lost)	1
Lemmings	–	2	2
Reindeer	3	2	5

CHAPTER 5

The Wintering

20 October 1852. The captain went ashore on Dealy Island to select a site for the burial of poor Mobley, and immediately a work party set to work to dig a grave, a task which is extremely difficult now since the ground is frozen as hard as a rock.

We are starting to make our major arrangements for the winter. The deck has been completely cleared and it has been covered with a mixture of earth and snow which forms a very hard, firm mortar, about 6 inches thick. From past experience of ships which have wintered in these regions this outer layer keeps the heat inside but has the inconvenience of producing some humidity.

Around the ship we have built a wall of snow 5 feet high and 4 feet thick [Plate 14], whose rounded top rests against the sides of the ship, while its base is about a foot away, thus leaving a passage a foot wide all around which allows the air to circulate and thus prevents dampness inside. This wall was easily built using large rectangular blocks cut from the snow with knives and saws; one then places them like dressed stones, cementing them and filling the gaps with snow mixed with a little earth.

21 October 1852. Very bad weather; the cold, penetrating north wind is raising blowing drift so thick that *Intrepid*, which is only 100 m off our beam, is completely hidden.

22–23–24 October 1852. Captain McClintock arrived today after an absence of nineteen days, having placed his depot on Nias Point in Liddon Gulf.[1] According to his report he had had to contend with extraordinary difficulties in crossing the peninsula; irregularities in the terrain were numerous and when ravines 300 or 400 feet deep presented themselves he had to take such precautions that the distance covered in twelve hours of effort sometimes did not exceed two or three miles. Thus Captain McClintock had taken ten days to cover thirty-two miles.

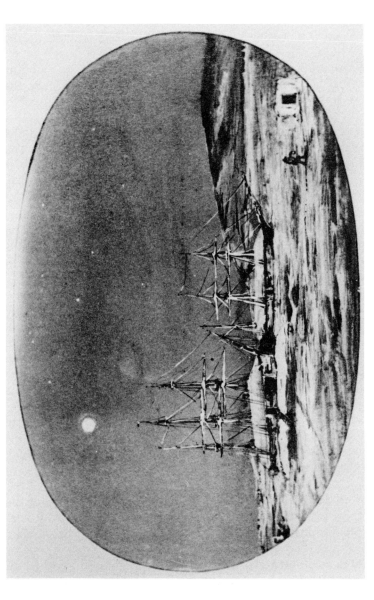

Plate 14 De Bray's painting of *Resolute* and *Intrepid* in winter quarters at Dealy Island by moonlight; the hulls are banked up with snow and housed over with tenting.

26 October 1852. At 10 o'clock this morning the officers and men of *Intrepid* came aboard to help conduct poor Mobley to his last resting place. The coffin was placed on a sledge pulled by six men; a file of marines with rifles reversed marched on either side; then came the men, marching in pairs; and the officers brought up the rear.[2]

I have never seen a more mournful spectacle; the surrounding landscape added singularly with its sad, desolate aspect. Since the cold was very keen, everyone was wrapped up as well as possible, and not a word was exchanged.

We soon reached the spot where the grave had been prepared; the coffin was placed alongside it, covered with the Union Jack. The captain read the funeral service and at the first verse the coffin was lowered into the grave; everyone filed past and bowed his head to bid a final farewell to our poor comrade.

The grave was only 3 feet deep and was covered with earth and large rocks to prevent the animals from getting into it; it was dug on the east side of Dealy Island about 200 metres from the shore, and is surmounted by an oak headboard 3 feet high on which is carved an inscription with the man's name and the date of his death.[3]

27–31 October 1852. Throughout this period we have noticed a fairly significant drop in temperature; everything indicates that the sun will leave us soon. Hence we are hurrying to make our final preparations for winter. The men are still working on banking up the outside of the ship; the after hatch has been secured to try to maintain a reasonable temperature in the wine store, and the others are equipped with rims and doors which close with counterweights in order to prevent draughts as far as possible.

1–2 November. At 10.00 a.m. the moon was above the horizon and one could see Venus, Aldebara,[4] and Saturn.

3 November 1852. We had the spectacle of a magnificent paraselina around the moon, i.e., four very distinct moons joined by a circle of light.

4 November 1852. At 10 o'clock we spotted the upper edge of the sun peeping over the horizon; at noon the centre of the disc was at 17' and the luminary presented the appearance of a slightly flattened cogwheel.

To say farewell properly, the sun gave us magnificent weather all day. The remarkably clear atmosphere allowed us to see Cape Bounty clearly, while to the south the sky was tinged with the most brilliant colours, the clouds being bordered with purple and gold.

Winter begins today, and soon bad weather will confine us to the ship. To prevent the men from stagnating in deadly inactivity, all the distractions we can arrange are being put into operation. Every evening the officers will run a school for those who wish to acquire some knowledge of navigation and elementary mathematics.[5] We have already begun classes in reading and writing and there is nothing more comical than to see these rough sailors struggling their best to trace the letters of the alphabet or spelling out words from books which one normally sees only in the hands of children. Preparations for the theatre also occupy a good part of our time. The captain, Dr Domville, and Mr McDougall have unanimously been voted the directors. Mr Hamilton will fill the office of prompter, and the master carpenter is busy with construction of the theatre which will be on the deck between the foremast and the mainmast. I myself am working with silk and lace to produce a full court outfit of the reign of Charles II;[6] at the same time I am giving Mr McDougall a hand at repairing the decorations used on the last expedition, and which we fortunately thought of bringing.

5–9 November 1852. Just at breakfast time on the 5th we were deafened by frightful shouts; on going on deck we discovered that the cause of all the noise was nothing but the great ceremony of Guy Fawkes, whereby the English commemorate the famous Gunpowder Plot.[7] Fawkes was represented by a horrible effigy pinioned to a chair and around which the crew was dancing, jeering at him. In the evening the effigy was burned amidst the vociferations of the crowd and to the sound of the most extraordinary instruments, altogether amidst a veritable racket.

10–11 November 1852. On the 10th there was a violent north and northwest wind blowing, as usual carrying a vast quantity of drifting snow. Towards evening the wind abated, swinging into the south, and on coming back from *Intrepid* where I had spent the evening, at 1 o'clock I heard an extraordinary noise to the south: a sort of prolonged rumbling accompanied by a shrill whistling. I moved a few paces in that direction but although it was a very clear night I could not distinguish anything.

12 November 1852. After breakfast this morning, since the weather had ameliorated a little I took a stroll in the direction of where I had heard the noise two days earlier. About a mile south of the ship I was stopped by a large crack, partly piled high with enormous blocks of ice shattered by the pressure of the ice from the south against the ice in which we were imprisoned.[8]

Plate 15 De Bray's painting of the theatre on *Resolute*'s main deck.
The French *tricolore* is prominently featured at upper left.

The subterranean rumbling which I had heard certainly derives
from the friction of the floes as they ride up over each other, and the
whistling from the water surging into the fissures.

We are thus now enclosed between the land and a ridge of hummocks extending almost from Cape Bounty to our anchorage. In the
opinion of the officers who have already wintered in this country
this situation is very favourable, since the floe is sure to break
against this line of hummocks during the next bout of pressure, and
in the event that our floe does not break up we would have only a
mile of ice to cut to free the ships.

13–22 November. Everyone is busy with classes and the theatre;
the parts have been learned and it has been decided that tomorrow
will be the opening performance.

23 November 1852. The great day has finally arrived; everyone is
astir aboard ship. The theatre poster was displayed this morning in
the orlop deck, announcing that the doors would open at 6.30. Mr
Hamilton, the stage-manager, is satisfied with the rehearsals in general and has announced that everyone knows his part perfectly.

At 4 o'clock, after a hurried dinner, everyone got busy dressing; the ladies shaved and put on their wigs and hair pieces. I was not left idle since it was my task to handle the make-up. I was using magnesium successfully as a substitute for white, while a jar of Chinese rouge which was found on board allowed me to give a lily-white or pink tinge to all the more-or-less tanned faces.

Finally everyone was made up, and having drunk several glasses of champagne to give ourselves courage, each actor took up his position, ready at the drop of a hat to dash onto the stage.

The audience, consisting of the officers and men of *Resolute* and *Intrepid*, took their places on benches, the officers in the front row since the house had no boxes to offer. Captain Kellett sat at the foot of the mainmast in an armchair surmounted by a canopy formed of flags and decorated with his coat of arms[9][Plate 15].

At 6.30 precisely the orchestra, consisting of six fifes, an accordion, a drum, and a triangle, attacked the opening number and soon came the obligatory three knocks calling for silence and the public's attention. The curtain rose on a very appropriate scene, representing *Assistance* beset in the ice; a subterranean rumble was heard and the King of the Hyperborean Lands, bent beneath the weight of his years, appeared. Dr Domville, playing this character, uttered a prologue composed for the occasion by Mr McDougall,[10] then left the stage amidst thunderous applause.

The orchestra played two or three pieces and the curtain rose again. From the polar regions we found ourselves suddenly transported to the court of Charles II.[11] The subject of this little play was very amusing, dealing with one of that monarch's bourgeois adventures, and the officers who played all the parts were an immense success. The costumes were magnificent and the one which I had made, and which had given me so much trouble, produced a tolerably good effect beside that of Mr Mecham who played the part of the king and wore a costume made in England. As for the women, they were as presentable as possible and a critic could in no way reproach Mr Nares for his debut in the role of Miss Clara.

Unfortunately, since flowers are very rare in this country, the spectators could express their enthusiasm only by prolonged cheers. After this piece the show was varied by means of dances and songs to give the actors time to prepare. This time only members of the crew were on stage to give their interpretation of a comedy entitled 'Who Speaks First.'

Unfortunately one of the actors was overwhelmed by numerous

libations and was incapable of continuing his part, and they were obliged to lower the curtain.[12] The orchestra then played the national anthem, 'God Save the Queen,' accompanied by the entire audience, standing with bared heads. We then retired, but only after calling the entire personnel of the theatre back to the stage and cheering them wildly. A charming supper which awaited us in Captain Kellett's cabin ended the evening.

The temperature, which was -9°C outside, was raised to -5°C by means of four stoves placed in the wings. Despite this the ladies suffered from the cold; nothing could be more amusing than to see them sitting astride a chair, their skirts hitched up, smoking long pipes and drinking mugs of grog. As for the audience, their only recourse was to blow on their fingers and to stamp their feet during the intervals.

Thus ended our first theatrical evening in the arctic regions, and by all reports it would have been perfect except for the unforeseen accident during the second play.

24 November 1852. The carpenters set to work this morning to dismantle the theatre, and by noon there was nothing of it left; everything was stowed in the hold until the date of the next production.

Today the temperature has dropped so much that we have to congratulate ourselves on having opened the theatre yesterday, since today we would have suffered even more.

25–29 November 1852. We have been taking advantage of the intervals between spells of bad weather to continue our work.[13] The dogs which we bought at Disko are starting to be put to work; we harnessed them to sledges to haul the gravel which we are stowing in the hold for ballast. Since the ice is fairly good between Dealy Island and here, they can easily pull 600 kg.

The autumn trips revealed a defect in our sledges and the carpenters are busy remedying it; all the supports which were made of elm broke, and we are replacing them with oak.

5 December 1852. The tracks of ptarmigan having been spotted on Dealy Island[14] I went out hunting to try to procure some of this excellent game bird, but after a very tiring chase through the snow I came back aboard without having seen a single live bird.[15]

7 December 1852. Today we had the spectacle of a magnificent aurora borealis stretching from SW to NE, the centre of the arc being about 10° above the horizon.

9 December 1852. During my watch, from midnight to 4.00 a.m., a north wind, which had been blowing all day, became very violent; at

2.30 when I tried to go out to retrieve a thermometer which I had left outside, I was almost blown off my feet.

The squall lasted about ten minutes and during this time the temperature dropped suddenly by 5°, rising again when the weather became a little calmer.

12 December 1852. We again have to deplore the loss of one of our men, Drover, captain of the forecastle aboard *Intrepid*, who had been suffering as a result of his autumn trip with Captain McClintock.[16]

19 December 1852. The officers and men of *Resolute* and *Intrepid* paid their last respects to Drover.[17] Although the ceremony took place at noon a man had to hold a lantern for the Captain while he read the prayers.

The new grave was located near that of Mobley on Dealy Island. It was not dug without some difficulty. The weather was so bad that we were obliged to pitch a tent to provide some shelter for the men; for seven days they had to use every means possible to dig a grave 2.5 feet deep. The ground was frozen so hard that they had to light fires to try to thaw it.[18]

23 December 1852. Following our example, *Intrepid* has also started theatrical productions. Mr Krabbé made his first appearance as a conjuror.[19] This time the stage was in the orlop deck since the temperature of -27° would have forced everyone to blow on his fingers.

Several men of the crew sang comical songs and at 10 o'clock the evening ended with a supper hosted by the officers of *Intrepid*.

25 December 1852. A great day, especially in England – Christmas Day. Preparations for the holiday have long been under way and in the evening everything was ready for dinner. Each seamen's mess, consisting of eight men, was decorated with flags and centrepieces, while four chandeliers hung in the orlop deck illuminated the scene splendidly.

Everything the country or the ship could provide appeared on the tables, which were arranged along either side. When everything was ready the Captain, accompanied by the officers, made a tour of the orlop deck; scarcely had he disappeared when the meal began.

For a moment one could hear only the noise of knives and forks; by the end of ten minutes the astonished eye had nothing left to contemplate but a vast field of carnage. Once the vigorous appetites had been assuaged somewhat the fun began. Now it was time for songs and laughter.[20]

As for ourselves, an excellent dinner to which we had invited *Intrepid*'s officers awaited us in the wardroom. All the resources of the country appeared on our table: muskox, hare, and ptarmigan, together with an enormous roast of reindeer [21 lbs] which was certainly the most delicious venison I have ever tasted.

31 December 1852. During each of the past few days the men have been busy with various tasks, including digging away the drifted snow which had piled up against the sides of the ship during the blizzards and was threatening to overwhelm us.

Everyone is preparing his equipment for the next sledge trip and is making boots, helmets, and mittens. Everyone is very inventive and generally finds that what he has made is best.

Time is passing; we are starting a new year, and we all hope that it will be eventful both in terms of work and our search.

1 January 1853. At midnight on 31 December we left the captain's cabin, he having invited us to supper. Toasts to our families and friends were proposed and drunk joyfully, toasts to their health and happiness during the year which lies ahead of us.

At the last stroke of midnight a flag was hoisted on the summit of Dealy Island and two rockets were fired.

7 January 1853. Since the temperature is still very low,[21] forcing us to stay aboard or run the risk of frostbite, the men are employed at clearing and cleaning the hold and the water tanks. The bacon which had been stowed on deck under the fo'c's'le had become as hard as a rock and we have moved it to near the stove to thaw it out.

While taking a walk on Dealy Island Mr Pim killed a very fat ptarmigan [22] in its magnificent winter plumage, i.e., entirely white.

8 January 1853. Another ptarmigan was shot on the island today; on opening it we found its stomach filled with the buds of a little shrub which grows under the snow.[23] This fact of two ptarmigan killed here over the course of the winter would make one suppose that these birds do not emigrate completely and that those which stay find the means to survive despite all the rigours of the climate and the poverty of the vegetation.[24]

14 January 1853. Since the weather has improved a little and appears to be promising to stay fine, the after housing was removed [on 10 January] to provide a little air and light.

On going on deck this morning I was struck by the sight of an immense poster announcing the arrival in the vicinity of a rival to Robert Houdin, who was to make his appearance that very evening in the theatre aboard *Intrepid* and was to astonish the gentle company by the most extraordinary feats of legerdemain. The evening was to end with a magic lantern show.

Delighted to be able to spend some pleasant moments in the evening, we besieged *Intrepid*'s doors; her orlop deck was soon invaded by a crowd of spectators. The poster had not deceived us and the prestidigitator, in the person of Mr Pim, really excelled himself.

The magic lantern show, featuring some incidents of our campaign, set the crowning feature to the liveliness and gaiety of the company and we did not leave *Intrepid* until 4.00 a.m. after a pleasant supper, our path lit by a brilliant aurora.[25]

22 January 1853.[26] Mr Roche killed a hare on Dealy Island[27] and Mr Hamilton captured a totally white lemming alive.

23 January 1853. When a bear approached the ship preparations were made to receive it; despite all precautions to take it by surprise the animal spotted some movements on board and immediately took flight.[28] We set off in pursuit but it soon disappeared behind the hummocks and we missed a fine opportunity to provide a bit of food for the dogs which are starting to be in real need of it.[29]

31 January 1853. The crew is still busy preparing the sledging equipment and we are starting to assemble on Dealy Island the provisions depot which we are to leave there. The dogs are employed in hauling gravel aboard.

Preparations for a second theatrical performance are also keeping us busy[30] and it has been decided that I shall make my debut this time.

1 February 1853. A large poster displayed this morning in the orlop deck [Plate 16] announces that the theatre doors will open this evening at 6. In order to avoid the inconveniences of the last performance the first play was staged by the members of the crew; it was entitled 'Raising the Wind' and was very well presented with great vivacity.

The show continued with dancing and songs and was terminated with an excellent farce, 'King Glumpus,' written in verse by Sir John Barrow.

In this play I was entrusted with the part of a lady of the court, Lady Lollypop, and since I was unable to find a dress to fit me I was obliged to transform myself into a Bloomer girl.[31] I do not believe I have ever been so cold as during this performance;[32] my feet were imprisoned in satin shoes and were half frozen. After the show I was obliged to soak them in warm water to revive them.

All of this again went off marvellously, and having provoked loud applause from our audience we ended by singing a general rendering of 'God Save the Queen.' Then everyone hurried to get out of our inappropriate clothing, then took refuge in the captain's cabin, where a good fire and cigars awaited us.

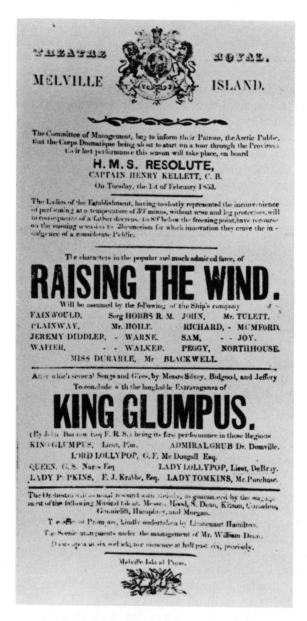

Plate 16 Playbill produced on board *Resolute* for the second theatrical
performance of the winter. De Bray is cast as Lady Lollypop in the
comedy *King Glumpus*.

The crew received a double ration and after one or two hours of conversation, all was quiet on board.

2 February 1853. First thing this morning the carpenters set about dismantling the theatre and by noon everything was gone.

All these distractions have not prevented us from thinking about serious things and for several days a morning inspection has been made of the outfitting of the sledges so that we are always ready to get under way, and the whole morning is spent in preparing and perfecting clothing and items of equipment.[33]

Today joy is reflected on every face; our dark days of winter are finished and the longed-for sun has reappeared. At 11.30 the upper edge of the luminary appeared above the horizon after an absence of ninety-three days, greeted by our joyful acclamations from the summit of Dealy Island where we had climbed to enjoy this pleasant spectacle even earlier.[34]

5 February 1853.

Observation by sextant   0° 23' 30"
Correction   20' 26"
Hence   0° 3' 4" above horizon
By calculation   41' 42" below horizon
Refraction   44' 46"   Therm. 37
Barom. 787

8 February 1853. We have begun sanding the channel which the ship entered to take up her winter quarters, so as to make the ice melt faster when the sun has a little more strength. The dogs have been hauling the sand from Dealy Island and have done marvels: on each trip five dogs have hauled 1,000 lbs on average. Admittedly the ice along their route is good and the distance is only one mile.[35]

In general a dog should not haul more than 120 lbs if one wishes to cover a long distance with some speed. The Eskimos of the west coast of Greenland cover an average of 150 miles per day with only two men, some provisions and furs on the sledge, a team consisting of five to seven dogs. Experience has shown that three dogs harnessed to a sledge weighing 100 lbs can cover a mile in six minutes, and during his voyage with *Fury* and *Hecla*, Parry reported that several times on the same day he saw nine dogs easily hauling 1,611 lbs a distance of a mile in nine minutes.

If the ice were always passable it would thus be very advantageous to use only dogs with the sledges, but since one generally encounters many hummocks and deep snowdrifts one has to have recourse to a more considerable, if slower, force and one uses men who, with their natural strength and moral power, are more apt to overcome all difficulties than any other being in creation.

Observed a magnificent aurora borealis stretching from NNW to SSE, the arc measuring 8° with periodically brilliant corruscations shooting up towards the zenith.[36]

10 February 1853. It is a remarkably fine day, the sun shining in all its splendour. Despite this, since the low temperature makes walking essential to obtain a little warmth, the ship was soon completely deserted by officers and men, with a view to enjoying this pleasure, of which we have been deprived for so long.

11 February 1853. On going ashore today around noon to take my usual walk on Dealy Island I was stopped by shouts coming from the ship, and on returning to see what was going on, I spotted a bear heading slowly towards me, completely cutting off my retreat. I had my gun, without which I never go walking, but it was almost useless, it being impossible for me to fire since I was in line with the ship; the same applied to the people on board, who might have wounded me. It was a critical moment and a moment's hesitation might have compromised me. I decided to return aboard and advanced boldly to meet the animal, my finger on the trigger of my gun. The bear stopped suddenly then began fleeing at top speed. I took advantage of the opportunity; I too began running and had soon reached *Intrepid,* where I was safe.

Having run for some time the bear stopped, and after sniffing in our direction, seeing that nobody was moving, it cautiously began approaching the ship. Everyone was ready to fire; soon it got to within 50 m of *Intrepid*'s stern and, standing on its hind legs, began sniffing in our direction. The moment was right; five shots rang out and the animal made a terrible leap, rolled on the ice for a moment, then got up and fled as fast as it could given its injuries, leaving a long trail of blood.

We immediately gave chase with the dogs, but although badly wounded the bear was rapidly outdistancing us. Since the wind was freshening, raising a lot of blowing snow, the pursuers began losing ground and I was left with just Messrs McClintock and Mecham vigorously continuing the chase, aided by two of our dogs. On turning off to try to intercept the animal's route, I ran into a range of hummocks which made for very difficult going. The drifting snow was getting thicker and since I guessed that I was already five or six miles from the ship and, moreover, had lost sight of my companions, I judged it prudent to return on board, where I arrived after a terrible journey, half-frozen.

The weather was so thick that at 100 paces one could not see the

ships; the thermometer was reading -39°C and we began to be anxious about the two officers who had not returned. By 4 o'clock the
concern had reached a pitch and we began firing a cannon every
quarter hour, as well as rockets and Bengal flares; at the same time
all the officers set off with some men in various directions.

The wind was extremely strong, right in the faces of our two poor
comrades. Finally at 5 o'clock they arrived aboard in a pitiful state,
almost blinded by the drift and so stunned by the wind that they
seemed like two drunks.[37] A bowl of hot wine had been prepared and
we celebrated their safe return with them.

Despite all our efforts the animal escaped, even although it had
one leg broken. By 5.30 everyone was back aboard and we once again
had a full complement after a day of keen anxiety.

12 February 1853. During the night a full gale was blowing and the
drift was so thick that we could not see *Intrepid*.[38] Around noon the
wind dropped and the temperature rose a little.

17 February 1853. Since we are running out of food for the dogs we
are obliged to take all the bacon rinds, bones, and condemned canned
meat, grind it all up, boil it with whale oil, and put it in tins.

For the moment the poor animals are having a complete rest in
anticipation of their forthcoming departure for Banks Land, since
orders appeared today to the effect that Messr Pim and Domville are
to hold themselves ready to leave at the first fine weather to go in
search of *Investigator*, Mr Pim with a sledge and seven men and Dr
Domville with a second sledge and five dogs.[39]

26 February 1853. The weather seems to be improving but the
temperature is still very low and at 8 this evening some mercury
placed outside in a saucer became totally solid.[40]

27 February 1853. Around 8.00 p.m., being aboard *Intrepid* for a game
of whist, we were alerted by a violent shock; we immediately went
on deck to see what had happened. Examining the ice more carefully
I noticed that the ship's stern had been raised by about 10 centimetres
without any apparent cause. I can only explain this circumstance as
being due to the excessive drop in temperature, which results in a
certain contraction in the ice, thus producing cracks which, as they
open, inevitably exert strong pressures on certain parts of the ice.[41]

28 February 1853. The opinion I formed yesterday evening on the
shock we experienced aboard *Intrepid* was confirmed for me today
by a crack about a foot wide between the old and new ice.[42]

3 March 1853. The sledges for Banks Land are loaded and ready to
go, but the weather does not seem settled enough yet, and it is more

prudent to wait, since the temperature is still very low. The men who are to go are no longer standing watches and are preparing their effects. The rest of the crew is employed at ballasting and at stowing the hold.

10 March 1853. At 8 o'clock this morning Messrs. Pim and Domville set off with their sledges;[43] the colours were hoisted on board and on Dealy Island and they were saluted by cheers from both ships. Mr Roche with a sledge and ten men is to accompany them to assist them if necessary as far as Winter Harbour. Mr Mecham and I also accompanied these gentlemen.

About a mile from the ship, while crossing a ridge of hummocks, Mr Pim's sledge, which was a little overloaded, overturned, and one of the runners broke in the middle. Fortunately one of *Intrepid's* sledges was ready and could be brought up and loaded immediately. Five miles from the ships we took leave of our two comrades; we exchanged firm handshakes and wished them good luck and success in their enterprise. Although their sledge was very heavily laden, the dogs seemed to me to be running marvellously and the two men accompanying the doctor were obliged to run to keep up.

In the evening Mr Roche arrived aboard, despite the bad weather which was just beginning and despite drift thick enough to hide us completely from Dealy Island. He had been sent by Mr Pim with the dogs to ask for another sledge since the one he had been given by *Intrepid* did not seem strong enough. The first day's travelling had been quite good and they had covered about ten miles.

14 March 1853. Since the 10th the weather has been so terrible that Mr Roche has been unable to leave and it was only today, with the wind dropping a little, that he was able to rejoin Messrs Pim and Domville,[44] whose tents we can see from the top of Dealy Island.[45]

20 March 1853. At 9 a.m. I spotted a sledge about four miles off to the west. Mr Nares went to meet it and at 11 o'clock Mr Roche arrived aboard with his men, having left the Bank's Land sledges on 16 March near Point Hearne. The officers and men were all in good health although they had suffered from cold during the three days following their departure, during which they had been confined to their tent. But one of the men, Sergeant of Marines Hobbs, had been sent back by the doctor, who did not judge him strong enough to continue the trip, since he had developed a heavy cold. He was immediately replaced by one of Mr Roche's men.[46]

At noon I noticed with delight that the snow was melting from the heat of the sun on the sides of the ship.

CHAPTER 6

Sledging to Cape de Bray

21 March 1853. Orders have been issued for the spring journey and everyone knows the route he is to take. I am in command of a sledge manned by a crew of eight and I will accompany Captain McClintock to explore the northwest coast of Melville Island. I have selected my men and have started making them take long walks to accustom them to marching. In the mean time I have been finishing my preparations. Everyone is busy trying to resolve the problem of taking the most possible in the least possible volume, something which is not always easy. Provisions cannot be reduced, although pemmican allows one to take a good amount of food in minimal volume. This preparation is used by Canadian trappers, and the pemmican we have was prepared following the recipe supplied by Dr Richardson. One takes good-quality beef (the rump is the best cut), cuts it into very thin slices, removes the fat and membranes, then dries it in an oven fired with oak wood until all moisture has totally disappeared and the meat is completely dried.

The meat is next ground and mixed with about an equal weight of beef fat. To give it a more agreeable taste and make it less binding one adds a small quantity of redcurrants and a little sugar. Once this mixture is complete one pours it into tins and lets it cool; to close the tins without air getting in one fills them with melted fat which one pours in through a little hole left in the lid. This hole is then stopped up with a tin plate which is soldered on.

In the process of drying the meat loses more than three quarters of its weight; as an example one may cite that to make 8,000 lbs of pemmican we needed 33,651 lbs of fresh beef; 1 lb of pemmican costs about 1 fr. 30 [91/2d].

The Indians and the Canadian trappers use reindeer meat which they dry in the sun, maintaining a small fire beneath it to keep the flies away; the meat is then ground between two stones on a bison skin. One can produce a very superior grade of pemmican by mixing the finely ground meat with beef marrow and the dried fruit of the shadberry.

As I have already mentioned, when equipping a sledge the first thing to consider is keeping the weight to a minimum; hence one must know what I shall call the constant weight, i.e., the total weight of all items of equipment, which does not vary unless things get wet, which happens quite often. The sledges are always manned by ten men or by seven and an officer.

These sledge outfits are kept to the absolute minimum and may be taken as a starting point in that the length of the trip may affect the constant weight; however, it never exceeds 40 kg per man.

Under normal circumstances, i.e., on fairly smooth ice, a man can haul a weight of 250 lbs without difficulty, using the sledges with which we were supplied. Hence for an eight-man sledge, for example, with the constant weight being 31 kg, this leaves 94 kg per man as the permissible weight of food. This is entirely adequate.

Equipment for eleven men			*Equipment for eight men*	
1 tent	29	kg	18	kg
4 pikes to support tent	14	kg	11	kg
1 buffalo robe	16.5	kg	11.5	kg
1 blanket	11.2	kg	10	kg
2 cooking apparatus	24	kg	17	kg
1 medicine chest	2.5	kg	2 5	kg
1 axe	1	kg	1	kg
1 bag containing wicks, thread, sail-needle, palm, matches, nails, etc.	4	kg	4	kg
11 sleeping bags	38.6	kg	28	kg
1 sledge sail	8	kg	6	kg
1 shovel and 1 pick	9	kg	9	kg
1 bag containing spoons and the day's lunch	5	kg	3.5	kg
1 rifle	3	kg	3	kg
1 bag containing ammunition	3	kg	3	kg
knapsacks and changes of clothing	44	kg	32	kg
sledge, complete	75	kg	45	kg
Macintosh sheet	11.5	kg	9	kg
1 brush	1	kg	1	kg

2 spars for mast	16	kg	16	kg
1 yard	13	kg	7.5	kg
Total weight	329.2	kg	216	kg
Per man	32.92	kg	30.85	kg

In the explanation which I am about to give of the major items of sledge equipment I shall confine myself to a crew of seven men and an officer, although I shall also quote the details for a ten-man crew's equipment [Plate 17].

The eight-man tent is 3 m 35 by 2 m 15 in area and 2 m 15 high; it may be designed in two styles as to its shape, since the canvas is invariably the same, having to combine strength and lightness. The sides may be rectangular, as in Figure 1, or with a slope to both ends, as in Figure 2. This latter design has the great advantage that it offers less surface to the wind when the tent is pitched. Four openings located in the upper part of the tent allow air to penetrate when the door is closed. These openings are covered by small canvas flaps so that snow cannot get inside the tent.

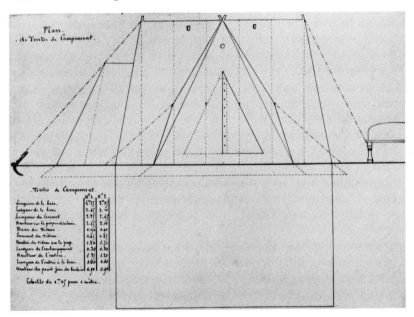

Plate 17 De Bray's sketch of the design and dimensions of the tents used on the sledging trips

The tent is supported by four boarding pikes, two at the front and two at the back. Then a rope, anchored to the sledge at one end, runs over the ends of the pikes, thus holding the ridge of the tent taut, and is fastened to a peg or pick sunk into the ice. As far as possible this rope should be made of horsehair, as being lighter and less susceptible to becoming stiff when cold.

The tent entrance is fastened on the inside by means of strong fasteners, while two curtains on each side of the entrance, made fast to the front tent pole, are very useful in preventing drifting snow from blocking the entrance, and at the same time provide some shelter to the cook or sentry, if there is occasion to have one.

To pitch the tent, either on land or on the ice, one starts by locating a site which is as level as possible; the sledge is placed about 3 m from the tent site and at right angles to the wind direction so that when the tent is pitched the wind will strike only the rear end.

The pikes are then slipped into sleeves made for the purpose at the top of the tent; the back guy is made fast to the middle of the sledge, leaving a slight slope to the back of the tent. When the front guy is tightened the tent is raised into position, the pikes are adjusted so as to form a rectangle as far as possible, and are thrust into the ground or into the ice. The pick with which every sledge is equipped serves as the point of attachment for the front of the tent. To complete the operation one piles pebbles, if they are available, all around the tent, or else snow or earth, in order to secure the tent and at the same time to stop the air from blowing in. For a crew of eleven men the tent should be 4 m 25 by 2 m 15 in area and 2 m 45 high.

As soon as it is pitched the first thing to put in the tent, in order to form the bed, is the Macintosh sheet with the rubber side down, to prevent the damp from penetrating. This Macintosh must be larger than the interior of the tent, i.e., 3 m 65 by 2 m 75 for eight men and 4 m 55 by 2 m 75 for eleven men. On top of this one then spreads the buffalo robe, hair side up. It should be of the same dimensions as the Macintosh.

The sleeping bags in which the men wrap themselves for the night are made of very thick blankets sewn along three sides and covered with canvas to keep the wool from contact with the snow. When all the men are in their bags one spreads a canvas or very light blanket over them, a little larger than the tent; this serves to protect them from the cold and the fine snow produced by condensation of the steam.

Every morning before the sledge is stowed all the sleeping items must be well brushed and shaken and before going to bed the officer must assure himself that the sledge serving as the rear anchor for the tent is well wrapped in the sail and that all the items of equipment are well stowed on it, so that nothing gets lost if it snows or drifts.

The major problem on sledge journeys is the means of cooking food, since it is impossible to take fuel such as wood or coal for a trip which may often last three months, in a country devoid of trees. Moreover, the weight alone would be an obstacle and one has to remedy these difficulties by using alcohol or an oil lamp.

The apparatus we use [Plate 18] consists of a round container, equipped with a lid, and large enough to contain all the cooking equipment. The sides of the container are made of two layers of tin, leaving a space of about 0.03 cm between, filled with solidified coal dust; coal being a poor conductor, it prevents the heat from escaping and concentrates it inside the apparatus. In making this container one should, as far as possible, not use solder, rivets being much better. The bottom of the container is pierced with round holes 2 to 3 cm in diameter and the entire apparatus rests on a round tin stand

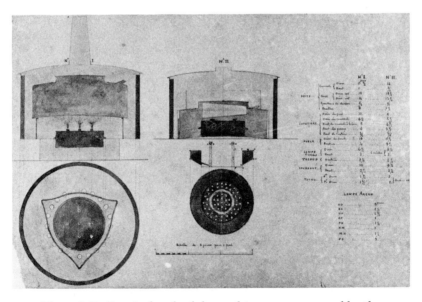

Plate 18 De Bray's sketch of the cooking apparatus used by the
sledging parties

which is also pierced with holes to allow an air flow and to provide a draught for the lamp.

If the fuel used is alcohol, the lamp is pierced by five holes, each of which has a wick, in the case of an apparatus for eight men, and by six holes in that for eleven men. Each wick is covered with a little copper hood when it is not lit to prevent the alcohol from evaporating, and it is worth noting that these little hoods should not screw on but should just slip on, since it often happens that it is impossible to unscrew them when it is cold. When the wind is quite strong one is obliged to cook inside the tent to avoid the flame flickering; this necessity has serious consequences, since the heat of the lamp is converted into steam which soaks one's clothes and the sleeping bags.

A lamp burning stearine or pure essence of mutton fat gives as much heat as one burning alcohol, but it has the disadvantage that it produces a lot of smoke and dirties the cooking utensils and especially the men's faces and hands. This last effect should be taken into consideration, since it is almost impossible to wash one-self effectively, the fuel ration being only 6 centilitres of alcohol and 750 grams of stearine for cooking breakfast and dinner for eight men and also for melting snow for water to fill the bottles which each man must carry with him.

In cold countries thirst is perhaps even a greater torture than in warm countries and it is very important that each man have a small supply of water for the day in order to avoid eating snow to quench his thirst; this latter produces the opposite effect and results in terrible griping pains, while ice, in the severe cold, makes one's mouth bleed.

The apparatus consists of a low copper coffee pot with a capacity of 9 litres in the case of eight men and 13 litres in the case of eleven men. It can be used for melting snow to provide a supply of water and for making tea. A sort of tin saucepan [illustrated in Plate 18] with slightly raised edges is used to cook meat and is placed in the container on top of the coffee pot. A tripod is placed over the lamp to support the coffee pot and the saucepan.

When the lamp is lit and the coffee pot placed on top of it the lid, which is slightly convex, is placed on top of everything to retain the heat. A single round hole is located in the middle of the lid; into it fits a little tin tube which helps in providing a draught for the lamp. When the temperature is very low it is also a good idea to cover the apparatus with a piece of blanket or unmilled felt to retain even more heat.

The apparatus is equipped with a strike-a-light for sulphurated matches and a little funnel for filling the lamp; everything is stowed in the coffee pot.

Every sledge should be equipped with two cooking apparatuses, one for alcohol, the other for stearine; these can then be used alternately.

The results achieved with these portable stoves have been very good until present, especially when using alcohol, and during my autumn trip, during which my dinner consisted of canned meat and tea, the meat was generally ready in forty-five minutes. But if the wind was a little strong and the temperature low, the meal would take an hour or even ninety minutes.

The sledges we use [Plate 19] are of two sizes and are made in such a way that when loaded with the weight they are designed to carry, the flat sections of the runners are 5 feet long in one case and 7 feet in

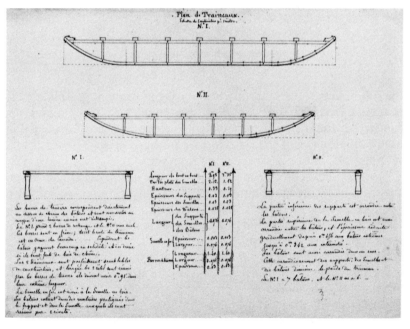

Plate 19 De Bray's sketch of the sledges used by the man-hauling parties

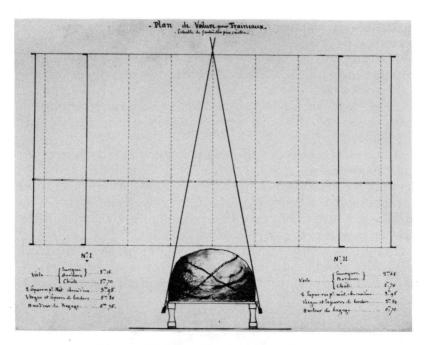

Plate 20 De Bray's sketch showing how to
set a sail on a sledge

the other. When the loads are removed, the runners possess a continuous curve. The supports from the runners and the crosspieces
connecting them should be rounded to reduce weight. Elm wood is
used by preference in the construction of these sledges. A sail can be
set [Plate 20], but only with a wind from aft.

The mast consists of two pikes, which are also used as tent poles,
crossed and secured at their shod ends by a little strop; two stays are
run forward and two back, made fast to the ends of the supports.
The bottom ends of the pikes rest in two leather shoes joined by a
strop rigged over the sledge. The sail halyards run through a thimble
on the strop which joins the two pikes and the yard consists of the
spare pike. Two pikes lashed together form a second lower yard
for the sail, to spread it as much as possible. This lower yard
is made fast in the middle to the front of the sledge. Two moor-
ing lines are sufficient to serve as braces for the yard. This rig is
very solid and sometimes I have seen a sledge under sail alone, gliding at a speed of 4 to 5 knots, the men being forced to drop their

hauling lines in order to run after the sledge and steer it.

The means of traction is via two ropes secured to an eye on the rear end of the sledge, then running forward along the supports and made fast to the front ends. These two ropes then join about 3 feet in front of the sledge by means of a cross-shaped lashing, beneath which run the hauling ropes with which each man is equipped. It is absolutely essential that these hauling ropes can be easily unhitched, since if the sledge were to break through the ice the men would inevitably be dragged under if they could not unhitch themselves rapidly.

The men should be provided with warm clothing, especially that made of flannel. A jacket and pants made of sealskin are excellent, and are even better if they are underlain by light woollen garments in order to prevent contact between the other clothing and the sealskin, which is almost always covered with ice produced by the condensed vapour which escapes from the body.

The boots should be made of very supple felt or some other material which is soft on the feet; leather must be avoided completely since it freezes and hardens so fast that it is impossible to put on one's footwear again once one has taken it off. In addition, one must always take the precaution of putting one's boots in one's sleeping bag at night if one wishes to find them in a good state in the morning.

Canvas boots are excellent but they must be cut very wide so that one can get one's foot in when it is enveloped first in a woollen stocking, then in a piece of woollen blanket, and finally in another very thick stocking reaching to the knee over one's pants. A piece of canvas forming a sort of gaiter encloses the heel of the boot and laces in front to stop any friction on the foot as much as possible and also to support the foot.

The provisions vary a little depending on the length of the sledge trip and on the difficulties of the route.

All the information which I have just given as to sledge equipment should be taken only in a fairly general manner and may serve as a base, but many improvements and changes can be made in it.[1] In outfitting my own sledge, as I shall describe later, I acted according to my own ideas, and I believe I arrived at what was absolutely essential, but without compromising the well-being of the men, which is so important on such excursions.

22 March 1853. Mr Hamilton shot a muskox yesterday in Bridport Inlet[2] and today Messrs Mecham and Nares with fourteen men and

a sledge, went to retrieve it; they returned in the evening.[3] They had found the animal still alive and the numerous tracks of wolves and foxes visible all around indicated that the poor animal had experienced some rough assaults during the night.[4]

27 March 1853. The boats have been cleared of the snow which covered them.

The carpenters are busy making small, very light sledges 1 m 50 long which will be issued as supplementary sledges to officers who have to make short side trips. They can be easily hauled by two men, with provisions and a small tent. The great advantage of these sledges, which we call satellites, is that they will allow the officer to explore the inner part of a bay or gulf while the main sledge simply crosses its mouth; they will thus be able to complete the exploration of the coasts or lands which they may discover.

29 March 1853. Mr Hamilton with twenty men and a cart laden with provisions set off for the head of Bridport Inlet in order to establish a depot for the use of the sledges which will be heading in that direction.[5] In the evening the weather turned bad and one of Mr Hamilton's men came aboard to inform the captain that one of his companions [Jeffries] was so fatigued that he could not walk any farther. A light sledge was immediately sent out and by .00 pm. Mr Hamilton and all the men were back aboard.[6]

Orders were given today to clear the deck of the layer of snow and gravel which was put there at the start of the winter.

3 April 1853. For the past three days everybody on board has been in an upheaval; the departure of the sledges has been set for tomorrow, 4 April.[7] The provisions are completed, the sledges are stowed, and above each one floats the flag which has been passed on to each officer by the captain on behalf of charming ladies who have embroidered them with their own hands. I think I shall never finish my preparations; every other minute I remember some item I have forgotten, and yet I do not want to exceed the weight fixed for each man, including changes of clothing, which is set at 7 kilograms.

My letters are finally finished, since I am hoping that a sledge will communicate with Beechey Island during my absence and I do not want to miss a single opportunity to send news home.

Tomorrow is thus the great day which we have been awaiting so impatiently, since our winter's rest has become so tedious that we are all looking forward to getting a bit of exercise. Moreover we have a great goal, the search for those unfortunates who, if they are still alive, have been counting the hours and the minutes for so long, always hoping to see a friendly hand appearing to succour them ...

I shall copy verbatim the report which I addressed to Captain Kellett on my return from the trip.

Journal of the sledge *Hero*, auxiliary to Captain McClintock, Captain of *Intrepid*, Northwestern exploration of Melville Island

Sir,

In compliance with your instructions I have the honour of addressing to you a report on my journey in command of the sledge *Hero*, auxiliary to Captain McClintock for the exploration of the northwest coast of Melville Island.

(Copy of my orders)

Issued by H. Kellett, C.B., captain of *Resolute*.

I have great pleasure in being able to appoint you to the command of H.M. Sledge *Hero*, auxiliary to so active an officer as Commander McClintock, one who is so well acquainted with Arctic travelling, whose journey will be so extended and whose example you will do well to follow.

You will place yourself under his command for your future proceedings and I feel assured that from the zeal you have manifested in the equipment of your sledge as well as in other matters connected with travelling, you will do great credit to the distinguished service to which you belong.

Given under my hand on board

H.M. Ship *Resolute*

in winter quarters, Dealy Island, 2d. of April 1853

Equipment of the sledge Hero
8 men and 1 officer

Item of equipment	Weight (kg)	Provisions	Amount	Clothing (worn)	Spares
1 tent for 7 men, enlarged by 1 width of canvas	19.75	pemmican	500 g	1 flannel (vest)	1
6 pikes for tent poles, yard & mast	17.5	bacon	250 g	1 knitted wool shirt	1
1 Macintosh	9.5	preserved meat	375 g	1 serge jumper	1
1 buffalo robe	14.5	bacon	375 g	1 pair woollen drawers	1

1 blanket	13.125	biscuit	375 g	1 pair cloth		
		biscuit		pants		1
1 sail (complete)	8.00	powder	40 g	1 pair over-		
10 sleeping bags	33.00	potatoes	80 g	trousers		2
9 knapsacks	63.00	tea	10 g	1 pair long		
1 iron shovel	2.5	sugar	20 g	stockings		2
1 bag containing		chocolate	10 g	1 pair		
needles, sail-twine,		sugar	10 g	mocassins		
ropes, etc.	3.75	rum	6 cent.	(with soles)		2
3 cooking apparatus	21.00	alcohol	50 cent.	1 pair gloves		2
1 medicine chest	2.25	stearine	500 g	1 woollen hat		1
1 sledge and rigging	58.5	tobacco		1 piece blue		
1 rifle and		(week)	120 g	crepe		
ammunition	5.0			1 mask		
1 bag of powder and				1 sealskin hat		
lead	6.5			1 woollen scarf		
1 bag matches, fuses,				1 sealskin		
rope-yarn, etc.	5.5			blouse		
1 axe	.0			1 pair canvas		
1 brush and canvas				boots		
cover for sledge	3.0					
2 pairs fur boots	3.0					
9 tin pots and						
alcohol containers	3.0	Constant weight per man 36.671 kg				
——Total——	293.375					

Notes: The shortage of fuel was made good with bacon fat and the fat contained in the preserved meat cans.

The only possible extra items would be a pair of Eskimo boots; the hauling belt must be adjusted as snugly as possible.

Names of men	Rank	Age	Ship
E.F. de Bray	Enseigne de vaisseau	–	*Resolute*
John Cleverley	Gunner's mate	29	*Intrepid*
John Drew	AB	30	"
Robert Ganniclift	"	27	"
William Walker	"	24	"
Thomas Hartnell	"	32	"
Samuel Dean	Carpenter's mate	25	"
James Miles	Leading stoker	32	"
Alexander Johnson	Steward	27	"

4 April 1853. *

Course steered   NW
Distance covered   10 miles
Encamped   13 hrs
Lunch   30 min.
Marched   9 hrs 30 min
Wind   ENE to NE
Temp.   -16°C

At 7.30 a.m. left the ship in company with *Star of the North*, Captain McClintock, *Erin*, Captain Kellett, *Hope*, Mr Hamilton, and *Beauty*, Mr Roche, exchanging three cheers with Messrs Mecham and Nares and the small number of those who will remain on board the two ships and whose number, including officers, totals sixteen.

The weather overcast and snowy and the ice generally good; we had lunch at 12.20 p.m. on the north shore of Bridport Inlet. From there on the hauling became very difficult although the land was covered with snow and we camped at 5.30 p.m. on a lake [Plate 21].

Having spotted several muskoxen, I gave chase with Mr Hamilton but without success. I tried to dig a hole through the lake ice to get water but had to give up after reaching a depth of 4 feet without success.

5 April 1853.

Course   NW1/2W
Distance   5.5 miles
Encamped   14 hrs.
Lunch   30 min
Marched   9 hrs 30 min
Wind   NE to NW
Temp.   -19°C

Breakfasted at 6.30 a.m., stowed the sledge, and set off. We soon reached the entrance to a deep ravine in the bottom of which the snow had accumulated to a considerable depth and obliged us to take the slope above, which we managed to reach only by assigning three crews, i.e., twenty-one men, to each sledge.

Lunched at noon near a cairn surmounted by a bamboo pole placed here by Captain McClintock last autumn. After our meal set a course across a plain about 600 feet above sea level.

Weather cloudy and snowy. Camped at 5.00 p.m.; after dinner everyone went to sleep, very tired with the efforts of the day.

* This version of de Bray's sledging report represents a direct translation of his own journal. Where this diverges significantly from the official report submitted to Parliament and published in English (de Bray, 1855b), such divergences will be noted.

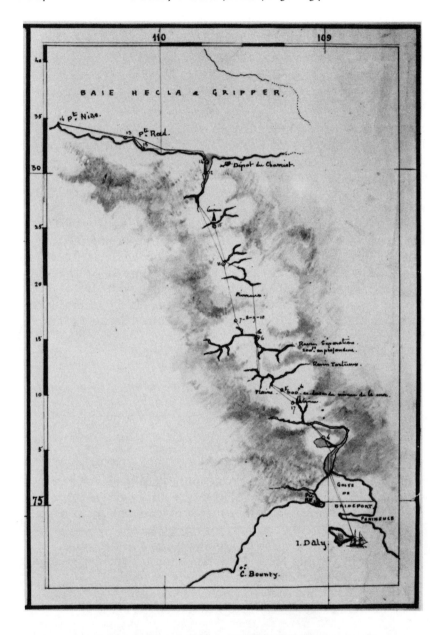

Plate 21 De Bray's manuscript map of his sledging route from Dealy Island to Point Nias and back. For comparison with the modern map, see Plate 10.

6 April 1853. Course N33°W
Distance 6 ¹/₄ miles
Camped 14 hrs
Lunch 30 min
Marched 9 hrs 30 min
Wind NNW
Temp. -22°C

Breakfasted at 7.00 a.m., stowed the sledge, and set off; we soon reached a second ravine to which we gave the name Crooked Ravine because of its many sinuosities, located about five miles from the bamboo cairn.

Lunch at 11.45 and set off again at 12.15. By 2.00 we were in another ravine whose depth of 200 feet caused us some difficulties, since the route was almost sheer. The snow in the bottom was very deep, and since our sledges were heavily laden we progressed only slowly. Camped in the ravine at 4.50 p.m.

We again spotted some muskoxen today but they were out of range. The weather was foggy, with a little snow in the morning but cleared up toward evening.

7 April 1853. Course NW
Distance 3 miles
Camped 14 hrs 10 min
Lunch 30 min
Marched 4 hrs
Wind NNW
Temp. -26°C

At 7.00 a.m. set off along the bottom of the ravine with a strong wind and very heavy drift.

Despite the bad weather Captain Kellett left his tent and sledge and accompanied us with his crew to help us in ascending the ravine and by 10 o'clock we were on a plateau which we named Stony Plain because of the large number of rocks with which it was strewn. Here the captain took his leave of us to return to the ship and we continued on our way.[8] At 11.00 the drift became so heavy that we were obliged to camp although the sky was still clear. Lunched at noon; dinner at 6.30 p.m., the thermometer reading 14° inside the tent.

8 April 1853. Wind NNW
Temp. -30°C

Confined to the tent by a strong NNW-erly wind which is raising such a heavy drift that one cannot see two paces.

9 April 1853. Wind NNW
Temp. -32°C

Confined to the tent by the same weather. One of my men, Johnson
by name, is complaining of general weakness, which I attribute to
the fatigue caused by such a long rest at such a low temperature. I
administered a very hot drink with half a spoonful of spirit of
ammonia.

Towards evening the weather had cleared a little and I had the
men shake their sleeping bags and all their spare clothing to get rid
of the snow produced inside the tent by freezing of the vapour and
at the same time by the drift which penetrates even the smallest
openings.

10 April 1853.   Wind   NNW
                                Temp.   -32°C

Still inside the tent with the same weather. But the wind is not
as strong and I was able to go out to visit Captain McClintock,
whom I found suffering from a slight attack of snowblindness. In all
the other tents they were in good health, without even any signs of
frostbite. This morning, having had a better night, Johnson was
completely recovered.

11 April 1853.   Course   N6°W
                                Distance   6 miles
                                Camped   14 hrs 30 min
                                Lunch   30 min
                                Marched   9 hrs
                                Wind   NNW
                                Temp.   -15°C

Since the weather seemed quite good and a little clearer, after
breakfast we stowed the sledge and set off at 8.30 a.m. The going
was very bad due to the large number of rocks which have been
blown clear of snow by the wind, and we were obliged to make long
detours. Lunched at 1.30 p.m.; got under way at 2.00, crossing a
little ravine. Camped at 6.00; the weather very clear and calm
towards the evening.

12 April 1853.   Course   N6°W
                                Distance   8 miles
                                Camped   14 hrs
                                Lunch   30 min
                                Marched   10 hrs 35 min
                                Wind   SSE
                                Temp.   -24°C

Breakfast at 8 a.m.; stowed the sledge and got under way with a
light breeze from the SSE; the fine weather allowed us to put our
gear to dry by hoisting it on the masts of the sledge.

The going was quite good and the snow cover quite deep and

hard. Lunch at 1.15 p.m.; got under way at 1.45 with the wind freshening from the SSE.

Passed a cairn called the Cart Cairn, from where I got a view of the panorama of the north shore of Hecla and Griper Bay.

With the help of the fair wind we soon reached a small cairn at the entrance to the last ravine which we have to cross, and in descending which we made rapid progress. About two miles from the sea ice we were stopped by the snow which filled the ravine, and were obliged to double the crews on the sledges to reach the ground above; there we found the going quite passable.

Camped at 7.00 p.m. in the ravine half a mile from the sea ice. My thermometer, which was in a gutta percha case, was found to be broken, probably due to contraction caused by the intense cold we have had.

13 April 1853.

Course   W
Distance   7.5 miles
Camped   13 hrs 30 min
Lunch   30 min
Marched   9 hrs
Wind   SSE & SSW
Temp.   -21°C

Immediately after breakfast I set off with one man and one of the satellite sledges to take a case of pemmican and one-and-half cases of bacon to the Cart Cairn.

I had previously unloaded my sledge to examine the runners and found only two rivets missing. All my men are in good health and I held an inspection of feet and hands without finding any frost-bite.

Set off at 8.30 a.m. accompanied by Messrs Hamilton and Roche, the former having left his tent and sledge at the campsite. At 9.00 I shook hands with these gentlemen and set off westwards along the land since the ice was too rough. Weather clear; light breeze from the SSE; hoisted the sail. Lunch at 1.00; set off again at 1.30. I went ahead with Captain McClintock with a saw and an axe to try to relocate a tree he had seen last autumn. We found it without difficulty, although it was partly covered with snow,[9] and we immediately began cutting it up. Soon afterwards both our sledges arrived and we were able to load two days' fuel. At 3.00 the wind got up very fresh from the SSW with heavy drifting. Camped at 5.30 p.m.[10]

14 April 1853.

Course   W6°N
Distance   8.5 miles
Camped   14 hrs 30 min
Lunch   30 min

Marched   9 hrs 30 min
Wind   NW to W
Temp.   -25°C

Breakfast; stowed the sledge and set off at 8.00; the weather clear with a light breeze from the NW.

With Captain McClintock taking charge of the sledges I set off in search of game and had the good fortune to kill a hare, which I literally decapitated with my ball. Lunch at 1.30; set off at 2.00 with the wind swinging all around the compass. Camped at 6.00 at the Point Nias depot.

15 April 1853.

Course   NW
Distance   2 miles
Camped   13 hrs 30 min
Lunch   30 min
Marched   4 hrs 30 min
Wind   SW to NW
Temp.   -26°C

Employed all morning at replenishing our supplies from the Point Nias depot and at burying another depot of eleven days' supplies for my return trip.

The weather foggy and snowy; wind fresh from the SW with much drift. Lunch in the tent at 12.30; stowed the sledge and set off under sail at 1.00; at 4.00 p.m. the wind suddenly swung into the NW after a brief calm and strengthened so much that we were obliged to camp at 5.30. The ice is very bad due to the large amount of snow covering it.

16 April 1853.

Wind   NW
Temp.   -30°C

Confined to the tent by a NW gale and a temperature which is too low to be able to continue our march.

17 April 1853.

Course   NW
Distance   8 miles
Camped   14 hrs
Lunch   30 min
Marched   9 hrs
Wind   NW to SW
Temp.   -19°C

Breakfast at 8.00; stowed the tent and set off to the NW; the weather cloudy with snow at intervals. In the evening the wind swung from NW to SW.

Severe glare which severely affects the eyes. Lunch at 1.00; set off at 1.30; weather the same. Camped at 5.30.

Very bad ice which impeded our progress a little at some points.

18 April 1853.

Course   NW
Distance   6.5 miles
Camped   14 hrs
Lunch   30 min
Marched   9 hrs
Wind   SE
Temp.   -24°C

Set off at 7.00; weather overcast, light breeze. Lunch at noon and set off again at 12.30.

A very pronounced mirage made the land ahead seem very close, although we were two to three miles away.

Camped at 5.00; noticed two fresh reindeer tracks on the ice heading from Melville Island towards Sabine Land [Peninsula]. The snow on the ice is still very deep.

19 April 1853.

Course   NW
Distance   7 miles
Camped   14 hrs
Lunch   30 min
Marched   9 hrs
Wind   SSE
Temp.   -24°C

Breakfast at 7; stowed the sledge and headed for a low point which forms the northern tip of Hecla and Griper Bay and named Cape Fisher by Parry in 1820 [Plate 22]. On rounding this point we found a very deep bay and another point bearing NW. Headed for this point, where we had lunch at noon. Set off again at 12.30.

Previously I had been sent by Captain McClintock to explore this point, and found some pieces of coal. Having sighted two muskoxen, I immediately gave chase and succeeded in wounding one, but it managed to escape although one front leg was broken.

This point was named Middle Point and the bays on either side Twin Bays.[11] At the head of the northerly bay there is a very high bluff which Parry sighted from Point Nias and named Bull Bluff. This bluff is the start of a chain of mountains running to the NW.

Before starting this morning we inspected our sledges which have suffered greatly these past few days. There are thirty-three rivets missing from the runners of Captain McClintock's sledge *Star of the North* and the runners were split in the middle. There were only fourteen rivets missing from mine and there was only a slight crack in the starboard runner. Camped at 4.30. The ice quite good along the coast.

20 April 1853.

Course   NW
Distance   9 miles

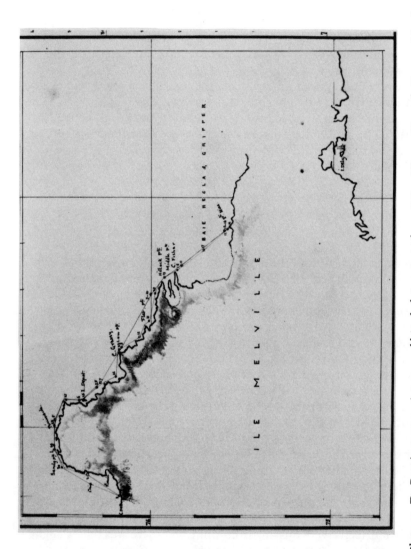

Plate 22 De Bray's manuscript map of his sledging route from Point Nias to Cape de Bray and back

Camped   12 hrs 45 min
Marched   7 hrs 15 min
Wind   SE
Temp.   -27°C

Set off at 5.15 in very clear weather with a light breeze from the SE. Hung our gear to dry. At 8.00 the weather became foggy and since the wind had freshened we hoisted sail. Found blue ice along the coast.

Having sighted three muskoxen, I set off in pursuit with Captain McClintock and succeeded in killing one. The other two abandoned the dead animal only after being subjected to a hail of rocks which we threw at them; we did not want to kill them unnecessarily, since we cannot overload our sledges.

As the wind was freshening rapidly and snow falling heavily, we camped at 12.30. The fresh meat was divided between the two sledges and we had the pleasure of a good steak for dinner, skipping lunch. We saw several reindeer during the day. The point we passed today was named Hillock Point.

21 April 1853.   Course   W1/4NW
                        Distance   10 miles
                        Camped   14 hrs 15 min
                        Lunch   30 min
                        Marched   9 hrs 25 min
                        Wind   NW to SE
                        Temp.   -12°C

Set off at 2.45 a.m. after a substantial breakfast of muskox and a good cup of chocolate. Weather snowy with a light NW breeze. The ice very good for six and a half miles. Lunch at 8.30 a.m.; set off again at 9.00 with a SE wind; the ice very bad because of the large amount of snow which fell yesterday, which is lying to a depth of 12 inches. Camped at 12.40; noticed numerous lemming tracks on the ice coming from the NE and heading for Melville Island.

We were marching all day along a very low coast and at times had difficulty in distinguishing land from ice. Walker having very sore eyes, I bandaged them after applying a drop of wine of opium.

22 April 1853.   Course   N1/4NW
                        Distance   7 miles
                        Camped   13 hrs 20 min
                        Lunch   30 min
                        Marched   9 hrs 30 min
                        Wind   N
                        Temp.   -10°C

Set off at 2.00 a.m.; the weather snowy, light breeze from the north.

Lunch at 7.00; got under way again at 7.30. The glare off the ice is very trying on the eyes. On climbing a hill near the coast I saw a landmass which I thought at first was separated from Melville Island, but as we progressed we could see that it was only the tip of a very low point bearing N1/4NW [Long Point].

We soon reached this point, where the ice was very bad due to the numerous hummocks and the large quantity of snow. Camped at noon.

Walker's eyes are much better; I removed his bandage.

23 April 1853.
Course   NW
Distance   8 miles
Camped   12 hrs 30 min
Lunch   30 min
Marched   9 hrs 30 min
Wind   N to NW
Temp.   -21°C

Set off at 12.30 a.m; very fine weather; light breeze from the N. Since the ice was very bad, we were obliged to travel across some low points which one could distinguish only by some small hillocks protruding above the snow.

Lunched at 5.30; set off again at 6.00. Since the wind freshened rapidly from the NW with drifting snow, we headed for quite a high point bearing NW; camped at 10.30.

24 April 1853.
Course   NW
Distance   8 miles
Camped   14 hrs
Lunch   30 min
Marched   8 hrs 50 min
Wind   NW
Temp.   -17°C

Set off at 12.30 a.m.; weather foggy; wind fresh out of the NW with heavy drifting.

We soon reached a point with quite a high hill which we called Grassy Cape because of the large amount of grass covering it. The land becomes very low again to the W and SW. Lunch at 5.30; set off again at 6.00 along the coast on quite good ice.

At 8.00 the weather cleared, allowing us to see a high land to the NW. Camped at 9.30 a.m.

Today I saw a ptarmigan on Grassy Cape and a herd of eighteen reindeer; I had the good fortune to kill a reindeer; its meat was shared between the two sledge crews.

25 April 1853.
Course   WNW
Distance   8 miles

Camped   15 hrs 10 min
Lunch   30 min
Marched   9 hrs 30 min
Wind   NW
Temp.   -25°C

Set off at 1.00 a.m. Clear weather with a light NW breeze.

Lunch at 6.00; set off again at 6.30, heading for a point which we could see ahead of us and which forms the entrance to a wide, deep bay.

The weather turned squally with heavy drift; the ice is fairly level but the deep layer of snow which covers it makes the work of hauling the sledges very laborious. Camped at 11.00 a.m.

26 April 1853.   Course   NW
                                    Distance   7 miles
                                    Camped   19 hrs 15 min
                                    Lunch   30 min
                                    Marched   7 hrs 40 min
                                    Wind   NW
                                    Temp.   -24°C

Set off at 11.50 p.m.; the sky clear with a slight haze on the horizon; light breeze from the NW.

Lunched at 4.20 a.m. and set off again at 4.50.

At 8 o'clock we camped on a little island two and a half miles long and two miles wide, lying about two miles off the coast [Depot Island]. The ice quite good all day.

27 April 1853.   Course   N1/4NW
                                    Distance   9 miles
                                    Camped   14 hrs
                                    Marched   9 hrs 30 min
                                    Lunch   30 min
                                    Wind   NW
                                    Temp.   -25°C

We set off at 10.10 p.m. leaving a depot of provisions on the island, which is intended for Captain McClintock on his return, and a case of pemmican for me.[12]

We found good ice for about three miles along a ridge of hummocks extending from the island to the coast, but then the hauling became very difficult because of the soft snow. Light breeze from the NW. Lunch at 3.45 a.m.; set off again at 4.15 a.m.

The land is very low, with an appearance quite different from what we have seen until present in terms of vegetation. Camped at 8. Observed some muskox and reindeer tracks heading eastwards.

28 April 1853.   Course   W
                                    Distance   9 miles

Camped   14 hrs
Lunch   30 min
Marched   9 hrs
Wind   W to WSW
Temp.   -18°C

Set off at 10.00 p.m. Weather clear; light breeze from the W; the ice very rough and covered with deep snow. Very strong refraction reveals land stretching very far to the N1/4NW, to the N and to the NNE.[13]

Lunched at 3.45 a.m.; set off again at 4.15; the wind freshening from the WSW with some drifting. Camped at 7.40 a.m.

The view of the land which lies ahead of us lets us suppose that we are in a channel running between Melville Island and the land to the north; this channel appears to be encumbered with old ice without any pressure ice visible along the coast.

29 April 1853.   Course   SW1/4S
Distance   9.5 miles
Camped   13 hrs 10 min
Lunch   30 min
Marched   9 hrs 30 min
Wind   NW
Temp   -18°C

Set off at 8.50 p.m. heading for a point which we can see ahead of us [Cape Scott]. This point forms the tip of a peninsula whose isthmus the sledges crossed to avoid a long detour.

I deposited a document on this point. Land appears to surround us on all sides as if we were in a large bay; to assure himself of this fact Captain McClintock took his lunch with him and headed north towards the land. I soon lost sight of him due to the very strong refraction.[14]

Camped at 6.50 a.m. Captain McClintock returned after a march of ten miles without having been able to assure himself of the position of the land. By 8.00 the refraction had ceased and we could no longer see any land. Weather very clear all night with a light breeze from the NW.

Saw three muskoxen and two ptarmigan today.

30 April 1853.   Course   SW
Distance   10 miles
Camped   13 hrs 55 min
Lunch   30 min
Marched   9 hrs 30 min
Wind   WSW to SW
Temp.   -13°C

Set off at 8.45 p.m. I went ashore to examine the coast; no vegetation on the land, which is covered with a layer of snow.

Clear weather; light breeze from the WSW; the ice appears quite good and yet the hauling is very difficult. Lunched at 2.45 a.m.; set off again at 3.15 a.m.

Ahead of us to the SW the land appears to be very high and from their appearance the mountains appear to be part of a chain which starts at Cape Fisher. The land to the WNW and NW appears to consist of several islands.[15]

Refraction is still very strong and makes the land seem very high, sometimes producing three distinct images. Camped at 6.45 a.m. Noticed three tracks of lemmings and one of a fox coming from the west of Melville Island. Several very fresh tracks of foxes and ptarmigan and foxes on land.

1 May 1853.

Course   SSW
Distance   9 miles
Camped   13 hrs 45 min
Lunch   30 min
Marched   9 hrs 30 min
Wind   Calm
Temp.   -19°C

Set off at 8.30 p.m. Sky cloudy; calm; the ice still quite bad, making the work tedious.

Lunched at 2.00 a.m. and set off again at 2.30 towards a hill which seems to be the tip of a point. The refraction is very severe.[16]

Noticed several tracks of reindeer and foxes; while crossing the ice two ptarmigan passed us, flying over the sledges.

2 May 1853.

Course   SW
Distance   9 miles
Camped   14 hrs
Lunch   30 min
Marched   9 hrs
Wind   N to NE
Temp.   -21°C

Set off at 8.30 p.m.;[17] weather clear; light breeze from N to NE. We hoisted the sail, although it was of little help. Lunched at 2.00 a.m.; set off again at 2.30 heading for the coast in the hope of finding better ice.[18] While we were resting for a moment three ptarmigan came and landed near the sledges; one of my men fired but missed. The ice near the land was very good; the snow sheltered by the mountains was hard and smooth. Camped at 6.00 a.m. on a little point where Captain McClintock is placing his major provisions depot.

Began building a cairn. The land in sight to the NW seems very high and about fifteen miles away.[19]

3 May 1853.

Course   NE
Distance   9.5 miles
Camped   14 hrs
Lunch   30 min
Marched   9 hrs 30 min
Wind   SSE

Having decided, after examination, that his sledge could not go any farther with such a heavy load, Captain McClintock took mine, which was in good condition compared to his own, and which was missing only a few rivets from the supports.

I also took three of his men: Hood, who had strained himself and could not work, and also two stokers from *Intrepid*, Smithers and Coombes.[20] I gave him one of my men, Drew, to complete his eight men. All the items of equipment were exchanged and my provisions completed to eleven days' rations for eleven men. In addition I received the following instructions for my return:

Proceed along shore, examining the beach in such parts as were not traversed in our outward journey as far as Depot Island; do this with all the speed you can and return to Point Nias as fast as possible. Take up my depot of seven days' provisions. Having carried out this depot to Cape Fisher, return to the ships.

Leave records and cairns at Depot Island, Grassy Cape, Cape Fisher, and Point Nias, at the Cart and in any other positions you deem suitable.

Dig up and copy Parry's record at Point Nias and leave it on the surface that I can easily find it and add my news to it.

At 9 o'clock I shook hands warmly with Captain McClintock, then, with the two crews saluting each other with three cheers, I set off along the coast [i.e., on the homeward journey] at a good pace, leaving them all in good health and full of high spirits. Weather foggy; light breeze from the SSE.

I sent my sledge across a fairly wide bay while I explored all its sinuosities, walking along the shore. Since the weather had become squally, I lost sight of my sledge for some time and did not rejoin it until 2.30 for lunch. Set off again at 3.00, with the weather clearing in the north.

By my estimate the bay I explored today might be three miles deep and three miles wide at its entrance;[21] had the good luck to kill three ptarmigan on my excursion. Camped at 7.00 near a remarkable hill in the shape of a coin.

The large depot we left is located about two miles from a cape which Captain McClintock graciously named Cape de Bray. From this cape the land appears to run south and I presume that Captain McClintock and Mr Mecham will meet shortly.

From today onwards I cannot record the temperature since I no longer have a thermometer.

4 May 1853.

Course   NNE
Distance   15 miles
Camped   13 hrs
Lunch   30 min
Marched   9 hrs 30 min
Wind   NNE to NE

Set off at 8.00 p.m.; weather clear with a light breeze from the ENE. We marched along the coast for about six miles then from there I sent my sledge directly across to a point bearing NE1/4E while I continued to explore the shoreline.

Lunched at 1.30; got under way again at 2.00; the weather became foggy and the wind suddenly freshened from the NE.

At one point along the coast I found salt water on the ice, probably coming from a crack in the ice caused by a strong tide. The ice is very good, especially for a sledge as light as mine is now; camped at 6.00 a.m. Saw three ptarmigan during the march.

5 May 1853.

Course   ENE
Distance   13 miles
Camped   14 hours
Lunch   30 min
Marched   10 hrs
Wind   NE

Set off at 8.00 p.m.; weather clear; light breeze from NE, freshening a little. Headed for a peninsula which we reached at 2.00 a.m. and had lunch.

Built a cairn on this point [Cape Scott again]; deposited a document which I added to the one we had left there a few days previously. Set off at 2.30; weather dull and foggy with the wind starting to blow violently. Camped at 6.30 a.m.

6 May 1853.

Course   E and S1/4E
Distance   7 miles
Camped   13 hrs 45 min
Lunch   30 min
Marched   9 hrs 30 min
Wind   NE

Set off at 8.15 p.m.; weather cloudy and foggy. The ice was very bad, obliging me to move close inshore where I found the going better.

Lunched at 1.45 a.m.; set off again at 2.15; the weather is so foggy that one can see only a hundred paces ahead; the glare is very severe and is affecting our eyes. Light breeze from the NE, almost calm at times. Camped at 6.15 a.m. Saw three ptarmigan.

7 May 1853.

Course SE1/4E
Distance 13 miles
Camped 13 hrs 45 min
Lunch 30 min
Marched 8 hrs 45 min
Wind all around the compass
Built a cairn 45 min

Set off at 8.00 p.m. heading for Depot Island; weather foggy, light breeze from NE. Since the ice was very bad we had to travel along the shore for most of the way.

I reached the depot at 10.00 p.m. and built a cairn in which I placed a paper informing Captain McClintock that I had found no trace of the Franklin expedition.

I took a case of pemmican from the depot and set off again at 10.45 p.m. Lunched at 1.45 a.m.; set off again at 2.15; camped at 6.00 a.m. Saw a ptarmigan.

8 May 1853.

Course SSE
Distance 12.5 miles
Camped 14 hrs
Lunch 30 min
Marched 8 hrs 30 min
Wind W to SW

Set off at 8.00 p.m.; weather cloudy and foggy; light breeze from the W; hoisted the sail.

Lunched at 2.00 a.m.; set off again at 2.30, heading for Grassy Point where I built a cairn and left a document. The ice is generally bad but the sail helps us greatly, although the wind is light. On going ashore at Grassy Cape I found the wind very fresh from the NE. The weather was very dark and the glare from the light on the snow affected our eyes viciously.

Camped at 5.00 a.m.; shot two ptarmigan.[22]

9 May 1853.

Course SSE
Distance 18 miles
Camped 15 hrs 15 min
Lunch 1 hr
Marched 8 hrs 45 min
Wind WNW

Set off under sail at 8.15 p.m.; sky overcast; fresh wind from WNW. At 12.30 a.m. the weather became so foggy and the drift so thick that I lost sight of the land and it was even impossible to tell if I were on the land or on the floe. To avoid wasting time, I pitched

the tent for lunch, the sky appearing to clear a little. At 1.30 I
sighted land bearing ESE and I got under way again under sail, but
the ice was so bad and the wind so fresh that I was obliged to reef
the sail so as not to capsize the sledge, which was gliding so fast
that the men were obliged to run to avoid being dragged along.

My men being very tired by today's march, I camped at 6.00.

10 May 1853. Confined to the tent by the bad weather; wind from
the WNW with drift and snow so thick that it was impossible to see
twenty paces. At sunrise the wind increased greatly, shaking the
tent in a menacing fashion. Wind WNW.

Lunched at 2.00 a.m., in the morning took advantage of a moment
of respite in the weather to rid our tent of the snow accumulated
all around it, and under the weight of which the pikes acting as tent
poles were starting to bend.

11 May 1853.

Course   SE
Distance   15 miles
Camped   14 hrs
Lunch   30 min
Marched   9 hrs
Wind   NW

The wind having moderated a little, set off under sail at 8.00 despite
the drift and the snow.

The floe very bad due to the numerous hummocks; hence I moved
close inshore, where I found the ice level and blue in some places.

Despite the reef in the sail, the sledge was running so fast that I
was obliged to have seven men ride on it; the other four had their
hands full to guide it. Lunched at 1.00 and set off again at 1.30; one
of the men, named Dean, was unable to walk after the sledge ran
over his leg, although without serious injury. Camped at 5.30.

Saw three muskoxen, but the weather was so bad that I was
unable to go after them.

12 May 1853.

Course   SE
Distance   16 miles
Camped   17 hrs
Lunch   30 min
Marched   8 hrs
Wind   NE

The wind was very violent throughout the day but moderated a
little around 10.30 p.m., and I set off despite the very thick drift.[23]

Since the sledge was in poor shape, and since I was afraid of
smashing it due to the jolting caused by the numerous hummocks,
I was forced to furl the sail on the reef-band.

Lunch at 4.00; a piece of cold pemmican as we are short of

biscuit because of the day I was forced to spend in the tent; set off again at 4.30.

Despite the men's fatigue, at 6.00 I spotted Point Nias through the telescope. At 7.00 a.m., when I was about two hundred metres ahead of the sledge looking for the best route, I saw the men signalling and one of them running towards me. I returned immediately with a presentiment that an accident had happened; I found the man Coombes stretched out unconscious on the sledge. I camped immediately and used all the means at my disposal to revive him, including boiling water at his feet and on his stomach. I tried to make him swallow the only stimulant I had in my medicine chest: forty drops of aromatic spirit of ammonia in a little glass of brandy. But all my efforts were in vain and I discontinued them only when it was quite evident that the man was dead.

In the morning Coombes had been in perfect health; two days earlier he had complained of a slight bodily derangement (looseness of the bowels) and I gave him an opium pill which produced a very good effect. The men told me that he had stopped for a moment to satisfy a need, and on hearing him calling for help they had turned round just as he fell to the ice. I arrived just at the point when he had been picked up and placed on the sledge.

The men seemed to be keenly affected by this sudden death, and since I judged the case to be very grave I decided to return aboard as quickly as possible with Coombes's body.[24]

13 May 1853.	Course	EI/2S
	Distance	9.5 miles
	Camped	14 hrs
	Lunch	30 min
	Marched	9 hrs
	Wind	NW

Having wrapped the body in a piece of canvas, it was placed on the sledge and I set off at 9.00 for Point Nias, which I reached at 10.30 p.m. Camped and gave the men a substantial breakfast of preserved meat. I tried to dig up Parry's document as I had been ordered, but having demolished part of the cairn without finding anything, and since time was pressing I was forced to abandon this task.

After breakfast stowed the sledge, taking my depot of ten days' provisions, and set off at midnight, leaving a message for Captain McClintock in which I reported the sad accident which had occurred.

Lunched at 4.00 a.m.; set off again at 4.30; wind freshening from the NW. Cut up a blanket and gave a piece to each man to put in his canvas boots. Camped at 8 o'clock at Point Reed.

14 May 1853.

Course   E1/2S
Distance   7 miles
Camped   14 hrs
Lunch   30 min
Marched   9 hrs
Wind   NW

Set off at 8.45 p.m.; weather clear and calm; the bad ice conditions forced me to travel along the shore although the snow was very deep there making the work very strenuous. Lunched at 2.30; set off again at 3.00 a.m.

I went ahead, heading for Cart Depot, where I left a message for Mr Hamilton, asking that if he had any provisions left on his return he might leave them for Captain McClintock. Camped at 7.00 at the entrance to the ravine.

15 May 1853.

Course   S1/4E
Distance   7 miles
Camped   14 hrs
Lunch   30 min
Marched   9 hrs
Wind   SE

Set off at 9.00 p.m.; took three and a half hours to get out of Cart Ravine because of the limited amount of snow on the land. Weather very clear; light breeze from the SSE. Lunched at 2.00; set off again at 2.30, with the wind freshening and raising a bit of drift; weather foggy. Camped at 6.30 about half a mile from the Cart Cairn.

16 May 1853.

Course   SSE
Distance   12 miles
Camped   14 hrs 15 min
Lunch   30 min
Marched   9 hrs 30 min
Wind   SE

Set off at 8.45 with a fresh SE breeze. On finding the going very bad along our old route, since the snow had almost completely disappeared, I led the sledge along a series of little ravines in the bottom of which I found snow.

Lunched at 1.45 a.m. within sight of a cairn surmounted by a broken pike, erected by Captain McClintock in the autumn of 1852.

Set off again at 2.15 down a ravine which led me to Separation Ravine (where we had left Captain Kellett). Here I camped at 6.45 on the same campsite.

The appearance of the country has changed completely due to the snow melt. Noticed numerous tracks of reindeer and muskoxen.

17 May 1853.

Course   SE1/4S
Distance   7.5 miles
Camped   14 hrs
Lunch   30 min
Marched   9 hrs 15 min
Wind   S to W

Set off at 8.45 p.m.; sky overcast; light breeze from the S freshening towards morning and swinging into the W. Lunched at 2.00 a.m. in the middle of Crooked Ravine and set off again at 2.30. Hauling very difficult due to the lack of snow on the land.

Camped at 6.30 half a mile from Bamboo Cairn; saw two ptarmigan and some very fresh tracks of reindeer and muskoxen. During our rest the sun was so hot that we were obliged to sleep outside our sleeping bags.

18 May 1853.

Course   SE
Distance   15 miles
Camped   14 hrs
Lunch   4 hrs
Marched   12 hrs
Wind   SE

Set off at 8.30 p.m. down the ravine leading to the lake, which I reached at 12.30 a.m. I had the pleasure of meeting Messrs Scott and Purchase who had been out hunting for several days and gave us a piece of fresh meat. I pitched the tent to let the men have a good meal and we boiled some water to wash, something of which we were all in great need.

Set off at 5.00 a.m. accompanied by Messrs Scott and Purchase;[25] since the snow had disappeared from the land, I was obliged to take the sledge down a deep ravine on the east side of the lake, where the going was better.

Water from melting snow already covered the land between the ravine and the sea ice. But I was fortunate enough to find a cart onto which I loaded the sledge, and was thus able to reach the ice without too much difficulty.

The weather was so foggy that they could not see us from the ships; we arrived back at 1.00 p.m. with my flag at half-mast.

In conclusion, allow me, Captain, to express my deep gratitude for the confidence you have placed in me. I am proud to serve under such officers and with such men and it is with the greatest pleasure that I report the zeal and good conduct of the men placed under my orders. All have done their duty, and if one of them is missing at roll-call, I am pleased to be able to say that he died gloriously at his post.[26]

I append to my journal some sketches which will perhaps add a little interest to the conciseness of my narrative; my sole regret is that I did not have more opportunity to exercise my pencil.

Having lost my thermometer due to an accident, I was able to record the temperature only while I was with Captain McClintock.

E. de Bray,
Enseigne-de-vaisseau.

Abstract

Number of days	Outward	29	45 days
	Homeward	16	
Total hours travelled	Outward	221 hrs 35 min	262 hrs 05 min
	Homeward	140 hrs 30 min	
Distance covered	Outward	190.25 miles	381.25 miles
	Homeward	191 miles	
Total hours camped	Outward	340.30 hrs	562 hrs 30 min
	Homeward	212 hrs	
Lunch stops	Outward	12 hrs	24 hrs 15 min
	Homeward	12.25 hrs	
Detained by bad weather	Outward	132 hrs 45 min	170 hrs 45 min
	Homeward	38 hrs	
Mean daily distance	Outward	7.59 miles	9.84 miles
	Homeward	12.70 miles	
Mean hourly distance	Outward	0.86 miles	1.08 miles
	Homeward	1.3 miles	

Remarks on Provisions

375 g of biscuit is insufficient; it should be increased to 500 g. Pemmican is the best food for travelling; it cooks very quickly and is very substantial. 375 g of pemmican instead of 500 g, with 40 g of biscuit dust would be quite sufficient. 250 g of bacon is adequate. The fuel is also sufficient.

Tea before one rolls into one's sleeping bag after hard work and when it is cold is absolutely essential.

Remarks on Bedding and Clothing

Instead of the buffalo robe and the Macintosh blanket, I would prefer two felt blankets. The buffalo robe becomes stiff and very heavy and sometimes the Macintosh is so hard that it is impossible to spread out.

Mocassins are much better than boots for travelling when it is very cold, especially those made from sealskin with the hair outside and with a walrus-hide sole. I have tried these with excellent results.

The duck jumper and trousers should be soaked in water for several days before being used to prevent ice from accumulating on the inside of the garments.

Abstract of Weights

Constant weight	293 kg 375
Thirty-four days' provisions including packages	455 kg 550
Nine days' depot	131 kg
Six days' depot	92 kg 500
Total	972 kg 425
Weight per man, leaving Point Nias	121 kg 553

When I arrived on board the captain was absent; he had been busy for several days surveying around Cape Bounty. Mr Pim set off immediately with a sledge and dogs to warn him and he arrived on board at 2.00 a.m.

I explained the reasons which had forced me to return without having been able to finish my work, and the captain expressed his satisfaction at my having brought back Coombes's body.[27]

My men were very tired and three of them were obliged to place themselves in the hands of the doctor for rheumatism and stiffness in the legs. I made the offer to the captain of taking fresh men and setting off again to move Captain McClintock's depot to Cape Fisher, although I was suffering violently from rheumatism and from a strain I had given myself a few days before. But the captain would not agree to let me set off in the state I was in, and since he was anxious to see this depot in place, he immediately dispatched Mr Pim with a sledge and seven men.[28]

It was with true joy that I got back to my little cabin and my bunk; I had not undressed for forty-five days and I felt the need to recuperate a little and become human once again.

CHAPTER 7

Rescue of *Investigator*'s Crew and Preparations for Sea

Before continuing my journal I have to report some important events which had occurred during my absence.[1]

Around noon on 19 April several sledges were sighted to the west. Captain Kellett and the officers left aboard went to meet them and were soon shaking hands with the good Captain M'Clure, who had arrived from Mercy Bay accompanied by his master, Mr Court, and Dr Domville.[2] Mr Pim arrived soon afterwards, proud and happy at the success of his expedition.[3]

The arrival of Captain M'Clure gave rise to a real celebration aboard *Resolute*, since it was almost a miracle to see him safe and sound among us, along with his crew who were soon to arrive.

Mr Pim had hurried to reach Mercy Bay[4] and while crossing the bay had found no sign of *Investigator*; he then supposed that the ship must have left the bay, and continued westwards along the coast hoping to find some clue. Just as he was leaving the bay, one of his men pointed out a black object a great distance away, and on spying with his telescope, he immediately recognized a ship, then some people walking nearby. He immediately started running and got within 100 metres of the ship before anyone noticed him, since they mistook him for one of their own men. But Captain M'Clure and one of his officers soon realized he was a stranger and advanced towards him with an air of suspicion. Other men who were working on the ice also noticed Mr Pim's arrival and soon the news was flying from mouth to mouth. In a moment the deck of the ship was crowded with people; the sick men even left their hammocks and dragged themselves painfully on deck to see the newcomer.[5]

Soon the men with Mr Pim's sledge arrived and the joy reached a peak. All these unfortunates who only a few moments earlier were a prey to despair could barely find words to express the thoughts which filled their hearts.

For eighteen months the crew had been reduced to half a pound of meat and 12 oz. of flour per day, and yet Captain M'Clure did not wish to abandon his ship. But everything comes to an end, and only a few days before Mr Pim arrived he had decided to pick out the healthiest half of his crew; part of them, under the command of Mr Haswell, were to proceed to Cape Spencer to try to find a whaling ship, while the other group, under the command of Mr Cresswell was to head for the Mackenzie River.[6] He himself, with the other half, would stay on board to try to get the ship out the following season, and if they were unsuccessful, would try to reach Port Leopold and make contact with the whalers.

Fortunately Captain Kellett had anticipated the possibility of the abandonment of *Investigator* and Mr Pim had set off as soon as the season had allowed. Thanks also to the speed of his travel, he had arrived in time to prevent this departure which could have proved fatal to these poor men who had already experienced such cruel sufferings. Providence had reserved for them a reward worthy of their courage and preseverance.

On 27 April Mr Hamilton and Mr MacDougall left the ship with a sledge to explore Hecla and Griper Bay.[7] On 28 April Mr Roche came aboard, having placed a depot on Cape Mudge for Mr Hamilton.[8]

On 3 May the lookout on Dealy Island signalled sledges in the direction of Cape Bounty and a work party was immediately sent to help them. At 4.00 p.m. Mr Cresswell of *Investigator* arrived with four officers and twenty-four men, all in a terrible state of health.[9] Scurvy had begun to make terrible ravages among the crew, yet there had been only three deaths since the ship sailed. One of these had occurred the day before Mr Pim's arrival, the man having poisoned himself due to carelessness.[10]

There was nothing more to decide now but the serious question of abandoning *Investigator*, which was in fact in a very difficult position. This delicate question was debated for a long time, and it was decided by Captain Kellett that Captain M'Clure and Mr Court would return to Mercy Bay accompanied by Dr Domville who, assisted by Mr Armstrong, surgeon aboard *Investigator*, would examine the health of the entire crew. If it were possible to find twenty fit volunteers apart from the officers, Captain M'Clure was to stay aboard and try to get the ship out. Failing this, *Investigator* was to be abandoned with the shortest possible delay and the entire crew was to move aboard *Resolute*.

On 5 May Captain M'Clure, Mr Court, and Dr Domville left

Resolute with two sledges manned by five men from *Investigator* who were pronounced fit,[11] and seven of our men, to return to Mercy Bay. On 6 May Mr MacDougall returned aboard, having accompanied Mr Hamilton to Point Reed.

On 7 May Mr Roche, accompanied by Messrs Cresswell and Wynniatt of *Investigator* and *Resolute*'s bosun [Mr Chandler], left the ship with ten men to travel to Beechey Island where *North Star* was lying, in order to reduce the number of men to feed.[12] These men had been selected as unfit for further service.

Hunting was now organized on a grand scale and we were able to procure the fresh meat so necessary, especially for *Investigator*'s men.[13]

When I arrived on board I found the ship unhoused and ready to be stowed for sea, although it would be another three months before that long-awaited moment arrived.

22 May 1853. Today, Sunday, having conducted an inspection aboard *Resolute*, Captain Kellett went aboard *Intrepid* to inspect her crew too. He expressed his satisfaction to the men who had accompanied me on my trip and thanked me in the most flattering manner. Having held divine service, we all proceeded to Dealy Island to pay our last respects to Coombes. I led the funeral procession, the body having been placed on a sledge manned by its crew and flying my flag at half-mast.[14]

There are now three men buried on Dealy Island: the same number as was left on Beechey Island by Franklin after his first wintering [Plate 23].

When Coombes died during my return trip, several reasons decided me to come back immediately to the ship although my task was not completed. First there was my rank as a foreign officer; then I thought I could detect among my men a reluctance to leave the body of their comrade behind. Incidentally this death was simply the result of an ordinary accident; the autopsy performed by Dr Domville revealed that Coombes was in perfect health and that he had succumbed to a heart attack.

31 May 1853. When the weather permits, the men are working at caulking the ship and transporting ashore the equipment and provisions which are to form the depot which we are leaving on Dealy Island [Plate 24].

At 3.00 a.m. a sledge under sail was sighted to the west and at 4.00 Mr Nares arrived aboard after an absence of fifty-seven days, having left Mr Mecham and his crew in good health, continuing their way

Plate 23 The three graves from Kellett's expedition on Dealy Island,
as they appear now

west along a land which he had discovered.[15] On comparing notes
with Mr Nares, by a strange coincidence I found that he had left
Mr Mecham the same day I had left Captain McClintock, leaving
him with the same amount of provisions and having covered about
the same distance, although I had not been absent as long.

3 June 1853. Since the weather has been very fine, we have been
taking advantage of it to dry the sails. Captain Kellett left with two
men and the dogs for Cape Bounty to make some observations. At
the same time Mr Nares with four men and twelve days' provisions
left the ship to transport a cart from Winter Harbour to Liddon Gulf
to be available for Mr Mecham's return.

5 June 1853. Around 4.00 a.m. I was wakened by an unusual noise
on board; I heard bursts of laughter from the wardroom and at the
same time a strange voice which was not totally unfamiliar. I dressed
hurriedly and was very surprised to see Commander Richards, second
officer of *Assistance.* We soon learned the circumstances which were
responsible for this unexpected visit.

Commander Richards had left *Assistance* with the intention of
exploring the north coast of Melville Island,[16] little suspecting that

we were already in that area, when on 17 May he met Mr Hamilton who was then 127 miles from the ship.[17] He learned from the latter the directions taken by our sledges, and seeing that there was nothing left for him to do in this direction, he decided to head for *Resolute* where he had turned up to surprise us.[18]

He had left *Assistance* fifty-seven days before, accompanied by five auxiliary sledges and by Lieutenant Osborn, captain of *Pioneer*, who had headed for the west shore of Wellington Channel.

By quite an extraordinary chance, while crossing the thirty-two miles of country which separate Hecla and Griper Bay from Bridport Inlet he had found a cairn which I had left, giving the bearings of all the various cairns and the best route to follow. Hence he had taken only five days to cover a distance which otherwise might have taken twice as long.

We then learned that *Assistance* had been obliged to go into winter quarters four days after leaving us. The ice driving violently from the north had forced her to enter a very deep bay which she fortunately managed to find but from which she could not escape. This bay, located at 76° 58′N, 98° 8′W, was named Northumberland Sound.[19]

The crews and officers of *Assistance* and *Pioneer* were in good health and a new land, named North Cornwall, had been discovered.

Commander Richards had had orders to deposit his dispatches at a prearranged location, for which Mr Hamilton was heading when they met. All this news was passed on to us in a moment and the signal was immediately hoisted on Dealy Island to recall Captain Kellett.

6 June 1853. Since the captain had doubtless not seen the signal, I was sent with four men to alert him. I found him camped on one of the islands near Cape Bounty, and when I informed him of the unexpected arrival of Commander Richards he immediately returned to the ships with the dogs. Since my men were tired, I did not return on board till next day.

8 June 1853. Once the crew of Commander Richards's sledge had rested, they left *Resolute* to return to *Assistance* via Byam Martin Channel; this gives them about four hundred miles to cover as rapidly as possible, since the season is already very advanced and they may be caught by ice break-up in Wellington Channel.[20]

9 June 1853. Our topmen are busy working in the rigging, reeving the running rigging. On land, part of the crew is busy picking up rocks which will be used to build a house for the depot we are to leave on Dealy Island.

Plate 24 De Bray's painting of the ships in spring 1853, showing supplies being sledged ashore to the depot on Dealy Island

At 9.45 Mr Pim returned on board after an absence of twenty-two days, having placed his depot on Cape Fisher. He had found the going very bad and had stayed out longer than he had anticipated.[21] Fortunately the hunting had been quite good and had provided him with additional provisions.

At 12.30 a.m. while walking on deck I sighted a sledge in the direction of Cape Bounty and recognized Dr Domville's flag. I headed out to meet him and at 2.00 am. he arrived on board with two men from *Investigator* and an officer from that ship, Mr Sainsbury, whose health was so grave that he had been lying on the sledge all the way from Mercy Bay. A dog sledge was immediately sent off to take Captain M'Clure's dispatches to Captain Kellett, who at that point was at Skene Bay.

11 June 1853. The news brought by Dr Domville is very interesting. The health inspection aboard *Investigator* has revealed that few men were fit to stay aboard, and at the point when he left the ship, Captain M'Clure was preparing to abandon her.[22] Half of the remaining provisions had been moved ashore and the ship moored solidly with several anchors.

The doctor's sledge had broken down near Winter Harbour and he had been forced to leave half of his load there.[23] Mr McDougall is to go to retrieve it with a sledge and six men and take some bearings at the same time.[24]

13 June 1853. Since the foundations of the depot house had been badly built, and since, moreover, the ground is very wet, the entire structure collapsed and we have had to restart work on new foundations.

Part of the crew is employed at watering and at transporting six months' provisions on board *Intrepid*. At 6.00 this evening, accompanied by Mr Piers and one man, I left the ship with the dog sledge to go hunting at the head of Bridport Inlet. At midnight we reached the shores of the polynya, a lake located at the head of the inlet, where we found a tent which had been left here for hunters.

We began by being confined to the tent for two days by bad weather, while the snow melt, which had turned the slightest gully into a torrent, prevented us from making any long excursions. As a result, after six days I decided to return to the ship with three reindeer, two hares, and some geese and wild ducks.[25] Moreover, my zeal for hunting is somewhat dampened, since it is very dangerous at this time of year, as proved by the accident I experienced.

I had wounded a reindeer and was racing after it when, crossing a ravine, I suddenly sank to my armpits in the snow and saturated earth. I was incapable of stirring, since at the slightest movement I made to get out I felt myself sinking even more. I began to be seriously alarmed, especially since I was losing feeling in my legs due to the cold. I then decided on an extreme course and gathering my strength threw myself violently backwards. Stretching out my arms and sliding slowly on my back I was fortunate enough to get my legs free and to get back to solid ground. I swore, a little late admittedly, that I would never leave solid ground again.

19 June 1853. On getting back aboard after a very fatiguing trip, since Bridport Inlet was covered with 2 to 3 feet of water, I found something to warm me and make me forget my fatigue: two letters from France were handed to me. I believe I have never experienced such happiness as at that moment; I shut myself in my cabin to read and reread these two letters.

During my absence Mr Pim[26] had returned on board on 14 June after an absence of twelve days and on 17 June Captain M'Clure with his officers and the entire crew of *Investigator* also arrived, having left their ship on 4 June,[27] and having first taken all possible precautions to preserve what was left of the provisions.

Around 11.00 p.m. on 18 June a dog sledge was sighted to the east; this aroused keen curiosity since nobody was expected from that direction. Soon Mr Roche arrived on board with news from *North Star* and the welcome letters from Europe which we had scarcely expected. One can imagine the avidity with which we listened to the news, which was of great importance. *North Star* was driven ashore on Beechey Island but fortunately without any great damage, and Captain Pullen had refloated his ship with the spring tides.[28]

Our letters had arrived via *Isabel*, which had left England some time after us to explore Baffin Bay. Her captain, Captain Inglefield, had succeeded in penetrating to the north of Baffin Bay and in identifying Smith Sound, which he found much wider than Ross had supposed in 1819. Halted by the ice, he was obliged to coast along the west coast of Baffin Bay where his ship experienced some rough assaults by the ice.[29] Rounding Cape Warrender he had reached Beechey Island.

We learned at the same time that the ship *Prince Albert*, aboard which was my friend Bellot, had returned to Europe, having explored the west coast of Boothia, which they found to be split into two parts by a very narrow channel where they found a very violent current flowing from west to east.

Prince Albert's captain, Mr Kennedy, had explored this channel with a sledge and six dogs, returning to the ship in Batty Bay by rounding Cape Walker. The dogs which have arrived on board with Mr Roche are the same as those used by Mr Kennedy.[30]

21 June 1853. This morning Hamilton arrived on board after an absence of fifty-five days,[31] bringing with him Sir Edward Belcher's dispatches which he had found at the rendezvous. *Assistance* was in good state, her crew in good health, and she had lost only one man.

Since he was in a hurry to get back aboard, and since his men were very tired, Mr Hamilton had left his sledge and cart about a dozen miles from the ship at the north end of Bridport Inlet.

24 June 1853. The ship has finished watering, having taken on forty casks. Mr McDougall arrived on board after an absence of ten days, bringing the good news that the ice around Cape Bounty was in poor condition; he had found 2 or 3 feet of water in some places.

This news is not without significance, since it indicates the imminence of the ice break-up which we are awaiting so impatiently and which we would like to see happen as soon as all our sledges have returned.

30 June 1853. Throughout this last period the men have been employed in getting the ship ready for sea; the yards are crossed, the topgallant masts sent up, and the sails bent.

The carpenters have built a four-wheeled cart, as light as possible, to fetch the game which is being killed almost every day and which is providing us with some excellent food. Everyone is in great need of it after the fatigues of our long sledge trips.[32]

6 July 1853. Despite the bad state of the ice, I set off with a party of ten men to fetch the sledge and cart left by Mr Hamilton,[33] and at the same time I helped Mr Pim and Mr Court and George Kennedy to transport their provisions to the hill northeast of the inlet, where they were to stay for a few days' hunting.

On leaving them I had to cross Bridport Inlet, which I could only do by wading through waist-deep water. It was only after ten hours of very difficult travel that I managed to reach the slope of a hill where, despite the wetness of the ground, I was obliged to camp since my men were too exhausted to go any farther. I had the fire lit immediately to cook our supper, for which I had luckily provided by killing a reindeer shortly before we stopped.

19 July 1853. It was not until today that I got back aboard, bringing Mr Hamilton's things, and I believe this was the hardest work I have had to do until present. The continued bad weather, the torrential rain which soaked the ground, had prevented me from travelling as fast as I would have wished. I was obliged to load and unload my cart three or four times a day, to carry items individually, and I managed to make only two or three miles in twelve hours of work.

Ravines converted into veritable torrents blocked my route constantly and we managed to cross them only with great difficulty, with water up to our necks and at the risk of being carried away by the current, which was so violent that we could barely manage to keep our feet. It took twelve hours to cover twelve miles, and when I got back aboard my men were exhausted and I myself was suffering from violent rheumatism in my left leg. However, I had the consolation of having had some good hunting; I had shot six reindeer and several hares and wild ducks. The day after I set off, i.e., on 6 July, a sledge had been sighted to the west; immediately the colours were hoisted and emphasized by a cannon shot to recall Captain Kellett, who was absent from the ship. At 1 o'clock Mr Mecham arrived after an absence of ninety-four days,[34] with all his men in perfect health apart from some slight frostbites.[35]

On 18 July Captain McClintock arrived on board after an absence of 106 days; he had left all his baggage on the north coast of Melville Island, since the going was too bad to cross the island.[36]

We are all back aboard now and in relatively good health apart from rheumatism, which is a normal consequence of our heavy work.

Unfortunately these spring explorations have given us no clue as to fate of the unfortunate Franklin and his companions. However, 1,200 miles of coastline have been explored and discovered, and from the appearance of the ice which borders these coasts on the west, as ancient and heavy as that noticed by Captain M'Clure along the coast of Bank's Land, it can be assumed that no land exists between these new discoveries and Bering Strait, all this area being occupied by the polar pack.[37]

20 July 1853. For the first time since 10 March we were at full strength at table and we celebrated the occasion by drinking to our success several bottles of champagne kept specially for this event.

We have been very lucky up till now, since although we have not found any trace of Sir John Franklin, we have fulfilled our instructions to the letter. Our depot is securely established on Dealy Island[38] and we have been able to assist our brave companions from *Investigator*, who have thus escaped from certain death, since if they had undertaken to cross America, as Captain M'Clure had planned, not a single one of them would have reached England.

There is nothing left for us to do now but to think of our return, and to make every effort to avoid spending a second year here, totally uselessly.

25 July 1853. The ice is starting to break up around us and is becoming more spongy, a certain sign of imminent breakup. Hence, in order to check the ship's trim and to set up our masts, we are starting to saw the ice all around the hull to let her float freely, and thus to correct the list which she has had all winter.

28 July 1853. After three days of work we managed to rid the ship of her ice cradle, and we have even corrected the trim by means of the ballast kept for this purpose. The ship now draws 4 metres 32 forward and 4 metres 56 aft.[39]

1 August 1853. The topmen are busy tightening and painting the rigging, scraping the masts and painting the hull.[40] The store house on Dealy Island is completely finished [Plates 25 and 26]; it is as comfortable as possible and will certainly be found to be so by those for whom it has been built, if they ever have the luck to reach it. It contains all the provisions, clothing, and equipment for sixty men for a winter. A cairn 30 feet high, surmounted by a mast, has been erected on the summit of Dealy Island to serve as a landmark for ships which might pass within sight of the island, and a plaque fixed to one of the sides of the cairn provides directions necessary to locate the house in case it is buried under the snow.[41]

8 August 1853. The ice does not seem to want to start moving[42] and to contain our impatience we are undertaking all kinds of exercise. Today we organized races on Dealy Island; bets were laid and I myself laid a bet against Captain Kellett, against whom I gave a start of 25 metres over the 100 metres I had to cover. But as I raced off I strained my left leg, which a severe bout of rheumatism had left quite weak, and I had to abandon the race, thus losing my bet.[43] Since any kind of drink had been prohibited to the crew, there was no disturbance of order, not even for a moment. After a good day of exercise we went back aboard with the wind freshening markedly and bringing rain, which we all greeted with great pleasure since it is the greatest destroyer of the ice.

10 August 1853. Every day the ice is on the move but no openings have appeared. In order to check what may be happening some distance away, Mr Nares was sent with five men to try to reach Point Griffiths, thus getting a good view of Byam Martin Channel.

13 August 1853. Mr Nares came back aboard with quite bad news; he had been unable to get past Skene Bay; the ice extended across

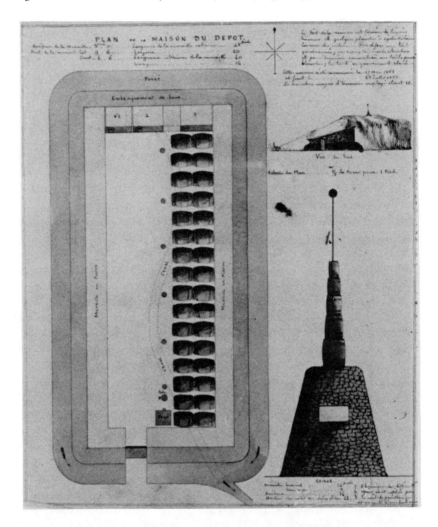

Plate 25 De Bray's plan of the storehouse on Dealy Island and views of
the storehouse and the cairn left on the summit of the island

that bay and was jammed against the coast in such a way as to
prevent him from hauling his boat over the ice. No opening was
seen in the floe, although it appears to be broken in every direction.

17 August 1853. The ice is still on the move but unfortunately
without any definite result. However, the strong wind which we are
expecting and which is to release us, now appears about to arrive; it

Plate 26 Kellett's storehouse on Dealy Island, July 1978, prior
to conservation

is freshening rapidly and the ice is starting to press against the south
point of Dealy Island. At the same time the cracks around us have
opened a little.[44]

CHAPTER 8

Under Way Again

18 August 1853. The wind is still increasing; it is blowing a whole gale and is having a miraculous effect on the ice. At 11.00 a.m. the floe which surrounds us suddenly broke up and we were obliged to lay out a chain with a heavy ice anchor to maintain our position. Around 3.00 the floe to which we were moored began to move southwards, the wind swinging from NNE to N to NW, and by noon it was impossible to recognize the spot where we had been detained for so long. The appearance of the ice has completely changed; the east coast of Dealy Island is washed by the sea and the floe which has become detached from it is the one to which we are now moored to the windward side. To the S and SE the ice is already out of sight. Nothing can give an idea of the speed with which our situation changed during this terrible squall. In an instant the floes were piling against each other forming veritable mountains, with a horrible and terrifying noise. We were so surprised that we left on shore one of our pumps, which had been used earlier for watering, and also one of our boats.[1]

Around 1.00 p.m. the floe to which we were moored began to swing upon itself towards the west, carrying us with it at quite a great speed, and we soon found ourselves in a channel lying between the land to the north and this floe to the south.[2]

The rudder was shipped, two reefs taken in the topsails so as to be ready to set sail, and we began warping, blowing up several floes which still blocked our route. Soon our energetic efforts were crowned with success and we again had the pleasure of feeling ourselves rocked by the waves, which we had not seen for eleven months. Joy shone on every face and we shook hands with each other, thinking of the great good luck of an imminent deliverance.

Intrepid, about which we had been quite fearful for a few moments, also got free and at 11 o'clock the two ships rounded Point

Ross, pushed by a good quartering wind, heading east without any obstacles in sight. Soon afterwards the wind became very variable; with the weather clearing, it allowed us to see the land which we hugged quite closely, the lead giving 34 to 37 fathoms.

19 August 1853. At 1.00 a.m. we sighted Point Griffiths and Byam Martin Island; the ice extended as far as we could see to the S and SW, but at the same time it was drifting rapidly eastwards.

At 7 o'clock the very clear weather allowed us to see the ice extending the whole width of the channel between the north point of Byam Martin Island and Melville Island, thus completely barring our passage.

We had hoped too soon, and today the prospects are not encouraging. But to assure ourselves that no passage existed we set off along this ice barrier, and it was only once we had convinced ourselves that we were blocked that we tacked to close with the east coast of Melville Island, which was ice-free, and hove-to three miles from land to spend the night.

20 August 1853. The ice still looks the same; the pack extends without a break between us and Byam Martin Island. We cannot hope to proceed eastwards now, but the ice, which for two days has been drifting south, gives us some opportunity to follow a route north of Byam Martin where the sea is perhaps clear.

Taking advantage of a light breeze from the SE we headed north in tow of *Intrepid*, running along the edge of the pack which consists of several floes three to four miles in extent.

At noon the weather cleared and the lookout signalled an opening in the ice to the east as far as the eye could see; but we are still continuing north without encountering any ice.

At 6.00, with the wind freshening from the NE, we moored to the floe, the lead giving 68 fathoms. Under the influence of this wind the ice drifted SE and packed together on all sides as it carried us along. At 10.00 the soundings gave 40 fathoms and at 11.00 12 fathoms with a mud bottom, which makes me assume that we are drifting quite close to land, although we cannot see it due to the foggy weather. When a natural dock offered about half a mile to the east, we hurried to get the ships into it in safety.

21 August 1853. The weather still foggy; the land is about two miles off to the SW and we are drifting NE with the pack. At 7.00 the ice seemed to be slackening a little and we shipped the rudder to be ready to take advantage of the least opportunity, but around 9.00 we were nipped again and we drifted south at a speed of 1 knot, the bottom varying between 33 and 17 fathoms.

22 August 1853. We are drifting south along the east coast of Melville Island about a mile offshore.[3] The fog, which clears from time to time, allows us to see Byam Martin Island and the pack ice, which is completely close in all directions.

23 August 1853. Since quite a considerable expanse of water had appeared between the ship and the east coast of Melville Island, Mr McDougall was sent in a boat to sound along the fast ice so that we might take refuge there in case of need, and found a depth of 10 to 13 fathoms within about 100 metres of the coast. At 8.00 the ice appeared to slacken, but without any passage opening for us.

When the weather cleared in the evening we were delighted to see that the ice had moved off Point Griffiths, leaving a passage three quarters of a mile wide; at the same time the ice opened to the south and to the east.

24 August 1853. At 7.00 we cast off our moorings and, taking a towline from *Intrepid,* we set off southwards between the pack and the land. The ice seemed to be in motion on all sides and to be slackening, and hence our hopes began to rise again. At 3.40 we cast off our tow and hove-to in order to send a boat to sound around Point Griffiths.[4]

At midnight there was no ice in sight to the south but we could see in the sky a white band stretching from WSW to N; this for us was a sure sign of the presence of ice.

25 August 1853. The breeze, which had been very light these past few days, is starting to freshen, bringing with it a dense fog, which hides the land from sight.

However, we cast off our moorings to close with the land and moored again to the floe in a sort of natural dock. Around 5.00 p.m., with the wind freshening in strong squalls, our ice anchor tore free and we began drifting along with the pack.

We immediately sent out a stronger anchor with one of our lighter chains, and shortly afterwards we had returned to our original position. The ice is still in motion; the pack extends about a mile to the east.

26 August 1853. Weather foggy and almost calm. Around 9.00 a.m. we were surprised by a very heavy rain, which gave us great pleasure since rain is the best destroyer of ice.

During the day we sighted seven muskoxen about four miles away on Melville Island.

27 August 1853. The ice is still close and leaves little hope of operating freely, although the lookout is still signalling that the ice towards the south is moving. In the evening the ice began moving along the land; catching *Intrepid* abeam, it gave her a severe nip which fortunately did not produce any damage.

A considerable flight of plovers passed over the ship, heading SE.[5]

28 August 1853. Weather foggy; the fresh, gusty wind had dropped by evening. Several seals showed themselves around the ship and we fired at several of them, without success.[6]

29 August 1853. Around 4.00 a.m. the wind rose, very fresh from the SE, clearing out the sky; it soon swung into the NW, making the ice move and opening it in every direction, but without producing any general movement.

Messrs Mecham and Pim set off with six men and a sledge to try to shoot some of the muskoxen which have been observed by us for three days as they graze quietly along the coast.

After a rough chase, the gentlemen succeeded in killing three of these animals, which were brought aboard; they gave us 181 kilos of meat. During the day we saw several flights of geese heading east and southeast.

30 August 1853. The temperature is dropping rapidly and, sadly, we see that the ice is not disposed to allow us passage. The prospect of a second wintering, especially in the middle of the pack, is not a very pleasant one, and yet I believe that everyone is beginning to resign themselves to the inevitable. The ice which formed around the ship during the night is already 3 inches thick and we have been blasting it to free ourselves.

At 10.00 a.m. *Intrepid* received orders to raise steam and, casting off her moorings, she headed off to the east to examine the state of the ice at close range. She returned to resume her position in the evening and brought us the bad news that the ice had not budged.[7]

31 August 1853. The lookout signals some openings to the east. *Intrepid*'s officers obtained permission to go hunting and shortly afterwards, on seeing that they had been successful in killing some muskoxen, I was sent with twenty men and two sledges to bring back the meat.

On reaching the site of the hunt, I had the pleasure of seeing ten muskoxen stretched out on the ground within a few paces of each other. The herd had been surrounded and all these animals had been killed *in situ*. In less than an hour they were all dressed and I returned on board with my sledges, transporting 1,590 lbs of meat.

Towards evening, with the wind freshening from the ESE, the pack began to drift slowly eastwards.

1 September 1853. We are still moored to the floe about three miles N of Point Griffiths and one mile from land; the weather is almost calm and the ice still has the same heart-breaking appearance. In the afternoon the ship was shaken by quite a heavy swell from the E, which would seem to indicate a great expanse of water in that direction. A herd of muskoxen appeared about four miles from the coast to the SW.

2 September 1853. The only opening we can see in the pack extends along the coast to the north; but to the south and east the ice appears even closer than ever.

Messrs Mecham and Domville set off to hunt the muskoxen we saw yesterday and by 9.00 two of these animals had fallen to their bullets; a sledge was immediately sent to bring them aboard.

At 10.00 the ice began to move, pressing against Point Griffiths and on another point to the N, and at the same time slackening to the SE. The ship is now lying in a patch of water two miles long between the pack and the fast ice.

The master carpenter [Mr Dean], who had gone ashore, came back with a fox and three cubs which he had surprised in their den. While he was busy digging them out the mother spotted him, raced towards him at top speed, and leaped at his face. He managed to get rid of her only by killing her with a shot.

At midnight I was able to count forty stars in different parts of the sky. This is an indication that the season is advancing and that the interminable winter nights are about to surprise us, for I am starting to fear seriously that we are beset.[8]

3 September 1853. Having observed since early morning a wide expanse of water which had formed during the night along the south coast of Melville Island, at 10.00 a.m. we cast off our moorings to run towards the SE under light canvas, but at 11.30 we were again stopped by the pack and obliged to moor. Climbing to the topgallant yard I could see the pack slackening a little and spotted several wide openings to the east. We had scarcely led out our moorings when the ice began moving and obliged us to warp, so as not to be completely surrounded. Our ice anchors were then sunk into a large floe with which we are drifting SE.[9]

4 September 1853. At 1.00 p.m., with the pack driving onshore, we were obliged to cast off our moorings to run in towards the fast ice north of Point Griffiths and at 2.00 we were in safety about two and a half miles NNE of that point. At midnight the pack was only half a mile from the ship, but appeared to be stationary.

5 September 1853. This morning, seeing that the pack was moving towards us, we led out a cable over the port quarter so as to warp the ship into a natural dock formed in the fast ice. At noon we sighted a large expanse of water to the south. By evening the pack was only 300 metres from us, thus leaving us only a small space to move.

Weather very calm and very fine. Several seals came to play around the ship and one was killed by Mr Hamilton.

6 September. The fresh breeze of this morning increased rapidly with heavy squalls; the ice is starting to move NNE, and everything presages a change in the weather. So as not to be caught off guard, and for fear of being separated from *Intrepid*, we transferred six months' provisions to her, hers being almost exhausted. A strong ice anchor with a chain was led out; the sails were furled and two reefs taken in the topsails.

In the evening we shipped our rudder to be ready to get under way. The pack is about three miles away and we can distinguish some openings in the middle and at its edges.

7 September 1853. At daybreak the pack surrounded us on all sides, except for a little passage to the east about four to five miles away. At 8.00 we cast off our moorings and set sail with two reefs in the topsails, sailing along the edge of the pack ice in search of an exit. But, having failed, we were soon forced to tack and head north. A large expanse of water lies SE of Point Griffiths and along the coast of Melville Island northwards.[10]

At 3.00 p.m. we moored again at our former site NNE of Point Griffiths.

8 September 1853. Our position is still the same and the appearance of the ice is far from reassuring; the weather looks foul and the drifting snow handicaps us greatly.

9 September 1853. Around 1.00 a.m. when the weather cleared we could see water seven to eight miles to the SE. We immediately slipped our moorings and headed ESE to try to find a passage; but at 2.30 we were suddenly stopped by a sort of sludge formed from the large amount of drift carried by the wind yesterday, which had accumulated on the surface of the water to a thickness of 5 to 6 inches.

Although the wind was very fresh and all sails set, we could not penetrate through this sludge; *Intrepid* was obliged to take us in tow and to steam at full speed. The towline soon broke and we had the greatest difficulty in passing another, since the steamer could scarcely manoeuvre herself.[11]

Finally, by 4.30 we were floating freely again and at 7.00 we led out our moorings to the fast ice near Point Griffiths, to give the crew some rest, since our position was not very good. At 9.00 we were taken in tow again, heading north along the land, and at 11.30 we finally moored with a heavy ice anchor and chain.

Several muskoxen had been seen along the coast and several officers went off hunting; they were lucky enough to kill eleven animals. The sledges were sent ashore immediately and we soon had 1,970 lbs of superb meat on board.[12]

10 September 1853. This morning the ice was out of sight.[13] At 9.30 Captain Kellett went aboard *Intrepid*, which slipped her moorings and set sail to go and check the state of the pack to the east. Around 3.00, despite the fog, we could distinguish *Intrepid* making signals to us to join her. In a moment everything was astir on board; this signal could only be an announcement of good news. The moorings were cast off and we made all sail. At 5.00 a boat was sent for Captain Kellett, and we set off towards the SE, forcing a passage through a sheet of new-formed ice.

Although the wind was very fresh, around 6.30 we were suddenly stopped by the ice, which became thicker as we progressed and was here about 3 inches thick. A boat was then slung beneath the bowsprit, with some men making it roll from side to side, and we were thus able to advance a little. Despite her engine *Intrepid* did not seem to be able to advance any farther to the east.[14] It was impossible to turn back since we could not tack against a very fresh wind and through quite a thick cover of ice. The prospects were becoming far from reassuring and we could only count on *Intrepid* to get us free. Finally, after great efforts, she managed to close with us, and passing ahead of us, tried to break the ice but this was in vain and we were soon reduced to total immobility. To crown our bad luck, *Intrepid* fouled our starboard boats and we barely managed to save them from total destruction.

We then tried to get free by blasting the ice around us, but the thinness of the ice prevented this since the mine simply made a hole without cracking the ice around it.

The weather, which had been threatening for some days, soon became terrible, due to a terrifying gale which might have caused serious damage in the rigging of a ship jammed as we were, but which fortunately served to free us from *Intrepid*. The latter took advantage of a little expanse of water which opened astern and succeeded in going astern and placing herself off our port beam about 200 m away.

The temperature is dropping considerably; the weather still remains foggy so as to prevent us from seeing the best course to take, so that I am starting to think that we are stuck here for the winter. Our position is far from pleasant, since we are in the middle of the pack and we do not have the resourcers of Dealy Island, whose proximity I miss.

Yet this morning when *Intrepid* made a signal for us to join her, the appearance of the ice was far from favourable but the terrible fog which rolled in in the evening prevented us from seeing the route to take and perhaps we have wasted a lot of time and overlooked the only route which might have led us out of the pack.

The prospects of another winter are not very encouraging but I hope it passes as happily as the last one.

11 September 1853. The wind is still fresh, and although we are solidly beset we are keeping the foresail set and the topsails with three reefs.

At 6.00 a.m. we sighted Melville Island and Byam Martin Island, but the ice is thickening around the ships with extraordinary speed. Around noon the wind fell and the drift stopped; with the clearing weather we could establish our position exactly. It is far from reassuring, since the lookout cannot see any water in any direction. Hauled down the topsails and clewed up the foresail.

12 September 1853. Not a drop of water in sight and we can no longer see the land; we have unshipped the rudder for fear of accidents. *Intrepid* is visible to the east, about 400 metres away.

13 September 1853. Since Captain Kellett wanted to communicate with *Intrepid*, a man was sent across to her; he accomplished his mission safely, which proves that the ice is already of a fair thickness. The ice is moving, however, since the ships are changing their relative positions. Today at noon *Intrepid* was a quarter mile to the ENE. At 1.00 p.m. we could see land stretching from WNW to N.

CHAPTER 9

The Second Wintering

14 September 1853. Any hope of escaping has almost vanished, and there is nothing left for us but to make our arrangements for a wintering. We are starting to cut the ice around us in order to swing the ship's bows to the north since experience has taught us that the prevailing winds come from that quarter.

15 September 1853. We are drifting quite rapidly towards the SE as indicated by the lead line; *Intrepid* is still the same distance from us.

16 September 1853. At 8 o'clock we sounded 127 metres, with the line indicating quite a strong drift to the SE; by 9 o'clock the ice pressure on the ship became awkward; to be ready for any eventuality the order was given to prepare the sledges with their equipment and provisions in sufficient quantity, in case we are forced to abandon ship.

17 September 1853. We are still drifting perceptibly towards the SE, with the depth varying rapidly from 128 metres to 178 metres. Towards evening the wind freshened and the ice began moving again.

18 September 1853. At 1.00 a.m. the ice pressure became considerable and the poor ship was cracking in every part with a sinister noise. Soon the ice took us on the starboard side and threw us violently over to port; accumulating due to the pressure, it climbed up onto the deck. The crew was busy, without respite, getting rid of this nuisance, which threatens to invade us completely.

At 4.00 a.m. the wind had dropped and the ice finally left us in peace; around 2.00 p.m. the wind rose again, from aft, and the ship advanced two to three lengths through the new ice. It was very fortunate that our rudder was unshipped, since the ice which was pushing us from aft would inevitably have smashed it. In the evening *Intrepid* seemd to me to be closer.[1]

19 September 1853. We were employed all day at hoisting provisions out of the hold and in transporting them to *Intrepid*. The ice is more or less still in the same state; about 50 metres from our starboard bow one can see a line of water stretching fairly far to the SE.

20 September 1853. We are continuing to provision *Intrepid* and the topmen are unreeving the running rigging and unbending the smaller sails and finally preparing the rigging for another winter, since the season is advancing and there is now little chance of us getting out of the ice.[2]

21 September 1853. We are completely beset and the captain has decided to start the work of wintering preparations. The topgallant masts have been sent down and the spars for the housing put in place. *Intrepid* is about 400 metres to the ESE.

22–23 September 1853. The crew is busy putting the ship in shape for the winter and a squad has been cutting a hole in the ice alongside to provide us with water during the winter. This operation involved some difficulty since the ice had accumulated to a depth of 21 feet.

Our deck is much more cluttered than last winter since we no longer have the land available for stowing a host of items, and we are already missing our Dealy Island. Also the ship's complement is increased by the men from *Investigator*,[3] and the hold and orlop deck have to be kept as clear as possible to give everyone air.

1 October 1853. Since the interior of the ship is very damp, we have lit the stove before starting to bank up the outside with snow. For the first time this autumn the snow has been falling very heavily.

2–3–4 October 1853. Our preparations for winter are almost finished; there is nothing left to do but to put the tent in place, but the weather is still not bad enough and we are taking advantage of the daylight for as long as possible. On the 4th the lead gave 175 metres.

5 October 1853. This morning we observed some cracks in the ice both ahead and astern of the ship, which is drifting slowly with the pack to the ESE, the lead giving 163 metres.

At 10.30 a loud noise like a cannon shot drew our attention and we saw the ice opening, leaving a narrow lead of water about three miles long and running SSE-NNW. The ice was about 16 inches thick.

6 October 1853. Observed a parhelion on each side of the sun, and sounded 157 metres.

We are starting to cover the deck with a layer of snow mixed with ashes, since we no longer have the land as a source of gravel; we are making it thicker this time, i.e., 13 inches.[4]

7–10 October. Since the 9th the ice has been constantly in motion, not leaving us a moment's rest, and poor *Resolute* is cracking in a terrible fashion.

On the evening of the 10th the wind increased sharply and there is every indication of bad weather ahead. Today the lead gave 110 metres.

11 October 1853. Around 4.00 a.m. the wind was blowing furiously and was making the drift whirl up so much that it was impossible to stay outdoors. Very fortunately there was no apparent movement in the ice and the wind soon dropped, swinging into the east.

At 9.00 p.m. the weather was very calm and we enjoyed the sight of a superb aurora borealis in the zenith, extending N-S.

12 October 1853. The wind dropped completely and the ice started moving, as always happens after a strong wind.

At 9.00 a.m. the lead gave 155 metres; at noon 110 metres, and immediately afterwards 103 metres; and at 11.00 p.m. 123 metres. This proves quite adequately that the ship is still moving despite the fact that she is beset. Since this movement is almost constantly towards the SE or ESE there must be a certain expanse of water in that direction.

13 October 1853. Throughout the night we heard the ice cracking in all directions but without any hazard to the ship.

At 7.40 a.m. the centre of the sun was just on the horizon; which is a clear indication that we will soon lose it. The lead gave 108 metres and there is not a drop of water to be seen. At noon, in admirably clear weather we sighted land at N79°W (true), probably Cape Cockburn. On climbing the rigging one could see Byam Martin Island about twenty-four miles to the west.

14 October 1853. At 2.00 a.m. the crack located near the ship opened to 2 metres; soundings taken in this lead revealed a depth of 73 metres, whereas in the fire hole near the ship we had 91 metres.

Although the ship is still drifting a little with the pack, she seems completely beset in her cradle and we have begun building the snow wall around the ship's sides. Since the snow is less abundant, as indeed is the gravel for which we have had to substitute ashes, we are making it only 5 feet thick instead of 6.5 feet.

At 9.30 a.m. we sighted Byam Martin Island to the west and

quite a high range of hummocks to the NE 1/4E, probably piled up on the bank discovered by Sir Edward Parry.[5] Towards the east the colour of the sky seems to indicate a large expanse of water, but around us everything is completely close.

15 October 1853. The weather is very calm; the lead line reveals a drift to the SE and the range of hummocks seen yesterday now lies to the ENE. To the south we can see quite a large expanse of water about ten miles off.

16 October 1853. We are still drifting with the ice, since the hummocks now lie about seven miles to the NE; the lead gives 125 m. Observations made as precisely as possible give our position as 75° 1'N, 104° 25' 30"W of Paris, with Cape Cockburn lying thirty-two miles to the E5°N, which would give an ice drift of three miles to the SSE in three days.

17–19 October 1853. We are continuing to build the wall of snow around the ship; soundings vary from 108 to 117 metres.

Since the ice is quite rough between us and *Intrepid*, we have cleared a passage of the snow and ice blocks which obstructed it, and along both sides of this route we have erected snow pillars so that in the dark or drifting snow we will have some landmarks. Several of these pillars have been sculpted using a knife, and represent the most extravagant figures; some have black buttons for eyes and the legs are adorned with old boots.

20–21 October 1853. The cold is starting to make itself felt and in the hold the temperature has dropped so much, despite the stove, that several bottles of lemon juice have burst, resulting in the loss of 48 litres of that precious liquid, the best antiscorbutic one can find.[6]

22 October 1853. When an owl landed on a hummock quite close to the ship I tried to get close enough for a shot but the ice was so bad that I had to abandon my attempt at getting within range. At 9.00 p.m. I saw a shooting star to the NE.

23–31 October 1853. During all this period the men were employed at various tasks on board and at collecting snow for covering the deck. Since the weather was very fine, the men not on watch took advantage of it to play ball[7] or pursue various exercises on the floe around the ship. Exercise was not uncalled for since the temperature has begun to drop, reaching -26°C, and one feels the need to keep moving.

The soundings vary between 117 and 133 metres; the ship is still drifting a little towards the SE.[8] Since the light is now quite limited during the day the tent was put in place, except aft, to give some shelter from the wind to the men working on deck.[9] Land in sight to the NE.

1 November 1853. We have started covering the deck [i.e., the remaining parts of the upper deck] with snow mixed with gravel and ashes; this forms a cement which, due to the low temperature, quickly becomes very hard and protects the interior of the deck from any moisture. The carpenters are adjusting the hatch coamings on the forward and after hatches and have hermetically sealed the main hatch. Sounded 127 metres.

2–6 November 1853. On the 2nd the wind freshened from the NNW; shortly afterwards a gale blew up, raising a vast quantity of drift; it was not until the 5th that we had a moment's respite, when the wind dropped suddenly.[10] On the 6th the sun disappeared according to our calculations, but due to the foul weather of the preceding period, it must probably have left us several days ago.

7–8 November 1853.[11] Sighted an owl whose plumage was totally white. In the evening watched a very remarkable shooting star at about 12° above the horizon to the SW. The land at Cape Cockburn in sight very distinctly to the NNE.[12]

12 November 1853. Observed two meteors, one to the NE, the other to the SSE; the weather very fine and the temperature dropping rapidly.

14 November 1853. I have to record a cruel loss, that of poor Sainsbury of *Investigator*.[13] This poor officer had had a chest ailment for a long time, even before he came aboard us. It was only thanks to the good care of our good Dr Domville that he has been able to prolong his existence, always in the hope of seeing home again.[14] But for some time he had been growing weak and the thought of spending another winter in the ice had affected his morale. Finally, despite all the care lavished on him, he expired at 11.30 p.m. today, at the age of twenty-six. Although we were all anticipating this death, it still made a strong impact since this poor lad was liked by everyone on board.

16 November 1853. Today Sainsbury's burial took place. This ceremony always made a strong impression on me whenever I have participated.

The prayers for the dead were read by Captain Kellett aboard *Resolute*, then we proceeded to a hole which had been chopped in the ice 200 m from the ship. There could be nothing more ominous than that mournful procession of officers and men from both ships, winding slowly across the snow, surrounded by darkness.

The corpse, wrapped in a piece of canvas and weighted, was carried on a sledge which soon reached the yawning opening which lay waiting for its prey, and I felt a terrible lump in my throat as I saw our poor comrade disappear into that icy water. Once the sad ceremony was over everyone returned on board in silence, their hearts profoundly saddened.

19 November 1853. The after housing has been put in place, since the cold is becoming more keen, with the temperatures fluctuating between -28 and -30°C.

21 November 1853. Today we observed a paraselina on either side of the moon and an elliptical halo whose greatest diameter was 52° and the least diameter 44°; the upper part was as brilliant as an aurora borealis.

Dr Domville has had the excellent idea of entertaining the men by giving lectures on popular subjects and the crew seems to have seized on the idea with alacrity. Hence today he began to put this plan into effect by reading a paper on chemistry as applied to the everyday usages of life. The chests on the orlop deck had been arranged as they are for seating for church service on Sundays and the lanterns were lit. Dr Domville gave this opening lecture amidst the most profound silence from a very attentive, quiet audience. The session ended after an hour amidst the warmest and highly deserved applause.[15]

I think this is an excellent idea and that it will be very successful, giving us another means of distracting the crews during the winter, since *Intrepid's* crew, which did not attend the first lecture, will be invited to subsequent ones.

22–26 November 1853. For several days everyone has been busy reorganizing our theatre; as the posters proclaim, the first production is set for the 30th, weather permitting.

At 5.00 p.m. on the 26th I observed a very curious aurora borealis whose arch ran from E to W through the zenith, but which also displayed a second arch parallel to the first, about 5° to the south.

During the night the wind began to freshen, which confirms what I have often noticed, namely that the wind always freshens when the aurora is very bright.

30 November 1853. Since the weather has cleared up again, the performance has not been cancelled and at 6.30 p.m. *Resolute's* deck was crowded with an audience waiting impatiently for the curtain to rise. To contain their impatience the orchestra played its best numbers, and one has to give credit to the musicians for the manner in which they handled their instruments; these consisted of six fifes, a violin, and a drum. The fifes had been made from hollow copper curtain rods and the tinsmith has spent many days in making the marvellous violin. With a certain amount of good will one could passably recognize the numbers, and they might have been a lot worse.

As regards construction details, the theatre was the same as last year and our leading carpenter had done marvels with regard to costumes and props.[16]

The evening began with a play by Shakespeare, arranged by Garrick, entitled *The Taming of the Shrew*, played by the men of the crew, with an extraordinary general effect and dash.[17] The officers then performed *The Two Bonnycastles*, a comedy very popular in England.

During the intermissions several men sang comic songs[18] and we found some excellent actors among *Investigator*'s men, among others a negro who recited a prologue composed for the occasion. Nothing could be more amusing than this negro coming on in black coat and white waistcoat to recite a piece of verse in his patois, and attempting to imitate the manners of a man of the world.[19]

Finally the success was crowned and the performance concluded by a chorus of 'God Save the Queen' and three cheers for the artists.

A bowl of punch was waiting for the officers in the captain's quarters, the whole enlivened by some songs. The men received a double ration of beer[20] and at midnight everyone except those on watch went to bed, delighted with the evening.

1 December 1853. Today everyone is at work dismantling the theatre, and by afternoon the ship had resumed its usual appearance.

2–4 December 1853. On the 4th, since the weather was very fine and the stars Arcturus and Vega very bright, we determined a latitude and longitude which will serve to fix our winter quarters definitively, since the ship is no longer drifting and the soundings are no longer varying. Thus determined our position is 74° 41' 34"N, 103° 42' 06"W of Paris. Cape Cockburn bears N34°E, twenty-eight miles off.

5 December 1853. Mr MacDougall, *Resolute*'s master, gave a lecture on arctic exploration, giving a resumé of the various voyages undertaken in the polar seas.[21] The crews of both ships attended this gathering. Today the thermometer dropped to -41°C.[22]

13 December 1853. Captain Kellett in turn gave a lecture on early ideas on astronomy, covering the subject right back to early times.

The temperature is very low today and the mercury is solid; very clear weather. Thus far the weather is noticeably better than last winter, which may be attributed to our distance from land.

At Dealy Island the weather was almost always overcast and the drifting snow very thick. Here the weather is always clear, the wind less violent, and there is less drift, since there are no mountains or deep gorges where it can accumulate and from where it can then escape in violent blizzards.

19 December 1853. Today Dr Domville gave a second lecture on practical chemistry, which was attended by the crews of both ships. In this lecture, which was much more instructive than the first, the doctor took for his subject the ventilation of houses in general, demonstrating the functions of the organs of respiration in man and animals. Some little experiments with the barometer, thermometer, and air pump completed this session, which was extremely well appreciated not only by the crews but also by the officers.[23]

20 December 1853. A strong wind with a great deal of drift which hides *Intrepid* completely. Observed a very pronounced halo around the moon.

21 December 1853. Around 3.00 a.m. there was a very bright paraselina with a diameter of 40°.

At 11.00 a.m. it was just bright enough to be able to read a paper with small print such as that in a newspaper. An aurora borealis, dark brown in colour, running through the zenith and starting in the NW.

22 December 1853. Taking advantage of magnificent weather, at 6.00 p.m. we went aboard *Intrepid* to attend a theatrical performance. Mr Krabbé, the incomparable conjuror, continued to astonish us with all kinds of tricks, and two members of the crew performed with great verve a very difficult little play entitled *Box and Cox.*

During the intermissions we had several comical songs, and a group of negroes produced a great effect.[24] The leader of the group (the solitary real negro) [Charles Anderson again] played the castanets while the others, who were admirably made up, accompanied themselves on tambourines.

After the performance and before setting off to return aboard *Resolute*, we moved to the wardroom where a good glass of punch awaited us, to help us withstand the outside temperature of -42°, and by 10.30 we were all under the covers.

25 December 1853. For several days we have been preparing for the great event of Christmas Day, which is a great celebration in England. The orlop decks were decorated with flags and brilliantly lit with theatre chandeliers; the tables were covered with the best of everything that could be procured.

The captain came to dine with the officers in the wardroom; on the table there were still some fine pieces of muskox and everything that still remained of our former splendour. Gaiety, in particular, was not lacking and we made an excellent night of it.

28 December 1853. Mr Nares, one of *Resolute*'s lieutenants, gave a lecture on the cause of winds and their prevalence, and the direction of land and sea breezes, with some remarks on local winds. This very interesting subject was well handled and strongly applauded by everyone.[25]

29 December 1853. Observed a very bright aurora borealis forming an arch of about 15° from the S to the WSW, with some corruscations towards the zenith.

30 December 1853. For several days I had been working with Mr Hamilton at putting our electric telegraph in order; once everything was ready the men were employed in erecting snow pillars at regular intervals between ourselves and *Intrepid* for carrying the conductor wire, and that evening we were in communication.[26]

31 December 1853. Since January 1st was a Sunday it had been decided that our New Year's dinner would take place today. Captains Kellett and M'Clure, as well as Mr Krabbé of *Intrepid*, were invited and at 4.00 p.m. we sat down at table to a superb dinner. The menu will give an idea of our resources although, admittedly, everything had been hoarded with religious care for this great day.

Puree'd hare soup
Preserved salmon
Quarter of reindeer, quarter of muskox, roast ptarmigan, muskox pâté, ham, with vegetables, green peas, turnips, potatoes
For the second course: plum pudding and a vast quantity of pies and cakes decorated with numerous Union Jacks.
Cheese. Grapes, almonds, figs, biscuits, olives.
All washed down with beer, champagne, port, and sherry.

Although the weather was very bad and it began to blow very strongly, some of *Intrepid*'s men who were part of our theatre orchestra came aboard to give us a short concert to close our dinner. When they arrived on board they noticed that one of them was missing and had presumably got lost in the drifting snow, which prevented one from seeing more than a pace in front of one. Everyone turned out in a moment, since in such a situation a man's life is always at stake.

Fortunately the telegraph to *Intrepid* had been installed and we were able to ask if the man was on board; after a moment of cruel anxiety the word 'Yes' was received and immediately everyone breathed more freely, since if we had not got an affirmative reply we would have had to send parties out in search of this unfortunate, and we might perhaps have had some accidents to lament.[27]

This incident provides the proof that the telegraph could be of great use to us. The singing and music, which had been interrupted for a moment, started up again even better, and we thus gaily celebrated the end of 1853, which certainly none of us expected to spend in the ice when we left Dealy Island in such a precipitate fashion. Relatives and friends were not forgotten and many toasts were drunk to them with great feeling.

The crew, for its part, celebrated just as heartily, and the old year was joyfully buried by everyone.[28]

The weather was so bad that Mr Krabbé was obliged to sleep on board, along with our musicians. The drift was so thick that we could not see *Intrepid* and it would have been unwise to hazard one's life out on the ice in such a blizzard.

2 January 1854. Hood, one of *Intrepid*'s men, who had been ill for some time, died during the night.[29] He had been a member of Captain McClintock's sledge crew who came back with me, suffering greatly from a rupture in the chest, and hence totally incapable of work. He had taken part in the last expedition and was one of those who reached Melville Island.[30] His constitution had been undermined by all the fatigues he had had to endure, and an autopsy revealed that he had died of a heart attack combined with a liver condition.

3 January 1854. This morning officers and men paid their last respects to Hood, whose body was slid down a hole chopped in the ice.[31]

In the evening Lieutenant Pim gave a lecture on geology. During the night there was some aurora borealis to the west.

6 January 1854. General muster of the crew and inspection of the ship by Captain Kellett, who went aboard *Intrepid* to proceed with the same operation there.

7 January 1854. Cleared the ship of the vast quantity of drift piled up by the wind, which had been blowing for several days.[32]

11 January 1854. Mr MacDougall gave us a lecture on arctic voyages and dealt with Sir John Franklin's overland expedition along the coast of North America [in 1820–3].

Sounded 125 metres in the fire hole.[33]

24 January 1854. Since the stove pipes were full of ice, we had to dismantle them to clean them. For several days we have been busy making an inventory of provisions and items of every kind on board.

26 January 1854. Mr Nares gave a lecture on elements of mechanics applied to industry.

27 January 1854. Since the daylight is increasing, we have removed part of the housing aft for the first time.

In the evening the sky was admirably lit up, in every sense, by the lights of the aurora borealis, especially in the south.

2 February 1854. Wilkie, ice quartermaster aboard *Intrepid*, died this morning of a heart complaint. Like Hood he was an old arctic hand and had taken part in three expeditions.[34]

3 February 1854. Officers and crews mustered to pay their last respects to Wilkie; the ceremony took place just at the moment when the sun returned after an absence of eighty-eight days. Our old friend has finally returned and we can almost consider the winter to be over.

The ice thickness in the middle of the floe was found to be 5.5 feet.

4 February 1854. The captain has issued an order charging Messrs Hamilton and Roche to hold themselves ready to set off soon for Beechey Island, i.e., during the first few days of March.

It is absolutely essential that we communicate with Sir Edward Belcher if possible, and in any case to learn if there is a ship at Beechey Island so that we can fall back in that direction if we cannot get our ship free. If Hamilton does not find Sir Edward Belcher at Beechey Island, Mr Roche will push on with his dogs to where he is wintering, and he will return aboard with his men to report on his trip.

All the men were immediately set to work to prepare items of equipment and sledges.

16 February 1854. Mr Hamilton is starting to train his men by taking long hikes on the ice towards Cape Cockburn.

For a radius of five to six miles around the ship the ice is very bad; the snow is soft and we need a good gale to pack it in order to make the going better for the sledges.

The poor dogs which are to go with Roche, seven in number, are in a pitiful condition and they will need a good feed before they set off. I really do not know how these poor animals have survived the winter with the small amount of food which we could give them. Finally, by concocting a terrible mixture of whale oil, bread powder, and ground sealskin we managed to produce a type of dog food, and since in general these animals are not very difficult to keep, after a very short time they were in a fit state to work, although not in quite such good condition as last year.[35]

26 February 1854. The wind which we have been waiting for to harden the snow has finally arrived and quickly developed into a gale, raising vast quantities of drift.[36]

28 February 1854. The wind has dropped, swinging into the south, and the temperature is much more bearable; the sun is starting to make all the snow melt from the bulwarks. A very strong refraction made Cape Cockburn appear, greatly elevated.

In the evening Mr MacDougall presented a vast memoir on arctic exploration.[37]

CHAPTER 10

Contacts with *North Star*
and *Assistance*

4 *March 1854*. Messrs Hamilton, Roche, and Court with nine men,
seven dogs and two sledges, provisioned for two weeks, left the ship
with the following orders:

> To Mr Hamilton, leader of the expedition:
> You will take command of the two sledges, manned by two officers,
> nine men, seven dogs and provisioned for two weeks.
> The first sledge is under the direct orders of Mr Hamilton, having
> with him Mr Roche, two men and the dogs; the second is under the
> orders of Mr Court, master of *Investigator*, with seven men.
> On leaving the ship you will make for the nearest land to deposit a
> message indicating the route you intend to follow so that Sir Edward
> Belcher's sledges, which may be sent in search of us, will be informed as
> to our departure for Beechey Island and our present position.
> Mr Court must then make all speed to reach Erebus and Terror Bay,
> where you will probably arrive a few days ahead of him.
> You will then adhere to the instructions which Sir Edward Belcher
> may give you if he is at Beechey Island or Gascoyne Inlet. In his absence
> Captain Pullen is to send Mr Court to Port Leopold to check the
> condition of the depot of provisions left by Sir James Ross in 1849.
> Mr Roche is to ascend Wellington Channel in search of *Assistance*
> and *Pioneer* and as soon as he returns you are to return aboard *Resolute*
> as promptly as possible to inform me of the result of your journey.

I was sent with Mr Nares and fifteen men to help our comrades
get clear of the vicinity of the ship, and after covering about three
miles, Hamilton, Roche, and the dogs set a course for Cape Cockburn,
accompanied by Nares with three men, while I and my men accompanied Mr Court who was heading east.

About five miles out I left Court, wishing him 'bon voyage' on what seemed to be very good ice. By noon I was back aboard.

5 March 1854. At 1.30 p.m. we were very astonished to see Roche arrive back with one man and five dogs, his sledge having broken in the middle while crossing a pressure ridge.

It appears that soon after Nares left them the ice became excessively bad; the dogs were soon exhausted and they were obliged to camp about sixteen miles from the ship.[1]

6 March 1854. At 6.00 a.m. Roche set off again with another sledge to rejoin Hamilton, accompanied by Nares and seven men, who returned at 11.00 having left him making good progress.

At 4 o'clock, just as we were starting dinner, we were interrupted by the telegraph bell; it was announced that Hamilton had just arrived aboard *Intrepid*, bringing back Roche who was dangerously wounded. Indeed Hamilton was soon on board, surrounded and encouraged by everyone.

We then learned that Roche had been wounded in the thigh by a bullet fired [by Lieutenant Hamilton] from a gun which was being carelessly jammed under the cover of the sledge, when it was being held by the barrel. He was then bandaged by Hamilton, for better or worse; the latter took him on his sledge and came back aboard at top speed, covering sixteen miles in three hours.[2]

Roche soon arrived on board, and once the wound was examined it was declared not to be dangerous; fortunately no muscles or arteries had been damaged by the bullet, which had passed through the fleshy part of the thigh, leaving a wound about 6 inches deep.

So as not to waste any time, Hamilton had left his tent and provisions in confusion on the ice and it was urgent that he set off again immediately so as not to give the bears time to wreak havoc.

However, the poor dogs are in an impossible state and they appear to be dying of hunger; hence we made them a monstrous pie consisting of everything we could find, and we can only hope that they will be in fit shape to set off tomorrow.

7 March 1854. Mr. Hamilton, accompanied by Nares as a replacement for poor Roche, left the ship to get back to their tent.

8–15 March 1854. We are preparing the equipment for the sledges which must get under way shortly, and everyone is making his arrangements. Commentaries of every kind are the order of the day and everyone is discussing the chances of getting home, or of another sojourn in the ice. In any case it has been decided in principle that *Investigator*'s crew will leave for Beechey Island as soon as the weather permits, around early April, since at the moment the weather is very harsh and we all feel sorry for our comrades Hamilton and Nares who at this moment are living under canvas at temperatures of -30 to -35°C.

20 March 1854. We have started to demolish the snow wall surrounding the ship and we are preparing provisions for the spring journeys; but nothing is yet decided as to the various directions to be taken.[3]

29 March 1854. The captain has decided that two sledges will head west. Mr Mecham, the 'lieutenant de bord' with a sledge and seven men is charged with visiting the islands where *Investigator* wintered the first year in Prince of Wales Strait, while the second sledge with seven men, under the orders of Mr Krabbé, *Intrepid*'s master, will go to *Investigator* in Mercy Bay to check the condition of that ship.

Both are to leave the ship at the same time with just fourteen days' provisions; they are to proceed to Dealy Island, where they can pick up all the provisions they need at the depot house, and from there will head for Bank's Land.

The after housing has been removed, as well as the coverings on the after hatch, and it is a great pleasure to have daylight in our wardroom again.[4]

31 March 1854. At noon today a thermometer exposed in the sun recorded 6°C: an enormous difference as compared to the temperature two weeks ago. Hence everyone is delighted, since it is with great pleasure that we look forward to the departure of the sledges.

3 April 1854. Messrs Mecham and Krabbé, who had waited until today, in the hope that Hamilton would return, set off accompanied by Mr Pim and a work party to get them under way and give them a good start on their first day.

4 April 1854. Captain Kellett has decided to set off himself for Beechey Island as soon as Hamilton returns to consult with the commander-in-chief, and hence his sledge and equipment are being prepared.

6 April 1854. At 11.00 a.m. a sledge was sighted to the NE and since we were anxiously expecting Hamilton, everyone was astir in a moment, ready to meet the new arrivals.[5]

As we approached, to our surprise we recognized Captain Richards, second officer aboard *Assistance*, with seven men and five dogs; great was our delight on learning that he was the bearer of letters and newspapers which had arrived via *Phoenix*, Captain Inglefield, who had made contact with *North Star* in August 1853.

We then learned that after her first wintering, our sister-ship

Assistance had been pushed south during breakup, escaping only by a miracle the danger of being smashed on shore, and had finally brought up about seven miles north of Cape Osborn, where she had spent the past winter, and that she was in a position such that she had little chance of getting free.[6]

The steamer *Phoenix*, commanded by Captain Inglefield, former captain of *Isabel*, had arrived at Beechey Island on 14 August 1853,[7] accompanied by the transport *Breadalbane*, loaded with provisions which were unloaded immediately.

Part of these provisions was lost, however. The ice began moving and since the transport was not very strong, she was stove in and sank about a mile off Cape Riley. *Phoenix* barely escaped this nip.[8]

At the same time I learned of the death of my comrade Lieutenant-de-vaisseau Bellot, who had already taken part in one expedition in 1852 aboard *Prince Albert*, commanded by Captain Kennedy, and had asked to be able to return aboard *Phoenix*. I cannot do better in describing this fatal accident than to reproduce the words of Sir James Graham, which he uttered at a meeting whose aim was to take the measures necessary to erect a monument to Bellot's memory:

> Captain Inglefield had left the ship himself ... , endeavouring to open a communication with Sir E. Belcher ... Captain Pullen, in his absence, was anxious to make a communication to Captain Inglefield. It was a dangerous expedition; Captain Inglefield's bright example was not easy to follow in that trackless region. Lieutenant Bellot volunteered for that service. His offer was accepted; and he left the ship with four British sailors, a sledge, and a slight India-rubber canoe. Very shortly after his leaving the ship arose that fearful storm of the 18th of August, which destroyed the *Breadalbane* which was in company with the *Phoenix*. The ice closing in on her in a gale of wind, such as had hardly ever been known in those arctic regions, the *Breadalbane* was crushed in a moment. The *Phoenix* was in the greatest danger ... In that fatal storm in which one ship was lost and another all but lost, Lieutenant Bellot and his four followers had to encounter the frightful gale. The first effect of that gale was to sever the ice from the beach. Lieutenant Bellot immediately when he saw that the floe on which he then was, was drifting from the shore, hastened to send two of the four men who were with him in the small canoe to dry land. They succeeded in effecting a landing; but to return became impossible. The floe drifted rapidly away, and the danger of these two men and of the gallant French officer became imminent and apparent. Observe, he was not the first himself

to go in the canoe to dry land. He saw the full extent of the danger. When the storm which was raging had almost destroyed himself with the two remaining Englishmen, he expressed the joy which he felt that the two other men were saved ... Snow was descending in large quantities. He taught them how to shelter themselves on the floe by accumulating the snow into something in the shape of a hut. They remained hutted. He twice went forth to see in which direction the floe was being drifted. A third time he went forth, and he returned no more ... ; his exhortations to those two men have been narrated to British officers ... He reminded them of their duty, that duty common to Frenchmen and Englishmen, ... not to be disheartened; and, above all, he exhorted them to look to that quarter from which alone in the last extremity assistance can be expected. He begged them to remember that overruling Providence which had saved them in the midst of so many and great dangers. It was the will of that Providence that he should not survive; it was the mercy of that Providence that the two men who were his companions should ... be drifted back almost to the very place where they had left their companions, and they have survived to tell the story (Anonymous, n.d., pp.106–7).[9]

The following letter announced this sad event in England and again shows how much my poor comrade was liked by all the British officers and seamen:

> Commander Inglefield to the Secretary of the Admiralty,
> Her Majesty's Steam Sloop *Phoenix*

Sir,

It is my very painful duty to acquaint you, for the information of my Lords Commissioners of the Admiralty, of the death of M. Bellot, Lieutenant of the French Marine, who was appointed to this ship on the 15th April last, by their Lordships, as supernumerary.

This gallant officer met with his death by drowning, whilst away on a travelling party up Wellington Channel, whither he had volunteered to go to seek for me. Captain Pullen had, however, availed himself of his experience in Arctic travelling to send forward their Lordships' despatches to Sir Edward Belcher.

The men who accompanied M. Bellot returned eight days after their departure, stating that on the evening of Wednesday, the 17th August, the party were landing from the floe by means of the india-rubber boat, when the ice suddenly broke up, leaving M. Bellot and two men still afloat. The former, after making arrangements (by building a barricade with snow) to protect the men from the gale which had set in, went to the top of a hummock, close to a crack five fathoms wide, and not returning shortly to the shelter, the men went out to seek for him, and could find nothing but the short stick he carried in his hand floating on the water; they have no doubt he was drowned as they remained on the floe thirty hours after, and never saw a trace of him.

By a miracle they succeeded in landing after this period at a spot a short distance from where the two other men had got on shore.

The independent evidence of the four men plainly proves the correctness of their statement, and there cannot be a doubt that poor M. Bellot was blown off the hummock into the crack by a violent gust of wind, when he indubitably perished by drowning, as unable to swim, he was much hampered with stiff, wet clothes, and a southwester tied under his chin.

The loss of this gallant officer has been deeply felt by all on board, for his amiable qualities, and bold adventurous disposition had rendered him beloved by all who knew him.

I am etc.
E. A. Inglefield, Commander (Inglefield, 1854b, pp. 19–20).

One can see from this letter how much Bellot was liked and appreciated by all those who knew him, and when we learned of his death aboard *Resolute*, where he was known only by name and from his previous expedition aboard *Prince Albert*, everyone was saddened.

A few days before the fatal event which ended his career so abruptly, and before leaving to join Sir Edward Belcher, Bellot had written me a letter, which I received only later, and which displays the charming grace of his manner and the fine feeling of comradeship with which he was animated. Here is that letter:

Erebus Bay, 8 August 1853

Dear Monsieur de Bray,

At approximately this time last year I received some letters which you were so kind as to take charge of for me,[10] and this year I am happy to be able to bring you the same pleasure those letters gave me; I know the cost only too well.

Apart from the letter which accompanies this one, and which I was hoping to be able to hand to you personally, you will find a small package of letters and newspapers which are addressed to you, among Captain Kellett's mail.

No doubt these letters will contain news which will be of most immediate interest to you, but I had the honour of seeing Madame de Bray since she wrote the last letter to you. At that time both she and your brother were enjoying excellent health, marred only by the grief caused by the absence of a son who is clearly tenderly loved.

Several times during my stay in Paris I had the honour of seeing some of your relatives and friends, among whom the similarities of our arctic adventures served as my passport and letter of introduction. I tried as far as possible, dear Sir, to reassure your excellent mother, and to convince her that you would soon return home, feted and lionized by everyone, having established firm title to the favours of the Ministry. Finally, in order better to prepare her mentally on this major point, I did not wish to leave her any illusions as to the fact that you would return this year, since I do not believe that you will do so myself.

I hope that Madame de Bray is now reconciled to considering the matter as a question of time and patience, since nowadays so many people are braving the rigours of one or two arctic winters with no ill-effects to their health.

Having returned to England last year, mainly because of scurvy which had debilitated us and reduced our crew of 18 men (all told) almost to nothing, I spent the winter in Paris. But Captain Inglefield also returned shortly after us; he had sailed in July 1852 aboard a little steamer, *Isabel*, belonging to Lady Franklin. During a voyage of just four months he had explored the northern part of Baffin's Bay and Smith Sound as far as 78°N, discovered that this sound extends beyond 80°N, enlarged John's [*sic*] Sound, and visited *North Star* at Beechey Island.[11]

An American expedition commanded by Kane had been organized to explore Smith's Sound and reach the North Pole by boat or sledge, and I was offered the position of second-in-command of that expedition,[12] but family affairs obliged me to decline this offer which otherwise I would have been very happy to accept. On the other hand I was very distrssed to see three or four arctic expeditions being organized without being able to take part in a single one of them, when Captain Inglefield, whom I met in Paris, proposed that I join the steamer *Phoenix*, which he commands, and whose mission is to escort to here a transport laden with provisions for your squadron. When the expedition left there was also a strong chance that it would spend the winter somewhere, to pursue the search and explore the country, and since during my service aboard *Prince Albert* I had acquired some specialized knowledge of arctic travelling I hoped that I might be able to make myself useful.

Hence, with the authorization of the Ministry, I joined *Phoenix*.

We left Woolwich on 18 May and Cork on the 26th, accompanied by *Barracouta* and *Desperate* which were towing *Breadalbane*, the transport laden with provisions for you, and *Diligence*, laden with coal for us. The two tugs having left us at Cape Farewell, we put into Holsteinborg, then at Lively and Upernavik, encountering no ice until well north of Devil's Thumb. After only eight days in the ice we rounded Cape York, then came flying into Croker Bay, where the state of the ice in Lancaster Sound forced us to wait for a week. *Phoenix* is a ship of 320 hp and this renders completely illusory the risks which normally accompany the passage of Baffin's Bay. We trans-shipped our coal at Lively (Disco), and from there *Diligence* returned to England, repatriating the crew of the whaler *Rose*, which had been crushed in Melville Bay. The captain's intention at the moment (8 August, within sight of Cape Herschel) is to land our provisions at Beechey Island, then return to Lively, and from there to Northumberland Inlet [*sic*] which we are to explore, north of Hudson Bay; and we will return to England towards the end of October. This, I think, is all our arctic news.

Please excuse, dear Sir, this chit-chat, which perhaps may tell you nothing new, and which I have only included because I am afraid that we may not meet, since it seems to me that the season is not sufficiently advanced that you may already have reached Beechey Island. Quite apart from any personal motive I should have liked it even more if, having told you in person everything I know, I could have had the pleasure of relaying news of you to your excellent mother on my return. I'm sure that would have made her very happy.

I hope that you have spent the winter in good health and the spring in delightful travels, and that you have found among your companions the same cordiality which I have encountered everywhere, both among officers of the British Navy and among individuals I have met in Scotland and England.

Last year we missed you by only 4 days at Beechey Island, which was a particularly great disappointment for me in that, having practically recovered from scurvy by that stage, I would have attempted to stay with the squadron, either with Sir Edward Belcher or with Captain Kellett. I have acquired a taste for these expeditions and I would have given a great deal to be under the command of men such as they, in the company of officers such as those who make up the squadron and almost all of whom I know (at least by reputation).

The great distance we both find ourselves from home and from our own service allows us to dispense with the conventional preliminaries; hence, dear Sir, allow me to shake you by the hand and express every good wish.

Your devoted comrade,

Bellot

Lieutenant-de-vaisseau.

We learned that *Phoenix* had left Beechey Island on 24 August to return to England, taking with her some of the men from *North Star* who had exchanged with men of her crew, and also Lieutenants Cresswell and Wynniatt of *Investigator*, the former carrying dispatches from Captain M'Clure to the Admiralty.[13]

10 April 1854. Lieutenant Haswell, Mr Paine, clerk-in-charge, and nineteen men from *Investigator* have left the ship with two sledges and fifteen days' provisions to join *North Star* at Beechey Island.[14]

11 April 1854. At 8.00 a.m. Mr Pim and Dr Armstrong left the ship with five men from *Resolute* and twelve from *Investigator*, also proceeding to *North Star*.

At 12.45 p.m. a sledge was sighted to the NE and soon Mr Hamilton came aboard with a man and seven dogs, having made contact with *Assistance* and *North Star*; he had thus made the journey in eight days at the almost incredible speed of thirty-four miles per day.[15]

He had met several sledges commanded by officers from *Assistance*, who were coming to deposit provisions for us along the northern shores of the strait; this gives us grounds to think that the commander-in-chief's intentions are to have us abandon the ship.[16] And yet nothing has transpired with regard to these intentions, which must be enunciated in the letters brought by Hamilton.

12 April 1854. At noon Mr Nares, with a sledge and six men, came aboard, coming from Beechey Island after a journey of sixteen days. Although his men had suffered during the first part of the journey, they arrived in good health; two of them were left aboard *North Star*, one due to a severely frost-bitten heel and the other to a stitch in his side and a violent cold.

Today for the first time since 28 October 1853, i.e., in 166 days, the thermometer recorded -18°C at 5.00 p.m.

13 April 1854. At 1.00 p.m. Captain Richards set off to return to *Assistance*, accompanied by Captain McClintock with one sledge, one man and twelve dogs and eight days' provisions, in order to take dispatches to Sir Edward Belcher. Hoisted the colours.

14 April 1854. Captain M'Clure, Mr Piers, assistant surgeon aboard

Investigator, and Mr Miertsching the interpreter left the ship with two sledges, seventeen men, and fifteen days' provisions, for Beechey Island.[17] Hoisted the colours.

19 April 1854. The carpenters are busy building sledges and in preparing a boat [*Resolute*'s ice boat], which is to be cached on Cape Cockburn to be used in case the ship is abandoned if the ice moves offshore.

20 April 1854. Having received orders to transport the boat to Cape Cockburn, I left the ship at 5.00 p.m. with nine men and ten days' provisions.

I had great difficulty in reaching the cape because of a very high line of hummocks I had to cross, which often forced me to unload the sledge and manhandle the boat across.

28 April 1854. I arrived back aboard *Resolute* having accomplished my mission, arriving at the same time as Captain McClintock; he had covered the distance to *Assistance* via Beechey Island and back in eleven days.[18]

We are preparing the ship for sea and are removing the housing from the deck.

At inspection today the captain informed the officers and crew that he had received orders to proceed to Beechey Island with everybody as soon as the ship was in good shape. Each man will be informed as to the weight he will be able to take, but all effects and other objects are to be carefully packed and the cases or bags marked so that everything can be found again in the event that the ship is reoccupied and if the commander-in-chief judges it to be appropriate.[19]

1–4 May 1854. The crew is employed trimming the ship; the boats have been hoisted on the davits and swung inboard; one of the rudders has been placed on deck, ready to be shipped and the other in the hold, along with two kedge anchors.[20]

On the 4th I received orders to hold myself ready to leave for Beechey Island with two sledges and the sick men; Dr Domville will accompany me in case of necessity. One of the sick men, Morgan of *Investigator*, is so sick and covered with scurvy sores that I am obliged to arrange a sledge with a hanging cot for him alone.

Although they are in poor health, the seven men who man the other sledge are capable of rendering some service, and in addition I am taking eight dogs which will give me a good, strong pull, especially if I have the good luck to encounter really smooth ice.

It has been decided by the captain that each officer can take 45 lbs of baggage and the men 30 lbs.

5 May 1854. Messrs Nares and Roche, with seventeen men, two sledges and eight days' provisions, left the ship to transport to Cape Cockburn the depots of provisions for Messrs Mecham and Krabbé on their return, bound for Beechey Island, since those gentlemen do not know that we have received orders to abandon the ship.[21] Mr Hamilton is holding himself ready to set off with one man and five dogs for Dealy Island, in order to leave the captain's new orders for Messrs Mecham and Krabbé. These orders enjoin them to proceed as rapidly as possible to Beechey Island instead of heading for *Resolute*; they also inform them of the depot left for them on Cape Cockburn.

Spotted two ptarmigan today but the dogs had scared them off before we could get a gun.

CHAPTER 11

Retreat to Beechey Island

8 May 1854. All my preparations are complete and the weather is promising to hold fair; I received orders to get under way. I was somewhat sad at heart to be forced to leave behind a number of items I would have liked to take, but I had to think first of useful things: firearms, clothes, etc., and the 45 lb limit we had been given did not allow much in the way of luxury. I packed up my things carefully and the door to my cabin was hermetically sealed.

Finally, at 7.00 p.m. I got under way with Domville, setting a course for Cape Cockburn, while Hamilton headed for Point Griffiths. I was saddened at thinking I was seeing poor *Resolute* for the last time, after she had sheltered me for two years; my companions were also keenly affected. We all had lumps in our throats and more than one glance was cast backwards until the ship disappeared from sight.[1]

The poor state of the ice, which forced us to exert all or strength, soon made us forget our sorrows; our only thought was to cover as much distance as possible, yet still taking the greatest precautions to prevent poor Morgan from suffering excessively.

We made the trip as quickly as the poor state of our sledge party would allow, and I arrived on board *North Star* on 25 May, and submitted my report to her captain:

> *North Star*, Beechey Island,
> 28 May 1854[2]
>
> Sir,
>   I have the honour to report that, in compliance with my orders,
> I left the *Resolute* at 7.00 p.m. on 8 May, accompanied by Dr Domville
> and having in charge two sledges, nine invalid men, and eight dogs. One
> of the sledges was loaded with provisions and travelling equipment, the
> other was fitted with a cot to accommodate the man Morgan.

The distance from the *Resolute* to Cape Cockburn was covered in four days, the bad state of the ice often forcing me to take one sledge at a time in crossing the hummocks.

Two days after I started I met Messrs Cheyne and Shellabear, then Mr Jenkins; all three had come from *North Star* and were on their way to *Resolute*.

From Cape Cockburn onwards the good condition of the snow on the land allowed us to progress rapidly. On 14 May I camped near Moore Island. Here Dr Domville judged that Morgan's state of health necessitated faster progress since the poor man was dying in terrible pain. Hence I gave him two men, four dogs, and six days' provisions and on the morning of the 15th he went on ahead.

Although my crew was greatly reduced, I travelled quite rapidly, thanks to a good WNW-erly wind, and was able to keep the doctor in sight for two days, but then I lost him completely.

On 17 May I camped two miles west of Brown Island. Saw two ducks and a raven.

My men were starting to get tired and one of them, Bailey, was obliged to ride on the sledge quite often. Fortunately the dogs were in good condition and were of great use to me.

On the 21st I reached Assistance Harbour; being short of fuel I tried to reach the depot with my sledge, but I had to give up because of the bad state of the ice and I was obliged to leave the sledge outside the pressure ice and walk to the depot with two men. I found the provisions damaged by bears and I did all I could to secure the depot, after taking about 10 lb of oil.

I reached Cape Hotham on 22 May [Plate 27] at the same time as Mr Court who had come from Beechey Island. Very luckily I found a small amount of bear meat there, which was a very timely find for my dogs, since some of them were already showing signs of weakness. Next day (the 23rd) I took two of Mr Court's men and set off for Beechey, and arrived aboard *North Star* at 5.00 a.m. on 25 May.[3]

I am happy to be able to tell you, Captain, that I have nothing but praise for the men placed under my command; they displayed remarkable zeal and good conduct.

I have the honour to be, with respect,

Captain,

Your very obedient servant,

E. de Bray.

Dr Domville had arrived on 19 May with poor Morgan, who died a few hours after they arrived and was buried on Beechey Island, alongside the men from *Erebus* and *Terror*.[4]

28 May 1854. The officers and crews of *Resolute* and *Intrepid* reached the island and were quartered aboard *North Star*, where everything had been prepared to receive them and house them as well as possible.[5]

After I had left *Resolute* and as soon as Messrs Nares and Roche had returned, work began on restowing the holds of the two ships; the running rigging was rove, the boats hoisted aboard, and an extra lashing passed around the topsails and lower courses. Finally the ships were ready for sea.

Messrs Cheyne, Shellabear, and Jenkins, whom I had met, were charged with caching provisions at Cape Cockburn, along with several items belonging either to the ships or to the officers. The day of 14 May was spent in completing all the preparations; Captain Kellett inspected both ships, then all hatches were closed and completely caulked.

At 7.00 p.m. flags were hoisted at the peaks and on the mizzen masts and the pilot flag at the foremasts, then the captain, officers, and crew of *Resolute*, accompanied by Captain McClintock and the officers and crew of *Intrepid*, set off for Cape Cockburn, en route to Beechey Island, having first given three hearty cheers for *Resolute* and *Intrepid*.

This convoy consisted of eleven officers, thirty-one men and four sledges provisioned and equipped for fifteen days.[6]

1 June 1854. Communications with *Assistance* are frequent, and four tents with sleeping gear have been set up permanently on Innes Point, Bowden Point, Cape Grinnell and Cape Osborn [Plate 27]. This eliminates encumbering the sledges with these items and we can carry more provisions.[7]

11 June 1854. A bear was sighted heading for the ship, chasing the dogs; I immediately grabbed my rifle and, walking towards him I opened fire at about 400 metres. The animal fell motionless. The conical bullet had cut his jugular and emerged behind the shoulder. This was one of the finest shots I have ever made.[8] It was a magnificent, full-grown animal and must have been provoked by great hunger to attack the dogs; on opening him we found the stomach to be totally empty of any kind of food.

12 June 1854. We were pleasantly surprised by the arrival of Mr Mecham in good health; he also gave us news of Messrs Krabbé and Hamilton, who were a day's march behind him. The latter had given

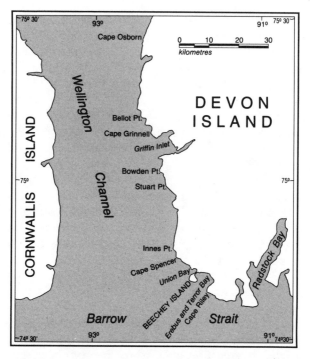

Plate 27 Map of southwestern Devon Island

him his sledge and dogs so that he could more quickly bring us the important news concerning *Enterprise*, Captain Collinson, of which he had found traces.

Having left us on 3 April, he had reached Dealy Island on the 12th after a difficult trip; the men had suffered severely from sore eyes and swollen legs.

He found the depot house in perfect condition; having replenished his supplies, he set off again on the 13th accompanied by Mr Krabbé to travel to Cape Providence, from where he was to take his point of departure for Baring Island, which he sighted on 24 April. On the 25th he pitched his tent near Cape Russell, where he cached eleven days' provisions for his return, and detached Mr Krabbé who was to visit *Investigator* at Mercy Bay.

On 4 May he reached Princess Royal Islands and in the cairn erected earlier by Captain M'Clure he found a document announcing that *Enterprise* had penetrated this strait as far as Point Peel in 1851 and then, turning back, had followed the coast of Baring Island to

72° 55′N, and had wintered in 1851-2 at 71° 35′N, 117° 40′W. Also that more detailed information on the movements of the ship had been deposited on a little island at 71° 36′N, 119°W.

Mr Mecham immediately set off southwards to visit this islet; reaching it on the 9th he found the document referred to, buried 10 feet to the north (magnetic) of a little cairn built on its summit.

According to this new document, *Enterprise*'s sledges had visited Point Hearne on Melville Island and the north and south coasts of Prince Albert Land.

When he left on 27 August 1852, Captain Collinson intended ascending the channel between Wollaston Land and Prince Albert Land, whose entrance lies at 70° 30′N.

On 27 May Mr Mecham returned to Dealy Island where he found orders, left by Mr Hamilton, to the effect that he should proceed to Beechey Island with all speed.

He arrived aboard *North Star* on 12 June, completing one of the most magnificent journeys ever made in the arctic regions.[9] One can easily summarize it in the following table.

Number of days absent	70
Number of days confined to tent by bad weather	8.5
Number of days travelling	61.5
Distance covered	1,157 miles
Distance covered per day	18.5 miles

One hour after Mr Mecham's arrival I set off with a sledge and ten dogs to take this news to the commander-in-chief. I took twenty hours to cover the sixty miles which separated us from *Assistance* and I stayed there for two days.[10]

Assistance seemed to me to be in quite a bad situation, yet it is not impossible that she will get free with a good easterly gale. If, on the other hand, the winds blow from the W or NW, there is a very strong chance that she will be pushed ashore by ice driving in from seawards.

15 June 1854. When I arrived back aboard *North Star* I found Messrs Hamilton and Krabbé there; they had arrived the day I had left to sledge to *Assistance.* They were extremely fatigued, especially Hamilton, who appeared to be in a pitiful state.

Having left Mr Mecham near Russell Point, Mr Krabbé had headed for *Investigator* and spotted the ship as he rounded Back Point. The flag was still flying, but in tatters and a large amount of snow had piled up against the north end of the ship; this allowed them easy access to the deck, which was also covered with snow.

The ship's head was facing N30°W (true), with the cable hanging slack from the hawse-hole. The ship was heeled about 10° to starboard, but there was no sign that she had suffered at all from ice pressure, although there was oakum hanging out of almost every seam.

Below decks nothing had moved on the orlop deck, but in the hold one could see that she had made some water during the previous spring. Forward she was filled with ice to the orlop beams and aft to within 10 inches of those beams. The ship was a little down by the head.

Having recovered the various items he had been ordered to remove and having secured the ship as well as possible, Mr Krabbé started back for Dealy Island, where he arrived on 26 May; here he found the order to assemble at Beechey Island. He completed his journey in seventy-one days which breaks down as follows:

Number of days absent	71
Number of days aboard *Investigator*	5.5
Number of days confined to tent by bad weather	8
Number of days travelling	57.5
Number of miles covered per day	15[11]

From June onwards work began on cutting a channel around *North Star*, sawing the ice and removing some pieces so that the ship would be afloat and could be trimmed more easily. The average ice thickness was found to be 7 feet.

There was a continual coming and going of sledges between *Assistance* and *North Star*,[12] and several hunting parties were sent in various directions to try to procure a little fresh meat.[13]

16 July 1854. The commander-in-chief, Sir Edward Belcher, reached Beechey Island[14] and took up residence ashore in the depot house[15] which provides him with a much more comfortable refuge than here on board ship, where we are a little crowded.

A cairn similar to that on Dealy Island has been erected on the summit of Beechey Island, on the same site as the one built by Franklin. A monument has been placed near the depot house, in honour of the dead of the expedition.[16]

24 July 1854. Mr Court left *North Star* with a sledge and 6 men to go and examine the state of the ice in Wellington Channel; he returned on the 26th having found no change.[17]

31 July 1854. The ice does not appear to be moving and yet leads are opening in every direction. Unfortunately the winds are persistently from the east and south, whereas they would have to come from the north and northwest to clear out the channel.

5 August 1854. The weather is foggy, with a light breeze from the SE by E. The channel-cutting operation is advancing quite slowly since, as we have nowhere to float away the pieces of ice we are cutting, we are obliged to haul them out on to the ice.[18]

7 August 1854. Two sledges have left under the command of Messrs Krabbé and Court, one bound for Bowden Point the other for Cape Hurd.

We are delighted to see a large lead which has opened at the entrance to the bay and only a short distance from the ship, and we have moved some of our saws there to try to free ourselves sooner.[19]

20 August 1854. By hard work we have finally succeeded in getting an escape route by cutting a channel 1,280 metres long by 15 metres wide.[20]

Barrow Strait appears to be completely clear and we are hurrying to warp ourselves out and to moor to the edge of the ice.[21]

CHAPTER 12

Homeward Voyage and Aftermath

21 August 1854. We are finally truly afloat and out of the bay. Sir Edward Belcher has now decided to go and visit *Assistance* and *Pioneer* and to see if there are grounds for abandoning them totally.

Over the past few days, thanks to some strong northerly squalls, these two ships had left their winter quarters and had advanced about twelve miles south, following the east shore of Wellington Channel, but an ice barrier twenty miles wide still separated them from the open sea. If the northerly winds were to continue they could easily be driven ashore, since the land swings sharply to the west in the southern part of Wellington Channel.[1]

25 August 1854. Since the wind has freshened from the WSW, it was judged prudent to cast off our moorings and to stand out to sea off Beechey Island under shortened sail. I admit that I felt a certain pleasure, shared by everyone incidentally, when I felt the ship moving freely again and especially at the prospect of an open sea ahead of us.

Towards evening the wind dropped and we moored to the floe edge again.

26 August 1854. Sir Edward Belcher arrived aboard, preceding his crew and officers who are to arrive soon with the boats, leaving *Assistance* and *Pioneer* abandoned.[2] Captain Pullen of *North Star* then received orders to embark everyone, and to hold himself ready to set sail for England with a total complement of 263 men.

We are continung to stand off, making short tacks, waiting for the boats from *Assistance*. Then at 1.00 p.m., just as Captain Richards came alongside with two boats, the fog cleared to the south and to our great surprise we spotted a steamer rounding Cape Riley.

Once the initial surprise had passed a great shout of delight went up from our ship, since we had completely abandoned any idea that a ship might arrive at this point. Every telescope on board was trained on the welcome vessel. As the fog cleared completely we soon identified not one ship but two: *Phoenix* towing *Talbot*.

Soon a boat was heading towards us from *Phoenix* and Captain Inglefield climbed to the deck shouting: 'Great news! War with Russia! France is allied with England!.' As one can imagine, poor Captain Inglefield had his work cut out to reply to all our questions, especially since they were posed by people sequestered from the outside world for so long.[3]

All the ships moored to the floe edge and the crews were immediately employed at unloading the transport's provisions, of which we were starting to feel the need.

I moved my quarters since there were too many of us aboard *North Star*, and I was sent aboard *Phoenix*, where I was welcomed with cordiality, being preceded by those fine sentiments of friendship which my poor comrade Bellot also received last year.[4]

27 August 1854. I went ashore with the commander-in-chief, Captain Kellett, Captain M'Clure, and some of the crew to participate in the erection of a marble tablet dedicated to the memory of Bellot and brought from England by *Phoenix* [Plate 28]; it was placed on the monument erected near the depot house and was saluted by three rifle volleys.[5]

At 2.00 o'clock *Phoenix* took *North Star* and *Talbot* in tow and we left the floe-edge off Beechey Island, bound for Port Leopold.[6] But we had not counted on the ice, which blocked our route and forced us to sail directly out of Barrow Strait, since the sea in that direction appeared completely free of ice. The ice also prevented us from making contact with the Eskimos at Dundas Harbour.

29 August 1854. In the evening we reached Navy Board Inlet and immediately began watering from *Phoenix* and *Talbot*. At the same time we took aboard 18 tonnes of coal, part of the depot left by Captain Saunders in 1850. The Eskimos were probably responsible for the disappearance of twenty-six barrels of rum, while all the casks of flour were riddled with holes.[7]

30 August 1854. In the early morning a violent northeasterly squall made *North Star* drag her anchor, and she was able to avoid being driven ashore only by abandoning a bower anchor and 40 fathoms of anchor chain.[8] Around 4.00 in the evening, once the wind had slackened, *Phoenix* took *Talbot* and *North Star* in tow.

While we were passing a towing hawser to *North Star*, the hawser fouled the bottom and on heaving it up with a great deal of effort we were astonished to find we had brought up an anchor and 60 fathoms of chain which *North Star* had lost four years before.[9] Once this

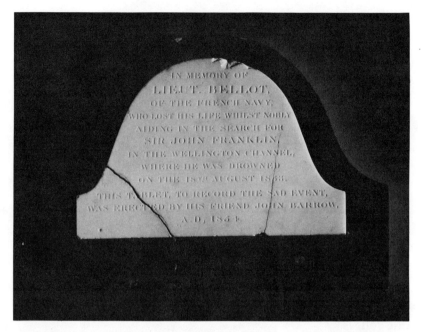

Plate 28 The memorial tablet in memory of Lieutenant Bellot, erected on
Beechey Island and unveiled by de Bray on 27 August 1854

anchor was aboard we got under way, heading along the south shore
of Lancaster Sound.

31 August 1854. We passed Cape Liverpool and Cape Bathurst, encountering some isolated floes, and at 3.00 o'clock we were at the
entrance to Pond Inlet.

Phoenix cast off *Talbot*'s and *North Star*'s towlines and anchored
at the head of the bay near a former Eskimo encampment which we
found unoccupied; as a result, it was impossible to gather any evidence
as to the culpability of these Eskimos, whom we suspected must be
those who pillaged the depot at Navy Board Inlet.[10]

At 10.00 we rejoined the two ships and identified Lievely as our
rendez-vous in case we were separated while crossing Baffin Bay.

1 September 1854. This morning we were wakened by an unusual
noise coming from the engine, which was stopped immediately; it
was discovered that one of the joints in the propeller shaft had come
loose.[11] With the wind freshening from the NW, we bore away to the
south with a rather rough sea.

2 September 1854. Ice is beginning to appear but it is not very heavy; once our engine was repaired, and since the wind swung into the SW, we took *Talbot* and *North Star* in tow again.[12]

3 September 1854. Very little ice in sight and we are making good progress with our two consorts in tow.

Today to our amazement we spotted a bear swimming among floes near the ship; at this point we were about two hundred miles from land, which leads one to suppose that these animals can make long sea crossings and can stay in the water for a very long time.

4 September 1854. The fresh SSW wind has swung into the SSE and there is a large number of icebergs in sight. We cast off our tows and headed for land, leaving Svart Hoek bearing NE1/2E. By 8.00 p.m. we had lost sight of our consorts.

5 September 1854. During the morning we spoke a Danish brig bound for Umanakfiord from Upernavik.

We followed the east coast of Disko, where we found the winds very variable in strength and direction. Still many icebergs in sight. At 11.30 p.m. we stopped engines and brought-to off Lievely.

6 September 1854. At 6.00 a.m. we dropped anchor in the roadstead at Lievely and immediately began coaling and watering. A Danish brig was the only other vessel in the anchorage.

8 September 1854. *Talbot* in sight off Disko at 6.00 p.m.; she fired a gun and we sent our boats to tow her in.

By 8.30 she was moored alongside *Phoenix* and we transshipped the coal she still had on board.

9 September 1854. The inspector for the north of Greenland and his wife and sister-in-law, accompanied by the governor of Lievely, came aboard and received a nine-gun salute.

Some Eskimo women of our former acquaintance also came aboard after dinner and we danced with them until 10.00 p.m., finishing the celebration by setting off some rockets and mines.

10 September 1854. *North Star* has anchored off the entrance to Lievely and Captain M'Clure has left that ship to come aboard *Phoenix*.

11 September 1854. At 8.00 a.m. *Talbot* set sail to leave Lievely and join *North Star*, which had already weighed; at 9.00 o'clock *Phoenix* got under way, exchanging salutes with the shore. A fairly fresh wind varied between NE and SE.

This time we said farewell to the beauties of Lievely, to the governor and his secretaries, Messrs Andersson and Saxtorph, who had welcomed us with the greatest cordiality.

12 September 1854. With a variable wind from the north quarter *Talbot* and *North Star* are sailing in company and we are heading south, holding sixty miles off the land.

17 September 1854. With the wind freshening from the NE we lost sight of our two consorts.[13]

22 September 1854. Wind very fresh from the N to NW; squally weather; we are making good progress.

28 September 1854. Finally, after quite a fair voyage, we dropped anchor at Cork in Ireland and immediately Sir Edward Belcher and Captains Kellett and M'Clure left for London to announce our arrival.[14]

On 2 October we came up the Thames and moored at Woolwich, from where we had sailed on 21 April, i.e., after an absence of two years, five months, and nine days.[15]

Our arrival in England was greeted with keen expressions of pleasure and it was with great interest that people followed the debates of the court martial which was convoked for the purpose of ruling on the abandonment of the five ships in the arctic seas.

The court held its sessions on board *Waterloo* at Sheerness,[16] with Admiral George Gordon presiding; it consisted of captains Sir Thomas Pasley, Wyvill, Tucker, Keith Stewart, Seymour, and Franshawe. The judge advocate was Mr Hayward.

Captain M'Clure appeared first and justified his action on the basis of written orders he had received from Captain Kellett for the abandonment of his ship under absolutely exceptional circumstances. After withdrawing, the court martial declared that Captain M'Clure, his officers and crew deserved the highest commendations and that they were all fully acquitted.[17]

Captain Kellett then appeared to give his account of the loss of *Resolute,* and produced the orders he had received from Sir Edward Belcher for the abandonment of *Resolute* and *Intrepid.* A large number of letters were read, some of them confidential; they proved that, despite the opinion of Captain Kellett and all his officers, who declared that the ships would not suffer at all during the impending breakup, Captain Sir Edward Belcher, by a letter dated 25 April, had peremptorily ordered them to abandon *Resolute* and *Intrepid* and proceed to Beechey Island to await further instructions.

Having thus been cleared of all responsibility, Captain Kellett was honourably acquitted and in returning his sword the president expressed his complete satisfaction with the manner in which he had comported himself in the difficult circumstances in which he had found himself.[18]

Sir Edward Belcher was then called[19] and read a lengthy statement in which he recounted all the details of our campaigns which tended to justify the abandonment of the ships and, moreover, built his case on the instructions he had received from the Admiralty. After ninety minutes of deliberation the judge advocate read the following extract of the judgment handed down:

> The Court is of opinion that the abandonment of Her Majesty's Ship *Investigator* was directed by Captain Kellett, who was justified in giving such orders. The Court is of opinion, from the great confidence reposed in Captain Sir E. Belcher by the Lords Commissioners of the Admiralty, and the ample discretionary powers given to him, that he was authorized and did not act beyond his orders, in abandoning Her Majesty's Ship *Resolute* and her tender the *Intrepid*, although, if circumstances had permitted, it would have been advisable that he should have consulted with Captain Kellett previously.[20]

The court hence ordered the acquittal of Captain Sir Edward Belcher, and his sword was returned to him.

The abandonment of the ships of the arctic expedition was a phenomenon keenly debated by a large number of people, from a wide range of points of view. It is certain that in taking upon himself to abandon the ships without consulting the various captains, the commander-in-chief was assuming an enormous responsibility.

In interpreting his instructions to the letter Sir Edward Belcher cannot be blamed, but as we will see later, far from proving that he was right, subsequent events demonstrated that at least two of the five ships, *Resolute* and *Intrepid*, could have got free during breakup in 1854.

We still had enough provisions and spare parts for another year; we were all in perfect health and filled with great anticipation in thinking of our planned spring voyage which would have led to us finding traces of, or even meeting, Captain Collinson. It might even have led to something akin to Captain McClintock's voyage of 1858 [sic] when he found the relics of Sir John Franklin on Prince [sic] William Land. The order to abandon our ship was a distressing surprise to us and it was with real regret that we were obliged to abandon all our hopes.[21]

It now remains for me to discuss one of the most extraordinary facts which the history of navigation can record, namely the almost miraculous return of *Resolute* to England. The account is derived from the *New York Herald* [of 27 December 1855].[22]

On the 29th May last, the whaling barque *George Henry*, Captain
James M. Buddington, set sail from New London, Conn., on a voyage
to Northumberland Inlet [*sic*] and Davis Straits. The bark was manned
with a crew of 17 men, including the first and second mates. On the
14th June, and while in latitude 54°, Captain Buddington encountered,
quite unexpectedly, large fields of ice, through which he dare not
penetrate. However, wishing to arrive at his destination as soon as
possible, he followed the edge of the 'pack' as far as Latitude 67°. As
the ship was much damaged by the floating ice Captain Buddington
concluded to wear out the season here, and accordingly the crew of
the bark were employed in catching whales in, and about Disko Bay,
with only tolerable luck, however. The floes are represented as being
very extensive, stretching far and wide to the north, and completely
blocking up the channel to Davis Straits. From the masthead of the
George Henry nothing could be distinguished but masses of ice. Even
with the aid of the telescope nothing but mountains could be described
in the distance.

On the 20th August, and while off Cape Walsingham, in lat. 67°N, the
ice became. to a certain extent, penetrable, and the barque was forced
through it in a south-west direction for about 150 miles. At this time a
heavy gale from the north-east sprung up, which, lasting three days, the
George Henry became unnavigable, and was drifted in the floe in a
south-west direction. Captain Buddington saw land, but could not say
to what continent it belonged.

On the 10th September, lat. 67°N, and, while in this field of ice,
Captain Buddington discovered a ship in the distance, bearing northeast, about twenty miles from Cape Mercy. He ascended the rigging of
his craft, and, looking at her through the glass, pronounced her, from
her appearance, to be an abandoned vessel.[23] The head of the stranger
appeared to be due east, and during the whole of that day and the
following, the course of the ship did not vary more than a point or so
from the east. 'We kept gradually nearing one another,' as Captain
Buddington says, 'although I could not exactly say what caused the
thing to come about, except, perhaps, the ship may have been struck by
a counter current from Davis Straits, and driven towards us in that
manner. For five days we were in sight of one another, and continued to
drift towards each other.' On the sixth day after making the discovery,
and when the ship was about seven miles off, Captain Buddington
ordered the two mates and two of the crew[24] to proceed to the aban-

doned vessel across the packed ice, and, after inspecting her, to return to the barque as soon as practicable.

Soon after the departure of the party a south-easter sprung up, and, in consequence thereof, no communication was had with those on board the ship for two days. As soon as the weather subsided, and it was safe for the party to retrace their steps, they left the ship, and, after a tedious and hard march, arrived on board the barque in safety. They immediately represented the facts to Captain Buddington,[25] saying that the abandoned vessel was Her Britannic Majesty's ship *Resolute*[26] ...

The *Resolute* being entirely free of water, preparations were made to bring the ship to the United States. Captain Buddington decided to sail the vessel himself, and accordingly, taking eleven men with him from his own barque, he began in good earnest to release the abandoned vessel from her ice-bound situation. The rigging had to be hauled taut, and the sails put in order, before he could venture to start. These jobs occupied him some time, but were successfully accomplished. Captain Buddington was in a great dilemma for proper navigating instruments, and the wherewith to bring him to New London after being released from the ice. His compass was not at all trustworthy; he was without a chronometer, and had no other map or chart to steer by, than a rough outline of the great North American coast, drawn on a sheet of foolscap. With his lever watch, a quadrant, and a miserable compass, the brave fellow bade adieu to his comrades in the barque *George Henry*, and, trusting to Providence and his experience in those latitudes, prepared to bring home the prize he had so cleverly won.

From the time that Captain Buddington took charge of the *Resolute*, up to the 16th of October, she continued to drive in a SW direction with the pack of ice, when she succeeded in getting clear. Wishing to be in company as long as possible in the barque, Captain Buddington waited on the outside of the floe for three or four days, with the hope of meeting her, but the vessels missed one another, and did not meet again during the remainder of the eventful voyage.[27]

While here waiting for the *George Henry* the British barque *Alibi* hove in sight, and, on being signalled, came alongside the *Resolute*. The news of the recovery of the *Resolute* was communicated to Captain Stuart, of the British barque, and a pair of Captain Kellett's epaulettes, found on board the abandoned vessel, were entrusted to him by Captain Buddington, with instructions to have them forwarded to the owner as speedily as possible. They were sent by Captain Stuart to Mr Barrow, who forwarded them to Commodore Kellett in the West Indies, and were duly received by him in perfect order for attending a drawing-room if required, not being soiled in the slightest degree. A letter for the owners of the *George and Henry*, informing them of what had occurred, was also placed in the hands of Captain Stuart, who promised to mail it immediately on his arrival in Great Britain ...

... Short-handed, poorly rigged, and unfitted for the long voyage as the *Resolute* was, Captain Buddington found it no easy task to bring the ship into port. The ballast tanks had burst in the hold long before he came in possession of her, rendering her very light and apt to roll heavily in the trough of the sea. Gale after gale was experienced; yet the brave fellow laboured day and night, and at last was successful in the praiseworthy effort made to rescue the abandoned vessel, driving across the mouth of Northumberland Inlet [*sic*] down to Cape Elizabeth. The open sea was gained, and on the 20th October the homeward voyage commenced. After a succession of strong gales and headwinds, the New London lighthouse was made on the 24th December...[28]

As soon as *Resolute* had arrived the Queen waived all claim to the vessel,[29] leaving her at the disposal of Captain Buddington, who at risk to his life had succeeded in extricating her from her icy prison.

Everything inside the ship was found in a deplorable state, except for the salt provisions, but the hull, by miraculous luck, had received no serious damage although the ship, left to her own devices, had drifted amongst islands, rocks, and shoals, and had covered a distance of about one thousand miles. It is impossible to establish exactly the route the ship may have covered, tossed by winds, currents and ice.

As soon as it was learned in America that the Queen of England had waived all rights to *Resolute*, Congress bought her for 200,000 francs [$40,000].[30] She was taken to one of the navy yards, refitted with great care; it was then decided that she should be given back to England, ready to begin a new polar campaign.

On 13 November, under the command of Captain Hartstene of the United States Navy, *Resolute* sailed from New York and on 12 December she dropped anchor at Spithead; the American and British flags were flying together from the mainmast.[31]

The Queen wanted to visit *Resolute*, and came aboard with a numerous suite.[32] The officers and several distinguished Americans were in attendance at the head of the gangway and were presented by Captain Hartstene. He then addressed the Queen:

Allow me to welcome Your Majesty on board the *Resolute*, and, in obedience to the will of my countrymen and of the President of the

United States, to restore her to you, not only as an evidence of a friendly feeling to your sovereignty but as a token of love, admiration, and respect to Your Majesty personally.

The Queen replied, 'I thank you, Sir,' and inspected the ship which was then opened to the numerous visitors. Captain Hartstene was invited to dinner by the Queen at Osborne and £100 was distributed among the crew.

During their short stay in England Captain Hartstene and his officers were showered with invitations of every kind and *Resolute* became the object of a sort of pilgrimage.[33] It was not until 30 December that the ship was officially returned to Britain.

At 1 o'clock Captain George Seymour of *Victory* came aboard with a party of seamen and a few moments later *Victory* hoisted the American flag to her masthead, to a twenty-one-gun salute. At the same time the American flag was hauled down aboard *Resolute*, and she once again hoisted the Union Jack at her peak, the flag which she had carried so nobly in the arctic regions and which one day she may perhaps take to the Pole.[34]

Translator's Postscript

Before leaving *Phoenix* at Cork, Captain Kellett had handed de Bray a letter which he would cherish for the rest of his life:

> H.M.S. Phoenix off Cork, 28 Sept. 1854
>
> My dear de Bray –
>
> I have already expressed to Sir Edward Belcher commanding the Arctic Expedition my opinion of your conduct whilst serving in Her Britannic Majesty's Ship 'Resolute' under my command. But I cannot allow you to leave me without expressing to you personally my admiration of your promptness and zeal in undertaking any piece of service and your ability in its execution.
>
> You *have* Mr de Bray done credit to the distinguished service in which you belong.
>
> Thrown amongst us a perfect stranger not even speaking our language with ease, you have so perfectly identified yourself with everything common to us, our duties, amusements and teaching as to have won the esteem and regard of all on board and of none more than of yours.

Almost immediately on reaching London, Sir Edward Belcher wrote to the secretary of the Admiralty, commending de Bray's contribution to the expedition:

> Admiralty in waiting
> 30th September 1854
>
> Sir,
>
> Having submitted the names of the officers, belonging to Her Majesty's Navy to the consideration of My Lords Commissioners of the Admiralty.
>
> It affords me infinite satisfaction to be able to speak in the highest terms of praise of the conduct of M. Emile de Bray whilst serving more

immediately under the command of my gallant coadjutor Captain
Henry Kellett of H.M. Ship 'Resolute', who has already given to him a
special letter, the burthen of which is to the effect, that his conduct
reflects infinite credit on the service of which he is so truly a noble
specimen.

Like the lamented Bellot, who [*sic*] has acquired the warmest sympathy of all who have had the pleasure of his society.

I earnestly hope that our sentiments may be made known to his
Government, and that his merit may meet with the distinction which
he so richly merits.

Hamilton, secretary to their Lords Commissioners, relayed a copy
of this letter to de Bray, conveying to him 'the expression of their
Lordships' high admiration of your conduct, which they have not
failed to communicate to your Government' (Hamilton, 1854). As
Hamilton had promised, Lord Cowley had forwarded a copy of the
above letter to the French minister of foreign affairs, who in turn
passed it to Theodore Ducos, the minister of marine. The latter,
having also received de Bray's official report (see Appendix 2) sent de
Bray his official congratulations:

Paris 13 October 1854.

Sir,

I have received the report you sent me on the voyage you made with
the Arctic Expedition sent in search of Sir John Franklin. I have read
this report with the keenest interest and it is not without a feeling of
deep satisfaction that I have perceived the part played by one of the
officers of our Navy in work whose importance and usefulness are of
interest to such a high degree to science and navigation.

I found attached to your report a map of the route followed by the
expedition in the arctic seas and I shall receive with pleasure all the
documents you may have gathered during your explorations. The
British Government has sent me the most flattering testimonials on
your conduct during the long, tedious voyage. These testimonials bring
honour on the officer who has earned them and at the same time reflect
on the service to which he belongs.

In relaying them to you, it is my pleasant duty to have to reiterate
here my entire satisfaction for services which are appreciated and which
will not be lost from sight (Ducos, 1854).

The previous day the minister had ordered a copy of Belcher's letter sent to the newspaper *Moniteur Universel*. It was published (in translation) in the issue of 12 October, alongside Belcher's letter written to de Bray in June in Wellington Channel.

Thereafter the honours came in rapid succession. While de Bray was still in the Arctic, he had been awarded the Croix de Chevalier de la Légion d'honneur by Napoleon III on the occasion of the Fête de l'Empereur on 12 August 1854. Following normal mid-nineteenth-century French practice this award was in no small amount due to the representations on his behalf by de Bray's mother, who had written at least twice to the ministre de la marine to present her son's case on the basis of his service in the Arctic (de Bray, J. 1854a). It is interesting to note that in her accompanying précis of her son's service career, she somewhat exaggerated his involvement in the discovery of the Northwest Passage: 'Enseigne-de-vaisseau de Bray who accompanied lieutenants Pim and Hamilton is thus the sole Frenchman who thus far has traversed these unexplored regions; as a result his name is associated with that valuable discovery which had been sought vainly for four hundred years.'

On 29 October de Bray received the supreme honour: he was received in private audience by Napoleon III at the Château de Saint-Cloud (Rouch, 1944:7; Henrat, 1982:111). The Emperor insisted on hearing a detailed verbal account of the voyage.

Simultaneously, however, de Bray was pursuing the matter of compensation for the belongings he had had to leave aboard *Resolute*. He wrote to Captain Kellett to ask for certification that he had been ordered to abandon his belongings. On 14 November Kellett wrote to the secretary of the Admiralty, including precisely this certification. Kellett also took the opportunity to reiterate his very high opinion of his former junior officer:

> I take this opportunity of stating to their Lordships my estimation of M. de Bray's conduct whilst serving under my command.
>
> M. de Bray, by his personal exertion, his ability, and the zeal he always manifested in the performance of every service he was appointed either to second or in command, has done credit to the distinguished service to which he belongs.
>
> His amiable disposition, and desire to please by the exercise of his manifold accomplishments, have won for him the esteem of both officers and men (Kellett, 1855b).

A copy of this letter was forwarded to the French minister of foreign affairs. One hopes that de Bray received some compensation for his abandoned belongings.

At this time another flattering and encouraging letter was on its way from London to France. On 16 November Sir John Barrow, second secretary to the Admiralty, wrote to de Bray's mother, in response to an earlier letter from her. He commented on de Bray's recent audience with the Emperor and noted that: 'I cannot but think that he will soon hear of some honour conferred upon him in the way of promotion' (Barrow, 1854), although he suspected that the Crimean War might delay promotion. On the other hand he assured Mme de Bray that:

> When the Minister of Marine becomes fully aware of his great exertions, the dangers gone through, difficulties overcome and privations suffered, I am sure that he will not allow them to pass by unrequited and particularly when he learns that standing *alone* as he did in a Foreign Service, in the remotest and most inhospitable regions of the globe, he upheld the honour of his nation by his energy, intrepidity, and patient endurance of much hard service, and succeeded in making himself as much *respected* in the Squadron as he was beloved.

Barrow's prophecies came true fairly rapidly. A recommendation for promotion was presented to the Conseil d'Amirauté on 9 December 1854. Once again, de Bray's mother played a role in promoting his case, writing to the Emperor, expressing the hope that 'Your Majesty's government would accord him the signal honour of retaining the rank of Lieutenant-de-vaisseau in which he served for two years in the British Navy' (de Bray, J., 1854b). On 5 October 1855 de Bray was promoted Lieutenant-de-vaisseau at the age of twenty-six. By then he was on active service in the Baltic.

There were further honours to come. On 25 July 1857 Stewart, British ambassador to France, wrote to Count Walewski, minister of foreign affairs:

> M. le Conte,
>
> The Queen having been graciously pleased to grant a medal to all the officers and men engaged in the arctic seas in the search of Sir John Franklin as a mark of Her Majesty's high approbation and recollection of their perilous adventure, I have been instructed at the request of the Lords Commissioners of the Admiralty to transmit two of these medals, as herewith enclosed, to your Excellency, the same being respectively

destined for the Lieutenant Emile de Bray of the Imperial Navy, who shared the perils of the voyage in Her Majesty's Ship 'Resolute' and for the relations of Lieutenant Bellot, who unhappily lost his life, while nobly aiding in the search referred to.

Your Excellency will, I am sure, have pleasure in requesting the Minister of Marine to deliver these honorable testimonials to the persons for whom they are destined, and the Lords of the Admiralty are further desirous Admiral Hamelin should have the kindness to convey to M. de Bray the expression of their utter appreciation of his valuable exertion, and to the relations of Lieutenant Bellot the assurance of their Lordships' sympathy; and I need scarcely add that the feelings thus expressed by their Lordships are fully shared by all classes of the Queen's subjects (Stewart, 1857).

De Bray was the only living Frenchman ever to receive the Arctic Medal. It had been Queen Victoria's intention to honour him with an even higher decoration, namely that of the Order of the Bath (de Bray, G., 1926:4). But since this could be awarded only to officers of high rank, it was agreed that this honour should be deferred until de Bray reached the appropriate rank. In fact, his premature death denied him this honour.

Lady Franklin was truly grateful for de Bray's efforts and maintained a correspondence with him and his mother for many years. She sent him a framed portrait of her husband with the dedication: 'En reconnaissant et affectueux souvenir de ses très habiles et zélés services dans la recherche de son bien aimé mari, Jane Franklin' (de Bray, G., 1926:4). She also sent him a portrait of Bellot and a large painting of the Arctic Committee. Probably one of the most treasured of de Bray's mementoes of his years in the Arctic was the flag from his sledge *Hero* which McClintock sent him.

De Bray's Later Career

Immediately on his return to Paris de Bray had requested a six-month furlough (de Bray, 1854; Henrat, 1982:112), but in fact he was permitted only three months leave. This was followed by three months of duty (1 February–23 April 1855) at the Dépôt des cartes et plans, the forerunner of the Service hydrographique de la Marine, a posting which was relatively undemanding and allowed him to put his journal of the expedition in order. Then, after a brief interlude as sous-aide-major at Brest, on 6 June he joined the steam gunboat *La*

Poudre at L'Orient, about to sail for the Baltic, as executive officer. Launched at Nantes on 30 April 1855, *La Poudre* was commanded by Lieutenant-de-vaisseau Lafond. *La Poudre* sailed from L'Orient on 1 August, bound for the Gulf of Finland where she was to join the squadron of Rear-Admiral Penaud, then participating in the Allied actions against the Russian Baltic fleet during the Crimean War. No doubt to the great disappointment of de Bray and his fellow officers, by the time the gunboat reached Penaud's squadron on 14 August they had missed the major bombardment of Sveaborg (Suomenlinna), the massive fortification protecting the harbour of Helsinki which was the last major offensive of the Baltic theatre of the war. *La Poudre* was assigned briefly to the much less exciting duties of blockading the Russian and Finnish coasts; but even these duties were shortlived; on 16 September Admiral Penaud decided to send home five of his eight gunboats, including *La Poudre*. After a protracted visit to Christiansand she returned to Cherbourg in mid-November and was paid off on 1 December.

For de Bray personally there were certain compensations. As we have seen, it was during the homeward voyage from the Baltic that he learned of his promotion to Lieutenant-de-vaisseau. And on leaving the ship he received a truly glowing report from Lieutenant-de-vaisseau Lafond: 'Great aptitude for the profession of the sea ... Capable officer, in whom I have the greatest confidence. I have nothing but praise for his services while under my orders. He has a great sense of command' (Henrat, 1982:113).

On shore once again, de Bray was posted to the Dépôt des cartes et plans once again. On 19 May 1856, having first requested and received the official approval of the minister of marine, he married the 29-year-old Laetitia-Constance-Marie Le Bleis, the daughter of a Pont-l'Abbé merchant (Henrat, 1982:114). She would bear him six children; two of whom would die in infancy.

After a three-month leave during which he finished the work on which he had been engaged at the Dépôt des cartes et plans, on 1 August 1856 de Bray took up the duties of the captain of a recruiting company at the Dépôt des équipages at Brest (Henrat, 1982:115). For the next eighteen months he carried out his rather lacklustre duties in this post efficiently and conscientiously. On 3 March 1858, leaving his wife, then expecting her second child, he joined the paddle-steamer *Gassendi*, Capitaine-de-vaiseau Clement de la Roncière-Le Noury, bound for Saint Pierre et Miqueleon to act as flagship of the small detachment of fisheries protection vessels stationed there.

Gassendi sailed from Brest in early April, and reached her destination on 18 May. It was a very late spring and de Bray must have felt he was back in the Arctic. On 30 June de la Roncière-le Noury wrote:

> The winter has been one of exceptional rigour and length. The majority of our fishing vessels were beset by the pack ice for more than a month before they were able to reach the east coast, and today several are still waiting for a favourable opportunity to enter their respective harbours ... Indeed this sort of situation has not been seen to last as long as this since 1826 when the pack did not disperse until 8 July. Numerous icebergs are lying grounded several miles off the island and there is a large quantity of ice drifting near the coast at the will of the wind and the currents, so that one day narrow leads will open, only to close again the day after (Henrat, 1982:117).

Fortunately the ice dispersed on 2 July, allowing the small fleet to go about its varied duties: assisting the cod-fishermen, delivering mail, visits to the British authorities, showing the French flag off the shores of Newfoundland, hydrographic work in these little-charted waters, and protecting the fisheries of the 'French Shore' from encroachment by British and other fishermen. In early October de Bray was briefly (for three days) given command of the schooner *Gentille*, but then, along with the officers and crews of most of the other fisheries protection vessels, he was posted back to France for the winter. He sailed aboard *Gassendi* on 4 October, reaching Brest on the 18th, from where he soon joined his family at Versailles.

In the early spring of 1859 de Bray was ordered to rejoin *Gentille*. This time he decided to take his wife with him. The couple reached Saint Pierre et Miquelon on 29 April and two days later de Bray rejoined his command. The *Gentille* was a minuscule vessel: 17.5 metres from stem to stern and displacing 35 tonnes, carrying a crew of twenty and six guns. In this little vessel de Bray carried out the varied duties of a fisheries protection vessel in poorly charted waters and amidst some of the worst weather in the world, with frequent fogs and gales, and, of course, with the added hazard of ice. Moreover, the status of French and British fishing rights in these waters was a confusing one, which had to be handled with tact and diplomacy. In execution of these demanding duties de Bray excelled. The comments on his performance by his commanding officer, Capitaine-de-vaisseau Montaignac, are replete with phrases such as: 'speaks English perfectly,' 'an intelligent officer with whom I have been very satisfied,' and 'a perfect aptitude for the profession of the sea' (Henrat, 1982:122).

After three seasons based at Saint Pierre et Miquelon, de Bray boarded the military transport *Perdrix*, reaching Brest on 22 October. He was now due a three-month leave after his duties in Newfoundland waters. At the end of that time, however, it became apparent that his health had been severely strained, presumably from the combination of his two years in the Arctic and the three years in Saint Pierre et Miquelon. On 31 December 1861 he asked for a two-month extension of his leave; the request was supported by a medical certificate to the effect that he was suffering from a 'vague rheumatic affliction' which affected 'successively his knees, shoulders and thorax' (Henrat, 1982:122).

On 14 March 1862 de Bray joined his new vessel, *Breslaw*, a screw steamer, commanded by Capitaine-de-frégate Geoffroy. During the summer it was decided that *Breslaw* would transport men and horses to Mexico as part of the French intervention in that country. Under the command of Capitaine-de-vaisseau Robin, and having taken on board 921 officers and men, eighteen horses, ten vehicles, and a vast array of guns, ammunition, and military stores at Cherbourg, on 4 September *Breslaw* put to sea as part of a convoy. She reached Vera Cruz on 28 October 1862 and was back at Brest early in 1863, where de Bray left her on 20 January.

By now, his health was seriously undermined. Some four years later the surgeon-major of *Breslaw*, Lallour, attested that de Bray had suffered severely throughout the voyage from a rheumatic predisposition. The attacks had been so severe in the tropics that Lallour had been seriously worried that they might be fatal. He warned that further service in hot climates would lead to a total breakdown of de Bray's health (Lallour, 1867; Henrat, 1982:125–7).

For the moment, however, there was no likelihood of a return to the tropics. De Bray's next posting was to the ship-of-the-line *Inflexible* moored at Brest, which housed the School for Ships' Boys; de Bray was made captain of the fourth company and in this capacity served from 20 January 1863 until 20 January 1865. In April 1865 there followed a further shore posting; for the next ten months de Bray was a sous-aide-major at Brest, under the direct orders of the new major-general, Contre-amiral Mequet. The latter's assessment of de Bray, written on 20 October 1865, was entirely positive and ended with the words 'Proposed for a command' (Henrat, 1982:128). Mequet's opinions must have carried some weight: on 24 February de Bray was appointed to the command of the brand new screw steamer, *Cher*, 64 metres in length, 1,700 tonnes and with a complement of seventy-nine (Henrat, 1982:129).

De Bray's new vessel had been assigned, together with *Pandore*, to provide support for the French fishing fleet in Icelandic waters. *Cher* sailed from Cherbourg on 22 April 1866, made rendezvous with *Pandore* at Burntisland, and then proceeded to the east coast of Iceland. That coast, however, was blockaded by ice, and it was not until early June that *Cher* was able to start her duties; she reconnoitred harbours, her carpenter and caulker gave assistance where needed to the crews of French fishing vessels; she gave medical help to a severely wounded Danish seaman; she transported to Reykjavik the crews of two Breton schooners which had been crushed by ice; her officers sounded and charted a shoal near Reykjanes which had been inaccurately plotted on the chart; and de Bray assembled statistics on the fishery. This was the pattern of *Cher*'s activities around the coasts of Iceland for the entire summer; by mid-October de Bray had brought his ship safely back to Cherbourg.

De Bray's health appeared not to have suffered at all during this northern cruise, and he was probably looking forward to a return to those same waters in the summer of 1867, but it was not to be. Early in the new year *Cher* was ordered to Vera Cruz to help repatriate the last elements of the French expeditionary force sent to Mexico to support the Emperor Maximilian. Despite his medical problems on his previous tropical voyage, de Bray raised no objections. The results were disastrous: when *Cher* returned to Cherbourg late in March, her medical officer reported that de Bray was suffering from dyspepsia and a rheumatic disposition. Examined in turn by the Health Council at Cherbourg, then by the Superior Health Council of the navy in Paris, then again by the Cherbourg council, de Bray was declared to be unfit to serve in hot climates for at least one year. Reluctantly, he had to relinquish command of *Cher*, which was about to sail for Senegal (Henrat, 1982:133).

De Bray was now authorized to take a leave of four months at Brest and Quimper. On 25 May, however, he was provisionally assigned to the staff of Vice-Amiral Dupouy, Préfet maritime de Brest. It is encouraging to note that during the two years he spent on this shore posting de Bray's health appears to have stabilized. He also had the satisfaction of knowing that his performance of his duties was highly appreciated by his commanding officer; Dupouy recommended him for the Croix d'Officier de la Légion d'honneur on 20 October, repeating his recommendation on 23 June 1868, shortly before his death. His successor, Contre-amiral Martin, renewed the application in October of that year.

In the meantime other honours came his way; on 17 April 1869 he was posted to the most prestigious of the Imperial yachts, *Aigle*, commanded by Capitaine-de-vaisseau Surville and then lying at Toulon. Unfortunately he served aboard her for only six weeks, during which time she put to sea only once, on a two-day trip to Ajaccio (Henrat, 1982:135). The event that terminated de Bray's period of service aboard the imperial yacht was his promotion, on 22 May 1869, to Capitaine-de-frégate.

For the following fourteen months the details of de Bray's career remain a little vague although he was attached to the Préfecture maritime de Brest. On 2 June 1870 he took a thermal cure at Aix-les-Bains, prescribed by the Health Council of Brest because of 'general chronic rheumatism.' While at Aix-les-Bains, however, he received word of a more specific posting; on 30 June 1870 he was appointed first aide-de-camp to the Préfet maritime de Brest, Vice-Amiral Reynaud (Henrat, 1982:137). This was to be only a brief interlude, however. With the outbreak of the Franco-Prussian War on 17 July 1870 it was quickly realized that the navy could make a useful contribution towards holding the Prussian advance on land. Thus on 7 August Capitaine-de-frégate de Bray received orders to take command of the 3rd Naval Battalion, which had just been formed at Brest, and to move it to Paris as quickly as possible. When the siege of Paris began on 19 September, its defenders included nine thousand sailors and almost two hundred naval guns, sent from naval bases around the coasts.

Among them was de Bray; for much of the time he was adjunct to Capitaine-de-frégate Coudein, commander of the battery at Saint-Ouen. For a brief period in mid-November he was appointed to the command of the 1st Brigade of the 6th Division, but this unit disappeared in another reshuffle and he returned to his post as second-in-command of the Saint-Ouen battery, taking command when Coudein was posted elsewhere on 23 November. Until the armistice on 28 January 1871 he and his battery bombarded the Prussian artillery positions at Orgemont and Epinay, the French sailors inflicting and suffering heavy losses. De Bray's services did not go unrecognized; on 15 December 1870 Coudein had recommended him for the Croix d'Officier de la Légion d'honneur; the recommendation was repeated by Vice-Amiral de la Roncière-le Noury on 27 December. Finally on 23 January, in the last bitter days of the Siege of Paris, by a decree of

the Président du Gouvernement de Défense nationale, de Bray was
promoted to the rank of Officier de l'Ordre nationale de la Légion
d'honneur (Henrat, 1982:142)

In March 1871 de Bray returned to Brest and resumed his duties as
aide-de-camp to the Préfet maritime. On 24 May 1872 he was posted
as second-in-command to what would turn out to be his last ship
(Henrat, 1982:143). She was the iron-clad corvette *Armide*, which he
joined at Toulon; she was for her time a formidable vessel: 3,800
tonnes, with engines of 1,900 horse power, developing a speed of 12
knots, and with an armament of six 190-mm and four 120-mm guns.

But de Bray's service aboard *Armide* was brief; he was ordered to
return to Brest on 29 July, and on 12 October received permission to
move temporarily to Pau, probably for reasons of health (Vice-Amiral
Préfet maritime de Brest, 1872; Henrat, 1982:144). And while there he
had to cope with a different type of stress; on 31 October his wife died,
aged only thirty-five.

From this point on, de Bray's dossier becomes rather sparse, but it
seems probable that he spent the next three years at Pau for reasons
of ill-health, although still officially attached to the Majorité générale
de Brest. There was some suggestion of him returning to sea in
October 1876, but this was not realized; shortly thereafter he received
permission to move to Pont-l'Abbé 'en residence libre' (Vice-Amiral
Préfet maritime de Brest, 1877; Henrat, 1982:145) and he seems to have
stayed there until 27 March 1878 when he was posted to the Majorité
générale de Cherbourg. There he was entrusted with training reserv-
ists and was assigned to various permanent committees, but his
health allowed him to handle these duties in only a sporadic fashion.
Thus on 17 May 1878 the Health Council of the Port of Cherbourg
attested that he was 'afflicted with a gouty condition, which had led
to serious nutritional problems and to a major accumulation of cal-
cium in the metatarsal joints' (Conseil de santé, Cherbourg, 1878;
Henrat, 1982:146); the council members prescribed a two-month cure
at Vichy.

Shortly after his return to Cherbourg he was appointed second-in-
command of *Tilsitt*, which was on the Indochina station. Perhaps, in
view of the serious state of de Bray's health, the minister was hinting
that it was time for him to retire. Certainly this was how de Bray
interpreted this posting; on 25 September 1878 he applied for retirement. This was granted on 30 September; prematurely aged and in
poor health, he retired to Brest at the age of forty-nine. But he was
not to enjoy his retirement for long; he died on 19 March 1879 at

3 rue de la Poterne, Brest and was buried in his wife's family's grave
plot in the cemetery at Pont-l'Abbé.

According to Rouch (1938) and Henrat (1982:147) the nickname which
de Bray enjoyed throughout his later career was 'De Bray Pôle Nord.'
But there are also two more substantive sequels to his arctic experiences. For a number of years he was a friend of Jules Verne, and the
latter relied heavily on de Bray for technical details while writing
his two-part novel on the adventures of Captain Hatteras in the
Arctic (Verne, 1866a; 1866b).

On a different level, in the mid-1860s de Bray was approached by
Gustave Lambert, who offered him command of his vessel *Boréal*,
originally the British three-master *Ismaelia* (Beaujeu-Garnier,
1990:134), on his planned attempt at the North Pole. Lambert (1866;
1868) had been on a whaling cruise to the Bering Strait area, and had
convinced himself that in view of the light ice conditions he had
seen in the Chukchi Sea, this was the most promising starting point
for a French attempt at the North Pole. On his behalf the Société de
Géographie began raising funds by public subscription and also by
an appeal to the government; Napoleon III led the subscription list
with a donation of 50,000 francs.

De Bray, by this stage father of four young children and in rather
poor health, was forced to decline Lambert's invitation, but he did
offer his advice and assistance with regard to organization. However,
Lambert fell foul of the president and members of the committee of
the Société de Géographie when, without authorization, he spent
some three-quarters of the funds collected on the purchase of the
Ismaelia; the matter went to the Cour de Paris, which ruled against
Lambert. Even had these complications been overcome, Lambert's
death at Buzenval during the Franco-Prussian War ended any hope
of this French polar attempt being realized.

De Bray's contribution to the Royal Navy's arctic expedition of
1852–4 had been a very commendable one. His two major sledge
trips from Dealy Island, one to Cape Providence in September–October 1852, and the other to Cape de Bray in northwest Melville Island
in support of McClintock in May–June 1853, compare very favourably
with any made by his British fellow officers. Moreover, his surveying and mapping of the coast of northwestern Melville Island, carried
out during the latter trip, represent a valuable contribution to the
cartography of arctic Canada. His supplementary sledge trips, such
as the one with the party of invalids from *Resolute* and *Intrepid* off

Cape Cockburn to Beechey Island in May 1854, or his dash north by dogteam from Beechey Island with urgent dispatches for Sir Edward Belcher later that same month, are not only quite impressive but also further demonstrate the trust placed in him by Captain Kellett.

Perhaps the most telling incident during de Bray's arctic sojourn was the fact that on his return journey from Cape de Bray he acquiesced to his men's request that they haul Coombes's body directly back to the ships, although this meant postponing part of the official program. It was a difficult decision, but both captains Kellett and McClintock clearly thought he had acted correctly.

Like all journals kept aboard the Royal Navy vessels during the Franklin search, de Bray's journal would have been available for official scrutiny, either during or at the end of the cruise. As a result one would not expect it to be particularly personal in its tone, or in the details which it reveals. Nonetheless, passing references in the journal, and in those of de Bray's shipmates, reveal a considerable amount about the man's character, how he interacted with his fellow officers and with the men, and how he was seen by them. The picture which emerges is of an officer who quickly overcame the problems of differences in language and culture to become a valuable and popular member of the expedition. His offer to try to repair Dr McCormick's watch (at a very early stage in the expedition), his role as French tutor to William Mumford, *Resolute*'s assistant carpenter, his participation in the Dealy Island races, or in various capacities in the shipboard theatricals, and his being asked by Captain Kellett and Sir Edward Belcher to draw plans of the Dealy Island store house and the Beechey Island monument, respectively – all these involvements in the life of the expedition reveal a man who was valued highly for his accomplishments and skills but also a man who was approachable and happy to assist, as well as keen to take a full part in every aspect of the life of the expedition.

In that de Bray and Bellot were the only two French naval officers engaged in the search for Franklin, it is almost inevitable that they should be compared. At the outset, however, one has to recognize that there are significant differences between de Bray's arctic experience and Bellot's first expedition (which embraced the majority of his arctic experience and is the best-known one). Whereas de Bray was a member of an expedition mounted by the Royal Navy and manned by naval personnel, Bellot's first arctic expedition (aboard *Prince Albert* in 1851–2) was a private expedition dispatched by Lady Franklin. The leader of the expedition was William Kennedy, a Métis

from Cumberland House (then in Rupert's Land, now in Saskatchewan) with considerable experience of travel in the Canadian
North, both as a lad around Cumberland House and as a Hudson's
Bay Company employee in Labrador and Ungava in the early 1840s.
But his nautical experience was confined to two years as master of a
vessel on Lake Huron in 1848–50 (Shaw, 1982). Thus, while de Bray
was only one of a number of officers on board *Resolute*, Bellot was
only one of two officers on board *Prince Albert*, and indeed was the
more experienced of those two. The men under his command,
moreover, were not under naval discipline.

Bellot appears to have been highly emotional and, had the word
been in vogue, one suspects that contemporary descriptions of his
physical appearance and character would have included the word
'cute.' When *Prince Albert* sailed from Aberdeen in May 1851 Sophia
Cracroft, Lady Franklin's niece, wrote of the occasion as follows:
'Our parting with our dear little French friend was really painful –
he sobbed like a child as he took leave of my Aunt. It was some
time before he got courage to say the word. We are really *very* fond of
him – his sweetness & simplicity & earnestness are most endearing'
(Sophia Cracroft, quoted in Woodward, 1950:398).

Neither Lady Franklin nor her niece met de Bray and hence we
have no comparable remarks as to the impression he made on them;
at the same time no other contemporary source contains remarks
even remotely resembling the above applied to de Bray.

In strong contrast to de Bray, in his account of the expedition
Bellot betrays a strong desire to be accepted by the men under him.
As Hodgson has suggested (1974), he played almost the role of a
mascot for them, somebody for whose welfare they felt responsible.
During one sledge trip in the fall of 1851 he describes eating some
pemmican,

> ... to which I alone added a little biscuit, the men having slipped a few
> pieces into the provision bag ... because they thought that, not being
> accustomed to an exclusively meat diet, it might disagree with me.
> Many a time in this short trip I had reason to be inwardly grateful for
> such delicate attentions, which are always the more touching when
> they are offered by persons outwardly rough; and the first night, when I
> was half asleep, I saw them, one after another, come and wrap me up,
> and make sure that my feet were not frozen (Bellot, 1855, vol I:337–8).

Hodgson notes quite correctly that it must have been difficult for

Bellot to maintain discipline having allowed such a relationship with his men to develop (although, as we will see, his performance as an officer and arctic traveller does not seem to have suffered as a result). Nonetheless, the contrast with de Bray is extremely striking; rather than the men 'tucking him up' at night, he specifically notes that it is the officer's responsibility on a sledging trip to spread a blanket over the men under his command before settling down for the night.

Kennedy's attitude to Bellot appears to have been somewhat ambivalent. At several points in his account of the expedition Kennedy gently pokes fun at his second-in-command. Thus at one point during the wintering at Batty Bay he notes: 'Mr Bellot makes daily pilgrimages to a hill in the neighbourhood, where he occasionally succeeds in getting a meridian observation of the sun, and *always* succeeds in getting his fingers frozen in the operation' (Kennedy, 1853:87).

On another occasion Bellot's sledge and dogs tumbled into a pit in the sea ice, 'and Mr Bellot after them, into an an abyss at the bottom, where the only indication of the catastrophe that could be seen was some six inches of Mr Bellot's heels above the surface of the snow. We dug him out "a wiser and a better man" for the rest of the journey' (Kennedy, 1953:97).

Yet only a short time later, when Kennedy almost dropped into a crack in the sea ice, he gratefully remarked: 'But for Mr Bellot's presence of mind, and the keener vision of his younger eyes, I verily believe that he and myself would then and there have ended our mortal career' (Kennedy, 1953:101).

And Kennedy's remarks concerning Bellot in his letter to the secretary of the Admiralty on his return to London, dated 9 October 1852, are unequivocally laudatory: referring to the main sledge journey he wrote:

> ... I cannot find words to express my admiration of the conduct of
> M Bellot, who accompanied me throughout this trying journey, direct-
> ing at all times the course by his superior scientific attainments, and at
> the same time taking an equal share with the men in dragging the sled,
> and ever encouraging them in their arduous labours by his native
> cheerful disposition (Kennedy, 1853:181).

His high regard for Bellot was certainly deserved. When Kennedy and a party of men became separated from the ship at Port Leopold in the fall of 1851, Bellot competently took charge of the ship, placed

her in safe winter quarters at Batty Bay, and after a couple of false
starts, led a sledge party to Port Leopold to rescue Kennedy and
party. The activities of Kennedy and Bellot on their spring sledge
trip in 1852 clearly demonstrate the stuff of which both men were
made. Between 25 February and 30 May they sledged south to Bellot
Strait (which they discovered), then west to Peel Sound, across Prince
of Wales Island to Ommanney Bay and back, then round the north
and east coasts of Somerset Island back to the ship at Batty Bay.
This sledge trip, covering some 1760 km was one of the longest of
any party during the Franklin search and provides ample proof that
in a crunch Bellot could certainly match de Bray's performance in
arctic sledging.

In striking contrast to the largely unadorned, factual narrative of
de Bray's journal (even after he had later reworked it for publication)
Bellot's narrative is long and tortuous, full of obscure philosophizing
and morose self-examination (Hodgson, 1974; Woodward, 1950). If
de Bray had any self-doubts he kept them to himself, although one
should note once again that as a naval officer he could anticipate
that his journal would be examined by his superior officer at the end
of the expedition, and wrote accordingly.

That Bellot's name is relatively well known (at least among those
with an interest in arctic history) while de Bray's name is practically
totally unknown is undoubtedly due to the contrasts in their careers
and fates. Bellot published a book about his first expedition which
was almost immediately translated into English (Bellot, 1855) and was
very popular in both languages. And most importantly, he died in
the Arctic. As we have seen, despite plans to publish his journal, de
Bray failed to do so, and he died in his bed at home. Bellot's memory
is honoured by a huge obelisk on the bank of the Thames near the
Royal Naval College at Greenwich and by a monument at Rochefort.
De Bray's achievements are commemorated only in the name of a
remote cape on the northwest coast of Melville Island.

The Fate of Franklin Discovered

It was probably a matter of real regret to de Bray that he and his
shipmates were unable to add anything to the knowledge of the
ultimate fate of the Franklin expedition. By a coincidence *Resolute*
and *Intrepid* were still in the Arctic when the first news of the
missing expeditions was obtained, by an overland expedition dispatched by the Hudson's Bay Company, and led by that redoubtable

traveller, Dr John Rae. His objective was to survey the west coast of Boothia Peninsula and the search for Franklin was only a secondary goal. Having wintered at Repulse Bay in the winter of 1853–4, on 21 April 1854, near Pelly Bay, Rae and his Inuit companions met an Inuk who reported that in the spring four years before, (i.e., in 1850), off an island some distance to the west, about forty white men were seen travelling south on the sea ice, dragging a boat and sledges with them (Rich and Johnson, 1953:274–5; Rae, 1855:831–9). Later that same season the Inuit had found about thirty bodies and graves at a site on the mainland and five bodies on an island nearby, about a day's journey northwest of the mouth of a large river, which Rae later identified as the Back River. Rae purchased from the Pelly Bay people a number of silver forks and spoons with crests identifiable as those of Robert Orme Sargent, mate aboard *Erebus*, Captain Francis Crozier of *Terror*, and of Sir John Franklin himself. He also bought a number of coins and assorted pieces of watches. None of the Pelly Bay people had seen the white men themselves, either dead or alive, but had heard the story from others, from whom they had also acquired the various items in trade. It was not until Rae returned to his winter quarters at Repulse Bay that he was able to determine through questioning the local Inuit that the disaster had occurred on King William Island and on Adelaide Peninsula. Had he known this earlier, he would presumably have tried to locate the various sites himself.

Rae's report of his discoveries reached John Barrow, second secretary to the Admiralty, on 24 October 1854. Only three days later their lords commissioners of the Admiralty were pressing the Hudson's Bay Company to send an expedition down the Back River to its mouth to investigate the details of what Rae had reported (Hamilton, 1855:846–7). As a result, an expedition led by Chief Factor James Anderson and James Stewart descended the Back River with two canoes in the summer of 1855 (Anderson, 1940–1). On 30 July 1855, just below the rapids at the outlet from Lake Franklin, they met a group of Inuit from whom they understood that a party of white men had starved to death on the coast after their ships had been wrecked. In their tents they found copper and tin kettles. They also found various pieces of poles and boards of ash, oak, white pine, and mahogany and the head of a pair of blacksmith's tongs. Communication was difficult for lack of a competent interpreter, so Anderson learned nothing about documents.

On 2 August Anderson and party found a variety of items which had clearly come from the missing ships in a cache on Montreal Island (Anderson, 1941:10–11); these included a tin kettle, a cold chisel, a shovel, a piece of wood with 'Erebus' on it and another with 'Mr Stanley' inscribed into it (Stanley was *Erebus*'s surgeon). Further progress by canoe was blocked by ice on 6 August and hence Anderson decided to walk on from this point on the east coast of Ogle Peninsula. Having reached Maconochie Island without finding further traces, on 8 August he reluctantly decided to turn back.

Despite these promising yet tantalizing clues as to the fate of the Franklin expedition, the Admiralty was not prepared to dispatch any further expeditions to discover the whole story; but Lady Franklin was certainly not yet ready to give up and in 1857 she mounted a private expedition. Captain Leopold McClintock sailed from Aberdeen aboard the yacht *Fox* on 2 July 1857 (McClintock, 1859). The vessel became beset in the ice of Melville Bukt and drifted south the full length of Baffin Bay and through Davis Strait over the winter of 1857–58. Once his ship broke free, McClintock headed north again and entered Lancaster Sound; the expedition spent its second winter in winter quarters in Port Kennedy at the east end of Bellot Strait.

During a sledge journey in February–March 1859 McClintock met a group of Inuit at Cape Victoria on the west coast of Boothia Peninsula, who were well aware that a group of whites had starved to death on an island to the southwest. They had various relics from the Franklin expedition in their possession: McClintock purchased silver spoons and forks, a silver medal which had belonged to Alexander McDonald, assistant surgeon aboard *Terror*, and several buttons (McClintock, 1859:233–4). The Inuit also reported that a ship with three masts had been crushed by the ice west of King William Island.

Having returned to his ship, on 2 April McClintock set off once again, accompanied by Lieutenant William Hobson, to make a thorough search of the shores of King William Island. On the west side of Boothia, some distance north of Cape Victoria, they encountered the same band of Inuit whom they had met a few weeks earlier. McClintock was now able to buy more items which had clearly come from *Erebus* and *Terror*. This time questioning revealed that two ships had been seen west of King William Island; one had been seen to sink in deep water; the other had been driven ashore by the ice.

At Cape Victoria on 24 April McClintock and Hobson separated; McClintock continued south down the east coast of King William

Island, aiming to travel clockwise around the island. Meanwhile Hobson headed straight for the west coast of the island, intending to confirm the report of a ship having been driven ashore there. On 7 May at an Inuit camp on the east side of King William Island McClintock saw and purchased six silver spoons and forks with crests or initials of Franklin, Crozier, Fairholme, and McDonald and a variety of other items from the missing ships. At a single snow house off Point Booth on 10 May he saw eight to ten fir poles, a kayak paddle made from two oar blades, and two large snow shovels, 1.2 metres long, made from what had probably been the bottom boards of a boat.

McClintock now cut south from Point Ogle to Montreal Island, which he searched carefully but where he found only a few metal remains. His party then headed west, crossed Point Ogle and Barrow Inlet, then cut northwest towards Simpson Strait, emerging a few kilometres west of Point Richardson. Crossing the strait on the sea ice, McClintock reached the coast of King William Island again, just west of the Peffer River. About midway between Gladman Point and Cape Herschel McClintock found the first skeleton. From the remains of the clothing he appeared to have been a steward or officer's servant. The skeleton was later identified as that of Harry Peglar, captain of the foretop aboard *Terror* (Cyriax and Jones, 1954).

Reaching Cape Herschel, McClintock easily located the massive cairn left there by Dease and Simpson in the summer of 1839 during their impressive canoe trip along the mainland coast. Some 19 kilometres west of here McClintock found a cairn which Hobson had left six days earlier. The most exciting part of the message left in the cairn was the news that he had found a document in a cairn at Point Victory. It was rather a complicated document, written by various hands on a standard printed form, in a number of languages, asking that the finder contact the Admiralty. The first part, evidently written by a small exploring party in the spring of 1847, read as follows:

28 of May 1847
H.M. Ships 'Erebus' and 'Terror' wintered in the ice in lat. 70° 05'N, long. 98° 23'W. Having wintered in 1846–47 at Beechey Island, in lat. 76° 43' 28"N, long. 91° 39' 15"W, after having ascended Wellington Channel to lat. 77°, and returned by the west side of Cornwallis Island.
Sir John Franklin commanding the expedition.
All well.

Party consisting of 2 officers and 6 men left the ships on Monday 24th
May, 1847.   Gm. Gore, Lieut
                                              Chas. F. Des Voeux, mate
                                              (McClintock, 1859:283–4).

As McClintock has pointed out, there is an obvious error in this
report since clearly, from the dates on the graves found there, the
ships wintered at Beechey Island in 1845–6 and not in 1846–7. However, the general tone of the record is quite positive, even optimistic.
But the remainder of the message, written almost a year later in
Crozier's handwriting around the margins of the document, is one of
disaster and despair:

> April 25, 1848. H.M. ships 'Terror' and 'Erebus' were deserted on the
> 22nd April, 5 leagues N.N.W. of this, having been beset since 12th
> September 1846. The officers and crews, consisting of 105 souls, under
> the command of Captain F.R.M. Crozier landed here in lat. 69° 37' 42"N,
> long. 98° 41'W. This paper was found by Lt. Irving under the cairn
> supposed to have been built by Sir James Ross in 1831, 4 miles to the
> northward, where it had been deposited by the late Commander Gore in
> June 1847. Sir James Ross' pillar has not, however, been found, and the
> paper has been transferred to this position, which is that in which Sir
> James Ross' pillar was erected.
>   Sir John Franklin died on the 11th June, 1847; and the total loss by
> deaths to the expedition has been to this date 9 officers and 15 men.
> (Signed) F.R.M. Crozier   James Fitzjames
> Captain and Senior Officer   Captain, H.M.S. Erebus
> and start tomorrow 26th for Backs Fish River (McClintock, 1859:286).

It has to be assumed from the closing phrase that Crozier planned
to ascend the Back River by boat, heading for the nearest Hudson's
Bay Company post, namely Fort Resolution on Great Slave Lake. It
lay almost two thousand kilometres from the point where the document was found, measured by the route which Crozier was proposing
to follow.

Encouraged by Hobson's message, McClintock continued his search
westwards and northwards round the coasts of the island. On 29
May he reached the western tip of King William Island, which he
named Cape Crozier, and on the 30th encamped beside a ship's boat,
which Hobson had already discovered, partly drifted over with snow.
It was mounted on a solid, heavy sledge; McClintock estimated the

total weight of boat and sledge at about 640 kilos. In the boat lay two skeletons (minus skulls), two double-barrelled guns, and some books, including a Bible and a copy of the *Vicar of Wakefield*. There was also a large amount of assorted clothing, seven or eight pairs of miscellaneous footwear, and an amazing array of twine, nails, saws, files, bristles, candle ends, sailmaker's palms, powder, bullets, shot, cartridges, wads, a leather cartridge case, clasp knives, dinner knives, needle and thread cases, lengths of slowmatch, bayonet scabbards cut down into knife sheaths, and two rolls of sheet lead. McClintock was astounded that any sledge party would have attempted to haul so much largely useless dead weight. The only signs of food were some tea and about 18 kilos of chocolate.

In terms of identifying the members of the party associated with the boat, some clues were provided by twenty-six silver spoons and forks; of these eight bore Franklin's own crest while the rest had the initials or crests of Gore, Le Vesconte, Fairholme, Couch, Goodsir, Crozier, Hornby, and Thomas. One of the watches bore the crest of Mr Couch of *Erebus*.

On the morning of 2 June McClintock reached Victory Point, where Hobson had found the note with the sketchy clues as to the final outcome of the expedition. Here McClintock placed a copy of the all-important record in the cairn, along with records of his own and Hobson's visits. Scattered all around was an incredible assortment of abandoned clothing and equipment which suggested that having sledged it all ashore, possibly over a fair length of time, the party had selected what was deemed essential for the sledge trip south and had abandoned everything else here. The discarded items included four sets of boat's cooking stoves, pickaxes, shovels, iron hoops, old canvas, a large single block, a small medicine chest, a Robinson dip circle, and a small sextant with the name 'Frederick Hornby' engraved on it. The abandoned clothing formed a heap 1.2 metres high. Every item was searched but all the pockets were empty and no names were marked on any of the clothing.

McClintock ended his own search here, although Hobson had earlier found two more cairns and relics between here and Cape Felix. Both men were convinced that the section of coast from Cape Crozier to Cape Felix had not been visited by the Inuit since the Franklin expedition had disintegrated here.

The following year yet another expedition set off in search of Franklin relics or survivors. The contrast with McClintock's search, or even more, with the massive operations of the Royal Navy, could scarcely have been greater. It was mounted by a single-minded American printer, Charles Francis Hall, who was convinced that some of Franklin's men had survived and were simply waiting in the Arctic to be rescued (Loomis, 1972). Hall's one-man expedition went north aboard the whaler *George Henry* in the summer of 1860, bound for the Frobisher Bay area; Hall's intention was to sledge west from there to the general area of King William Island. Unfortunately *George Henry* was wrecked and Hall was forced to restrict himself to a study of the Inuit and the landscape of the Frobisher Bay area (Hall, 1864).

Undaunted, two years later Hall headed north again, this time aboard the whaler *Monticello*, intending to start his search from Repulse Bay. He was to stay in the Arctic for five years. As early as September 1864 the Inuit at Repulse Bay told him of two ships which had been lost near Boothia Peninsula, and of their crews dying of starvation, although they also asserted that four men had survived (Nourse, 1879:64).

It was almost another two years before Hall heard anything more of the Franklin people. In June 1866 he was visited at his camp at Repulse Bay by a group of Inuit from Pelly Bay. One of the men told of how he had visited King William Island three years previously. He reported that he had found two cairns, one of which had contained a small 'tin cup,' evidently a record cylinder which had contained a paper; it had been given to the children or thrown away as being of no importance (Nourse, 1879:276). Nearby lay a skeleton and a pile of white man's clothing.

It was not until 10 April 1869 that Hall finally found some tangible relics of the Franklin expedition. At a Netsilik encampment at Pelly Bay he found a one-gallon stone jug, a copper *kudlik* (blubber lamp) measuring 75 x 30 centimetres and weighing about 2.5 kilos, a sword tip 10 centimetres long, and a wooden snow shovel made of spruce or pine; the Inuit said they had made the latter from a plank from a ship near King William Island. The ship had allegedly sunk soon after the Inuit made a hole in it to get timber out of it. Hall's Netsilik informant also reported that when the Inuit had discovered remains of whites on King William Island they had observed that arms, legs, etc., had been cut off with a saw, judging by the marks on the bones (Nourse, 1879:392).

On reaching the sea at Sheperd Bay on the west coast of Boothia, Hall encountered a further Netsilingmiut encampment; he was shown a large silver spoon with Franklin's eel-head crest, which had come from a large island where many whites had died. In one of the snow houses Hall was shown further articles from the Franklin ships, and their owner drew a map of King William Island and vicinity. The most interesting features and sites marked on the map were an island called Kee-wee-woo (O'Reilly Island) off which one of the ships had sunk; a site on the northwest side of King William Island where the Inuk had found two boats; a small island (Kee-u-na) off the southeast coast of King William Island (possibly one of the Todd Islands), where he had seen the remains of five whites, one of whom he believed was Too-loo-a (which may have been Crozier). Finally, a boat and the remains of a large number of whites had been found on a small island on the west shore of the inlet immediately west of Point Richardson (Nourse, 1879:398).

On the basis of these reports Hall decided to visit the Todd Islands. He reached them on 11 May. Unfortunately the islands now lay under deep snow and Hall was able to find only part of a human thigh bone. One of the Inuit accompanying Hall now reported that when he had first seen the five bodies here, they had been lying close to each other, fully dressed and unmutilated.

Hall next crossed to King William Island, where two more of Franklin's men were said to be buried. Near the mouth of the Peffer the Inuit uncovered a skeleton after digging away the snow. Hall hoisted the American flag to halfmast, built a cairn 1.5 metres high and fired a salute over the remains. A strong gale and deep snow inhibited any further search. On a long, low spit farther east the Inuit indicated the site where another white man was known to be buried. Deep snow covered this site too and Hall simply built a cairn without trying to locate the remains. Returning to the Todd Islands, Hall was forced to abandon his search because, to his frustration, his guides refused to go any farther. Hence he was unable to locate any further remains of the Franklin expedition. On the other hand he was able to collect a surprising number of reports from the Inuit concerning visits to one of the ships, and of seeing a group of whites dragging a boat on a sledge southwards on King William Island. Perhaps most intriguing were several references to whites having been seen alive on northern Melville Peninsula, and of a group of whites who survived for several years and then departed, heading south by way of Chesterfield Inlet. These various stories have been critically evaluated by Cyriax (1944), who has argued convincingly that these reports almost certainly represent confused recollections of Dr John Rae's travels on Melville Peninsula in 1847, and of his later travels to and around the Pelly Bay area in 1854, all of these possibly being further confused with recollections of meeting Sir John Ross and other members of the *Victory* expedition thirty years previously.

No doubt de Bray followed with enormous interest the newspaper accounts of these various expeditions and their findings over the years. It is a little ironic that the last expedition to make any really significant contribution to our knowledge of the fate of the Franklin expedition had not yet returned south when de Bray died. This was the expedition led by Lieutenant Frederick Schwatka of the US Third Cavalry, which sailed north aboard the whaling schooner *Eothen* in the spring of 1878 (Gilder, 1881; Stackpole, 1965; Klutschak, 1987).

The expedition had been provoked by rumours picked up from the Inuit by the American whaling captain Thomas Barry over the period 1871–6 at Repulse Bay and Marble Island, concerning 'a stranger in uniform who had visited them some years before, and who was accompanied by many other white men' (Gilder, 1881:3) and, more significantly, concerning a large quantity of papers which the uniformed stranger had left in a cairn, allegedly on an island in the Gulf of Boothia (Stackpole, 1965:13).

James Gordon Bennett, influential editor of the *New York Herald*, conceived the idea of fitting out an expedition to try to find this cache of documents. John B. Morrison, of the New York whaling firm, Morrison and Brown, offered the use of his schooner *Eothen*, under Captain Barry's command, to transport the expedition to Hudson Bay. And finally Judge Charles Daly, president of the American Geographical Society (of which Morrison was a member) arranged for the society to sponsor the expedition.

The expedition consisted of only four white members: Schwatka himself, Colonel William Gilder, acting as reporter for the *New York Times*, Heinrich Klutschak (who had previously wintered with the whalers at Repulse Bay) as artist and surveyor, and Frank Melms, who had also wintered previously at Repulse Bay. Two other important members of the expedition were 'Eskimo Joe' or Ebierbing and his wife Hanna (Tookolitoo), natives of the Cumberland Sound area, who had accompanied Hall on all his expeditions, and who spoke English well.

The expedition was landed (with minimal supplies) at Camp Daly (near Depot Island) on the northwest shores of Hudson Bay on 9 August 1878; several Inuit families settled near the expedition's camp, and the expedition members spent the fall and winter learning everything they could from the Inuit in terms of travelling and living in the Arctic.

Setting off with three dogteams and a total of seventeen people (including women and children) in April 1879, the party headed north across the interior of the Keewatin to the lower Hayes River (which Schwatka named after the president) and Committee Bay. Among the Netsilik camps along the northern shores of Adelaide Peninsula Schwatka and his companions began to run across innumerable items which could only have come from *Erebus* and *Terror*; the Inuit also told them numerous first-hand accounts of having seen survivors of the Franklin expedition. One old woman confirmed the report obtained earlier by Hall, that a box of papers had been found, but that they had been given to the children to play with (Klutschak, 1987:73).

Crossing to King William Island, Schwatka and his men searched the south and west coasts of that island as far north as Cape Felix. They found innumerable traces of the retreat of the Franklin expedition, including, near Victory Point, the desecrated grave of Lieutenant John Irving, one of *Terror*'s officers (Klutschak, 1987:83). His scattered remains were assembled and taken back south by Schwatka, for ultimate reburial in Edinburgh. The party also found the remains of the great heap of clothing, etc., which Hobson and McClintock had discovered, as well as the remains of the boat they had found, farther south. The Inuit had been at both sites and there was relatively little left, although Schwatka and his men did retrieve a substantial section of the stem of the boat. Near Victory Point one of the Inuit women in the party discovered the note which McClintock had left, along with his copy of the all-important document left by Gore and Crozier (Klutschak, 1987:86). And scattered along the shores of King William Island Schwatka and his party found numerous remains of human skeletons (estimated at being parts of between fifteen and thirty bodies, Klutschak, 1987:135) which were carefully gathered together and buried.

Having spent the late summer and autumn on the shores of Simpson Strait, the party started south again on 1 November. One party, led by Klutschak, at this point visited Starvation Cove, the location on the mainland where the scatter of skeletons and relics indicated that a boatload of the Franklin people had perished, indeed the most southerly significant concentration of such remains. Klutschak buried the remains and erected a cross-shaped cairn (Klutschak, 1987:132). The party then started back on the long trek to Camp Daly, travelling through temperatures of -50°C. They reached their goal on 4 March 1880, having covered a distance of 5,287 kilometres in eleven months! As the longest recorded sledge journey ever made by whites to that date, this sets the Schwatka expediton in a class by itself, quite apart from what it had added to the knowledge of the fate of Franklin.

Unfortunately de Bray had died only shortly before the party had set off northwards from Camp Daly in the spring of 1879. Hence he was not fated to learn of their various finds, which confirmed, in much greater detail, the clues which McClintock and Hobson had discovered twenty years earlier.

Report of Enseigne-de-vaisseau de Bray to the Minister of Marine

To the Minister of the Marine and the Colonies,
on board *Resolute*, Whalefish Islands,
28 May 1852

Dear Minister,

An opportunity has presented itself to write to France and I hasten to inform you of my arrival at the Whalefish Islands on the west coast of Greenland at 68° 59'N, 55° 50'W.

We left Woolwich where the ship had fitted out and proceeded to Greenhithe at the mouth of the Thames. There a committee led by the Duke of Northumberland came to inspect us and on 21 April we started for the Orkneys, towed by three steam frigates. On the 25th we reached the anchorage at Stromness where we lay for three days to take on fresh provisions and to await the arrival of a courier who was to bring the Admiralty's final orders to the Commander-in-Chief of the expedition, Sir Edward Belcher. On 28 April, still accompanied by the steam frigates, we set off for Cape Farewell. The steam frigates did not leave us until the 22nd W meridian, when they returned to England.

On 20 May after quite a pleasant crossing we sighted the first ice and on the following day we rounded Cape Farewell. From there to the Whalefish Islands the weather has been very fine although with much snow and a temperature of -5° Réaumur. We will probably lie at this anchorage for about two weeks since it is much too early to penetrate into Barrow Strait by swinging around Baffin Bay; in Barrow Strait we are to proceed to Cape Walker where we are to make a further call.

The squadron sent in search of Sir John Franklin consists of five vessels:

Assistance, 424 tons, 61 men, commanded by Sir Edward Belcher;
Resolute, 424 tons, 61 men, commanded by Captain Kellett;

North Star, 500 tons, 30 men, commanded by Captain Pullen;

Pioneer, steamer of 60 horse power, 30 men, commanded by Lieutenant Osborn;

Intrepid, steamer of 60 horse power, 30 men, commanded by Lieutenant McClintock.

The first two ships, *Assistance* and *Resolute* are rigged exactly like whalemen, but they have double planking, even on the decks, and the forward part of the hull has been reinforced by iron sheathing 2 cm thick, secured to the actual stem since the ship has no cutwater apart from what is necessary for securing the bowsprit gammonings (chains).

An economical stove located in the hold at the main hatchway distributes its heat via vents which have been cut at regular intervals throughout the length of the ship.

North Star, a former corvette with covered batteries, is fitted out in almost the same fashion. The two small steamers are screw vessels and have a good spread of canvas which allows them to keep up with the sailing vessels without burning coal, which it is necessary to husband as much as possible.

Every ship is supplied with provisions and and spare parts of every type to last for three years; in addition *North Star* carries a load of provisions which she is to cache at Beechey Island where she is to winter, and where there is already a depot of coal and provisions established by Captain Parry in 1848. It is at Beechey Island, too, that the ships are to separate: *Assistance* and *Pioneer* will ascend Wellington Channel while *Resolute*, the ship on which I am embarked, along with *Intrepid*, will head for Melville Island where if at all possible, we should have arrived and begun our wintering by around 15 September. *North Star* is to explore the entire expanse of ice lying north of Beechey Island.

The search can not begin until spring; our plan, as far as *Resolute* is concerned, is to make contact, either with the ship if she can proceed, or with sledges, with two other ships, *Enterprise*, Captain Collinson, and *Investigator*, Captain M'Clure, who sailed two years ago and have orders to head in our direction via Bering Strait. The distance to be covered to effect this meeting is not very great, 800 to 900 miles at most, but the route presents great difficulties and the length of the campaign will be dictated by whatever time is needed to cover that distance and then on our further operations, depending on what clues we may find as to the fate of the two ships, *Erebus* and *Terror*, commanded by Sir John Franklin.

From what I have managed to learn we are not to attempt to make new discoveries; our sole goal is to search the area allocated to each of the ships.

The crews consist of men who have already taken part in previous arctic expeditions or of men who have gone whaling in the polar seas; as a result they are all completely inured to the inclemencies of the climate and to the privations of all kinds which they will have to endure. All the ships are equipped with an electric telegraph so that they can communicate during the winter when they are beset in the ice and when movement from one ship to another is interrupted, as well as with an electric battery sufficiently powerful to blow up very thick ice and thus force a passage in case of necessity. We have also brought small balloons covered in coloured silk which will be sent in all directions and will serve as signals to indicate to the crews of Franklin's ships that a search is being mounted for them. The generally widespread belief in England is that *Erebus* and *Terror* have been crushed by the ice in a major onslaught and that having hurriedly abandoned the ships the men have established a camp where they are safely awaiting the ships which they are counting on being sent in search of them.

This then, Mr Minister, is for the moment all that is known to me and that might be of some interest concerning the expedition. If occasion arises in the future I shall keep you posted as to the various incidents of the campaign which, moreover, I am carefully noting day by day in a journal which I shall have the honour of presenting to you on my return.

Please accept, Mr Minister, the assurance of my deep respect.

E.F. De Bray,
Enseigne-de-vaisseau

Report of Enseigne-de-vaisseau de Bray to the Minister of Marine on the Expedition aboard 'Resolute'

Mr Minister,

I have the honour to address to you an account of the voyage of *Resolute*, one of the ships sent in search of Sir John Franklin and to which I was appointed by the British Admiralty.

Assistance, Sir Ed. Belcher;
Pioneer, tender, Captain Osborn;
Resolute, Captain Kellett;
Intrepid, tender, Captain McClintock;
North Star, Captain Pullen.

The five ships forming the arctic expedition under the command of Sir Edward Belcher left Woolwich on 16 April and proceeded to Greenhithe and from there to Stromness in the Orkney Islands, in order to await final orders. On 29 April we left the latter port, having on board provisions and fuel for three years, and being equipped with all the tools we will need to battle against the ice.

The first ice was sighted on 20 May 1852, about 50 miles north of Kap Farvel, but it did not impede our course, and on 29 May we reached the anchorage at Kron-Prins (the Whalefish Islands) on the west coast of Greenland. *Assistance, Resolute* and the two steamers completed their provisions from the transport *North Star* and on 5 June we left Kron-Prins for the better anchorage of Lively (Disko Island) where we arrived on the 6th. This place being one of the main Danish establishments in Baffin Bay we were easily able to procure Eskimo dogs, articles of clothing and sealskins for mocassins.

According to the information provided by the Governor at Lively the season was seen as being favourable and we attempted to pass through Waigat Strait between Disko Island and the mainland of Greenland. But we were blocked by ice and were obliged to retrace our route and to pass Disko on the west, northward bound for the settlement of Upernavik where we arrived on 19 June, encountering a large amount of pack ice and some icebergs.

On the evening of 20 June a strong snow squall forced us to put to sea hurriedly; *Resolute* escaped only by a miracle from being wrecked on reefs which are located at the entrance of the bay and which the thickness of the weather had prevented us from spotting.

From that date on we properly entered the ice, making our way through immense floes (or fields of ice) and attempting to push north along the west coast of Greenland. The steamers now demonstrated their enormous usefulness in navigation of this type; they would charge at the ice at full speed, acting like a wedge driven by an enormous force and forcing the ice to open a passage for us. Sometimes we were obliged to use mines and saws to cut a dock into which the ships could be hauled, thus sheltering them from the pressures caused by floes several miles in extent drifting before strong northerly and northwesterly winds which are common at that season. But on several occasions the ice drove down on us so rapidly that we were unable to execute this operation in time and the ships had to withstand violent pressures. On one of these occasions *Resolute* was heeled over violently to port and the ice piled up against the ship until it reached the chains. On 30 June we encountered the whalers at the entrance to Melville Bukt, where they were waiting for a favourable moment to cross to the west of Baffin Bay.

Finally, after a month of hard work and having had to battle against the embrace of the ice and against all the dangers of this type of navigation, *Resolute*, accompanied by *Intrepid* and *North Star*, reached Kap York on 1 August 1852. We had hoped to encounter *Assistance* and *Pioneer* there, since we had lost sight of them several days earlier; but on not finding them there we communicated with the Eskimos, giving them some gifts, and set a course for Cape Warrender, the northern cape at the entrance to Barrow Strait, the sea ahead of us being open. On 9 August we reached Beechey Island where *Assistance* and *Pioneer* joined us three days later. The island was carefully examined during our stay but nothing was discovered which might add to the ideas already obtained by the previous expedition. The three graves with inscriptions and dates prove beyond any doubt that Sir John Franklin spent a winter at Beechey Island, but everything else is a mystery since nothing has been found which might indicate what his intentions might have been as to the route he had resolved to follow.

Beechey Island having been chosen as the centre of future operations *North Star* received orders to prepare to take up winter quarters there while *Assistance* and *Pioneer*, under the command of Sir Edward Belcher, proceeded via Wellington Channel, leaving us and *Intrepid* to pursue our course westwards under the orders of Captain Kellett.

Crossing the entrance to Wellington Channel, we coasted along the south coast of Cornwallis Island; here *Resolute* ran aground but fortunately experienced no serious damage, losing only part of her false keel. Since the ice did not permit us to proceed westwards for long, we headed for Lowther Island where we were detained for twelve days. Finally, after a strong gale from the northwest which cleared the ice from the north shore of Barrow Strait, we set a course for Melville Island and on 7 September reached the entrance to Winter Harbour where Sir Edward Parry had wintered in 1819.

A depot of provisions was sent ashore for the use of the sledge parties which were to head in this direction in the following spring; then, retracting our steps, we took up our winter quarters here, 1 mile from Dealy Island. Preparations for the wintering began immediately and by 13 September the ice had formed around the ships.

Five sledge parties were immediately organized to advance depots of provisions in various directions; in command of one of these I set off on 22 September for Cape Providence, returning on board on 8 October. I arrived only a few days ahead of Lieutenant Mecham who returned with very important news.

Having carefully visited Winter Harbour he had found there a document left by Captain M'Clure of *Investigator*, containing the information that that ship had succeeded in forcing a passage through the ice from the west and, having coasted along the north coast of America had reached Banks Island in Barrow Strait, thereby solving the celebrated problem of the Northwest Passage.

On 4 November the sun disappeared below the horizon, not to reappear until 5 February 1853.

So as to pass the interminably long hours of winter as pleasantly as possible everything was put in hand to keep the men occupied; to this end a theatre and a school were established, as well as regular exercise hours, either on the floe when the weather allowed or on deck if it did not. A permanent system of ventilation was organized in all parts of the ship; using the stove this allowed us to maintain an approximately even temperature constantly. The lowest temperature recorded by the thermometer during this first winter was -52°C.

The early part of 1853 was used to make preparations for the spring journeys. The search plan was divided into four sections: Captain McClintock (of *Intrepid*) was charged with exploring northwestern Melville Island; Lieutenant Mecham, western Melville Island; Lieutenant Hamilton its eastern part; while Lieutenant Pim was to proceed to Mercy Bay, *Investigator*'s last known winter quarters.

Lieutenant Pim set off first, leaving the ship on 10 March with a sledge and seven men, accompanied by Dr Domville with a sledge and 6 dogs. On 4 April all the other sledges set off in their various directions and only seven men were left aboard the two ships under the charge to two officers. I was in charge of a sledge and 8 men and I accompanied Captain McClintock on the first part of his journey.

Crossing Melville Island we reached the head of Hecla and Griper Bay; from there we headed along the coast towards the northwest, carefully examining this coast. We thus reached 76° 30'N, 118°W (from Paris); here the land swung abruptly southwards giving us reason to think that we were about to meet Lieutenant Mecham who was heading west along the south coast of Melville Island. To avoid such an encounter Captain McClintock left Melville Island and headed off for a distant land mass which we had been seeing for some days to the northwest. I took leave of him on 2 May, leaving him with provisions for 56 days, and returned to the ship which I reached on 18 May; I brought back with me on my sledge one of my men who had died suddenly along the way.

During my absence Lieutenant Pim had returned, having found *Investigator* at Mercy Bay; when I arrived some of the crew of that ship were already aboard *Resolute*. The last officer to return aboard was Captain McClintock, after an absence of 105 days during which he had explored 1,148 miles of coast.

Lieutenant Mecham had been away from the ship for 94 days and had explored 1,006 miles; Lieutenant Hamilton had explored 585 miles in 54 days, and in so doing had made contact with a sledge sent out by *Assistance* to the rendezvous.

No trace of Sir John Franklin had been found by these various officers despite their exertions and their careful examination of the coasts; it now appears evident that *Erebus* and *Terror* never advanced their search in the direction of Melville Island.

Preparations for sea were started immediately after the sledges had returned; at the same time the internal arrangements of the ship were altered to accommodate the officers and men of *Investigator*. A house had been built on Dealy Island and in it were depos-

ited 200 days' provisions for 66 men; these were to be for the use of
Captain Collinson of *Enterprise* in case he was obliged to abandon
his ship. A mast was placed on the summit of the island to attract
the attention of any travellers who might pass within sight and a
tin box containing all the documents concerning our ship was attached to it.

Finally, at 1:00 a.m. on 18 August 1853 the ice began to move under the influence of a violent northwesternly wind and in the short
space of three hours we were under sail, eastward bound, and all
the signs promised a fast run back to Beechey Island. But we were
not taking the ice into consideration and it soon brought us to a
halt off the east coast of Melville island and held us there until 10
September. Since the season was advancing rapidly it was decided
to make a last effort and taking advantage of a fresh northerly wind
we cast off our moorings and headed southeast where we had spotted a wide expanse of open sea through the fog. We made only very
slow progress, despite the use of steam, due to the ice which had
started to form and in some places had reached a thickness of 5 cm. By
12 September, the ship having been brought up standing despite all
our efforts and a very fresh wind, we began to realize that our return
home was a very uncertain proposition. But we did not abandon all
hope until 26 September; we then began to prepare our winter quarters in the middle of Barrow Strait at 74° 4′N, 103° 43′W (from Paris);
since the 12th we had drifted a distance of 180 miles with the ice, or
69 miles eastwards in a straight line.

During this second wintering every effort was made to maintain
the health of the men; there were very many more of us than in the
previous winter, since we had the crew of *Investigator* in addition.
With the aid of the fresh meat which we had been able to procure
on Melville Island we were able to avoid scurvy, which occurred
only to a very minor degree.

On 4 March 1854 a sledge was dispatched to Beechey Island to
make contact with Sir Edward Belcher; it returned on 11 April
bringing orders to abandon *Resolute* and *Intrepid* and to bring the
men to Beechey Island where *North Star* was still lying.

The ships were prepared towards that end; they were made ready
for sea, properly trimmed and with the steam engine ready to go, so
that in the event that we encountered them as we emerged from
Barrow Strait we would find them in a state to be reoccupied.

On 8 May I left the ship, in charge of the sick and reached Beechey
Island on the 25th; three days later Captain Kellett of *Resolute* also

arrived with all the officers and men of both ships.

On 3 April two sledges had been sent off: one, under the command of Lieutenant Mecham was bound for the Princess Royal Islands in Price of Wales Strait (*Investigator's* first winter quarters) to check that *Enterprise*, following in the tracks of the latter, had not reached the same goal. The other sledge, commanded by Mr Krabbé, master of *Intrepid*, was bound for Mercy Bay to see what state *Investigator* was in.

These two officers, who had been informed of the abandonment of *Resolute* and *Intrepid* by Lieutenant Hamilton, who had been sent to meet them with that aim, headed straight back to Beechey Island where they arrived on 12 May.

In the depot at Princess Royal Islands Lieutenant Mecham had found a document deposited by *Enterprise*, indicating that Captain Collinson had followed the same route as *Investigator* along the coast of America and had reached those same islands; finding Prince of Wales Strait blocked by ice he had tried to round Baring Island on the west in order to gain entry to Barrow Strait but unable to succeed in this had been obliged to retrace his steps and take up winter quarters in Walker Bay in August 1851. Lieutenant Mecham headed south with a view to reaching Walker Bay if possible; on reaching Ramsey Island he found a further document which reported that Captain Collinson's intention was to continue his voyage by hugging the coast of America, and to try to penetrate east through Dolphin and Union Strait. Having obtained these important documents Lieutenant Mecham immediately retraced his steps; with this stimulus he achieved a journey unique in the annals of arctic travel, covering a distance of 1,157 geographical miles in 70 days, 8 days of which were spent weatherbound in the tent.

I was immediately sent with a sledge and a team of 10 dogs to carry this news to the commander-in-chief aboard *Assistance* which was lying north of Cape Osborn in Wellington Channel. I covered this distance of 60 miles in 12 hours; having remained aboard *Assistance* for 2 days I returned to Beechey Island.

The wind blew from the east for almost a month, preventing any movement in the pack and it was not until 15 August that the ice around Beechey Island cleared out.

On the 26th Sir Edward Belcher arrived aboard *North Star* with his crew and that of *Pioneer*, having been obliged to abandon *Assistance*.

On that very same day we were surprised by the arrival of a

steamer, *Phoenix*, Captain Inglefield, and of a transport *Talbot*. The provisions brought by the transport were immediately deposited ashore in the depot house and on 27 August we left Beechey Island; *Phoenix*, to which Captain Kellett and I had transferred, took *North Star* and *Talbot* in tow.

We were favoured by magnificent weather for crossing Baffin Bay and we saw very little ice. On 6 September, we arrived at Lievely (Disko Island) having first called at Navy Board Inlet and Ponds Bay.

Having taken aboard all our coal at Lievely, we sailed from that harbour on 12 September, bound for England; on the 28th we spotted Cape Clear in the south of Ireland.

It will always be a source of great pleasure for me to recall my sojourn aboard *Resolute*, where the excellent Captain Kellett and all the officers tried by every means in their power to make me forget that I was among strangers.

If you wish, Mr Minister, I would consider it an honour to send you a more detailed report on my voyage as soon as I have put all my notes in order and have finished some drawings to illustrate the voyage.

I hope, Mr Minster, that I have met your expectations, having upheld worthily the honour of the French Navy through my conduct.

I am, respectfully, Mr Minister, your humble and very obedient servant.

E.F. de Bray,
Enseigne-de-vaisseau

Letter from Enseigne-de-vaisseau de Bray to His Mother

At sea, on board *Resolute* ...

Dear Mother,

In the hope that we will encounter some whalemen who may take charge of our mail I shall start this letter without knowing when it will reach you, but better late than never. Thus far the voyage has not been very interesting, but at least there is the element of novelty for me and here are some details which may interest you ...

My last letter was dated from my arrival at a little port called Krons-Prins in the Whalefish Islands, a Danish settlement which consists of about thirty Eskimos and a few Danes who hunt seals whose oil and skins are carefully harvested. The appearance of this country is far from pleasant; there is no vegetation; it is all rock and ice and walking is extremely difficult, seeing that one sinks to the waist in the snow at every step ... The inhabitants of this charming country are as beautiful as it is. They live in a sort of cellar dug in the ground; a sort of roof is constructed of sods in the shape of a somewhat flattened dome, 3 or 4 feet thick; I can state without lying that there is not a single animal which would want to live in such a den. The door is so low that one is obliged to crawl in, and before reaching the hut one passes through a passage as low as the door and usually with a right-angled elbow so as to allow as little air as possible to enter. The bed consists of a few sealskins and reindeer skins on which the entire family sleeps jumbled together. The clothing of men and women is approximately the same and is made entirely from sealskin. It consists of a close-fitting jacket, the only openings of which are at the neck and the sleeves, pants which extend a little below the knee and mocassins; the hair side is always outside except for the footwear. In winter they also wear beneath this another complete suit made from reindeer skin, while a hood covers the head so that one can see only the oval of the face. The men have no particular hairstyle; they leave their hair long and tangled, full of seal oil which gives them a foul stench. The women are a little cleaner; they wear their hair in a Chinese style; they pile their hair on the top of the heads in a clump which they tie up with the prettiest ribbon which they can obtain. Women with children at the breast have a large pouch contrived in the back of their jackets the entrance to which is via the hood; the child is placed in this hood in such a way as to leave the mother's movements entirely free. The Eskimos live on seal meat which they dry to preserve it, since the winter is often too rigorous to allow them to leave their huts; sometimes they are besieged by famine. In that case they use their dogs for food although this is a great sacrifice for them since these animals represent their main form of wealth. They harness them to sledges and can cover up to 15 to 20 leagues per day across the ice. You will see from this description that our visits to the local inhabitants are quite rare since it is impossible to stay in their huts for more than 5 minutes; even then one emerges suffering from a terrible nausea. I left this place on 5 June; that evening we were anchored at another Danish settlement called Lievely on the coast of Disko Island. This settlement is the centre for all the operations which this nation undertakes on the Greenland coast; the inhabitants are almost all half Danish and are a little more civilized than the others. Their houses are made of wood and are quite clean, to the extent that one can contemplate visiting them ...

The bay where we are anchored is surrounded by high mountains; on the morning of 7 June, along with two other officers I undertook the project of climbing one of them. We set off immediately with our guns and some provisions; after six hours of walking, all uphill, and helping oneself up on hands and knees we reached the summit which was covered with snow; I estimate its height at 2,500 feet above sea level. After we had recovered somewhat we began looking for a route we could descend down another side. For most of the route we were wading through waist-deep snow, greatly hampered by our guns which were not of much use to us, since we encountered only a solitary fox, at which we were unable to fire since our guns were full of snow. Finally at 10 p.m. I found a route which seemed not quite as bad as the rest, but it still looked so uninviting that my two companions positively refused to try it. Despite this I attempted the descent; ten minutes later I was in a very embarrassing position being able neither to descend nor climb back. I took my courage in my hands and sliding down the snow on my back I was lucky enough to encounter a rock and was able to cling on to it with all my strength in order to slow my speed, since I was travelling much too fast. Having overcome the bad section there was only a slope of soft, shallow snow which I descended in 30 minutes. My two companions finally found a route which they judged to be less dangerous and did not arrive back until three hours after me; during this time I had walked to the houses where I was fortunate enough to meet the officers from *Assistance* who offered me a glass of whisky; I was in great need of it since I had been on the move for 15 hours during which I had had only a piece of cheese and biscuit and a little brandy to sustain myself. I can assure you that that evening I retired to my bed with great pleasure and that it was not long before I fell asleep.

On 10 June we left Lievely and proceeded to Upernavik, which lies a little farther north at 72° 50′N, 58° 35 W (from Paris). During this passage, which took us nine days we encountered a great deal of drift ice which blocked our passage and forced us to work our way through it. Fortunately the ice was only 3 or 4 feet thick and we were able to break through it fairly easily; on the other hand we were sometimes blocked by icebergs as high as the ship's masts, and which we were forced to circumvent ...

At this port of call something quite unpleasant happened to me. I had gone ashore with another officer to purchase some Eskimo boots and other very useful items; the wind was quite fresh and the Commander set a rendezvous for the boat to pick us up at 8 p.m. Having taken care of all our business, around 7 o'clock we started back for the shore since the huts lay quite far from the anchorage, behind a small hill. Reaching the summit of this hill; we were quite astonished to see *Resolute* and the little steamer *Pioneer* under sail and hurrying to leave the bay, with *Pioneer* missing a mast. We then signalled to *Assistance* to come to pick us up since the wind had become very strong and the snow was fallng so thickly that one could barely see 50 paces at times, but apparently it was not judged convenient to do so, since we were left for two hours, our backs to a rock trying to shelter as much as possible from the wind and snow ... Finally we were spotted and a boat from *Intrepid* which had been aboard *Assistance*, charitably came to pick us up. We spent the night aboard that vessel, somewhat more comfortably than we would have done on the rocks. Next day we returned aboard *Resolute* where we learned that the night before the wind had become so violent that the moorings had snapped; *Pioneer*, which had been lying to leeward, had been unable to avoid *Resolute* as the latter drifted down on her, and had lost one of her masts. On 20 June we left Upernavik bound for Melville Bay. Until 30 June there was nothing of interest to relate, except that every other moment we were brought up by ice which we were obliged either to saw through or blow up. Today, as I end my letter so abruptly we have just encountered a ship crushed by the ice and we have just spotted a ship to which I am sending this letter ...

Goodbye, dear Mother, give everyone a hug for me. All the best to all our friends. Tell Georges that I am making a collection for him, and please accept a thousand big kisses from your son who loves you with all his heart.

E.F. de Bray
30 June 1852

Latitude 75° 30' N   30 June 1852
Longitude 60° W   On board *Resolute*, in ice

I have reopened my letter since the ship we sighted is an American and we will not be passing any mail to her; I shall continue my report. This morning we spotted the wreck of a ship alongside a floe; we stopped immediately and established that in all probability the ship had been caught between two floes and literally crushed, probably two days before when *Resolute* all but experienced the same fate. On that day we were already preparing to grab our bags when the ship righted herself, but I can assure you that we had a narrow escape. In any case we all have our bags packed with some clothes and some food since that sort of incident is quite a common occurrence and one has to be ready for all eventualities ... The ship which had thus been crushed was British; her entire crew had been picked up by another whaler which we now sighted in company with several others but quite far away; we will not reach them until this evening ... I hope to find a French vessel among these whalemen, since I need several things which I forgot to buy in England. In particular I need glasses with coloured lenses, the most indispensable thing one can bring to these regions since the reflection of the sun off the snow blinds one and sometimes damages one's vision not to the point that one is permanently blind but that one can not look steadily at an object which is at all bright.

2 July 1852

We have been beset for two days along with the whalers and I do not know when my letter will leave since it is one of these ships, *Treuleove,* which will probably take it. At this point I can scarcely write; yesterday while out hunting on the ice I fell into the water and I can assure you that a bath at 4 or 5 degrees below zero is far from warm. In addition I have a terrible pain in my right arm and shoulder and I can scarcely move them. In any case I am closing this letter since the mailbag may be closed at any moment and I do not want to be late. Goodbye again, my dear Mother; take leave of yourself; my normal refrain as usual. My compliments to Mr Vogel and hug my aunts and uncles for me as well as all the children. I hope that Monsieur Fremy is pleased with Georges and that he is giving you some peace; hug him for me too.

Your son who loves you dearly,

E.F. de Bray

When you receive this letter, around October or November you can tell yourself: Emile is really cold since we will be at a season when one can barely put one's nose outdoors: 30 or 40 degrees below zero if not even colder ...

My sketching is poor since I am in a hurry, but this will give you an idea. [In the original the drawing reproduced in Plate 7 appeared above this line.]

Letter from Enseigne-de-vaisseau de Bray to His Mother

Melville Island, 2 April 1853

Dear Mother,

I finally have a chance hurriedly to write you a few lines; it has just been decided that a sledge will be sent with mail; it has little chance of arriving but at least it is worth the attempt ... You must have been anxious as to my fate since it is a very long time since my last letter dated from Melville Bay must have reached you and since then many events have occurred. But, thank God, I am in good health and have not suffered in the slightest since I left; so please rest assured on that point. I can not give you any great amount of detail on our voyage since I am pressed for time because tomorrow at 6 a.m. we leave on our spring explorations which are the major goal of our expedition. The Commander, who has been exceptionally kind to me, has entrusted me with the command of a sledge; I will be supporting the captain of the steamer *Herald* [sic], which is accompanying us; he himself will be commanding another sledge with orders to search the northwest coast of Melville Island. I will have about 500 miles to cover which will take 2 months of heavy work since although it is April the temperature is 29° centigrade below zero and since during the journey we will be sleeping on the ground covered by as light a tent as possible. These sledges, hauled by 7 men, must be as light as possible since we have to carry 2 or 3 months' provisions and I consider myself very lucky that my crew have only 230 lbs per man to haul. As you may judge this is not child's play since there are all sorts of dangers, especially bad weather, which is always accompanied by severe cold. It is not uncommon for one to have a foot or a hand frozen, but with the precautions one takes nowadays it is only a careless person who will find himself in this situation. For my own part this past winter, the worst I had to complain about was the loss of my nose for a week but, thank God, it returned to its natural state and shows no ill effects. We have survived the most severe winter ever experienced by any expedition in the polar seas; in January the temperature dropped to 54 degrees below zero, a totally unbearable temperature, I can assure you. However during these three months of winter during which we have not seen the sun at all, we have had to find amusements so as not to let the men languish in a mental idleness which is always fatal, especially in this climate. A theatre was set up and inconceivable though it might sound, we enacted several plays on the deck despite the temperature; the deck was roofed in with a very heavy tent and heated by two small stoves which raised the temperature to 10° below zero. I myself played the role of a woman, disguised as a Bloomer-girl; I assure you I was superb ...

Despite all these amusements, dear Mother, this is a hard life and I hope that we do not spend next winter here. It is impossible to say whether we will return to Europe this season, since an unforeseen circumstance has changed our plans. Last autumn we found on the coast of Melville Island a document which told us that *Investigator*, a British ship sent out by Bering Strait to discover the Northwest Passage, has succeeded in making her way along the north coast of America, and is wintering in our vicinity off a coast which she had discovered, about 160 miles from where we are located. A sledge has been sent to that spot and if the ship is still there, we will have to take her crew aboard and return promptly to England, since they are now on short rations having been out for three years. Alternatively we will have to find out where they have gone in order to assist them. To tell you the truth the length of the expedition has not been specified, but it cannot last beyond 1854. If we leave this spot it will not be before August since the ice will not begin to release us before that time, and we cannot be in England before October, perhaps even before this letter, whose only chance of reaching you is by way of the British whalers.

Now, dear Mother, let us talk a little about yourself; I hope that you are perfectly well and happy with Georges who, I have no doubt, is making a great fuss over you, since he has to fill that duty for both of us. You can tell him that he will be rewarded by the curios which I will bring back for him for science. I want to find you as happy as possible when I come back hence, dear Mother, none of those moments of sadness in which I have sometimes seen you, and which filled me with despair; grasp every opportunity for distraction which your friends, I am sure, will be keen to offer you.

Since I cannot write to everyone, show my letter to Aunt Adèle, Aunt Louise and finally to all those who take some interest in me. When you see Mr Bucquet at the ministry show him my letter, too, and remind him of me; he will show you on the map the spot where I spent last winter, i.e. at 75° latitude North and 110° 30′ longitude West. It is impossible for me to write to the ministry, since I have a very long report to write. I believe it will perhaps be better to present my journal to the Minister, since it has been written day-by-day with all possible details, as well as some sketches representing the different events of our progress through the ice.

I hope that Mr Vogel is as well as possible and that the chance I predicted for him has been realized despite all the obstacles he had to overcome. If, as I hope, they have been crowned with success I will say to him: better late than never since in this world talent often goes unrecognized and hence, when one triumphs one deserves double merit, that for one's talent and that for having opened the eyes of a large number of ignorant people who, unfortunately form a good part of the population. In anticipation that I may be able to add the deed to my words I send him a hearty handshake. The same to all my friends. Hug all the family for me, my aunts, uncles, Camille who I hope has come back home, Marie, Maurice and Lucie, in order of age and not of my affection since I love them all equally. Give Georges his share of hugs too; he will find appended just two words which I recommend to his close attention.

Goodbye, dear Mother, I embrace you, as I love you, i.e., from the bottom of my heart, and I yearn for the moment when I can hold you in my arms, and I hope that will be soon.

Your son,
F.E. de Bray

If Francis is in France, shake his hand for me, and that of his brother ...

When you write to St Petersburg do not forget to send some details to Papa and Maman Borrel and be sure to tell them that I embrace them with all my heart.

Do not pay too close attention to the French in this letter; I am so completely English that I have reached the point where I have had to look up some words in the dictionary.

Here is a hurriedly drawn map to show you the new discoveries and the location where I spent the winter. [The map reproduced as Plate 29 appears beside this line in the original of the letter.] If you follow the dotted line from the ship this will give you the direction in which I must march on the trip which I shall start tomorrow and which will take me through totally unknown terrain.

This map is based on the Greenwich meridian (ship's position: 75°N, 109°W).

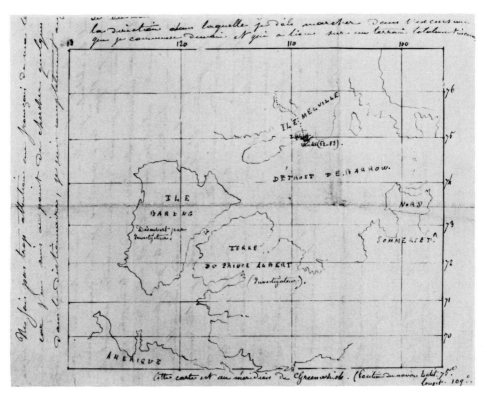

Plate 29 De Bray's sketch-map to accompany his letter to his mother dated 2 April 1853

Notes

Introduction

1 In 1818 Sir John Ross was dispatched by the Admiralty with two ships, *Isabella* and *Alexander*, to search for a Northwest Passage by way of Baffin Bay. The ships rounded Kap Farvel on 26 May and crossed Melville Bukt. Ross spotted the entrances of both Smith and Jones sounds but decided that neither of them promised a through route. Entering Lancaster Sound on 30 August, he shortly afterwards sighted mountains ahead which he named the Croker Mountains and hence decided that this, too, was a dead end (although the junior captain, William Parry, did not see the mountains and thought there was a passage west). The two ships coasted south along the coast of Baffin Island then headed for home (Ross, 1819).

Also in 1818 the Admiralty dispatched two ships northwards: *Dorothea* under the command of David Buchan and *Trent* under the command of John Franklin; their aim was to reach the Pacific Ocean from Svalbard by way of the North Pole. After visiting various sites on the coast of Spitsbergen the two ships pushed north to 80° 34′N before being blocked by impassable ice. They were beset for some time and after extricating themselves were damaged by ice during a gale. After calling at Spitsbergen to repair the damage, they started for home on 30 August (Beechey, 1843).

2 Parry commanded two bomb-vessels, *Hecla* and *Griper*, the latter under the command of Matthew Liddon. In the spring of 1820, using a cart pulled by twelve men, he made a trip overland across Melville Island, reaching and exploring the southern shores of Hecla and Griper Bay and the east end of Liddon Gulf (Parry, 1821).

3 On this, his first overland expedition, supported by the Hudson's Bay Company, Franklin travelled with a small party by the company's standard canoe route from York Factory via Cumberland House and Fort Chipewyan to Fort Providence. Having wintered at Fort Enterprise, the base which they built at treeline at the west end of Winter Lake, in the spring of 1821 the party descended the Coppermine River

by canoe, then coasted east along the shores of Coronation Gulf,
Bathurst Inlet, and Melville Sound. Owing to dwindling supplies
and unrest among the Québécois canoemen they turned back at
Turnagain Point on Kent Peninsula. It was decided to return to base
overland via the Hood River, Kathawachaga Lake, Contwoyto Lake,
and Point Lake. This trip became a dreadful ordeal. Altogether ten of
the party died, mainly of starvation; Lieutenant Hood was murdered
by an Iroquois canoeman, who in turn was executed by Dr John
Richardson. Reaching Fort Providence on 11 December 1821 the
survivors were nursed back to health by the local Indians and returned
to York Factory and England in the spring and summer of 1822
(Franklin, 1823; Houston, 1974, 1984).

4 During this second expedition, on which his second-in-command was
Captain George Lyon, Parry and his officers established close and
generally harmonious relations with the Inuit of the area. Hence their
narratives, but especially Lyon's, provide the first fairly detailed
account of the Inuit of the Central Arctic (Parry, 1824; Lyon, 1824).

5 Captain Frederick Beechey (HMS *Blossom*), was ordered to proceed to
Bering Strait and then await the arrival of Parry and/or Franklin,
coming from the east, through the summer and autumn of 1826.
Calling at Petropavlovsk in June–July 1826 Beechey learned that Parry
had already returned home, but it was assumed that Franklin might
still be on his way west to Bering Strait. Sailing north through that
strait, *Blossom* pushed north to Icy Cape; from there a boat under the
command of Thomas Elson coasted north to Point Barrow. He
rejoined *Blossom* in Kotzebue Sound on 9 September and a month
later *Blossom* sailed for home (Beechey, 1831; Gough, 1973).

6 On this, his second overland expedition, on which he was again
accompanied by Dr John Richardson, Franklin travelled by the fur
trade route to Great Slave Lake then down the Mackenzie River in
the summer of 1825. Having wintered at Fort Franklin on Great Bear
Lake, in June 1826 the party descended the Bear River and the
Mackenzie and split into two groups at the head of the Mackenzie
Delta on 4 July 1826. Franklin and George Back headed west along the
coast, but with winter approaching, turned back at Return Reef (148°
52'W) only 250 km from Point Barrow. They were back at Fort Franklin
by 21 September. Meanwhile Richardson and Edward Kendall coasted
eastward to the mouth of the Coppermine. Then they returned
overland to Great Bear Lake. The entire party then returned to England
over the winter of 1826–7 (Franklin, 1828).

7 Born in Halifax, Nova Scotia, in 1799, Belcher moved to England with
his family in 1811 and entered the navy as a first class volunteer the
next year. During postings to various ships on the Atlantic coast, the
West Indies, Africa, and the Home station he studied surveying and
natural history. His first major assignment was as assistant surveyor

aboard *Blossom*, under Captain Beechey (Stuart-Stubbs, 1972).

8 On his third expedition, once again aboard *Fury* and *Hecla*, Parry was badly delayed by ice and weather in Baffin Bay and was baulked by ice in his attempts to push south in Prince Regent Inlet, and wintered at Port Bowden on the west coast of Brodeur Peninsula. Soon after getting under way next season, in early August, *Fury* was driven ashore at Fury Point on Somerset Island and had to be abandoned. Both crews returned home aboard *Hecla* (Parry, 1826).

On his last expedition Parry tried to reach the North Pole from Svalbard using boats fitted with runners. He arrived aboard *Hecla* off the north coast of Svalbard on 14 May, where *Hecla* was beset for three weeks. Finding a suitable harbour for the ship at Sorgfjorden, Parry set off with his two boats on 21 June, at first in open water, then across the ice. After several weeks of effort Parry realized that the ice drift was carrying them south faster than they were travelling north. He turned back on 27 July at 82° 40'N, a record which would stand for fifty years (Parry, 1828).

9 John Ross's second expedition, aboard *Victory*, was a private endeavour, financed by Sir Felix Booth. With his nephew James Clark Ross as second-in-command Ross entered Prince Regent Inlet on 11 August. *Victory* settled down in winter quarters in Felix Harbour on the east side of the Isthmus of Boothia. During a sledge journey in the spring of 1830 James Ross discovered King William Island. The ice did not break up through the summer of 1830 and *Victory* spent a second winter in the same location. Ice conditions were still bad in the summer of 1831 and *Victory* covered only 25 km before being beset again and hence the expedition was forced to spend a third winter in the Arctic. In the spring of 1832 *Victory* was abandoned and her crew travelled north with the ship's boats to Fury Beach on Somerset Island. Picking up *Fury's* boats, the party set out on 1 August by boat, hoping to encounter a whaling vessel. When ice blocked the exit from Prince Regent Inlet they turned back and spent a fourth winter in a hut they built at Fury Beach. On 15 August 1833 they again set off in the boats and were picked up by Ross's former ship, *Isabella*, now a whaler, on 26 August in Lancaster Sound (Ross, 1835).

10 Early in 1833 George Back, who had participated in both of Franklin's overland expeditions, was dispatched to Great Slave Lake to search for John Ross, who by then had been missing for four years, by way of a river which, according to Indian report, rose near Great Slave Lake and entered the Arctic Ocean. Reaching Great Slave Lake via the fur trade route, Back made a reconnaissance in the autumn of 1833, during which he located the headwaters of the Great Fish River (now the Back River). Returning to Great Slave Lake, where a support party had built winter quarters at Fort Reliance, he received news that Ross was safe. He decided to explore the Great Fish River in any case.

Having built a boat on Artillery Lake, Back's party portaged to the
head of the Great Fish River and descended it to its mouth (in
Chantrey Inlet), then returned to Fort Reliance. After another wintering they returned to New York and England (Back, 1836).

11 In 1837 Peter Dease and Thomas Simpson, both employees of the
Hudson's Bay Company, were dispatched by the company to explore
all the still unexplored portions of the north coast of America.
Descending the Mackenzie River by canoe, they reached its mouth on
9 July 1837. Heading west they passed Return Reef (Franklin's farthest) on 23 July. Simpson completed the final four-day journey to
Point Barrow on foot. Returning to Great Bear Lake they wintered at
Fort Confidence on the northeast shores of the lake then, starting on
6 June 1838, they crossed to the Coppermine and descended it to the
sea, where they turned eastwards. Ice blocked their progress at
Turnagain Point but Simpson continued on foot to Cape Alexander
on Kent Peninsula. After another winter at Fort Confidence they
repeated their attempt to explore the coast eastwards in the summer
of 1839, pushing east almost to the mouth of the Murchison River on
the west coast of Boothia Peninsula; en route they discovered
Simpson Strait and on the return journey surveyed parts of the south
coast of Victoria Island (Simpson, 1843).

12 De Bray is in error here. The closest that Dr John Rae ever came to
Bathurst Inlet would have been when he searched the south coast of
Victoria Island for traces of the Franklin expedition in the spring and
summer of 1851 (Rich and Johnson, 1953: 180–214).

13 De Bray's narrative contains a few minor errors. In fact, the combined
complements of the two ships when they sailed from England was
134 men. Five were invalided home to England from Greenland and
hence 129 men proceeded on from there (Cyriax, 1939:28). Franklin's
last dispatch to the Admiralty, sent back with the transport *Baretto
Junior* was dated 12 July 1845, at the Whalefish Islands (Cyriax,
1939:62–63). And finally, he was last sighted in late July.

14 Now Wollaston Peninsula, southwestern Victoria Island.

15 Born in Paris in 1826, Joseph-René Bellot grew up in Rochefort and
attended the École Navale at Brest. As a naval cadet he sailed aboard
the corvette *Berceau* for the Indian Ocean in 1844. He was seriously
wounded in a joint English-French attack on the port of Tamatave
(Madagascar) in June 1845, and for his part in the action was made a
Chevalier de la Légion d'Honneur.

   After the Franklin expedition disappeared Bellot became intensely
interested in the Royal Navy's search for the missing ships and
offered his services to Lady Franklin. *Prince Albert* sailed from
Aberdeen on 22 May 1851. On reaching Port Leopold Captain Kennedy
landed but became separated from his ship. Bellot took the ship south
to Batty Bay, Somerset Island, established winter quarters, then,

pushing north overland, rescued his captain. During a sledge trip next spring Prince of Wales Island was searched and Bellot discovered Bellot Strait (Kennedy, 1853; Bellot, 1855).

1 The Outward Voyage

1 HMS *Assistance* and her identical sister ship, HMS *Resolute* had been built especially for Captain Horatio Austin's search for the Franklin expedition in 1850-1. Massively built of African oak, they were barque-rigged and had a displacement tonnage of 410 tons (Dunbar, 1961).

2 Henry Kellett was born at Clonacody in Tipperary on 2 November 1806. He entered the navy in 1822 and after five years service in West Africa was appointed to the survey vessel *Eden* under Captain William Owen. After four years aboard her in West African waters, in the summer of 1831, now a lieutenant, he was appointed to the surveying vessel *Aetna* under Captain Sir Edward Belcher. In 1835 he pursued survey work off the west coast of South America, then from 1840 surveys of the Zhu Jiang (Pearl River) and the Yangtze-kiang in connection with the hostilities in China. Promoted captain in 1842, in February 1845 he was given command of *Herald*, a small frigate dispatched to carry out survey work in the Pacific, especially the coast of Colombia. However, in three successive seasons she also made forays north through Bering Strait in connection with the search for Franklin. In 1848 she reached Kotzebue Sound where she was to rendezvous with HMS *Plover*, but when the latter did not appear Kellett headed south again. In 1849 he made contact with *Plover* at Kotzebue Sound and, pushing west along the edge of the pack in the Chukchi Sea, discovered Ostrov Geral'da before heading south. In 1850 *Herald* was again in the Chukchi Sea and briefly encountered *Investigator* on her way north. *Herald* then headed for home via Cape of Good Hope, reaching England in the summer of 1851. When he took command of HMS *Resolute* in February 1852 Kellett was forty-five (Laughton, 1892).

Sherard Osborn was born in England on 25 April 1822. In September 1837 he joined the sloop *Hyacinth* as a first-class volunteer. After seeing service in Chinese waters in *Hyacinth* and *Clio*, Osborn returned to England in 1843. He was appointed gunnery-mate aboard *Collingwood*, the Pacific Fleet flagship, and in the summer of 1849, by then a lieutenant, took command of HMS *Dwarf*, a small steamer, which was employed around the coasts of Ireland during the insurrection there. In 1850 he was given command of *Pioneer*, one of the steam tenders attached to Captain Austin's squadron. Hence he had wintered in the ice off Griffith Island in 1850–51. In the spring of 1851 he made a sledge journey of some 830 km during which he searched most of the west coast of Prince of Wales Island (Laughton, 1895; Osborn, 1852; Holland, 1972).

Francis Leopold McClintock was born at Dundalk, County Louth on 8 July 1819 and first went to sea aboard HMS *Samarang* as a first-class volunteer at the age of twelve. Over the next fourteen years he slowly made his way up through the system, seeing service in such diverse places as the Gulf of California, Brazil, the Irish Sea, the Channel, the Caribbean, Newfoundland, Bermuda, and Rio de la Plata. He made lieutenant on 29 July 1845. In 1848 he was appointed second lieutenant in *Enterprise* under Sir James Clark Ross, then fitting out (along with *Investigator*) for the Arctic. From winter quarters at Port Leopold on northeastern Somerset Island Ross and McClintock made the main sledge trip of the expedition in the spring of 1849. They searched the northern and western coasts of Somerset Island, covering some 800 km in forty days. In 1850 McClintock returned to the Arctic as first lieutenant aboard HMS *Assistance* under Captain Erasmus Ommanney, and wintered with the rest of Captain Austin's squadron off Griffith Island. In the spring of 1851 he made a major sledge trip west to Cape James Ross on the southwest coast of Melville Island, covering a distance of 1,240 kilometres in eighty days (Markham, 1909; Barr, 1987).

William J.S. Pullen was born at Devonport on 4 December 1813. Educated at the Greenwich Hospital School, he entered the navy as a first-class volunteer on 15 June 1828. Having served in the Mediterranean, in 1836 he left the navy, to become an assistant surveyor in South Australia. Returning to England in May 1842 he rejoined the navy as mate. From the summer of 1842 until 1848 he served aboard the survey vessel *Columbia*, surveying the Bay of Fundy among other areas. In 1848 he was appointed first lieutenant under Captain Thomas Moore aboard HMS *Plover*, which was to act as the base ship for the western division of the search for Franklin.

Having passed through Bering Strait Moore reached Wainwright Inlet on 27 July 1849 and dispatched Pullen with four boats to search the coast east to the Mackenzie. Pullen reached the Mackenzie Delta on 2 September and spent the winter at Hudson's Bay Company posts in the Mackenzie valley. Having started for home in the spring of 1850 Pullen received dispatches promoting him commander and ordering him to continue the search eastward from the Mackenzie. Starting down the Mackenzie from Fort Simpson on 11 July 1850 Pullen and party headed east by boat but were blocked by ice off Cape Bathurst. Returning upriver again the party wintered at Fort Simpson and reached home in October 1851 (Pullen, 1982).

3 All four ships had been recommissioned on 12 February at Woolwich (McClintock, 1852–4; Mumford, 1852–4) and since then had been undergoing repairs and renovations either in drydock or alongside the

wharf in the dockyard. *Resolute* and *Assistance* had required little in
the way of repairs but *Intrepid* spent a few hours in drydock while her
false keel was repaired; most of it had been lost during a collision
with an iceberg in Baffin Bay during the previous expedition. *Pioneer*
needed much more work; many of her timbers were broken and to
replace them a considerable amount of her double planking had to be
removed. Her boilers were also replaced at this stage (McClintock,
1852–4).

4 The move to Greenhithe was in fact made on the 15th (McClintock,
1852–54; Mumford, 1852–54), the vessels being towed downriver by the
steamer *Africa*, among others.

5 And the remainder of their Lords of the Admiralty (Mumford, 1852–4;
McClintock, 1852–4). This happened on 19 April.

6 The squadron set off from Geenhithe at 5.30 a.m. and dropped anchor
off the Nore at 10.30 to wait for the tide to change; while there they
were visited by the Port Admiral for Sheerness. They took on some
last-minute stores and *Resolute* took on an extra seaman to replace
one who had jumped ship at Greenhithe (Mumford, 1852–4).

7 By 8.00 p.m. on the 22nd the squadron was off Yarmouth and by 8 a.m,.
on the 24th within sight of Peterhead (Mumford, 1852–54).

8 Lieutenant George Frederick Mecham was born at Cobh, County
Cork, in 1828 and entered the Royal Navy in 1841. In 1850-1 he had
served as third lieutenant under Captain Ommanney on board HMS
Assistance, which had wintered with the rest of Captain Austin's
squadron off Griffith Island. In the spring of 1851 he had commanded
a sledge party which had supported Captain Ommanney's sledge
party and in this capacity had sledged south across Barrow Strait to
the north coast of Prince of Wales Island and back. A little later he
again sledged south across Barrow Strait to lay depots and also made a
circuit of Russell Island (Burant, 1985).

Lieutenant Bedford C.T. Pim was born in Bideford in 1826. Educated at the Royal Naval School, New Cross, he entered the Royal
Navy in 1842. In 1845 he was posted to HMS *Herald*, Captain Henry
Kellett, and participated in her Pacific surveys. He was on board
Herald in the Chukchi Sea in 1849 when Ostrov Geral'da was discovered and Ostrov Vrangel'ya sighted. For the winter of 1849–50 Pim
transferred to HMS *Plover* (Captain Thomas Moore) and wintered
aboard her at Chamisso Island in Kotzebue Sound. During that
wintering Pim made a journey by dog sledge south across the Seward
Peninsula and across Norton Sound to Mikhailovskiy (now St
Michael's) to question the Russian authorities and the people there
about rumours concerning whites who had been reported in the
interior of Alaska. After his promotion to lieutenant in 1851, Pim
attempted to mount a search of the eastern part of the arctic coast of
Siberia for traces of the Franklin expedition. With the support of the

Royal Geographical Society and the prime minister he managed to get to St Petersburg but he was dissuaded by the Russian authorities from proceeding with his scheme and returned to England early in 1852 (Neatby, 1982).

Richard Vesey Hamilton was born at Sandwich on 28 May 1829. Having been educated at the Royal Naval School, Camberwell, he entered the navy in 1843. After serving in *Virago* in the Mediterranean he went to the Arctic in 1850 as mate on board HMS *Assistance*, Captain Erasmus Ommanney and thus wintered aboard her off Griffith Island in 1850–1. In the spring of 1851 he commanded a sledge party which transported supplies across Barrow Strait to Russell Island in support of Sherard Osborn's party, then surveyed the shores of Young and Lowther islands on the way back to the ship (Callender, 1927).

George F. McDougall joined the navy in September 1839, serving in succession in HMS *Star*, *Tyrian*, and *Ranger*. From December 1842 until January 1847 he served as master's assistant in *Samarang*, under Captain Sir Edward Belcher. Having passed for second master in March 1847, he spent eighteen months as assistant surveyor to Captain G.A. Frazer on a survey of the southeast coast of Ireland. In the spring of 1850 he sailed for the Arctic as second master aboard *Resolute* under Captain Horatio Austin. In the spring of 1851 he made two sledge trips from the winter quarters off Griffith Island, one to lay depots on the shores of Cornwallis Island and the other to explore the land between Cornwallis and Bathurst islands. McDougall Sound, between those two islands, is named after him (Dawson, 1885, Pt. 2:165).

Dr William Thomas Domville entered the navy as an assistant surgeon in 1842. After a year's service at the Royal Hospital Plymouth he spent three years at sea in *Eurydice* and then one year in the gunnery ship *Excellent* at Portsmouth. From there he was appointed to the Royal Hospital at Greenwich in September 1847 and in February 1852 was promoted surgeon (O'Byrne, 1860:316).

Richard Roche had served as midshipman under Captain Henry Kellett aboard *Herald* and hence had had experience of arctic conditions during that ship's forays into the Chukchi Sea in 1848, 1849, and 1850 (Markham, 1875:46).

George Strong Nares was born at Straloch near Aberdeen on 24 April 1831. Having been educated at the Royal Naval School, New Cross, where he was prize cadet in his final year, he entered the navy in July 1845. After serving as a cadet, then midshipman in HMS *Canopus* on the Home Station, in 1848 he was appointed to HMS *Havvanah* on the Australian station and served aboard her in Australian waters until 1851 when he returned to England. On 16 February 1852 he was appointed second mate aboard HMS *Resolute* (Deacon and Savours, 1976).

9   Meanwhile the officers and men left on board were kept busy setting
     up rigging, watering the ships, etc. On the 27th Mumford (*Resolute's*
     assistant carpenter) reported that 'Each man in the expedition
     received a jacket and pair of trowsers of blue box cloth, a pair of
     fisherman's boots, souwester, drawers, boot hose and mittens, being
     the usual articles of summer clothing allowed by the Admiralty on
     these expeditions, and also a Meerschaum pipe' (Mumford, 1852–54).

10   The squadron passed Cape Wrath about 6 a.m. on the 29th and the
     Butt of Lewis about 3 p.m. (Mumford, 1852–4; McDougall, 1857:10).

11   None of the other narratives on the voyage include any mention of
     this tradition.

12   Captain Kellett also read the Articles of War (Mumford: 1852–4).

13   *North Star* lost one boat overboard during this storm and suffered
     other minor damage (McCormick, 1884). Some of the casks on
     Resolute's quarter-deck broke adrift 'and played a game of football over
     the gunroom skylights, rubbing the corns of several men who had to
     secure them' (Mumford, 1852–4).

14   The inner tier of casks from the upper deck was moved to the lower
     deck and lashed along the ship's side, somewhat constricting the
     accommodations there (Mumford, 1852–4; McDougall, 1857:14).

15   *Resolute's* bentinck boom carried away during this gale and over the
     next few days the carpenters were kept busy adapting a flying jib
     boom to replace it (Mumford, 1852–4).

16   Captain Kellett was confined to his cabin due to sickness for the first
     time on 8 May (Mumford, 1852–4).

17   Mr Mecham took divine service since Captain Kellett was still very
     ill. The supply of fresh beef also ran out on the 16th; from now on salt
     beef was issued and the daily issue of lime juice began (Mumford,
     1852–4).

18   Land was sighted briefly to starboard at dawn, identified variously as
     Cape Desolation (Mumford, 1852–4) or Cape Comfort (McCormick,
     1884:6).

19   Mumford reported seventy-two icebergs in sight from the foretop that
     morning (Mumford, 1852–4).

20   Mr Mecham again performed divine service since Captain Kellett was
     still too ill (Mumford, 1852-4).

21   This attempt at colonization occurred in 986; twenty-five ships set
     out from Iceland; only fourteen arrived safely (Jones, 1964).

22   Leif's voyage and other Norse voyages to North America have been
     discussed in detail by Helge Ingstad, in the light of his discovery of
     the remains of an incontestable Norse settlement at l'Anse-aux-
     Meadows in Northern Newfoundland in 1968 (Ingstad, 1969).

23   While the so-called West Settlement (Vestribyggd) (the Nuuk area)
     had been abandoned by *c.* 1350, the so-called East Settlement
     (Eystribyggd) (the Julianehåb area) was probably still surviving into the

sixteenth century (Jones, 1964). But by the time John Davis visited the area in 1586 there were no identifiable Norse left alive.

24 Graah's expedition (1828–31) was dispatched by the Danish government to locate the missing East Settlement, mistakenly thought to lie on the east coast of Greenland. Travelling by boat, from his base at Nanortalik he searched the east coast as far north as Dannebrogsø (65° 15′ 36″N) and established that there were no ancient Norse settlements on the east coast (Graah, 1837). There are, however, still substantial traces (ruins of farms, churches, etc.) from the Norse period in West Greenland. (See, for example, Ingstad, 1959.)

25 Part of the day was spent in getting ready ice-anchors, ice saws, ice chisels, etc. (McDougall, 1857).

2 Greenland and Melville Bukt

1 De Bray has again got his dates a little confused. The ships reached the Whalefish Islands on the 29th, not the 28th (Mumford, 1852–54; McClintock, 1852–4; McDougall, 1857), although land was sighted on the 28th. Another event worthy of note on the 28th was that the crow's nest was assembled and hoisted to *Resolute*'s main topgallant masthead (Mumford, 1852–4).

It was on 28 May, off the Whalefish Islands that de Bray started the report to the minister of marine which is reproduced as Appendix 1. It was probably taken to Europe by a whaler or by the regular Danish mail vessel.

2 The Eskimos came off in large numbers in kayaks and umiaks, and there was a lively trade in skin jackets, trousers, boots, and model kayaks, in return for cloth trousers, handkerchiefs, British currency, etc. (Mumford, 1852–4; McClintock, 1852–4). McClintock stressed that those who had been in the Arctic before were particularly keen to buy sealskin boots.

3 This gentleman, a carpenter by trade, was named Fritz Emil Torgenfead (McCormick, 1884, vol. 2).

4 On the 29th Dr McCormick, *North Star*'s surgeon, went on board *Resolute* to visit Captain Kellett 'who had been so ill as to have been confined to his cabin the whole of the way out. I found him sitting up in his cabin, with several officers around him. He was looking much reduced in flesh and strength, but in excellent spirits, joking with those around him ...' (McCormick, 1884:7).

5 McDougall, *Resolute*'s master, found the odour of the Eskimo houses equally repugnant (McDougall, 1857).

6 On this date the ship's blacksmith and his forge were put ashore on an island, where he and the carpenters were engaged in repairing the ship's boats. Mumford reports that a party of Greenlanders, male and female, came aboard in the evening, and that a dance was held, 'the voyage to the shore afterwards being found more circuitous

than usual by most of the gentlemen.'

7 On the 7th Sir Edward and a group of officers from the different ships started a survey of all the islands (Mumford, 1852–4; McClintock, 1852–4; McDougall, 1857:31).

8 On the same day Mumford, one of the carpenters repairing and painting the boats on shore, noted that: 'Having a pitch kettle on shore and a fire, the muscles [sic] have proved much to our taste' (Mumford, 1852–4).

9 By the evening of the 4th the boats had been hoisted aboard again. Also on that date the last of *Resolute*'s livestock (a sheep) was killed and the meat stowed on ice (Mumford, 1852–4).

10 This is confirmed by Mumford and by McDougall (1857:36). The tracks of Pim and his companions were also found on the summit by Dr Domville when he climbed the same mountain on the 8th (McCormick, 1884).

11 *Pioneer* also filled a boat with driftwood (McDougall, 1857: 39) and the sportsmen from all the ships were quite successful (McDougall, 1857; Mumford, 1852–4).

12 De Bray omits to mention that Kellett had first tried to tow his ship with boats to another iceberg, but that this effort was foiled by a strong current. The result was that 'the boat's crew had the pleasure of hauling in and coiling away 480 fathoms of wet line to which a cold drizzle added much comfort' (Mumford, 1852–4).

13 McClintock described how 'we saw three of the officers of the *Resolute* seated under a rock which sheltered them partially from the storm and looking anything but comfortable as they watched their ship driven off to sea'.

14 The men were allowed out on the ice and began playing football, cricket, and leap-frog (McDougall, 1857:48). Mumford and a few others had the misfortune to fall into the water.

15 Two dogs were abandoned according to McDougall (1857) and McCormick (1884). The Devil's Thumb, the Sugar Loaf, Three Islands, and Cape Shackleton were all in sight at this point (McCormick, 1884).

16 *Intrepid*'s engine broke down for a while and she herself had to be towed (Mumford, 1852–4; McClintock, 1852–4).

17 This in fact was a multi-vessel collision. The steamers (towing the other vessels) had been brought up standing by the ice, and the towed vessels proceeded to ram into them and each other. *Resolute* managed to ram into the ice but *North Star* fouled her, while *Assistance* collided with *Pioneer*, although neither suffered serious damage (Mumford, 1852–4).

18 McClintock has left a fuller description of *Resolute*'s predicament: 'Yet the ice looked so beautiful and the night so clear, calm and still, one unacquainted with the movements and power of the ice

could hardly have believed the ship was in danger. Those who were down below were the first undeceived and came rushing up, the pressure of the ice having caused the ship's timbers to creak and groan so loudly that they thought her sides would be squeezed in before they could get on deck.

The floe which had drifted down upon her was pressed steadily onward by others behind, the ship heeled over to starboard and the ice crushed up against her sides in large blocks until it was [blank] feet high. Her rudder was reduced almost to a scrap of splinters; her whole frame quivered under the enormous pressure; the bells rang and masts trembled; as the ice broke up, mass by mass, against her side, the short intervals afforded her momentary relief. Of course nothing could be done for the ship. Crew and boats were placed in safety on the ice.

19 This is one of the most detailed and lucid descriptions of the techniques of cutting an ice-dock and of manoeuvring a ship into it, available anywhere in the literature.

20 A major activity was the task of clearing the after hold to reach the spare rudder, which was then hoisted out onto the ice and assembled by the carpenters (Mumford, 1852–4).

21 This included such treasures as: 'damaged biscuit for the pigs, straw for the sheep, iron hoops for shoeing sledges, harpoons, sails, ropes, blocks, anchors, spars and every piece of wood to add to our store of fuel' (McClintock, 1852–4).

22 De Bray appears to have been unimpressed by the proceedings: some thirty boats rowed wildly around among the debris from the sunken ship, retrieving whatever they could from the flotsam. The most valuable prizes were vast numbers of barrel shooks (staves), retrieved for firewood, and a large number of turnips (McClintock, 1852–4; McDougall, 1857:6).

23 The welcome which they received was indeed quite bizarre. To quote Dr McCormick (1884:30):

Their crews had all assembled on the floe, advancing along its edge to meet us, with flags flying, and moving to the tune of the old Scotch air 'Rob Roy McGregor', played by a drummer and two fifers, one dressed in regimentals, the red jacket conspicuous amongst the motley group clothed in blue and drab habiliments, and of all ages, from the boy of fourteen or fifteen to the old man of sixty and upwards. Amid the throng was a sort of triangle, and a figure dressed as harlequin in mask and cocked hat. There were about thirty colours [flags] in all, pocket-handkerchiefs included; one or two, having a star in the centre, belonging to an American whaler amongst them. They carried a boat over the ice with them, and as they passed the leading ships of our squadron gave them three cheers, which were again repeated on passing us; continuing onwards, they cheered the *St Andrew*, whaler, after which they broke up into straggling parties, several coming on board of us to see the ship.

24 This peculiar custom is elaborated on, and in part explained, by McClintock:

... according to the whaling custom, it seems, they did not take the trouble to save any of her cargo, which might easily have been done, as the ice supported her for several days. The men took out a cask of spirits and a most shocking scene of riot and excess ensued. Rather than permit others to profit from their misfortune they hacked all the masts and yards, cut the ropes, sails, etc., set fire to the rudder which lay upon the ice, and then the carpenter in a state of drunkenness and excitement bordering on insanity, set fire to the ship.

We were told that some of her men sat in the cabin drinking wine they found there, altho' up to their knees in water, for the vessel was gradually settling down at the time. Of course all of them were drunk and they amused themselves by smashing the glass skylight with the empty bottles. The whaling captains say they have no power to check these revolting practises and that they dare not attempt it. The crew consists of 45 or 50 men who receive no pay unless the voyage is successful. This system induces a reckless, gambling sort of spirit. Failure makes the men desperate, and being the chief sufferers they solace themselves in the way I have described. Not only the crew of the *Regalia*, but of all the ships present were drunk for two or three days, and the masters were in a great state of alarm, lest their ships should catch fire.

25 The whalemen were: *Princess Charlotte* (Captain Deuchers) of Dundee, *Chieftain* (Captain Archibald) of Kirkcaldy, *Pacific* (Captain C. Paterson) of Aberdeen, *Rose* of Grimsby, *Jane* (Captain Walker) of Bo'ness, *Alexander* (Captain Sturrock Jr) of Dundee, *Orion* (Captain Wells) of Hull, *Advice* (Captain Robb) of Dundee, *Lord Gambier* (Captain Couldney) of Hull, *Truelove* (Captain Parker) of Hull, *McLellan* (Captain Quayle) of New London, *Horn* (Captain Sturrock Sr) of Dundee, *St Andrew* (Captain Smith) of Aberdeen, and *Anna* (McCormick, 1884:32; McClintock, 1852-4).

26 The shooting party consisted of Captain McClintock (*Intrepid*), Lt Mecham (*Resolute*) and Dr McCormick (*North Star*). The bear was 7 feet long and weighed 245 kg (McCormick, 1884:34-5; McClintock, 1852-4). McClintock gave the bear to Captain Kellett (McClintock, 1852-4; Scott, 1852-4). Shooting parties were also hunting birds at this point; thus parties from *Resolute* killed 140 murres and dovekies on the 2nd and 187 birds on the 3rd (Mumford, 1852-4).

27 As an American vessel whaling in Baffin Bay, generally a British preserve, the *McLellan* was something of a rarity. She had worked

these waters since 1846. In 1851 her captain, William Quayle, had attempted a novel experiment; he had left a wintering party of twelve men, including his first mate, S.O. Buddington, and George Tyson, later to become a famous whaling captain himself, to winter on a small island, Kemisuack (or Nimigen) in Cumberland Sound in order to hunt whales from shore in the spring before *McLellan* could get in there. This was the first known wintering by whites in the area since Frobisher's expeditions of the 1570s. In the event, the expedition was a success, since the party killed seventeen whales. After the loss of *McLellan* the wintering partly was picked up by Captain Parker in *Truelove* in September 1852 (Goldring, 1986; Ross, 1985; Blake, 1874).

28 When McDougall went on board he found four timbers on the starboard side below the water line, stove in and 1.2 m of water in the hold. Masthead tackles were rigged from her main and fore mastheads and the ship was hove-down to port, allowing access to the damaged parts of the hull. By 7 p.m. she was seaworthy again (McDougall, 1857; McClintock, 1852-4).

29 Captain Quayle in fact cut away the mizzen mast himself (McCormick, 1884:39).

30 Captain Sir Edward Belcher paid Captain Quayle for everything he took, giving him bills on the British government (Mumford, 1852-4; McDougall, 1857). *McLellan*'s crew were very indignant at being prevented by the Royal Marine sentries whom Belcher posted from pillaging and burning the ship as usual. In retaliation they chalked on the ship's stern and sides 'John Bull's prise' and 'Teddy Belcher, the pirate' (Mumford, 1852-4).

31 In the evening de Bray paid a visit to Dr McCormick on board *North Star*. There he met Lieutenant Pim, Dr Domville, and Captain Quayle, who had dined with McCormick (McCormick, 1884).

32 On the 14th the wreck of *McLellan*, now very low in the water, was blown up with a 10 kg charge of powder (Mumford, 1852-4). The wreck was still visible, but only barely, on the 22nd (McCormick, 1884:42).

33 The stove became overheated and set fire to some *lignum vitae* stowed near it, but the fire was discovered and extinguished before serious damage was done (Mumford, 1852-4).

34 During spring tides (i.e., with a full or new moon) the tidal movements tend to encourage the sea ice to slacken.

35 The mail bag was put aboard *Lord Gambier* (McClintock, 1852-4). In it was the letter from de Bray to his mother, reproduced as Appendix 3.

36 New ice had begun to form overnight and that morning it was 1.25 cm thick (Mumford, 1852-4).

37 The squadron was close abeam of Cape Walker and Melville's Monument (McCormick, 1884:42).

38 Both officers and men also got great entertainment from tobogganing down the sides of the iceberg (some 19 m high); many of the runs ended in duckings in the pools around the foot of the berg (Mumford, 1852–4; McDougall, 1857:69).

39 *Alexander*'s crew were becoming very concerned about the danger of being beset in Melville Bay and on this date asked the captain to 'go south ... which he at once refused to do in terms more decided than polite' (McClintock, 1852–4). McClintock suspected that *Alexander*'s men might have mutinied if the navy vessels had not been present.

40 This is the North Water, a large polynya (ice-free area) which remains open year round due to unusual configurations of currents and coasts. It occupies the northwest corner of Baffin Bay, with an arm extending into Smith Sound. It was commonly used by the whalemen in order to get to the whaling grounds off northern Baffin Island as quickly as possible.

3 West to Winter Harbour

1 These were the people who had first been encountered by Captain John Ross during his voyage to Baffin Bay in *Isabella* and *Alexander* in 1818, and whom he had named the 'Arctic Highlanders.' According to Ross this small group of people had 'until the moment of our arrival, believed themselves to be the only inhabitants of the universe' (Ross, 1819:123).
The group included Captains Kellett and McClintock, Dr McCormick, Lieutenant Pim, and Lieutenant Nares (McCormick, 1884).

3 This individual, whose name was rendered Kallihirua by other members of the expedition, and would be rendered as Qalasirssuaq in modern orthography, was named Erasmus York by Captain Austin. He had voluntarily joined HMS *Assistance* (Captain Erasmus Ommanney) to act as a pilot (Holland, 1985b; Sutherland, 1852: vol. I.
Having guided Ommanney to where *North Star* had spent the previous winter, he stayed on board *Assistance* for her wintering off Griffith Island and returned with her to England in the autumn of 1851. There he was placed in St Augustine's College in Canterbury, where he was taught to read and write and given instruction in religion and tailoring. In the autumn of 1855 he travelled to St John's, Newfoundland, for further religious training at Queen's College, with the intention that he would begin missionary work among the Inuit of the Labrador coast in 1856, but he fell ill and died in St John's in June 1856.

4 It was later learned that *Assistance* had stopped at Kap York the previous day and had made contact with the Inuit there (McDougall, 1857; McClintock, 1852–4).

5 The 'red snow' on snow slopes on the cliffs west of Kap York had first been observed by Ross in 1818, who examined it under a microscope, and deduced that the red particles were of vegetable origin (Ross, 1819). Red snow is caused by a number of species of criobiont algae, the commonest being *Chlamydomonas nivalis*, which are found on snow in both polar regions. For a discussion of the ecology of red snow, see Kol and Eurola (1974) and Newton (1982).

6 Captain Kellett obtained a small boat from *Alexander* in return for one of the McLellan's sails (Mumford, 1852–4).

7 Namely, the North Water.

8 This is an excellent description of the striking coastal topography of the southern Devon Island, developed on horizontal or gently dipping Ordovician and Silurian limestones and dolomites. For details of the physiography and bedrock geology, see Glenister and Thorsteinsson (1963).

9 De Bray's suggestion that Ross made a voyage from Sweden in *Mary* with only one man is erroneous; he must have misunderstood his informant. Ross did indeed bring *Mary* from Sweden, where he had been consul, with a view to using her for a North Pole expedition which he had planned, but she was towed from Elsinore to England (Rear-Admiral James Ross, personal communication, 1989).

   On his walk to Cape Spencer, de Bray was accompanied by Captain Kellett and Mr McDougall (McCormick, 1884:49).

10 The bodies of all three men, almost perfectly preserved in the permafrost, were recently exhumed by Dr Owen Beattie of the University of Alberta. John Torrington was exhumed in 1984 and John Hartnell and William Braine in 1986. Post-mortem investigations revealed that all three had suffered from tuberculosis and died of pneumonia. All three, however, recorded extremely high levels of lead in their systems and it was this poisoning which had weakened the men to the point that they easily succumbed to pneumonia (Beattie and Geiger, 1987).

11 De Bray is referring to fossil madrepore corals. Beechey Island is composed of the flat-lying limestones of the Read Bay Formation, of Silurian age, most of whose members contain an 'abundant and varied fossil fauna' (Grenier, 1963).

12 On the 13th all the carpenters of the squadron were sent aboard *North Star* to saw the salvaged masts from *McLellan* into planks for building the house which Captain Pullen was to build on Beechey Island (Mumford, 1852–4).

13 At midnight Captain Kellett dispatched de Bray and Mr Groves (of *North Star*) to invite Dr McCormick to join the fun. But the latter, who was meeting with obstacles, especially from Belcher, to his plans to mount a small-boat expedition up Wellington Channel, and who had retired at 11.00 p.m., could not be persuaded to join the revelry (McCormick, 1884:53).

14 After this ceremony Dr McCormick of *North Star* joined the officers of *Resolute* in a convivial evening around the gunroom table. De Bray took apart McCormick's watch, which had been immersed in salt water when the doctor fell through the ice. But de Bray found that a small part in the watch had been corroded through and he was unable to repair it (McCormick, 1884:53).

15 *Enterprise* (Captain Richard Collinson) and *Investigator* (Captain Robert M'Clure) had sailed from England in January 1850, bound for Bering Strait via Cape Horn. Having become separated, *Investigator* pushed east past Point Barrow and wintered (1850–1) at the Princess Royal Islands in Prince of Wales Strait. In the summer of 1851 M'Clure took his ship round the south end of Banks Island and north along its west coast, but had been blocked by the ice at Mercy Bay on the island's north coast. There *Investigator* had wintered, and was still there at the point when *Resolute* and *Intrepid* left Beechey Island, heading west (Osborn, 1857). *Enterprise* had also pushed north through Bering Strait some weeks later than M'Clure in the summer of 1850 but was unable to get past Point Barrow due to ice. Having wintered at Hong Kong, Collinson took his ship back north in 1851 and retraced M'Clure's route north down Prince of Wales Strait, then south around Banks Island and part way along its west coast. More cautious than M'Clure, he then turned back south and returned to the southern entrance to Prince of Wales Strait and put his ship into winter quarters at Walker Bay. By the time *Resolute* and *Intrepid* left Beechey Island, *Enterprise* was already working her way out of her winter quarters and was bound eastwards through Dolphin and Union Strait, towards Cambridge Bay, which would become her next wintering site. Collinson started back west in the summer of 1853 but was blocked by ice at Camden Bay on the north shore of Alaska, where he wintered yet again (Collinson, 1889).

16 De Bray appears to be a little confused here. Assistance Harbour is on the south coast of Cornwallis Island. The confusion may have arisen from the fact that while Penny's vessels (*Lady Franklin* and *Sophia*) and Sir John Ross's *Felix* had wintered in Assistance Harbour, Austin's ships (*Assistance, Pioneer, Resolute,* and *Intrepid*) had wintered off Griffith Island.

17 Even worse was the fact that it was almost high tide on the spring tide (McClintock, 1852–4).

18 This development caught Captain Kellett off guard; since things had seemed fairly quiet, the hands had been sent below for a combined meal of dinner and supper when the ship was heeled bodily over to starboard, 'making the masts bend like coach whips' (Mumford, 1852–4).

19 At this point the order was given to 'splice the main brace'; each man was issued half a gill of rum and half a pound of preserved meat (Mumford, 1852–4).

20 Captain McClintock, Lieutenant Mecham, and Lieutenant Hamilton were also members of the party (McClintock, 1852–4).

21 Captain Kellett, Captain McClintock, and Lieutenant Mecham went ashore and built a cairn, in which a message was deposited, on the east side of the island (Mumford, 1852–4; McDougall, 1857:100).

22 Using a sledge and a boat, a detail from *Resolute* watered the ship from the land on the 22nd (Mumford, 1852–4).

23 That morning the men aboard *Resolute* were issued with sealskin clothing (Mumford, 1852–4).

24 The party was to be relieved daily (Mumford, 1852–4).

25 McClintock makes the remark (rather poorly chosen in view of de Bray's presence with the expedition) that 'the movements of the ice [are] as closely watched as ever was the French Fleet' (McClintock, 1852–4).

26 The balloons (2.4 m in diameter) were filled with gas (presumably hydrogen) produced on board (Mumford, 1852–4). Examples of the balloon and of the little message sheets are displayed in the museum of the Scott Polar Research Institute in Cambridge, England.

27 The depot was placed about 5 km west of Allison Inlet (McDougall, 1857:108) and about 10 km from Cape Cockburn (Mumford, 1852-4).

28 The bearings for the month were pasted on a board and hung abaft the mizzen mast for use of the officer of the watch, and a special 'bearing plate,' i.e., an instrument for taking the sun's bearing, was set just forward of the wheel (McDougall, 1857).

29 This was felt to be a major achievement. McClintock signalled to *Resolute*: 'Accept congratulations,' to which Kellett replied: 'Same to you' (McClintock, 1852–4).

30 Some more hunters went ashore at this stage; one of them, Lieutenant Pim, was charged by a bull and narrowly missed being gored when his gun misfired (Mumford, 1852–4).

31 However, Captain Kellett did find a promising little harbour for winter quarters just inside Point Palmer (McClintock, 1852–4).

32 The party was led by Mr Krabbé; the eight animals (including two calves) represented an entire herd (McClintock, 1852–4), located about five miles from the ships. These eight animals provided 550 kg. of meat (McClintock, 1852–4).

33 Dr Scott (of *Intrepid*) makes the interesting, but erroneous, observation: 'I would account for the great number of muskoxen seen and shot by supposing that the Hudson's Bay Co. hunting them & driving them up far North, they are compelled to seek shelter far from their proper territories' (Scott, 1852–4). In fact the historic range of the species includes both the islands and the mainland and while the species was nearly exterminated (largely by the Hudson's Bay Company) on the mainland by 1917, this severe hunting pressure did not begin until 1860 or 1870.

34 On the 5th many of the men were allowed ashore to get some exercise in the afternoon (Mumford, 1852–4).

35 On the 6th each member of the crew was issued with a pair of cloth snow boots, boot hose, mittens, drawers, and comforter (Mumford, 1852–4).

36 This was the name which Parry applied to the larger embayment on the south coast of Melville Island, off which both Fife Harbour and Winter Harbour open (see chart in Parry (1821:28–9). The name was subsequently transferred (by Kellett) to the even larger embayment on the north side of the island.

37 De Bray is here confusing two different landmarks. The cairn left by Parry was located on 'Northeast Hill,' about 2.5 km north-northeast of the north end of Winter Harbour. 'Parry's Rock' (which consists of sandstone, not granite) (Parry, 1821:97) is located 200 to 300 m from shore in the southwest corner of Winter Harbour (Fisher, 1821:238–9). Very significant, in terms of later developments, is the fact that nobody visited Parry's Rock during this brief visit to Winter Harbour in September (Mumford, 1852–4).

4 Fall Sledge Trips and Preparations for Wintering

1   *Intrepid* cut her dock about 50 m closer to the island (Mumford, 1852–4).

2   Captain McClintock set off that morning with a party of three men, a tent, and a sledge to examine a creek at the head of Bridport Inlet to see whether it offered a route for hauling a depot across to the north coast of the island (McClintock, 1852–4).

3   There is no record of any of the messages from this or any of the other balloons released ever having been recovered.

4   Detailed accounts of this trip are to be found in Scott (1852–54) and in McClintock (1852–4; 1855). The provisions to be left in the depot, as well as those to be used on the journey are listed in detail by Scott.

5. Some 230 kg of bread (hardtack), 4 kg of tobacco, 4.3 kg of sugar and 350 g of tea had to be condemned (McDougall, 1857:128).

6   On the 19th the young ice was strong enough to allow a man to walk for a mile outside the ships (McClintock, 1852–4). On that same date the Sylvester stove aboard *Resolute* was lit for the first time; its daily allowance of coal was 27.5 kg. Other stoves included the galley stove (13.75 kg), the gunroom cook's stove (13.75 kg), the Captain's stove (5.65 kg) and the sick bay stove (2.25 kg). The ship's cook was allowed an extra 2.25 kg on brewing and washing nights (Mumford, 1852–4).

7   The six men were Joy, McLean, Patural, Hobbs, Harbourn, and St Croix (De Bray, 1855a:660).

8   A sail could be rigged on the sledge to take advantage of a following wind.

9   No mention of this accident appears in the official report (De Bray, 1855a:661).

10 De Bray is referring to his portion of the depot landed here from the ship on 7 September. He left twenty-two cans of preserved meat and just about eight litres of alcohol here (De Bray, 1855a:662).

11 William Mumford, the assistant carpenter, has provided us with an excellent description of the camping and cooking arrangements on these sledge trips, which nicely supplements what de Bray tells us here and elsewhere:

The tent is made just large enough to hold the sledge's crew, the length from the door to the end allowing each man to lie down on his side, and the breadth allows the men to lie at length. The officer of the party takes the end of the tent and lies his head on the right, the next man on the left and so on to the door, which is the place of the cook for the day, after which he moves up by the side of the officer. The next man takes his place & office. To pitch the tent a smooth patch of snow is selected and the sledge having stopped the crew (except the cook & cook's mate) take the tent and place its end to windward, setting the pickaxe in the snow to secure the rope to. It is then spread as tight as possible, the rope at the lee end being secured to the sledge, which is therefore as near the tent door as convenient. This having been done, the two men who were cooks last, having brushed their clothes and feet of drift go inside and first spread an India rubber cloth on the snow throughout the tent. Over this a 'robe' of buffalo skin or blanket is spread. The blanket bags (one for each man to lie in) are then placed alternately at each man's place. The other hands, having banked up the sides & end of the tent with snow, get into their bags as soon as possible, which is often not so soon by 1/2 an hour as agreeable, for the boots, stockings, boot hose & wrappers since the stopping of the sledge have generally frozen into one mass, and often occupy from 10 to 30 minutes to get them off the feet whole, which when done are laid down in each man's place, on which he lies to keep them thawed, ready for putting on again.

The cook in the meanwhile has brought his apparatus close to the tent door and which by this time under favorable circumstances is giving some hopes of the coming supper. The apparatus consists of a circular tin case in which is a tallow or stearine lamp, a stew pan and a kettle made to hold a pint for each man. Snow has first to be melted to obtain water, to do which and to bring the snow to boiling point occupies, according to weather & temperature and the lamp, from 1 to 3 hours, which also has a similar effect on the health & temper of the already tired-out cook, who is the last into the tent, and out again to cook the breakfast a similar time *before* the rest. The travelling provisions consist of pemmican, preserved meats, boiled bacon & biscuit, cocoa & tea. (Mumford, 1852–4: 4 April 1853).

It is clear from this description that the cooking was done *outside*, which goes a long way to explain why it took from one to three hours to boil water.

12 I.e., two crews would proceed with one sledge, leave it at a suitable place, then go back for the second one.

13 These latter formed the surplus part of de Bray's sledging rations.

14 The depot consisted of two cases containing 45.45 kg of bread, 545 kg of stearine, tea, chocolate, and sugar; 1 bag containing 18 kg of bread; 34 cans of preserved meat (61.8 kg); 2 cases of pemmican (50 kg); 2 cases of bacon (50 kg); and 10 litres of rum (de Bray, 1855a:663).

15 Mr Hamilton's party was in sight ahead (De Bray, 1855a:663).

16 This was M'Clean's knapsack (de Bray, 1855a:663).

17 De Bray and his men had covered 246 km (130 outwards and 116 on the return), at a mean rate of 12.95 km per day going out and 17.83 km per day coming back (de Bray, 1855a:664). Mumford commented that de Bray and his men were 'as black as sweeps.'

18 A small depot of provisions was even landed on the island for the sledge parties in case the ships were blown out to sea and were unable to return immediately (Mumford, 1852–4).

19 Details of this trip may be found in Scott (1852–4) and in McClintock (1855a; 1852–4). George Drover, one of Captain McClintock's men, was severely frostbitten on the foot on his return. Almost all the men had started off wearing leather boots, but had been unable to get them on after the second day because they were frozen, and had had to make moccasins out of blankets and canvas bags (Mumford, 1852–4). Perhaps not surprisingly, Drover fell ill on the first day out on the second trip and was escorted back to the ships by Dr Scott. His place was taken by Mr Purchase, the ship's engineer (McClintock, 1852–54; Mumford, 1852–4).

20 For example, on the 29th the task of covering the deck with an insulating layer of snow was begun, starting with the fo'c's'lehead; a layer of snow 20 cm deep was spread, then covered with a layer of snow, gravel, and water which quickly froze into a protective crust (Mumford, 1852–4).

21 During de Bray's absence the expedition's first polar bear had also been shot. It appeared close to the ship early on the morning of the 6th; and after being chased by the dogs for 3.2 km it was shot but could not be retrieved because the ice was dangerously thin (Mumford, 1852–4).

22 This version of M'Clure's message (translated by de Bray into French and now translated back into English) appears to be the only full version of the message available in published form, although McDougall (1857:137–42) has published extracts. Fuller details of what M'Clure had achieved in *Investigator* may be found in Osborn (1852), Armstrong (1857), and Neatby (1967).

23 *Plover* spent the entire period from 1848 until 1854 in the Bering Sea–
   Chukchi Sea area under the command of Captain Thomas Moore and
   Captain Rochfort McGuire, wintering at various locations, with a
   view to possibly intercepting Franklin's expedition if it emerged via
   Bering Strait, and to supplying search expeditions such as those of
   M'Clure and Collinson. The history of the Bering Strait component of
   the Franklin search is discussed very effectively by Bockstoce (1988).
24 Johann Miertsching, a Moravian missionary who had learned
   Inuktitut while serving on the Labrador coast (Neatby, 1967).
25 Travelling overland from Fort Confidence on Great Bear Lake,
   Dr John Rae of the Hudson's Bay Company reached Cape Baring on
   the north coast of Wollaston Peninsula (Victoria Island) on the night
   of 23–24 May 1851 (Rich and Johnson, 1953:187).
26 The previous day the party became marooned on a floe which broke
   away from the fast ice, but escaped that night when the floe drifted
   back in and made contact with the fast ice again (Mumford, 1852–4).
27 De Bray's dates do not quite agree with those quoted by Mumford,
   who was a member of the hunting party; according to the latter they
   set off on 19 October and returned on the 22nd. McClintock's diary
   agrees with Mumford's version.
28 It had been known for some time that Mobley had heart problems. On
   18 October he went out on deck without being properly clad and
   dropped dead (McDougall, 1857).

5 The Wintering

1 This is a slip on de Bray's part. Point Nias is on Hecla and Griper Bay.
2 The ships' bells were tolled as the funeral procession wound its way
  across the ice (McDougall, 1857).
3 The headboard, which was not placed until spring, read as follows:
  Sacred / To the memory of / Thomas Mobley, R.M. / HMS Resolute
  / Obit — / Aetat.   years / James 4C, V. 14&15 / Whereas ye know
  not what / Shalt be on the morrow / If the soul will we shall be.
4 A very bright star in the constellation Taurus.
5 McDougall offered a class in navigation to eight students (McDougall,
  1857).
6 McClintock commented that most of the dresses 'were made or fitted
  by Mr de Bray, who has all the skill of his countrymen in such
  matters' (McClintock, 23 Nov., 1852–4).
7 This was *Intrepid*'s Guy Fawkes, which had come to visit *Resolute*. To
  quote McClintock: ' ... at eight o'clock our people set off with the
  'Guy' sumptuously apparelled, and seated in an arm chair upon a
  sledge. It was very tastefully got up with powdered wig & numerous
  ornaments of colored paper. The men were uniformly dressed in fancy
  styles, excepting only the officer in charge of the state prisoner and

the state coachman; the former with preposterous cocked hat, plume & ample military cloak; the latter in a scarlet coat & cocked hat such as the Lord Mayor's coachman in those days probably wore. Altogether it was very creditable to those concerned. They looked well & sang the historical ballad with every appearance of loyalty – and sound lungs.' The 'Resolutes' produced a smaller Guy and the whole proceedings ended with 'splicing the mainbrace' (Mumford, 1852–4).

8 McDougall was also sufficiently curious to walk out to investigate the new pressure ridge. He likened the 'whistling' noise to the "soughing" of a dying gale through the cordage of a ship' (McDougall, 1857).

9 This was probably the royal coat of arms which normally embellished *Intrepid*'s stern and was moved to the theatre for the occasion (Mumford, 1852–4). Mumford, as assistant carpenter, has left the most detailed account of the setting-up of the theatre, with descriptions of making and installing a chandelier consisting of 'swords, bayonets, beads, festoons, variegated lamps and candles.'

10 The full text is quoted by McDougall (1857:159–60).

11 This first piece, presented by the officers, was the historical drama, *Charles the Second*.

12 The actor in question was the quartermaster, Thomas Joy, playing a footman called Potter; he missed several cues in a scene with Mumford but they managed to struggle through it. Once off stage, 'Potter at once measured his length behind the scenes and was duly "taken in tow" headfirst down the fore hatchway by Mr Dean and stowed "all standing" in his hammock' (Mumford, 1852–4).

13 A walking match took place between Pim and Nares from the ships round Dealy Island in opposite directions, a distance of 10.3 km, the prize being three bottles of wine. Nares won with a time of 82 minutes to Pim's 85 minutes (Mumford, 1852–4; McClintock, 1852–4).

14 They were seen by Messrs Krabbé and Ibbetts (McDougall, 1857:166).

15 On the 6th, lieutenants Mecham and Hamilton saw a herd of at least fourteen muskoxen on shore about 5 km from the ships; they ran off into the darkness. This was welcome news, as being clear proof that the animals did not migrate (McDougall, 1857:166; Mumford, 1852–4; McClintock, 1852–4; Scott, 1852–4).

16 Drover had been sick ever since he had been forced to turn back on the last sledge trip on 7 October. Anticipating the end, he had made his will on the 8th but then rallied on the 11th when he was even able to walk a few steps. But then he relapsed and died at 2 a.m. on the 12th (McClintock, 1852–4). He had been with Captain McClintock on two previous expeditions and the latter had great respect and even affection for him.

Intrepid's carpenters began work on Drover's coffin immediately; it was lined inside with flannel and covered outside with blue cloth

paid for by his messmates (Mumford, 1852–4; McClintock, 1852–4).
The body was placed in it and stowed on the upper deck until a grave
could be prepared.

17 The first part of the service was conducted by Captain McClintock on
the quarter-deck (i.e., under the housing) since it was -20°C outside.
The coffin was then hauled to the grave on a sledge by *Intrepid*'s
crew, followed by the rest of the expedition members carrying lanterns.
The headboard was erected immediately. It read: Sacred / To the
memory / of / George Drover, / Captain forecastle, / HMS /
Intrepid. / Died 12th Decr. 1852 / Aged 32 years. / Blessed are the
dead / which die in the Lord / XIV Revns. 13v. (McClintock, 1852–4)

18 On one occasion (14 December) during a severe gale with a temperature of -22° the men digging the grave missed the ships as they were
walking back from the island; fortunately they spotted a rocket and
heard the shouts of their shipmates who had been concerned about
them (Mumford, 1852–4).

19 Mr Krabbé, the 'Wizard of the North,' was assisted by Lieutenant Pim
as Senor Cigazzi. Tricks which involved an 'inexhaustible bottle' and
the drawing of rum from an old drunkard's elbow, were especially
popular (McClintock, 1852–4).

20 McClintock was particularly pleased by his men's behaviour: 'Their
conduct was equally praiseworthy. I have never seen so orderly a
Christmas on board ship, nor one so much enjoyed. It very rarely
happens that the day passes without a single case of inebriety, but
such was the fact here.'

Resolute's men seem to have been a little more rambunctious.
Mumford noted: 'Jollifications went on till 12 p.m., the First Lieut.
and other officers having great trouble to get some of the men to their
hammocks and acting more like messmates than superiors ... Some
hands very noisy from the time to turn in to the time to turn out ....
Got the irons up and placed them in the after cockpit ready for a
"noisy boy".' But apparently this precaution was unnecessary.

The expedition's band played a major role in the Christmas
festivities. It consisted of a drum, harmonica, piccolo, triangle, and
three flutes made from brass curtain rods (McClintock, 1852–4).

21 From the 2nd onwards the mercury froze for brief periods (i.e., colder
than -39.7°C) and from the 4th until the 13th it was frozen continu-
ously, the temperature dropping to -46.9°C on the 9th according to
Intrepid's thermometer (-51.7°C according to McClintock's own
instrument) (McClintock, 1852–4).

22 It weighed 1.125 kg and 563 g when dressed (McClintock, 1852–4).

23 These were shoots of arctic willow (*Salix arctica*); the crop contents
weighed 75 g and 'nearly filled a good-sized tea-cup' (McDougall,
1857:174).

24 Over the 11th and 12th three tanks were hoisted out of *Resolute*'s

hold and sledged ashore to form a major component of the depot to be left on Dealy Island (Mumford, 1852–4)

25 Afterwards *Resolute*'s men were issued an extra allowance of half a gill [62.5 milliliters] of rum, with the promise of a repeat of this issue on similar occasions 'conditionally that the men would go to their hammocks quietly, all good boys' (Mumford, 1852–4).

26 During the week before this journal entry a heavy easterly gale on the 16th resulted in a great drift of snow against *Resolute*'s starboard side, some 2.75 m in depth, depressing the ice and causing the ship to list 1° to starboard (Mumford, 1852–4). It was shovelled away on the 21st (McClintock, 1852–4). On the 18th the lists of sledge crews for the coming season were given out, and preparations begun on making and mending stockings, boot hose, face protectors, and caps (Mumford, 1852–4; McClintock, 1852–4). On the evening of the 18th McDougall gave a lecture on what *Investigator* had achieved (Mumford, 1852–4).

27 This was one of three hares seen on the island (McClintock, 1852–4)

28 The bear was first spotted (at very close range) by Silvey, *Resolute*'s quartermaster, as he was reading the thermometers on the ice alongside the ship at 1 a.m. (McDougall, 1857:176). It ran off when he shone his lantern on it. Mr Hamilton and Mr Dean went in pursuit (Mumford, 1852–4).

29 While moving coal from the forward hold to the engine room aboard *Intrepid* on the 23rd, Henry Smith fell into the hold and broke a rib and hence was eliminated from the spring sledging (McClintock, 1852–4; Scott, 1852–4).

30 Preparations began on the 29th, namely rigging the chandelier (Mumford, 1852–4).

31 In 1849 Mrs Amelia Jenks Bloomer designed and promoted the style of woman's dress named after her, namely a short skirt worn over loose trousers, gathered at the ankles. McDougall (1857:180) remarked that it 'is, or at least was, worn by decoy bar girls in London, as an inducement to *very* young men to expend a certain amount of capital on a glass of beer.' Mumford thought that de Bray's dress 'showed the greatest taste.' He also noted that de Bray sang a song in French.

32 The ladies were 'obliged to have recourse to a posture decidedly unlady-like – sitting with their legs extended over the stove' (McDougall, 1857:181).

33 A great deal of thought and ingenuity went into trying to reduce the 'constant weight,' i.e., that of non-consumables, on each sledge to a minimum (McClintock, 1852–4).

34 McDougall has painted an amusing picture in this connection: 'Officers, – aye, and sedate ones too, on most occasions, might have been observed jumping as high as the weight of their clothes permitted, fondly hoping to be the first to welcome the glorious source of light and warmth, to these inhospitable shores' (McDougall, 1857:182).

In the evening *Resolute*'s officers presented each mess with a bottle of rum 'to drink the sun's and Her Most Gracious Majesty's health' (Mumford, 1852–4).

De Bray went for a 'smart walk' with Captain McClintock, covering 18.78 km statute miles in three hours over rough ice and rocky tundra (McClintock, 1852–4). Since the temperature was -37°C with a sharp breeze, they were both slightly frostbitten.

35 The dogs were also being used to haul gravel from the island for ballast. This was in part to replace the weight of three tanks which had been moved ashore, each of which weighed 2 tonnes (McDougall, 1857:187).

36 About this time Lion, the lead dog of *Resolute*'s sledge team, had a battle with Naps, Captain Kellett's water spaniel; somebody grabbed Lion's tail in an attempt to separate them, damaging the tail. Thereafter it hung limply, rather than curling over his back (McClintock, 1852–4).

37 In his account McClintock makes light of this adventure and certainly makes no mention of being mentally impaired.

38 The northerly gale which arose on the 11th continued until the 17th. As McDougall noted (1857:191): 'The crisis of the gale occurred between midnight on Monday [14th] and 4 a.m. on Tuesday, when the wind blew a complete hurricane; the ship literally trembled; the masts shook like poplar-trees; whilst the awnings, ropes etc. kept up a continued noise.' Everyone was confined to the ships and communication between them was cut off. As McDougall further noted (1857:192), *Intrepid* 'was frequently completely hidden by the drift, which rolled past like a dense volume of steam, mast-head high.'

39 On the 18th, the gale having abated, the casks containing the depot were moved ashore to the island; it consisted of provisions for sixty-six men for 210 days plus plenty of warm clothing, being intended for the use of the crews of *Enterprise* and/or *Investigator* (McClintock, 1852–4).

40 But during a walk on the island on the 20th Mumford noticed that he could feel the heat of the sun on his cheek, although the shade temperature was -36°C. He also commented on himself and his shipmates 'from the long confinement and darkness having a French-white complexion, calling to mind the looks of a cellar-grown onion or potato.'

41 On Sunday 27th Lieutenant Pim's, Dr Domville's and Mr Roche's sledge parties mustered at divisions in their travelling gear (Mumford, 1852–4).

42 In a walking match with Lieutenant Pim Dr Scott (escorted by Captain McClintock) walked from the ship to the lake and back in just under 4 hours 40 minutes (a distance of 29.77 km). Nares tried the same distance next day but took 5 hours 30 minutes. Pim and Scott had seen fresh traces of muskoxen (McClintock, 1852–4; Scott, 1852–4).

43 On the basis of M'Clure's message found at Winter Harbour by
    Mecham in the autumn it was presumed that if *Investigator* had been
    forced to spend a second winter at Mercy Bay, M'Clure would
    abandon his ship as early as possible in the spring of 1853. Pim's
    orders were to try to reach Mercy Bay before that happened. If the
    ship were not there, on the basis of documents left by M'Clure, Pim
    was to attempt to follow him, sending Dr Domville back with details
    as to his intentions (McDougall, 1857:198–9). When the sledge parties
    left the ships the temperature was -42°C and even their rum was fro-
    zen. This was earlier by a month than any previous spring sledge trip
    in the history of the navy's arctic operations (McClintock, 1852–4).

44 Roche's party was seen to reach the tents at 8:30, and all three sledges
    got under way around 11.30. This was a great relief since Pim,
    Domville, and their men had been camped out in a blizzard with
    temperatures of -34 to -39°C since the 10th (McDougall, 1857:204;
    Mumford, 1852–4; McClintock, 1852–4).

45 On St Patrick's day Captain Kellett's sledge 'Erin' was launched down
    a snow ramp from the ship's side, with Mr Dean, its builder, sitting
    astride. Both ships hoisted their colours in honour of the day and the
    event (McDougall, 1857:204–5; Mumford, 1852–4; McClintock, 1852–4).
    Also on the 17th Captain McClintock, Mecham, and Hamilton saw
    two muskoxen during a walk to the north shore of the inlet
    (McDougall, 1857:205).

46 John McLean (McDougall, 1857:206).

6 Sledging to Cape de Bray

1 These descriptions of de Bray's in fact represent some of the most
   comprehensive accounts available of the domestic arrangements of the
   Royal Navy's man-hauling sledge parties.

2 In a ravine west of the lake (Mumford, 1852–4).

3 Having lunched on the heart, liver, etc. (Mumford, 1852–4). Lieutenant
   Nares and Captain McClintock continued overland to Skene Bay but
   saw tracks of only foxes and lemmings (McClintock, 1852–4).

4 On the 25th a breach of discipline occurred aboard *Resolute* which,
   significantly, was reported by Mumford but not by any of the officers.
   At lunchtime brandy (diluted one part brandy to two parts water) was
   substituted for the usual rum ration, similarly diluted, to the disgust of
   the men. In the evening, at 5:30, when the grog was being mixed, a
   deputation went on deck to inform the first lieutenant of the men's
   dissatisfaction at this substitution, but unfortunately he was not on
   board at the time. Then when 'grog' was piped, the man from each
   mess detailed to collect the ration made no move. The captain was
   informed, all hands were turned up, and Captain Kellett promised to
   derate the petty officers involved and to give the men involved four

dozen lashes each. The brandy was then poured out on the ice and the captain read the Articles of War. A detailed investigation was made next day, following which the petty officers were derated and the promise of floggings renewed. Port wine was served in lieu of rum on the 26th (Mumford, 1852–4).

5 The party had great difficulty in navigating because of fog; at noon, according to Mumford, who was one of the party, 'the sun bore on the port bow instead of right astern,' i.e., they were heading SSW instead of N.

6 Mumford makes the revealing comment that they were all 'dead tired but much consoled by knowing that this was only a "small taste" of what we had to expect, under which circumstance it was best to be jolly.'

7 The objectives of the various parties were as follows: McClintock was to explore the northwest coast of Melville Island, with de Bray acting in support. Hamilton was to relay a depot to the eastern shores of Hecla and Griper Bay for use by Kellett in the future; Roche's sledge was to act in support of Hamilton. Captain Kellett's sledge was to operate in support of all the above four parties for the first few days. Mecham was to head west to Winter Harbour, cross the land to Liddon Gulf, then explore the coast of Melville Island west and north from there. Nares would command a sledge in support of Mecham. As McClintock has pointed out, the sixteen officers and men left aboard the ships represented an extremely small reserve in the event of the sledging parties running into serious difficulties.

8 Captain Kellett got back to the ships at 5:00 p.m. on the 11th. McDougall's remarks, no doubt based on conversations with Kellett on his return, are very illuminating: 'the Captain had, until then, been ignorant of the description of labour and exertion required for arctic travelling, which he candidly confessed surpassed everything in the form of hard work he had ever seen, though his experience in the Navy embraces a period of upwards of twenty-five years, during which time he has seen much arduous service in every clime' (McDougall, 1857).

9 In the official report this tree trunk is reported as being partially covered with mud (p. 480).

10 The official report (p. 481) appends the additional information: 'Several fresh deer tracks along the shore going from the westward to the eastward. The neck of a rum can having been broken in packing the sledge, lost a pint.'

11 Middle Point, named by McClintock, was in fact the eastern headland of Middle Island and the Twin Bays are in fact a single embayment, now known as McCormick Inlet. Note that de Bray suspected the true configuration of the bay and island, as indicated with a dashed line on his map (Plate 22). The name Middle Point has now been transferred to the headland on the mainland to the north of Middle Island.

12 Thomas Hood, one of the Captain McClintock's men, was unwell, spitting blood and with a severe pain in his side (McClintock, 1852–4).

13 This was Emerald Isle, lying some 27 km to the north.

14 Two lines have been omitted here: 'Lunch at 2 h. 20 m. a.m. Started at 2 h. 50 m. a.m. making my way in the direction of the shore, keeping at 2 or 3 miles. The floe very rough' (de Bray, 1855b:483).

15 This was Prince Patrick Island, the nearest point of which lies about 30 km away across Fitzwilliam Strait.

16 It was probably due to this refraction that de Bray did not realize the dimensions of Marie Bay, whose mouth the sledges were crossing, and which he marked on his map and named, presumably after his fiancée, Loetitia-Constance-Marie le Bleis. In fact it extends some 35 km inland.

17 Before getting under way the entire party indulged in washing their faces, which McClintock described as 'refreshing' despite the pain caused by frostbite and blisters.

18 McClintock has described this coast as follows: 'it rises abruptly into lofty hills with bold outlines, and is intersected by numerous deep ravines. This part of Melville Island is very beautiful, dark land, not much covered with snow; found grass, saxifrages and poppy, but hardly any moss' (McClintock, 1855:550).

19 This land is reported as being 32 to 48 km miles away in the official report (p. 484). The distance to Prince Patrick Island to the northwest and to the northern tip of Eglinton Island to the west is about 25 km.

20 These stokers were needed on board *Intrepid* (McClintock, 1852–4).

21 One must assume that the bad weather again prevented de Bray from realizing the true extent of Marie Bay.

22 De Bray also saw a snow bunting, the first recorded for the year (p. 485).

23 The party had only one day's provisions left at this stage (p. 486).

24 This was a difficult decision for de Bray to make, since it meant disobeying McClintock's orders to relay provisions forward to Cape Fisher for him.

25 Having accompanied de Bray and party back to the ship, Dr Scott conducted a post-mortem on Coombes; cause of death was reported as 'congestion of the lungs caused by hyperthrophy of the heart' (Scott, 1852–4).

26 This sledge trip across Melville Island represented a very impressive achievement. In forty-five days de Bray and his men had covered 613 km. Taking into account the days when they were weatherbound, this represented a mean daily distance of 15.83 km (12.21 km on the outward journey and 20.43 km on the homeward journey).

From the evidence of the track chart appended to de Bray's report (Plates 21 and 22) he would appear to have been a workmanlike surveyor. Deviations from the modern map are readily explicable in terms of low, snow-covered coastlines, indistinguishable from sea ice, and often obscured by fog and/or blowing snow, or else camouflaged by the effects of mirages.

27 The fact that he had disobeyed orders in order to bring Coombes's body back immediately must understandably have been causing de Bray some anxiety and hence Kellett's sympathetic response must have been a great relief. On his return to the ship in July, McClintock was equally understanding: 'Sudden death is at all times a most awful visitation, & it is difficult to conceive anything more sudden than this poor man's transition to the other world! John Coombes was one of the most powerful men in the expedition. He was in the prime of life & in excellent health, when he fell dead upon the ice about two miles from Point Nias. Mr de Bray & his crew deserve great praise for bringing in the body for six long marches over the land' (McClintock, 1852–4).

McDougall, on the other hand took a different tack. Recognizing that the men's request had placed de Bray in an embarrassing position, since it was in conflict with explicit orders from his superior, he wrote: 'Nor is he, as a foreigner, to be in the least degree blamed for pursuing this line of conduct, although had any other officer of the squadron been in command of the party, his duty, I presume, would have been to have buried the body, and to have fulfilled his orders, after which, if the men had asked it, to have exhumed the corpse and brought it on board' (McDougall, 1857:242–3). Quite apart from his being a foreign officer, the fact that de Bray's men were all from *Intrepid*'s crew, rather than *Resolute*'s, with whom he must have been more familiar after the wintering, cannot have made his decision any easier.

28 William Mumford was one of the sledge crew and has left an excellent account of a very trying journey, plagued by bad weather, melting snow, and generally abominable conditions.

7 Rescue of *Investigator*'s Crew and Preparations for Sea

1 On 15 April Mr Richards (clerk-in-charge) set off with a party of seven men to leave a cask of provisions at the lake (Polyniya Lake) at the head of Bridport Inlet, for the use of any of the sledging parties who might have run seriously short of supplies. Richards and party returned on the same day (McDougall, 1857:212–13).

2 Dr Domville was a little ahead of the rest. McDougall has described the meeting as follows: 'As we grasped him by the hand (which, as well as his face, was as black as the ace of spades), his words, "The *Investigator* is found, and M'Clure is close behind," overpowered us with surprise ... ' (McDougall, 1857:213–14).

3 The group of new arrivals included J.H. Nelson, AB, who had injured

his leg when the sledge capsized on it, two days after leaving *Investigator*; thereafter he was 'in little better than a crippled condition, being compelled to drag my leg out of the deep snow by the help of my trowsers, at almost every step.' He barely managed to make it to *Resolute* under his own steam but there he 'met with a most cordial reception, being instantly supplied by our kind-hearted friends with comforts and even luxuries, never expected to again gladden our hearts in these regions of perpetual snows' (Nelson, 1850–4).

4 Pim and his men had overcome daunting obstacles. Apart from the initial delay when they had sat out a four-day blizzard within sight of Dealy Island with the temperature hovering around -38°C, they had encountered appallingly rough ice in M'Clure Strait after leaving Cape Dundas. A few quotations from Pim's journal will suffice:

Wednesday 23rd March ... Found the appearance of the floe from 'Cape Dundas' had not proved deceptive; the ice was thrown up in the wildest confusion and almost impassible, being heavy hummocks of apparently last year's formation. After a day of severe toil succeeded in gaining about three miles ...

Friday 25th March ... The floe, if floe it can be called, proved bad indeed: hummocks after hummocks followed each other in apparently endless succession, sometimes composed of very old, then young ice; on the former the surface was so glassy and uneven that the men could scarcely stand, on the latter the snow had filled up the interstices, into which men and sledges sank deeply at every step; in short after a hard day's work we only accomplished 2 1/2 miles WSS ...

Saturday 26th March. This morning we began work by breaking through some hummocks more formidable than ever; at last it became absolutely necessary to unload and carry our baggage over on the men's backs ... After much toil succeeded in getting through, but at 5:30, when we encamped, only 1/2 a mile had been gained in a WSW direction. (Pim, 1855:653)

On the 29th Pim's sledge broke down completely and Pim decided to push on with two men, Robert Hoyle and Thomas Bidgood, and the dog sledge, leaving Dr Domville with the unenviable task of relaying most of the provisions and the crippled sledge back over the abominably rough ice to Cape Dundas, where he was to await Pim's return.

5 This was one of the most dramatic meetings in the history of the Arctic, particularly in view of the fact the men of *Investigator* had not seen another European for three years, and of the fact that the bulk of her crew were about to leave their ship for various destinations within the next few days, an initiative which probably would have led to substantial loss of life.

Pim's own account of the event reads as follows:

Wednesday 6th April ... Arrived upon the sea ice and commenced

crossing the Bay of Mercy ... Having seen nothing to indicate the
vicinity of the 'Investigator,' I now made up my mind that she had
left the bay, and accordingly steered right across it with the intention of tracing the whole coast-line in search of her cairn. At 2 p.m.,
when already half-way over, Rt. Hoile reported that he saw something black up the bay; upon looking through the glass, I made out
the object to be a ship, and immediately altered course for her,
weather gradually clearing. 3 p.m. Left the sledge and went on in
advance. 4 p.m. Observed people walking about and made out a
cairn and staff on the beach ... 5 p.m. Arrived within 100 yards
without being observed; then, however, two persons taking exercise
on the ice discovered that I did not belong to the ship. Upon
beckoning they quickly approached, and proved to be Capt. M'Clure
and Lieut. Haswell.; their surprise, and I may add delight, at the
unexpected appearance of a stranger (who seemed as it were to drop
from the clouds) it is needless attempting to describe. One of the
men at work near them conveyed the news on-board, and in an
incredible short time the deck was crowded, every one that could
crawl making his appearance, to see the strangers and hear the
news. The scene which then presented itself can never be effaced
from my memory, nor can I impress any idea of the joy and gladness
with which my arrival was hailed. (Pim, 1855:656–7)
The same event, as seen from the other side, was described by M'Clure
as follows:

While walking near the ship, in conversation with the first
lieutenant upon the subject of digging a grave for the man who died
yesterday, and discussing how we could cut a grave in the ground
whilst it was so hardly frozen – a subject naturally sad and depressing – we perceived a figure walking rapidly towards us from the
rough ice at the entrance of the bay. From his pace and gestures we
both naturally supposed at first that he was some one of our party
pursued by a bear, but as we approached him doubts arose as to who
it could be. He was certainly unlike any of our men; but recollecting
that it was possible some one might be trying a new travelling dress,
preparatory to the departure of our sledges, and certain that no one
else was near, we continued to advance. When within about two
hundred yards of us, this strange figure threw up his arms, and made
gesticulations resembling those used by the Esquimaux, besides
shouting, at the top of his voice, words which, from the wind and
the intense excitement of the moment, sounded like a wild screech;
and this brought us both fairly to a stand-still. The stranger came
quietly on, and we saw that his face was as black as ebony, and
really at the moment we might be pardoned for wondering if he was
a denizen of this or the other world, and had he but given us a
glimpse of a tail or a cloven hoof, we should assuredly have taken to

our legs; as it was, we gallantly stood our ground, and, had the skies fallen upon us, we could hardly have been more astonished than when the dark-faced stranger called out: 'I'm Lieutenant Pim, late of the *Herald*, and now in the *Resolute*. Captain Kellett is in her at Dealy Island!'

To rush at and seize him by the hand was the first impulse, for the heart was too full for the tongue to speak. The announcement of relief being close at hand, when none was supposed to be even within the Arctic Circle, was too sudden, unexpected, and joyous for our minds to comprehend it at once. The news flew with lightning rapidity, the ship was all in commotion; the sick, forgetful of their maladies, leapt from their hammocks; the artificers dropped their tools, and the lower deck was cleared of men; for they all rushed for the hatchway to be assured that a stranger was actually amongst them, and that his tale was true. Despondency fled the ship, and Lieut Pim received a welcome – pure, hearty and grateful – that he will assuredly remember and cherish to the end of his days.

(Osborn, 1857:291)

6 Each party was to consist of fifteen of the weakest men. At Cape Spencer (near Beechey Island) Haswell and his men hoped to pick up a boat left there by Captain Austin of *Assistance* in 1851, and sail it to Greenland, if they did not first encounter a whaler. Cresswell's party was to head south to the depot left on the Princess Royal Islands in 1851, and using the boat left there, cross to the mouth of the Coppermine and ascend that river, presumably aiming, via Great Bear Lake, for the Hudson's Bay Company's post at Fort Good Hope (Osborn, 1857:273–4; Nelson, 1850–4). Either of these enterprises must almost certainly have ended in disaster, and it is probable that all thirty men would have died.

7 This sledge expedition is described in detail by McDougall (1857: 225–39); he was transporting supplies as far as Cart Cairn in support of Lieutenant Hamilton who was to search the coasts of Sabine Peninsula.

8 Mumford, who was one of the men hauling Roche's sledge, has left a lively account of this sledge expedition.

9 Johann Miertsching, the Moravian interpreter, was one of this group and has written a graphic account of the trip across M'Clure Strait (Neatby, 1967: 196–7). Each man was allowed to take only two pairs of spare socks. *Intrepid*'s lower deck was converted into a hospital for the nine scurvy cases (Scott, 1852–4). Dr Scott was grateful of the fact that Mr Piers, *Investigator*'s assistant surgeon, had come with this party. Two men, Anderson and Ross, were so sick that they had to be hauled on the sledges, while five were 'so miserable and lame that they can scarcely stand upright and follow the sledges that we draw' (Neatby, 1967:195). To make matters worse, two of the men, Lieutenant

Wynniatt and Mr Bradbury, had gone mad; the former was violent and had had to be locked in a strongroom aboard *Investigator* (Nelson, 1850–4). Twenty-two of the group were accommodated aboard *Intrepid*.

10 This was Boyle, the sick-bay attendant, who had drunk the dregs from a number of medicine bottles (Neatby, 1967:193).

11 They included James Nelson, who made the return trip to *Investigator* over the objections of Dr Domville, who was concerned that the injury to his leg had not properly healed (Nelson, 1850–4).

12 Lieutenant Cresswell and his party were evacuated home to England from Beechey Island aboard *Phoenix*, which called there to resupply the various expeditions in the summer of 1853. Thus he brought the first news of the achievements and fate of *Investigator* to England. Cresswell also delivered mail from Dealy Island, including de Bray's letter of 2 April 1853 to his mother, reproduced as Appendix 4.

13 Another minor sledge journey occurred just before de Bray's return. On 9 May Mr Richards, Mr Dean, and the gunner's mate set off with the dog sledge for Winter Harbour (McDougall, 1857:2401; Mumford, 18524). En route they were to relay Mecham's depot from Fife Point to a better location at Winter Harbour and then carve the ships' name in Parry's Rock. They returned to the ships, missions accomplished, on the 15th.

   Several hunting excursions had also taken place. On the 9th Lieutenant Pim, Mr Miertsching, and Mr Purchase set off for the lake for a few days' shooting (Mumford, 1852–4). Then on the 18th Mr Krabbé and Mr Dean encountered a herd of seventeen muskoxen near Skene Point. They shot two cows and a calf and captured one calf alive. It was brought on board and fed on 'preserved milk,' but it died after a few days (McDougall, 1857:243–4; Mumford, 1852–4).

14 Although the men spent three days in digging the grave, they were able to penetrate to a depth of only 63 cm into the permafrost (McClintock, 1852–4). The lines carved on the headboard were: 'Therefore be ye also ready; for in such an hour as ye think not the Son of man cometh' Matt. 14:44.

15 Nares and his party had escorted Mecham west to Winter Harbour, then overland to Liddon Gulf and down that gulf and west along the southwest coast of Melville Island as far as Cape Smythe, where they had cached their load for Mecham's return trip, on 19 May. Nares had then turned for home (Nares, 1855:608). The intent had been that Nares would relay a cart from Winter Harbour across to Liddon Gulf (for Mecham's use on his return) but one of his men, John Bailey, was so seriously ill will scurvy (Nares, 1855:609; McDougall, 1857) that Nares decided to come straight back to the ship.

16 Richards had set off from *Assistance*, wintering in Northumberland Sound in northwestern Devon Island, on April 10 with six sledges, two boats and fifty-seven men (McDougall, 1857; Richards, 1855a). Crossing

Penny Strait he left one boat (a whaleboat) at Cape Lady Franklin on the northeast tip of Bathurst Island, and the second one (an ice boat) at Boat Beach, east of Domett Point on the northeast coast of Melville Island. As prearranged, he had left dispatches from Sir Edward Belcher for Captain Kellett at Success Point, the northwest tip of Cameron Island on 30 April.

17 The meeting with Lieutenant Hamilton's party occurred on the sea ice between Cape Colquhoun and Cape George Richards on the northeast coast of Sabine Peninsula; at this point Richards felt that he and his men were good for another 320 km of exploration, and hoped to get to the west of Melville Island, not realizing that Kellett's sledge parties had forestalled them in this area.

Richards's journal reads as follows:

At 1 h. p.m. to our great surprise, we crossed a sledge track, which appeared very recent. I immediately halted the sledge, and followed them back to the eastward. After an hour's quick walking, we saw an encampment, and, on coming up to it, found it to be a party from the *Resolute*, under Lieutenant Hamilton. The surprise of himself and his party may be imagined, at being awoke from their dreams by the hail of a stranger. (Richards, 1855a:322)

From Hamilton they heard of the contact with *Investigator* and:

... the less pleasant information, that the *Resolute*'s parties had left to explore the north coast of Melville Island, about the same time that we had started from Northumberland Sound, thus cutting off all hope from us of further search or discovery in that quarter, at the moment, I am bound to say, a bitter disappointment to all. (Richards, 1855a:322)

18 En route he had also surprised Lieutenant Pim and his party, whom he encountered stormbound at Cart Cairn on Hecla and Griper Bay. Mumford has reported the event as follows:

Monday 30th. Confined to the tent by the gale not being able to see 20 yards ahead. At 9 p.m. the cook reported a sail, which news roused us all out in a hurry to meet the stranger. The sledge under sail came down on us in fine style and proved to be one from H.M.S. *Assistance* consisting of Commander Richards & 7 hands. Exchanged cheers and were all anxious to hear the news. Obtained 4 days rum, pemmican & spirits of wine from them as we only had 5 days provisions left. The party left us about 10 p.m. having the gale in their favor [sic]; but being dead against us we all turned in and made the best of it, Mr Pim congratulating me that I should not require my sealskin boots for a meal at present.

19 For full details of this wintering, see Belcher (1855a).

20 Commander Richards and party got back to their ship safely on 12 July, travelling by boat for the last lap across Penny Strait (Richards, 1855a).

21 Mumford was extremely glad to get home. He wrote that they 'reached the ship at 11.30 a.m. to the great joy of all engaged, who congratulated one another on a return from one of the most unpleasant excursions ever made over Melville Island, having endured the worst weather, the rough road and, worse than all, 129 hours confined to the tent by bad weather.'

22 The medical report by Drs Alexander Armstrong and Domville is quoted in full in Kellett (1855a:70-2) and in Osborn (1857:332-4). They found that all of *Investigator*'s crew showed 'with one or two exceptions, well marked evidence of scurvy and debility in various stages of development, with great loss of flesh and strength (Osborn: 332), and predicted disaster if they were 'exposed to the intense severity of another (the fourth) arctic winter, after the effects of a sojourn so long as that which has fallen their lot to have experienced' (Osborn, 1857:334). Captain Kellett had specified (Armstrong, 1857:571) that *Investigator* should be abandoned unless a minimum of twenty fit officers and men volunteered to stay aboard for another wintering. Only ten officers and men, including M'Clure (and including only four men) in fact volunteered to stay and hence, even if the results of the medical survey had been more encouraging, M'Clure would probably still have decided to abandon his ship.

23 One of the sledge runners wore through completely about 13 km west of Point Hearne (Domville, 1855:676). Having nothing with which to effect a repair, Domville was forced to cut the sledge in half and then, 'divesting the sledge, therefore, of every encumbrance excepting actual necessaries,' he pushed on to Dealy Island.

24 McDougall (1857:263) has described this brief trip in detail. He set off on 14 June and returned on the 24th having fulfilled his orders. Especially on the return trip, the travelling was execrable due to the vast quantities of meltwater on the ice. On 23 June their route 'lay through continuous pools of water knee deep *per mare per glaciem*,' while off Cape Bounty 'the floe was even worse than before, the men at times being obliged to extricate each other from the deep sludge, as well as to dig out their sledge, which often sank above the bearers' (McDougall, 1857:261).

25 Dr Scott (1852–4) has clarified the expedition regulations about game brought in: 'The rule of shooting is that if any one goes away, all small birds are his & the head & appurtenances of muskox or deer, the carcasses being given up. But if one is *sent* away on a regular, organized shooting party everything is given up.'

26 De Bray has made a slight error here. It was Nares who returned on the 14th, having set off on 3 June to transport a cart from Winter Harbour across to Liddon Gulf for Mecham. For Nares's report to Captain Kellett on his return see Nares (1855:610).

27 Many of *Investigator*'s crew were in a pitiful condition, as Miertsching

has described (Neatby, 1967:200): ' ... the melancholy spectacle which they presented I will never in my life forget. Two sick men were lashed on to each of the four sledges; others, utterly without strength, were supported by comrades who still preserved a little vigour, others again held on to and leaned on the sledges, and these were drawn by men so unsteady on their feet that every five minutes they would fall and be unable to rise without the help of their comrades, the captain, or one of the officers.'

Captain Kellett ordered fresh muskox beef and venison and a double allowance of lemon juice for all 'to improve their emaciated appearance' (McClintock, 1852–4). The results were quite dramatic. With liberal rations, including plenty of fresh meat, all these signs of weakness quickly vanished. 'At first they became full-faced & bloated, then fell off again, but subsequently regained their strength & healthier appearance' (McClintock, 1852–4).

28 *North Star* had been driven ashore by the ice on 28 September 1852, but Captain Pullen had managed to heave her off and she was more or less on an even keel by the end of October (Pullen, 1855:814–29).

29 Inglefield had also pushed quite far west into Jones Sound, sighting and naming headlands as far west as Cape Newman Smith (Inglefield, 1853:80). He had reached Beechey Island on 7 September 1852 and had sailed again from England almost immediately.

30 For full details see Bellot (1855) and Kennedy (1853). *Prince Albert* reached Beechey Island on 19 August 1852 and sailed again on the 24th. For a detailed report of Roche's trip back by dogteam, see Roche (1855:688–9).

31 Lieutenant Hamilton had in fact sent one man, Bombardier Ross, ahead with Sir Edward Belcher's dispatches on the 19th, since the party was making such slow progress. He had left the sledge and cart at the head of Bridport Inlet because of a shore lead 20 m wide between the ice and the shore (Hamilton, 1855:640).

32 There were at least two hunting parties out at this period. Dr Domville and Mr Roche, with three hands and most of the dogs, had gone to Skene Bay on the 27th, while Mr Haswell and Mr Couch had left for Cape Bounty on the same day. Dr Domville returned to the ships with two muskoxen on the 30th (Mumford, 1852–4).

33 This cart was known as 'Paddy's Mistake' (Mumford, 1852–4). It was left on the beach on 10 July 'in a damaged state, the wheels not "keeping step" with one another' and it took eight men to recover it (Mumford, 1852–4).

34 Mecham had explored and searched the southwest coast of Melville Island, the south coast of Eglinton Island, and the south and west coasts of Prince Patrick Island, as far north as Cape Discovery, which he reached on 26 June. On the way back he crossed Prince Patrick Island from West Bay to Walker Inlet, and searched the north coast of

Eglinton Island on the way home (Mecham 1855a). Mecham and his men had covered the remarkable distance of 1,871 km.

35 On the 11th work began on building a cairn 4.3 m high and 4.3 m in diameter at the base, 2.13 m in diameter at the summit, surmounted by a flagstaff 10.7 m high on which five casks were strung and which was topped by a black ball, on the summit of the island (Mumford, 1852–4; McClintock, 1852–4). It took about 42 tonnes of stone to build (Scott, 1852–4).

36 After parting from de Bray at Cape de Bray, McClintock had crossed to Prince Patrick Island and had searched the shores of Intrepid Inlet, the north coast of Eglinton Island, and then the northeastern and north-western coasts of Prince Patrick Island. He turned back from McClintock Point on the northwest coast, and on the way back searched the coasts of Emerald Isle (McClintock, 1855b). He had covered 2,137 km. For the last three days his party had travelled light, camping without a tent.

37 This is a perceptive assumption. The west coast of Prince Patrick Island, which both Mecham and McClintock examined, faces the Central Arctic Basin, with no land between it and the coasts of Siberia.

38 The depot was completed on 23 July, the work being supervised by Mr Dean, Resolute's carpenter. The stone walls were 91 cm thick, the east wall 2.7 m high, and the west wall 2.1 m high; the rear wall consisted largely of the tanks moved ashore from the ship. The roof, supported by pillars in the centre was covered with a layer of new tarred canvas, then with a layer of coal bags, and then with a final layer of new canvas painted white (Kellett, 1855a:79). The stores left in it, intended for Collinson and his men, were enough for sixty-six men for 210 days. The store house is still largely standing and was conserved by a multidisciplinary team from the Prince of Wales Heritage Centre in Yellowknife in the summer of 1978 (Janes, 1982).

39 The first slight movements in the ice were observed on the 29th, with cracks opening and closing and the ice pushing up on shore on the east side of Bridport Inlet (McClintock, 1852–4).

40 On the 1st Resolute's crow's nest was set up on the fore topgallant masthead (Mumford, 1852–4). Both crews were kept busy painting the ships for most of the first week of August.

41 This wooden plaque read as follows: 'H.M.S. Resolute, Henry Kellett Esqr. CB. Captn., & H.M.S. Intrepid, F.L. McClintock, Esqr. Commr., wintered 1852-53, S 82°E (true) 763 fms. from this cairn. Door of depot house, S 11° 15'E, 975 feet. Record will be found in house.' It was discovered at the cairn by Captain J.E. Bernier, from Arctic, in 1908 and moved to Parry's Rock, Winter Harbour (Bernier 1910:197). On 6 August the records were deposited in the house and the door barri-caded with rocks (Mumford, 1852–4).

42 Although M'Clure was optimistic, both Kellett and McClintock were

quite pessimistic about getting to Beechey Island with the ships in the 1853 season. McClintock noted in his journal: 'I think the chances are against us & have proposed starting a considerable number of men with boats on sledges. I think they will find water along the shores of this isld., Bathurst & Cornwallis & so will be able to pull 2/3rds of the way; the remainder must be done over rough ice. A sledge adapted to the purpose is ordered to be made for a preparatory trial. We have so little preserved meat remaining & so many mouths here (138) that it is desirable to try & push forward some of them in time to go home this autumn from Beechey' (McClintock, 1852–4). Then on August 10 he noted: 'No time is to be lost if parties are to go down with the hope of getting home this autumn; 3 weeks is the least we can allow for the journey. It would be unusually wet & laborious work & its ultimate success doubtful, yet I think it is worth the trial.' Not surprisingly, rumours of such plans soon spread throughout the ships. On the 10th Mumford remarked on 'the standard topic being the state of the ice and whether we shall ride or walk to Beechey Island.' On the 14th he noted: 'Much said of another winter, short allowance, etc.'

43 In another race Kellett, carrying McClintock, ran 50 yards (45.72 m) against Pim (with a handicap of 50 yards) for a bet of £3. Kellett won by 7.3 m. The handicap of 25 yards (22.86 m) in the Kellett – de Bray race represented the difference in their ages (Mumford, 1852–4). Mr Nares ran 100 yards (91.44 m) in 14 seconds and 300 yards (274.32 m) in 46 seconds (McDougall, 1857:302). In the evening each man received half a gill of rum and a 'grinning match' took place in *Resolute's* lower deck (Mumford, 1852–4).

44 To relieve the tension a little a sports day was held on Dealy Island; the competitions included wrestling, jumping, and sack races, with prizes being awarded from a 'whip-round' which had been held on both ships (Mumford, 1852–4). Salmon of *Intrepid* was the champion wrestler (McClintock, 1852-4; Scott, 1852–4).

8 Under Way Again

1 McDougall (1857:305n) argues very sensibly that a similar rapid and unexpected breakup of the ice might have surprised *Erebus* and *Terror* at Beechey Island and might thus account for the baffling lack of messages. This boat (and one from *Intrepid* which was carried away by the ice) was being used to cross the stretch of water between the ice and the land, some 60 m wide at high water (Mumford, 1852–4). *Resolute's* boat was discovered (and photographed) by Bernier in 1908 (Bernier, 1910:49–50).

2 Both ships experienced some heavy impacts from the ice as they were driving out to sea. With regard to *Intrepid*, McClintock noted: 'We were upon the weather edge of the ice & there was a considerable sea

up, beating us against it violently. Also large masses gave the ship most unpleasant thumps, making the plates and glasses jump up from the table.' However, this is a long way from Miertsching's sensational account in which he claimed the ships 'were flung this way and that by the heavy and tumbling ice, and took many hard knocks. The rudder of the *Resolute* and two boats of the *Intrepid* were smashed to pieces' (Neatby, 1967:204). Indeed, he claimed that *Resolute*'s rudder was smashed beyond repair and had to be replaced. None of the other accounts makes mention of such serious damage; it is difficult to understand why Miertsching should have resorted to fiction.

3 At the time there was real concern that the ships might be crushed and/or might have to be abandoned. Thus on the 22nd, lists of boat crews were announced in the event of abandoning ship, and on the same day *Resolute*'s crew mustered at divisions with packed knapsacks (Mumford, 1852–4). McClintock noted on the 25th that 'Some days we got tents, sledges, provisions & boats in readiness for instant departure, in case of sudden casualty to the ship. These things are to be always kept ready & the men know their stations & duties in such an event' (McClintock, 1852–4). But neither ship was ever in any danger; the worst situation noted was on the 27th when McClintock reported: 'A little pressure on the ship, occasionally making the timbers creak.'

Certainly there was nothing even vaguely resembling the crisis which Miertsching described on the 29th: 'This morning came a mighty storm in which the sturdy ships were flung around by the ice like nut-shells, and threatened more than once with being overwhelmed and sunk by the ice-masses heaving up around them' (Neatby, 1967:205).

4 McDougall was again selected for this task; he found ample water depths along the edge of the fast ice (8 to 13 fathoms), running in a straight line from Point Griffiths to a headland about 8 km to the north (McDougall, 1857:312).

5 According to Dr Scott (1852–4) a herd of sixteen muskoxen was seen on shore during the morning, but they were left in peace.

6 Already there was much talk of this probably being the ships' winter quarters (Mumford, 1852–4).

7 Captain Kellett and several officers went ashore to hunt but although 10 muskoxen were seen from the ship the hunters returned empty-handed (Mumford, 1852–54).

8 By McClintock's reckoning 'the chances are decidedly against our getting away.' He saw this as a mixed blessing: 'We look upon our present berth as our winter quarters with no disrelish, for game is abundant, but if we cannot take the Investigator's down [i.e., to Beechey Island] this season it will not only be a very serious detention for them – undoubtedly fatal to some – but will greatly diminish the

éclat of our expedition' (McClintock, 1852–4). At the same time he noted that if they wintered there they would have to send a large party back to *Investigator*, in view of the limited remaining stocks of preserved meats.

9 The ice on the melt pools on the ice had now frozen hard enough for the men to go skating (McDougall, 1857:319).

10 Various minor preparations for winter were already being made. For example, Mumford noted that the ship's organ 'came out again.' This is one of the few references in the journals to this instrument, which was presumably similar to the barrel organ which Sir William Edward Parry took on all four of his expeditions and which has recently been restored and stands in the museum of the Scott Polar Research Institute in Cambridge (Holland and Hill, 1972:413–4). Mumford remarked that of its ten tunes, the only one which it would now play, 'in rather a consumptive manner' was 'There's a good time coming boys'!

11 McClintock has reported that this sludge 'is exactly of the consistence [sic] of iced cream, and when it becomes more than a few inches thick it acquires a semi-frozen surface & a ship sticks as firmly in it as a fly in treacle, unless she is aided by steam, or favored [sic] by a strong breeze' (McClintock, 1852–4).

12 The party consisted of McDougall, Mecham, Haswell, Miertsching, and two hands (McDougall, 1857:321–3). These eleven animals brought the total number of muskoxen killed on Melville and Prince Patrick islands between September 3 1852 and September 1853 to 122 animals, of which eighty-four were killed in the spring and summer of 1853. Over the same twelve-month period, ninety-four caribou and 161 hares were killed (McClintock, 1852–4). By Osborn's estimate (1857:339) some 5 tonnes of muskox meat were obtained on Melville Island. He remarked: 'At one time the meat was festooned round the rigging of the *Resolute* and *Intrepid* until they resembled butchers' stalls far more than British discovery ships.' And as he also emphasizes (1857:342) the recovery of the health of most of *Investigator*'s invalids must be largely ascribed to the relative abundance of fresh meat.

13 Captains Kellett, M'Clure, and McClintock held a meeting to decide on future action (McDougall, 1857:323). M'Clure proposed transferred all the 'Investigators' to *Intrepid* and dispatching her to Beechey Island round the north end of Byam Martin Island (McClintock, 1852–4).

14 *Intrepid* was having problems with small pieces of ice choking her injection pipes every ten to fifteen minutes, which meant stopping engines and clearing them by blowing steam through them. McClintock in fact was convinced that 'the steamer, *alone*, could have got back to the land ice, but could do nothing with the *Resolute*' (McClintock, 1852–4).

9 The Second Wintering

1 This was the day on which Captain Kellett announced a reduction in rations for all hands. The major changes were 337.5 g instead of 450 g of biscuit or flour, a half allowance, of tea, cocoa and vegetables, and half a gill of rum [35 ml] in lieu of tea every second night (Mumford, 1852–4). Kellett's aim was to have enough in hand in case a third wintering became necessary. But in that case all the *Investigator*'s and half of the other crews would have to be dispatched to *North Star* in the spring (McClintock, 1852–4).

Perhaps the most serious aspect of the provisions situation 'is that we are obliged to use salt meat on five days out of the seven. We can only afford preserved meat *once*, and preserved soup with meat in it once a week. We cannot afford to increase the allowance of other provisions nor issue extra lemon juice. We may well feel grateful for the providential supply of 27 musk oxen at Point Griffiths, for without it we could scarcely have issued anything but salt meat' (McClintock, 1852–4).

2 Although, strangely, there is no mention of it in his journal, at McClintock's request Miertsching fired at a snowy owl and, having only wounded it, took it on board *Intrepid*, where McClintock kept it in his cabin and derived great pleasure from its appearance and its calm, philosophical behaviour (McClintock, 1852–4).

3 If Nelson was at all typical of the 'Investigators', they were quite philosophical about facing their fourth winter in the Arctic:

... we were fully prepared, as far as circumstances permitted, to enter the lists against our relentless and ever-present foes, frost and snow.

Although greatly disappointed at our want of success (for the reaching of Davis Straits this season had been looked on as a matter of certainty) still I must confess, there are many relieving features in our present condition, in comparison to that of last winter. In the first place we have received a plentiful supply of most nutritious food, viz. musk ox and deer flesh, the effect of which is pretty evident on most of us, and notwithstanding an existing necessity to reduce, in a slight measure, the present ration of provision, no hunger-dreams are again likely to be experienced nor, in fact, a second edition of Mercy Bay in any of its bitter details. Change of scene, new faces, two years subsequent news from England, in lieu of the old, old and unconscionably oft-repeated yarns, all tend to wile away hours that would otherwise pass by as if with leaden footsteps. (Nelson, 1852–4)

4 Since *Resolute* was listing 5° to port, the snow layer on the deck was made deeper on the port side than the starboard side (McDougall, 1857:331–2). Only the forward and after parts of the upper deck were 'snowed' at this point.

5 Parry had similarly spotted them on 28 August 1820 during his homeward voyage due to the presence of grounded floes; he sounded a depth of 5¾ fathoms to the west of the shoal (Parry, 1821:262).

6 The cases of lime juice had been stowed in the gravel ballast (McDougall, 1857:338).

7 The game was rounders (Mumford, 1852–4; McDougall, 1857:339) or, as Miertsching described it, 'a kind of game with a ball that occupies fifty to sixty men at a time' (Neatby, 1967:209).

8 Cape Cockburn was sighted to the northeast, 35 km off, on the 25th (McClintock, 1852–4). Mr Roche was sent a few miles in that direction to check the ice conditions, since there was still some thought of sending a party to Beechey Island, in order to reduce the number of mouths to be fed. Roche reported the ice practicable for a light sledge, but Kellett decided against it (McClintock, 1852–4). The idea was not finally abandoned until the end of the month.

9 On the 26th the 'Investigators' celebrated the anniversary of Captain M'Clure's discovery of the Northwest Passage (McClintock, 1852–4), having saved up their grog for the occasion. As Mumford diplomatically noted, 'Captain M'Clure did the same but more privately, Captain Kellett showing some signs of having helped in the ceremony.' The celebration continued on the 27th to the point where one of the 'Investigators' 'freshened up to a serious state of insubordination,' and ended up in irons under guard in *Resolute*'s main hold (Mumford, 1852–4). A reference to 'certain unfortunate preparations being made by the boatswain's mates on the 28th' would indicate that he was also flogged.

10 Guy Fawkes Day was celebrated with just as much verve and noise as on the previous year (Neatby, 1967:210; Mumford, 1852–4; McClintock, 1852–4), although out of consideration for Sainsbury's serious condition the noise level on *Resolute* was held down for most of the day.

During the preparations in the afternoon, what might have been a serious accident aboard *Resolute* was narrowly averted, and even concealed from the officers:

> In the afternoon while the men were engaged mixing up a 'devil' of rocket composition, gunpowder, turpentine, etc. on No. 6 mess table, a spark from a lamp ignited the whole with a tremendous blaze and filled the lower deck with smoke. Fortunately the officers were in the gunroom dining so that the blaze was not seen and the smoke was blamed to an airing stove in the steerage, which was laying on its side in the ash pan and has been cold for some time. (Mumford, 1852–4)

The day's events provoked McClintock to philosophize on the beneficial effects of such activities:

> The preparations for all this [the Guy Fawkes celebrations] were made privately by the men, as a sort of agreeable diversion not only

for themselves but also as a surprize to the officers. Men of war seamen excel all others in this; that they can always find amusement or employment for themselves, and to get up this affair has kept a number of them busy for several weeks. This is the cream of the joke: the man who is constantly employing his time has too much to do to get sick, keeps out of scrapes & does not burthen his mind with unprofitable reflections about getting out, getting home or getting crushed, or anything else which may befall us. Peace of mind & activity of body are almost safeguards against the scurvy. (McClintock, 1852–4)

11 On the 7th names were taken of those who wanted to take part in the next theatrical performance. On the 8th the *Taming of the Shrew* was selected as the piece to be staged, and on the 11th the carpenters began work on the theatre on board *Resolute* (Mumford, 1852–4).

12 By this time the ships had ceased to drift. The position of the winter quarters was determined to be 74° 41′ 30″N, 101° 22′W, in a depth of 137 m (McClintock, 1852–4).

13 The news was passed to *Intrepid* by 'that poor silly creature Bradbury' who went around the ship informing everyone he met in 'the same set phrase.' The irony was not lost on McClintock: 'This man is now a perfect simpleton, inoffensive & apparently happy. Having lost his wits he may be regarded as in a medium state between life & death, and in this view his mission this morning was not inappropriate, awakening a long train of melancholy thought' (McClintock, 1852–4).

14 According to Nelson, his shipmate, he had rallied noticeably on reaching *Resolute* but then deteriorated:

> For nearly two years past has this young officer been somewhat broken in health, and so debilitated that on Dr Domville's leaving the 'Investigator.' Mr Sainsbury had to be placed on the sledge, and never left it until he arrived on board the *Resolute*. But a marked change was soon visible, our young shipmate somewhat rallying, and when the vessels broke out, he might often be seen promenading the upper deck, as merry as we have known him in our halcyon days. It was during the terrible snowstorm, before related, & which so effectually barred our further progress, that our young friend became somewhat gloomy & hinted at his having given up all hopes of reaching England, seeking retirement and generally speaking extremely despondently. This state of things soon brought him to his bed, from which he never rose. (Nelson, 1850–4)

15 Dr Domville's original intention had been to read the lecture quietly in the sick bay to the small group of men who first requested it, but the size of the operation was expanded by popular demand (McDougall, 1857:343).

16 The carpenters' ingenuity was tested by demands for props such as a wooden leg of lamb (McDougall, 1857:344).

17 The men insisted on 'having a "real play". They hold mere farces in contempt. The most probable explanation of this is that they have heard *plays* were acted on board the *Assistance* last winter and they do not choose to be surpassed' (McClintock, 1852–4).

18 The songs included 'I'm only ninety-five' sung 'by an old Marine in the character of a stout spinster of that age, who having luckily discovered that the nasty men are base deceivers, eschews matrimony and in her song exposes their "flattering arts" by which they incessantly try to ensnare her still susceptible heart!' The effect was enhanced by the old marine 'being a very ugly man with coarse features & grizzled beard of a week's growth' who 'looked of course like a most hideous bedlamite when appropriately bedizened in a cap with frills, an antiquated bonnet, a huge grey shawl, short gown & strong laced-up boots, also armed with a substantial oak stick' (McClintock, 1852–4).

19 This was Charles Anderson, whom Miertsching dismissed as 'the most godforsaken of men' (Neatby, 1967:15). He also sang 'Poor Old Joe' (McClintock, 1852–4).

20 Mumford contradicts this, reporting that there was some real discontent when no extra allowance was issued, despite earlier promises, because of the 'advanced state' of some of the hands.

21 The topic was Ross's voyage of 1818 and Parry's voyage of 1819–20 (Mumford, 1852–4).

22 On the 11th the man who had been clapped in irons for insubordination on 27 October was finally released (Mumford, 1852–4).

23 McDougall was very impressed not only by the attentiveness of the men at this lecture but at their studiousness in general, and at the fact that many of them were keeping journals; one man would conscientiously entertain his messmates by reading aloud to them (McDougall, 1857:349). About this time Dr Scott informed Thomas Hood, who had been seriously ill for some time, as to the true state of his health and the sick man made his will (McClintock, 1852–4). Also William Mumford began studying French 'under the kindly offered instruction of Lieut. De Bray' (Mumford, 1852–4).

24 Two choral groups were involved: the Royal Arctic Choral Society and the Ethiopian Serenaders, both of which had been practising for several weeks.

25 Prior to this, presumably in preparation for rigging a telegraph system, Lieutenant Hamilton explained the principles of the electric telegraph and 'concluded with electrifying all that felt disposed to be operated on' (Mumford, 1852–4).

26 The wire was supported on boat oars (presumably stuck in the snow pyramids) about 30 m apart and at a height of about 3.5 m above the ice (McDougall, 1857:356). The first message relayed between the ships (on the afternoon of the 31st) was 'How are you off for soap?' (Mumford, 1852–4). Samuel Morse had transmitted his first public telegram over a 64 km line between Washington DC and Philadelphia on 24 May 1844, barely ten years earlier.

27 There are several slightly differing variants of this story. According to McClintock:

> ... a party of our men [i.e., from *Intrepid*] started with lanthorn and gong to escort back our 'band' from the *Resolute*. In consequence of the weather some of them came back & but two men, guided by the wires, succeeded in reaching the *Resolute* & not finding their companions there, gave the alarm. The wires soon satisfied me about these two missing ones & by them we arranged to keep onboard our ships until the weather improved. The weather was most severe & snow drift so thick that one could not see ten yards. (McClintock, 1852–4)

According to McDougall only one man, Hartnell, was missing. On reaching the first 'telegraph post,' only about 50 m from *Intrepid*, he had lost sight of the ship and was afraid to move. Crouching against the pillar he began shouting 'A man lost! A man lost!' until his shouts were heard.

At midnight, after the New Year had been welcomed in aboard both ships the telegraph was used to exchange the compliments of the season (McDougall, 1857:358–9).

28 Miertsching was not at all impressed by the Christmas or New Year celebrations. 'Christmas Day and New Year's Day are the only two festivals in the whole year, except Sunday, which are observed at sea; but unhappily not in an edifying manner, but by eating, drinking, and uproar, for which extra rations of food and spirits are issued – a truly English tradition' (Neatby, 1967:216).

29 Hood persistently refused Miertsching's attempts at intercession for his soul: 'This unhappy man has no rest night or day, but groans, curses and complains unceasingly. I go often to his bedside and try to awake him to a sense of his pitiful state and of the great danger he is in of being lost eternally ...; but unhappily, unhappily, all my words seem to be in vain. He absolutely refuses to listen; he has forbidden me to visit him, for he cannot endure religious instruction and does not believe in it' (Neatby, 1967:216).

30 In fact he had been on two previous expeditions, with Sir James Clark Ross in *Enterprise* and *Investigator* at Port Lepold in 1848–9, and with Captain Austin in *Assistance* at Griffith Island in 1850–1 (McDougall, 1857:363; McClintock, 1852–4).

31 Mumford has remarked very eloquently of this funeral: 'If the beautiful form of the burial service can appear more solemn at one time than another, it is when a small and decreasing, isolated party are rendering their last tribute to a deceased shipmate, while the gloomy, widespread monotony of the ice fills up the picture.' He also noted that there was enough light for Captain Kellett to read the service without using a lantern, but McClintock (1852–4) refutes this.

32 On the 7th de Bray and Lieutenant Nares made some experiments into

the maximum weight which could be hauled with a hauling belt; it was found to be 135 kg (Mumford, 1852–4).

33 On the 13th Mumford began making model sledges at the request of the officers, as souvenirs (Mumford, 1852–4).

34 Wilkie had become grotesquely swollen towards the end, 'like one far advanced in dropsy' (McClintock, 1852–4). But at the end his death was very sudden; he asked for a drink and before it arrived he was dead. To Miertsching's delight, he was much more responsive to his religious ministrations than Hood had been.

Wilkie had been with Sir James Clark Ross in 1848–9, with Austin in *Assistance* in 1850–1 (when he was one of McClintock's party which travelled to Melville Island), while on the present expedition he had taken part in the autumn sledge trips, but had not been well enough to take part in any of the spring sledge trips.

35 Not surprisingly, by 20 February Captain McClintock was having difficulty in thinking of projects to keep his men employed. On that date however, he had the men making brooms out of hair rope and some baleen, salvaged from *Regalia* and *McLellan*. Mumford, on the other hand, had plenty to fill his time. By the 11th he had completed eleven model sledges (Mumford, 1852–4).

36 The travelling party (i.e., those bound for Beechey Island), mustered in their travelling suits (Mumford, 1852–4).

37 The topic was arctic exploration from 1845 to the present, i.e., a survey of the Franklin searches.

A three-cornered fight broke out between *Investigator*'s boatswain, carpenter, and ice master; it was broken up by the first lieutenant and the sergeant of marines and they were hauled before Captain Kellett (Mumford, 1852–4).

10 Contacts with *North Star* and *Assistance*

1 Roche in fact set off to return to the ship immediately after the accident to the sledge on the 4th, but after four miles decided to return to where Hamilton was camped, since both he and the dogs were near exhaustion (McDougall, 1857:374).

2 Alexander Thompson, the dog driver, had thus covered 59.5 km running behind the sledge across rough ice in under nine hours, and hence was totally exhausted (McClintock, 1852–4). Mumford reported that his friends 'took charge of him and after some refreshment turned him into a hammock where he soon exchanged his dogs for "pigs" which he drove in good style.'

3 Mumford reported that on the 22nd de Bray's sledge crew for the impending journey was named, and that they were to transport depots to Cape Dundas on northern Prince of Wales Island and Cape Hardy in

Peel Sound, then back across Barrow Strait to Assistance Harbour and
Beechey Island.

4 As an experiment, on the 13th the return wire of the electric telegraph
was eliminated; instead earth wires leading down via the fireholes into
the sea from each apparatus were substituted and were found to be
equally effective (McClintock, 1852–4; McDougall, 1857:373).

5 Mr Roche was well enough to be one of the party which went out to
greet the new arrivals (Mumford, 1852–4). On 29 March he had
been able to walk from *Resolute* to *Intrepid* using only a stick, an
amazingly rapid recovery (McClintock, 1852–4).

6 For further details of *Assistance*'s wintering see Belcher (1855a).

7 For details of *Phoenix*'s and *Breadalbane*'s voyage see Inglefield (1854a).

8 Caught between the driving pack and the fast ice on 22 August 1853,
Breadalbane, which was not ice-strengthened, was sliced open by the
ice and sank within fifteen minutes. No lives were lost although some
men were undoubtedly badly scared: 'only roused out of their hammocks in the forecastle as the ice was crashing through her bows'
(Pullen, 1855b:784).

   The sunken ship was located by Dr Joe MacInnes using side-scan
sonar in July 1980 and, using a remotely piloted submersible, the
wreck was photographed the following summer (MacInnes, 1982).

9 The statements of William Johnson (who was one of the men with
Bellot on the floe at the time of his death) and of William Harvey (also
a member of the party, but on shore at the time) may be found in
Anonymous (n.d.:28–9). See also Barr, 1986:63).

10 *Resolute* had brought mail for Bellot to Beechey Island and he had
picked it up from *North Star* on 19 August 1852 when *Prince Albert*
called at Beechey Island, homeward bound (Kennedy, 1853:164).

11 For details, see Inglefield (1853).

12 For details of this expedition, see Kane (1856), Godfrey (1857), and
Hayes (1860).

13 The details of Richards' own sledge journey from *Assistance* to
Beechey Island then west to *Resolute* and *Intrepid*, bringing the mail,
can be found in Richards (1855b). He had started from Beechey Island
with seven sledges with supplies for Kellett's ships, but on meeting Mr
Court and his party, eastward bound just east of Cape Hotham on 21
March (Richards, 1855b:381) and having heard all the news of *Investiga-
tor*, *Resolute*, and *Intrepid*, Richards had ordered all the depots left at
Assistance Bay (McClintock, 1852–4).

14 Messrs Newton and Ford were also among the group (McClintock,
1852-4; McDougall, 1857:384). A detailed account of this journey is to
be found in Nelson's journal (Nelson, 1852–4). It took just under two
weeks, from 10 to 23 April 1854.

15 Alexander Thompson, as usual, was driving the dogs (McClintock,
1852–4).

16 This rumour quickly spread through both ships (Mumford, 1852–4; Nelson, 1852–4) but the three captains were utterly baffled by Belcher's totally confusing orders (one of which is reproduced in Belcher, 1855b). McClintock reported :

> I was sent for by Captain Kellett to read over all his orders from Sir E. Belcher, dated respectively Octr./53, Feby./54 and April/54, and to give my opinion as to their meaning. I did so. Some paragraphs in these long orders contradict each other. I could not make out any *distinct* order application [sic] to the present positions of the ships, which bore on their future disposal. It is implied that we are to abandon them. By his last orders Sir Ed. assumes that Capt. Kellett has determined upon abandoning his ships.
>
> Now this being exactly contrary to his intentions (which he fully explained to Sir Ed. in his letters by Hamilton) he feels greatly puzzled. (McClintock, 1852–4)

After consulting with Captains M'Clure and McClintock and Commander Richards, Kellett decided to send McClintock to *Assistance* for clarification.

17 This party included all the remaining 'Investigators' with the exception of Morgan, who was still too ill to travel (McClintock, 1852–4). As Miertsching reported, their departure was accompanied by a brief ceremony: 'Before we left the ships Captain Kellett assembled us all on deck and thanked us publicly for the regular discipline and exceptionally good conduct which to the very last had characterized the men of the *Investigator*; he handed to our worthy Captain M'Clure a letter to the Admiralty in which he gave the crew of the *Investigator* a character so good that one would rarely find other ships worthy of it' (Neatby, 1967:222). Miertsching has also provided some details of the journey to Beechey island (Neatby, 1967:221–6).

18 McClintock had reached *North Star* at Beechey Island on the 18th, having met en route a further four parties from *North Star* hauling supplies to *Resolute* and to Cape Cockburn; he directed them to cache their supplies at Assistance Bay (McClintock, 1852–4). After one night at *North Star* McClintock continued north to *Assistance*, covering the 84 km in twenty-four hours. He thought Sir Edward Belcher 'looked debilitated and old; more perhaps from want of fresh air, exercise and society than from all other causes put together.' After lengthy discussions with the commander-in-chief, McClintock started back for *North Star* and *Resolute* on the evening of the 21st. He and Thompson had covered 740 km in fifteen days, i.e., an average of 49 km a day. He reported:

> Sir Edd. gave me distinct orders for Captain Kellett to abandon both *Resolute* and *Intrepid*. He told me this was in accordance with the views of the Board of Admiralty which had given him the command, & also in anticipation of his orders, which he expects to

receive this year. I told him how strongly Captain Kellett's profes-
sional feeling of sticking to his ship to the last, operated on his
mind, and spoke most fully and freely on the subject. Sir Edd. thinks
differently from us all. (McClintock, 1852–4)

19 Quite sensibly, in view of the orders to abandon ship, the men were
allowed almost unlimited rations from the 29th onwards (Mumford,
1852–4), while the officers began 'making a very liberal use of the
remains of our mess stock, but shall not be able to finish it'
(McClintock, 1852–4). Strangely, perhaps, the men were not inclined to
gorge themselves. 'Plenty of work and plenty to eat but 7 months of
short allowance had so changed our appetites that none seemed to care
about the increase and dainty habits showed themselves for the first
time on board H.M.S. Resolute' (Mumford, 1852–4).

20 At the same time the engineers were reassembling Intrepid's engines
(Scott, 1852–4); they were ready for operation by 10 May.

21 Mumford was a member of the party that hauled the provisions to
Cape Cockburn and he has left a good account of the trip. Rough ice
forced them to 'double-bank,' i.e., relay the sledges, frequently. The
party got back to the ships on 12 May.

11 Retreat to Beechey Island

1 These emotions were shared by many of the officers and men who
were thus abandoning their homes of the previous two years. On
leaving Resolute for the last time on 15 May, Captain Kellett kissed
the ship's side in farewell (Mumford, 1852–4).

2 De Bray's official report to Commander Pullen was published in 1855
(de Bray, 1855c). It differs only in insignificant detail from the translation of the version which appeared in de Bray's journal.

3 Thomas Pullen, North Star's master, was clearly not greatly impressed
by de Bray's arrival: 'Regularly knocked up with a sore throat & severe
cold, fit for nothing. My health is I think breaking a little. I cannot
stand much. De Bray arrives in the morning, digging me out' (Pullen,
1853–4, vol. 2:63).

4 There had also been an accident at Cape Hotham which might well
have produced yet another fatality. Lieutenant Pim had fired at a bear
which was pilfering some supplies when his gun burst, badly injuring
his left hand (McClintock, 1852–4; McDougall, 1857:401–2), 'taking
away nearly all the inside of his hand, laying bare the thumb bone, and
also severely injuring the wrist' (Nelson, 1850–4). Dr Domville treated
the wound and Pim was hauled on a sledge to North Star, his men
covering the 56 km in twenty hours.

5 The entire party had to spend the night in tents for the first night
(28th) while quarters were being prepared for them on board (Mumford,
1852–4; McClintock, 1852–4). Since the crews of four ships had to be

accommodated, *North Star* was quite crowded. On the 29th the crews of *Resolute* and *Intrepid* were given a medical examination by the five medical officers on board (McDougall, 1857:404; Mumford, 1852–4).

6 This party, too, had experienced a near-accident involving firearms. On 29 May, abreast of Baker Islands, a small bear came close to the tents; McDougall came running out of his tent with his double-barrelled gun at full cock; he tripped over the end of a sledge and both balls narrowly missed Mumford and some companions (Mumford, 1852–4). McDougall (1857:399) seems to have been more concerned that he had endangered his own life; he maintained the gun was at half-cock.

7 On 30 May Mr Court was sent with a party to Assistance Bay to secure the depot there (McDougall, 1857:405), while a group of carpenters (including Mumford) was sent with him to Cape Hotham to repair a boat which had been sledged there and damaged in the process. Mumford has left a lively account of this little trip, from which he returned to Beechey Island on 8 June (Mumford, 1852–4).

8 Nelson, of *Investigator*, remarked: 'I must confess I never saw a bear killed with so little trouble' (Nelson, 1850–4).

9 Full details of Mecham's impressive journey may be found in Mecham (1855b). McClintock, who until Mecham's return held the record for longest sledge trip on the Franklin search, was delighted at his achievement: 'Mecham's journey is a most splendid feat, topping all previous ones in speed & probably in distance. His sledging amounts to 1,157 miles (mine to 1,148 & with walking examinations to 1,210) but Mecham is absent only sixty-nine days; his marches average eighteen miles. The longest one is thirty miles' (McClintock, 1852–4).

10 De Bray reached *Assistance* on the 13th. Belcher (1855a, vol. II:186–7) reported his arrival as follows: 'At noon of the 13th a dog-sledge was reported, and I went out to receive the visitor, which proved to be Monsieur de Bray. My salutation was: "Well, you bring me news of Collinson's safety?" "Yes, Sir, he is safe! and I have documents here for you," pointing to his knapsack.'

It was probably during this visit to *Assistance*, or possibly earlier, via the courier service between the two components of the squadron, that de Bray received a letter of high commendation from Belcher:

H.M. Ship Assistance June 1/54

Sir,

Not far from this spot your gallant countryman. Monsr. Bellot met his fate endeavouring to convey to me the despatches from my Government!

From the same position I have not only to acknowledge the receipt of your journal on your late trip from H.M.S. Resolute to Beechey Island – but I am informed, by my excellent friend Capt. Kellett, that I shall have the pleasure of forwarding to our Government his approbation of your services during the period in which

you have participated in our laborious search after our missing
countrymen!

I sincerely trust that your labours and meritorious services here
may be properly appreciated by your own Government – and I feel
assuredthat my Lords Commissioners of the Admiralty will not fail
to aid by transmitting to the proper authorities our humble approbation. (Belcher, 1854a).

11 Details of this trip may be found in Krabbé (1855).

12 Two of these trips were occasioned by a change in command: Lieutenant Hamilton started north with the dog sledge on 17 June, since he
had been ordered to replace Captain Sherard Osborn in command of
Pioneer, the latter having been superseded at his own request
(McDougall, 1857:420–1).

McDougall has left an excellent description of one of these late-
season sledge trips north to *Assistance* and back, over the period from
17 June to 11 July. By then there were vast melt pools on top of the ice,
as well as quite a few open leads:

The road from Cape Bowden proved to be the worst part of the
journey, for cracks varying from six to twelve feet were numerous.
The dogs were terrified at the water. There was, however, but one
course to pursue: the poor animals were forced across the water, and
their being started at full speed, rarely failed in drawing the sledge
across ...

After no slight toil, through a mass of hummocks near Point
Innis, where the road was almost indescribable, being composed of a
mixture of rugged hummocks, cracks, snow and water waist-deep,
we at length forded a noisy watercourse near Cape Spencer.
(McDougall, 1857:430–1)

13 Mumford, who accompanied Dr Scott on one of the shooting expeditions to Cape Spencer, has left an excellent description of this activity.
They were away from the ship from 3 to 13 July, during which time
they shot 307 birds (Mumford, 1852–4) (333 birds according to Dr Scott
(1852–4), of which 155 were sent south to *North Star* for the sick on
board. By the end of July the birds were getting scarce, however
(McClintock, 1852–4).

At Cape Spencer Dr Scott found 'near the ruins of an Esquimaux
encampment, a piece of tin (evidently part of Edward's potato tin)
about 12.5 cm square with H.M.S. '*Terror*' painted on it in white
letters' (Scott, 1852-4).

14 In fact Sir Edward arrived at 2.00 a.m. the next day, riding in his gig
mounted on a sledge (McClintock, 1852–4; Mumford, 1852–4). He was
met by Captains Kellett, M'Clure, Pullen, and McClintock (Belcher,
1855a, vol. II:21).

15 Northumberland House: a depot house which Pullen had built and
which was now refurbished for Sir Edward's use. On the 18th–19th a

cook house was built beside it, fitted with the galley stove, etc. from the *McLellan* (Mumford, 1852–4).

16 The cairn was built by a party of six men led by Mr Johnson, *Resolute*'s acting boatswain, who were detailed for the task on 16 June (Mumford, 1852-4).

   The monument was fashioned from the capstan salvaged from *McLellan* and nicknamed the 'parish pump' by the men (Mumford, 1852-4). It was an octagonal column, surmounted by a ball (McDougall, 1857:433), commemorating the thirty-two men who had died on the Franklin search since 1850 (Neatby, 1967:232). At Belcher's request, de Bray produced a detailed scale-drawing of the monument (Belcher, 1855a, vol. 2:62). Mumford was not impressed with where it was located, i.e., 'at the back of the house instead of at the graves where any one but Sir E. B. would have put it' (Mumford, 1852–4).

17 On the 20th Belcher ordered signal stations erected on Point Innis, Cape Bowden, Cape Grinnell, and Cape Osborn, in order to relay orders to abandon *Assistance* and *Pioneer* quickly if it became necessary. Work on these stations was pushed ahead over the next few days (McDougall, 1857:432; Mumford, 1852–4).

18 A shooting party returned from Cape Riley, having killed about four hundred dovekies in ten days (Scott, 1852–4).

19 On the 11th a messenger arrived from Commander Richards, aboard *Assistance*, to the effect that she and *Pioneer* had got free of the ice on the 9th and had advanced about 19 km south, to just south of Cape Osborn, but were again blocked by ice (McDougall, 1857:435–6; McClintock, 1852–4; Mumford, 1852-4; Scott, 1852–4).

20 Towards the end the men were cutting about 100 m of channel per day (McClintock, 1852–4). Mumford has included a detailed description of this back-breaking work. By his reckoning the entire operation of sawing the canal and getting the ship free involved sawing about 6.4 km of saw cuts.

21 During this period Captain McClintock tried his hand at 'calotypes,' i.e., photographs, and produced both landscape shots of Beechey Island and portraits (McClintock, 1852–4).

12 Homeward Voyage and Aftermath

1 On the 22nd Sir Edward left in his whaleboat to return to *Assistance* and *Pioneer*, accompanied by Captain McClintock, Drs Lyall and Scott, Mr Court, Mr Jenkins, and five men. It was Belcher's intention that they would stay aboard *Assistance* with a small crew for another winter if they thought the ships would drift free of the ice over the winter (Belcher, 1855, vol. II:217–19; McDougall, 1857:437; Scott, 1852–4). McClintock was to relieve Commander Richards if the latter's health were not up to another arctic wintering (McClintock, 1852–4).

2 McClintock has left an excellent description of this journey to
  Assistance and back (McClintock, 1852-4). Even before they reached
  Assistance and *Pioneer* Belcher had concluded that 'without a heavy
  gale, and probably a fatal result to the vessels, not the remotest chance
  of their extrication offered this season in time to reach England'
  (Belcher, 1855, vol. II:219). Perhaps more telling was the fact that of the
  crew under his command 'none volunteered to remain out' for another
  winter (ibid., 222).
     The crews of the two ships started south in the early hours of the
  25th. 'The ships were left with colors flying & their hatches battened
  down. They were both in very nice & very efficient order'
  (McClintock, 1852-4).

3 The atmosphere is perhaps best described by Captain McClintock:
     About noon I was awoke by loud cheers & jumping up found that a
     vessel was in sight thro' the fog, approaching from the eastwd ...
     Such a total eclipse of rationality I have seldom seen displayed
     outside the doors of a mad house as our people exhibited, anxious
     beyond measure for 'news'. Fellows who looked listless, vacant &
     apathetic beyond measure before, now looked either stupidly half
     drunk or wildly excited & up to anything. Before we were all
     wishing for beefstakes [*sic*] & cauliflowers, now no one seemed to
     care a fig about eatables ... Every one wandering about the decks,
     myself (altho' very tired after the journey of yesterday & last night),
     until one o'clock in the morning. (McClintock, 1852-4)

4 Belcher made a final pretence of consulting his officers on whether or
  not *North Star* should stay for another winter at Beechey Island:
     Sir Edd, meeting McClure, Pullen & myself in the cabin, told us he
     was ordered to consult the wishes etc. of his officers. He told us if
     we had anything to say to put it in writing at once. He said he was
     not ordered to look for Collinson & that a ship lying at Beechey
     would be useless ... Sir. Ed's communication was evidently only a
     form. He neither wanted our opinion nor intended altering his own.
     His mode of asking us showed sufficiently plain that he considered
     it merely as a burlesque (McClintock, 1852-4).

5 The tablet, the original of which is now in the Prince of Wales's
  Heritage Centre in Yellowknife, was commissioned by John Barrow; it
  read: IN MEMORY / OF LIEUTENANT BELLOT, / OF THE
  FRENCH NAVY, / WHO LOST HIS LIFE WHILST / NOBLY
  AIDING IN THE SEARCH FOR / SIR JOHN FRANKLIN / IN THE
  WELLINGTON CHANNEL / ON THE 18TH AUGUST, 1853 /
  This tablet / To record the sad event / Was erected by his friend John
  Barrow / A.D. 1854 /

6 The little convoy proceeded east to Gascoyne Inlet then headed south
  toward Port Leopold but reached the edge of the pack ice close to
  Leopold Island (Scott, 1852-54).

7 Captain Inglefield had already found this cache rifled when he called here outward bound on 21 August. He had found only 114 casks and cases out of the 608 left by Captain Saunders in 1850, and all of these had been stove-in (Inglefield, 1855:10). The details of the establishment of the depot may be found in Saunders (1851:62–6), where a detailed list of the contents is also to be found. Mary-Rousseliere (1980:38–40) has presented a convincing argument that the Inuit responsible for rifling the cache were Qitdlarssuaq and his companions at an early stage in their famous migration from Baffin Island to the Thule area of Greenland. He has suggested that they would have been greatly disappointed at the contents of the barrels.

Nelson has left a graphic description of the mess he saw:
Flour casks were stove, bread, tea scattered in all directions, carpeting the spot several inches in depth. In fact everything had been utterly destroyed, not consumed, for the Esquimaux had not made use of a single article, excepting the fat of the pork. One fellow must have had a sharp reminder, when busied in his work of demolition, for the marks of his teeth were distinctly visible on a lump of *blister salve*, a circumstance which I strongly suspect would have afforded considerable amusement to us, provided we could have been lookers-on. (Nelson, 1850–4)

8 *North Star* came within a ship's breadth of *Talbot*: 'fouling her would have been to lose both ships' (McDougall, 1857:442).

9 McClintock (1852–4) has included a sketch of how the towing line was entangled with the anchor; almost incredibly the line had taken a half-hitch around the fluke of the anchor.

10 In his journal entry for 31 August McClintock (1852–4) reported:
In the afternoon the Phoenix ran into Pond's Bay. Sir. Edd., Captns. Kellett & Englefield [*sic*] landed upon Button Point. Traces of natives were numerous & their caches of blubber of last spring still secure but they did not appear to have visited the place since it is evidently only a spring or summer station. Only the ruins of 3 winter huts were seen. Mr Miertsching left some marks upon a stone to indicate to them that some white men had been there & had gone away by sea.

In one of the huts Belcher found a skull, an English knife, and an iron-tinned spoon. He brought the skull back to England, in case it was one of Franklin's people, but it was identified as that of a female (Belcher, 1855, vol. II:236).

11 The shaft must have been significantly displaced; Mumford reported that it stove in several casks of oil and pickles.

12 Mumford has given a graphic description of the crowded conditions on board *North Star* (and presumably on board the other two ships also):
Plenty of rolls for supper on account of which I found it necessary to secure myself 'for sea' while asleep, for my perch consisted of the

top of the bins in the carpenter's store-room, which allowed me 16 inches in width to lie on, having the racks on one side and the deck three feet below on the other. But I was considered as a favoured lodger by being allowed such quarters till I should reach England.

13 By Mumford's account it was an extremely rough and unpleasant voyage. For example his entry for the 17th reads:

Gale from SE with heavy sea, a 'Cape Fareweller'. Set fore staysail which was soon split to rags and hauled down. The ship steering badly for want of head sail, and requring six hands at the helm. Axes prepared for the mizen mast in case of not steering. The lower deck all aflood and the bags & bedding that was stowed in the fore coal bunker drowned. At 11 a.m. a sea struck the ship on the port bow and stove in the bulwarks from the cathead to the fore rigging, breaking in the binns on the lower deck and seriously injuring some of the crew in the lee scuppers. Battened down & chined hatches & skylights and scuttled lower deck. Watches pumping ship.

The ship ran into another gale which raged from the 20th to the 22nd: the fore topsail yard was cracked and the ship was again making water seriously. *North Star* encountered the same ferocious weather over the period 17th to 21st (Nelson, 1850–4).

14 *Phoenix* also coaled and watered for the final run up the Channel (Mumford, 1852–4).

15 *Phoenix* was within sight of Longships Light by midnight on the 29th and by 7.00 p.m. on the 30th was in sight of Portland Bill, in hazy weather. She dropped anchor off Beachy Head at 4.30 p.m. on 1 October in thick fog, but when the fog cleared soon afterwards she got under way again and by 11.30 p.m. was off Deal (Mumford, 1852–4). Here de Bray, Groves and Lewis went ashore in the pilot boat (Mumford, 1852–4); we have no information on de Bray's homeward movements thereafter.

16 On 18, 19, and 20 October (McDougall, 1857:447). Mumford (and presumably all the crew members of the ships involved) were ordered to hold themselves available on board *Waterloo* for the period of the trial (Mumford, 1852–4).

17 The report of the verdict which appeared in *The Times* (1854a) read as follows:

that the Court having considered all the circumstances, and having heard the statement of Captain M'Clure and the officers of the ship Investigator, it was of opinion that no blame whatever attached to Captain M'Clure for the loss of the ship and that his conduct and that of the crew had been highly meritorious. The Court fully acquitted him and the officers of the ship, as they considered their conduct to be highly meritorious and praiseworthy.

The President, in presenting Captain M'Clure with his sword, highly complimented him on the meritorious service he had performed.

18 The coverage in *The Times* (1854a) read as follows: 'The Deputy Judge
    Advocate read the finding of the Court, which fully acquitted Captain
    Henry Kellett and the officers of the Resolute, as they had acted under
    the orders of Sir Edward Belcher.'
       The president, on handing Captain Kellett his sword, said: 'Captain
    Kellett, I have much pleasure in returning you this sword, which you
    have so long worn with honour and credit and service to your country.'

19 This was preceded by the trial of Commander George Richards for the
    loss of the *Assistance* and *Pioneer*; he pleaded that he had acted on
    Belcher's direct orders. The court 'completely exonerated Commander
    Richards from all blame, he acting under the orders of Sir Edward
    Belcher' (*Times*, 1854a).

20 The *Times* coverage continues: 'The President then returned Sir E.
    Belcher his sword without observation, and the Court was dissolved.'
    The contrast between the warmth of the complimentary remarks
    addressed by Admiral Gordon to M'Clure and Kellett and the total
    silence in which Belcher's sword was returned to him, spoke very
    much louder than words.

21 While the majority of the officers (certainly Kellett, McClintock, and
    McDougall) were in agreement with de Bray and were convinced that
    Resolute's and *Intrepid*'s crews could have survived another wintering,
    and that there was no need to abandon their ships, this view was not
    shared by Mumford:
       The abandonment of the 'Resolute' and 'Intrepid' by order of Sir E.
    Belcher was justifiable, for though Kellett was bent on rendering
    assistance to Captn. Collinson and the crew of the 'Enterprise' still
    by doing so he was risking the loss of more of his crew and would
    by remaining also have detained the 'North Star' or some other
    vessel at Beechey Island, to have received his crew in the event of
    his ships not breaking out in the following summer, and as in the
    meanwhile the 'Enterprise' might have reached home or at least
    have retraced her steps before her third winter and at the worst
    being on the northern shores of America and within reach of the
    Hudson's Bay territories either by boat or sledge journeys, the
    propriety of such orders was beyond question.
    Even if *Resolute* and *Intrepid* had been reprovisioned (as had been
    intended) one cannot but feel that Mumford's prediction of further
    serious loss of life during a third wintering was correct.

22 This account from the *New York Herald* may also be found in
    Crampton (1858a:2–5). A different version is to be found in Blake
    (1874:92–6); the latter is a first-hand account by George Tyson, one of
    the party which boarded *Resolute*. As Dunbar (1961:12) has pointed
    out, the latter is 'by far the most entertaining, but not necessarily the
    most accurate.' Tyson's account has recently been republished in Ross
    (1985:192–5).

23   According to Tyson (Blake, 1874:92), the vessel was in sight for several days: 'no one for a moment thought she was an abandoned vessel.'

24   According to Tyson the initiative was his and he had difficulty in overcoming the captain's objections. The four men were the mate, John Quayle, second mate Norris Havens, and the two boatswains Mr Tallinghast and George Tyson (Blake, 1874:92).

25   Tyson's somewhat imaginative account of their boarding of *Resolute* reads as follows:

> By this time Mr Quayle was so tired that I had to assist him in boarding the ship, myself and the other two following. We found the cabin locked and sealed; but locks and seals did not stand long. A whaler's boot vigorously applied to a door is a very effective key. We were soon in the cabin. This was no whaler, that was plain; neither was she an American vessel, it was soon discovered. English, no doubt of that. Every thing presented a mouldy appearance. The decanters of wine, with which the late officers had last regaled themselves, were still sitting on the table, *some of the wine still remaining in the glasses*, and in the rack around the mizen-mast were a number of other glasses and decanters. Some of my companions appeared to feel somewhat superstitious, and hesitated to drink the wine, but my long and fatiguing walk made it very acceptable to me, and having helped myself to a glass, and they seeing it did not kill me, an expression of intense relief came over their countenances, and they all, with one accord, went for that wine with a will; and there and then we all drank a bumper to the late officers and crew of the *Resolute* (Blake, 1874:93–4)

At first sight it would seem unlikely, given the effort spent on battening down hatches, etc., before *Resolute* was abandoned that a wine decanter and glasses would have been left sitting on the cabin table. On the other hand McDougall (1857:391) does record that one of Captain Kellett's last acts on board was that of 'drinking a glass of wine to the old *Resolute* and her crew.'

Tyson and his companions spent the night on board *Resolute* but a storm sprang up and they were forced to stay aboard her for a further three days, during which time they amused themselves as best they could:

> Among other things we found some of the uniforms of the officers, in which we arrayed ourselves, buckling on the swords, and putting on their cocked hats, treating ourselves, as *British officers* to a little more wine. Well, we had what sailors call a 'good time', getting up an impromptu sham duel; and before those swords were laid aside one was cut in twain, and the others were hacked and beaten to pieces, taking care, however, not to harm our precious bodies, though we did some hard fighting – *we, or the wine!* (Blake, 1874:94–5)

When the weather cleared they loaded themselves with food and started back across the ice to their own ship; almost all of them fell into the water several times when jumping from floe to floe 'but we were in such good spirits that these little mishaps, instead of inciting condolences were a continual cause of merriment' (Blake, 1874:95).

26 De Bray has opted to omit a lengthy passage from the *Herald* account at this point. It read:

The captain, knowing the history of Sir Edward Belcher's expedition to the Polar Seas, at once divined the reasons of the vessel being left in that condition; and knowing that the safe conveyance of that vessel to some port would be better than catching whales, and knowing withal that it would be quite a piece of glory to hand back the Britishers a vessel long since abandoned by them as being lost to the Queen's service for ever, determined at all hazards to try the bold and arduous task. Accordingly, he sent his mate back, with six men, giving them instructions to free the ship of the water with which she was burthened, and signalize this success to him. If they did not succeed in freeing the vessel, they were to hoist a signal, whereupon the captain himself would proceed to their aid.

As it took nearly a day to accomplish the journey to the ship, nothing could be expected from the mate's party that day. But the next morning, just as Captain Buddington anticipated, the signal was hoisted for his presence on board the 'Resolute'. Taking two men with him, and leaving the barque in charge of the second mate, the captain started, on the 10th of September, to the relief of his comrades. After a hard day's travelling over ice and through pools of water, half frozen, the little party succeeded in reaching the 'Resolute' in perfect safety.

He commenced immediately to search the vessel, in order to ascertain if she was seaworthy. On descending the hold it was found to be entirely full of water up to the floor of the first deck. The well was then sounded and seven feet of water was found to be in the ship. The pumps were then visited; and being of a new construction, none but Captain Buddington was acquainted with the mode of working them. One of them, which was a force pump of very great power, was rigged, and the following morning was got in working order. A gang of men were then set to work, and for three days the pump was kept busy. Fourteen hours out of the twenty-four were consumed in thus freeing the vessel. On the third day all the water was cleared from her hold, and the attention of the captain was turned towards extricating the prize from the dangerous position she was then placed in.

The appearance of things on board, as represented by Captain Buddington when he had leisure to examine the vessel, was doubtful in the extreme. Everything of a moveable nature seemed to be out of its place, and was in a damaged condition from the immersion in the water. The cabin was strewed with books, clothing, preserved meats, interspersed here and there with lumps of ice. There was one thing, however, which struck Captain Buddington as being very remarkable, and for which probably no satisfactory explanation can be given; and this was the presence of ice for several feet in thickness on the larboard side, while there was not a particle on the starboard. The only argument that can be presented to explain this curious freak of the elements is, that the 'Resolute', lying with her head to the eastward for probably more than a month, received the direct rays of the sun on her starboard quarter, and nowhere else, and thus a daily warmth was imparted to this side of the ship, while the other side, being without this heat, became as solidified with ice as though the sun never shone on it. This supposition may be very plausible and satisfactory to many, for, to the certain knowledge of Captain B., the head of the 'Resolute' never varied from the east for twenty days, notwithstanding she was constantly drifting in a south-west direction (the course of the pack). There was scarcely anything on board the abandoned vessel that was not more or less destroyed. There was a great lack of fuel on board, although, in the course of the search throughout the vessel, a little coal was discovered in the hold, but the quantity was very small, and entirely inadequate to supply the vessel more than a week. Of provisions there was enough, perhaps, to last a crew of seventy-five men (the number originally carried by the 'Resolute') for nine months. The salt meats were the only articles that were at all in a state of preservation. Everything had gone to decay. Even the ship's sails, found between decks, were so rotten that the sailors could thrust their fingers through them like so much brown paper. An attempt was subsequently made to rig a topmast studding-sail out of some of the canvas found saturated with water; but it blew out of the gearing and was scattered to the wind like chaff. The lower hold was found to contain the library of one of the officers of the expedition, valued at over a thousand dollars. The books were entirely valueless when discovered by Captain Buddington, and subsequently thrown overboard as worthless rubbish. (Crampton, 1855a:2–3)

27 *George Henry* broke free from the ice during a gale on 26–27 October but was badly damaged in the process (Blake, 1874:96). Only by constant pumping was her crew able to get her home to New London.

28 The remainder of the *Herald* article reads as follows:

... and the voyage was successfully accomplished with credit to all concerned, but especially to Captain Buddington, for he worked morning, noon and night. The condition of his hands at present is strong evidence of their having reefed sails and hauled taut ropes during the entire voyage. No doubt he must have felt proud when, entering the harbour of New London, he there safely anchored a valuable ship which had been locked up in the dreary latitudes of the Arctic regions for the space of two years. He did feel proud, and justly too, for he had the honour of adding another triumph to the well-directed skill and entreprise of the New England people.

The 'Resolute' now lies anchored in the stream off the town of New London, and is the chief object of attraction in the neighbour-hood. She is about 600 tons burthen, and is built in the strongest manner. Her bows are sheathed with iron, while her entire frame is coppered, and copper-fastened and bolted. The topgallant masts are down, having, as it is supposed, been used for fuel by her com-mander previous to the abandonment. She is very bluff in the bows, but is a pretty good sailer. Some idea may be formed of her strength, when our readers are told that she was forced through sheets of ice varying in thickness from five to eight feet, while going at the rate of six knots per hour. No danger was anticipated of her being sunk by the floes of ice, on account of her great strength. But there was a period in the history of that brief voyage, when the lives of all on board hung by a thread, as it were. When a little to the north of the Banks of Newfoundland, the 'Resolute' came in contact with an iceberg about 150 feet in height, on top of which there was a detached piece of ice of many tons weight, and which the captain expected every moment would tumble down upon the vessel, and sink the prize so gallantly obtained. So great was the danger, that the boats were in all readiness to push off, should the overhanging glacier be precipitated upon them. However, after a great deal of careful working and hard labour, the dangerous obstacle was cleared, and the star of success once more shone brightly upon the hardy and intrepid mariners.

It is the opinion of Captain Buddington, that if the crew of the 'Resolute' had remained on board of her, with the hope of eventually releasing her, they could not have effected the task any sooner than it was performed by the natural causes which eventually freed her, and hence, he thinks, that Sir Edward Belcher, who had command of the squadron, acted perfectly rightly in abandoning the vessels under the circumstances.

Among the articles found on board of the 'Resolute' was rigging and anchors valued at 2,000 dollars, whaling gear, full suits of winter clothing, and other things necessary for a voyage to the Polar seas. As these are goods subject to duty, a Custom-house officer has been stationed on board of the ship to look after the interests of Uncle Sam, until the destination of the 'Resolute' is finally determined upon.

The prize is valued at 50,000 dollars, although Captain B. informs us she was never fitted out for less than 100,000 dollars. The proceeds of the cruise will have to be divided among the owners and crew of the 'George Henry', for in whaling voyages the entire proceeds, no matter what turns up, are to be shared amongst the parties interested, namely the captain, crew and the owners.

The 'George Henry' it will be remembered, arrived a few days previous to the 'Resolute', having on board about 150 barrels of oil.

Whether the British Government will pay the finders of the 'Resolute' the value of the vessel or not remains to be seen. At all events, Captain Buddington deserves a substantial token of esteem at their hands for the intrepid and praiseworthy part he took in thus rescuing one of their service-vessels from a long captivity in the Polar regions. (Crampton, 1858a:4–5)

One aspect which this story omits to mention is that due to storms it took *Resolute* sixty–four days to reach New London, at one stage being driven as far south as Bermuda (Buddington, 1858).

29 The rather involved correspondence between the Admiralty, the Foreign Office, Washington, Henry Grinnell, and Messrs Perkins and Smith, owners of *George Henry* concerning *Resolute* may be found in Great Britain (1858:1–24). It is significant that earlier, on 10 November 1854, the British government had claimed a continuing right on behalf of the Queen to the abandoned vessel (Crampton, 1858b:1). But on 24 January 1856 Thomas Pinn, secretary to the Admiralty, wrote to the Foreign Office that:

My Lords have read with great satisfaction the acount of the exertions and skill evinced by Captain Buddington and the crew who navigated the 'Resolute' from Baffin's Bay to New London, and as the best mark of the sense which they entertain of his conduct, their Lordships will waive their right to the vessel, and leave her to Captain Buddington's entire disposal, or if he prefers giving her up to Her Majesty's Consul in Boston, their Lordships request that the Consul may be instructed to sell her, and to distribute the proceeds of the sale to Captain Buddington and his crew.

This information was relayed to Perkins and Smith, owners of *George Henry* by Mr Crampton on 12 February 1856 (Crampton, 1858c). At this point the owners felt obliged to point out to Mr Crampton that:

Some difference in the custom in the English ports probably induced you to think that the captain was the agent of all parties interested in salvage caused by whaling vessels.

By custom and the agreements of the shipping articles the agents of the vessels are the agents of the officers and crew, and whatever of value is to be disposed of for their benefit, is to be so by the agent. (Perkins and Smith, 1858)

Hence, rather than *Resolute* being left to Buddington's 'entire disposal,' Perkins and Smith suggested that the British government should 'abandon to Perkins and Smith, agents for account of parties interested in salvage on barque "Resolute," all right and title the English government have in her, said salvage to be distributed and apportioned by said Perkins and Smith, in conformity with the terms of the shipping articles and the custom of the port of New London' (Perkins and Smith, 1858).

Perkins and Smith also asked Mr Henry Grinnell to write to clarify the situation. The latter did so very succinctly, pointing out that 'the officers and men who remained on board the "George Henry," as also the owners of that ship, should be participators agreeable to the shipping articles entered into between the owners of the ship "George Henry" and the officers and crew, viewing the capture of the "Resolute" in the same way as the capture of a whale. The shipping articles of a whale-ship give the officers and crew about one-third of the oil, bone, or any other article that may be procured.' (Grinnell, 1858). To this their Lordships acquiesced.

30 It was Mr Henry Grinnell who suggested to several members of the US Senate that a proper disposition of *Resolute* 'would be for the United States' Government to purchase and return her to Her Majesty's Government, as a mark of courtesy' (Lumley, 1858). The outcome of this was that the idea was broached, in a tentative fashion, by Senator Mason of Virginia and Senator Foster of Connecticut in early June 1856 (as reported in the *National Intelligencer* on 12 June. Senator Foster had already made inquiries as to what might be a reasonable price; Perkins and Smith had quoted a price of $40,000 on 11 June. The outcome was that on 24 June Senator Mason introduced the following resolution:

> In token of the deep interest felt in the United States for the service in which this ship [i.e., HMS *Resolute*] was engaged, and of the sense entertained by Congress of the act of Her Majesty's Government in surrendering it to the salvors, the resolution requests the President of the United States to cause the ship, with all her armaments and equipments, and the property on board when she arrived in the United States, to be purchased of her present owners, and to be fully repaired and equipped at one of the navy yards of the United States, and then sent back to England, under the direction of the Secretary of the Navy, with a request to Her Majesty's Government that the United States may be allowed to restore the ship. For the purchase of the ship and her appurtenances it is proposed to appropriate 40,000 dollars, or so much of that sum as may be required. (*National Intelligencer*, 1858)

The resolution was passed unanimously.

31 On 13 December Mr G.M. Dallas of the United States legation wrote to the Earl of Clarendon (the foreign secretary) to announce the ship's arrival:

I am now specially instructed by the President, while conveying to your Lordship the assurance of his cordial gratification in directing such a measure of comity to a friendly Power, to fulfil the Congressional injunction by tendering the barque 'Resolute' to Her Majesty's Government, and by requesting that the United States may be allowed to restore that vessel, with all her armament, equipment and property, preserved in good condition, to Her Majesty's service. (Dallas, 1858)

The Earl of Clarendon replied on the 16th:

I have received Her Majesty's commands to acquaint you that she gratefully accepts the offer thus made of the restoration of the 'Resolute' to her service. I beg to assure you that the friendly feeling on the part of the Senate and House of Representatives which prompted this measure, and the generous and complete measure in which it has been carried into effect by the President and his Government, are most highly appreciated by the Queen and Her Majesty's Government, and, I am confident, by the British nation at large. (Clarendon, 1858a)

32 As a token of her appreciation, on 16 December Queen Victoria inspected *Resolute* at Cowes, and was introduced to Captain Hartstene and his officers, *Resolute* having been towed from Spithead to Cowes and back for the occasion (Clarendon, 1858b).

33 On his return to the United States Captain Hartstene received a presentation sword from Queen Victoria, 'as a memorial of an event which has been so gratifying to the Sovereign, the Government and the people of this country' (Clarendon, 1858b).

34 In fact, *Resolute* never returned to the Arctic and was something of a white elephant. The British government had abandoned all hope of finding *Erebus* and *Terror* and had no intention of sending further expeditions in search of them. Even when Lady Franklin requested that *Resolute* be placed at her disposal in order to mount a private expedition (Franklin, 1858) the request was refused. Particularly at a time when the Royal Navy was starting to change from sail to steam, a sailing ship, heavily strengthened for work in ice, was totally redundant.

Resolute was broken up in 1878 (Dunbar, 1961:16). In recognition of her interesting history a desk was made from her timbers and was 'presented by the Queen of Great Britain and Ireland to the President of the United States as a memorial of the courtesy and loving kindness which dictated the offer of the *Resolute*' (Dunbar, 1961:16). In 1961 President John Kennedy moved the desk from the Broadcast Room in the White House to the Oval Office, where it still remains.

Bibliography

Abbreviations

NAC   National Archives of Canada, Ottawa
SHM   Service Historique de la Marine, Château
        de Vincennes, Paris
SPRI   Scott Polar Research Institute, Cambridge, UK

Anderson, J. 1940–1. Chief Factor James Anderson's Back River
  journal of 1855. *Canadian Field Naturalist* 54:63–7, 84–9, 107–9, 125–6,
  134–6; 55:9–11, 21–6, 38–44.
Anonymous. n.d. *The arctic dispatches, containing an account of the
  discovery of the North-West Passage by Captain Robert Maclure.*
  London: J.D. Potter
Armstrong, A. 1857. *A personal narrative of the discovery of the
  North-West Passage; with numerous incidents of travel and adventure
  during nearly five years' continuous service in the arctic regions while
  in search of the expedition under Sir John Franklin.* London: Hurst and
  Blackett
Asher, G.M. 1860. *Henry Hudson the navigator.* London: The Hakluyt
  Society
Back, G. 1836. *Narrative of the Arctic Land Expedition to the mouth of the
  Great Fish River, and along the shores of the Arctic Ocean in the years
  1833, 1834 and 1835.* London: John Murray
– 1838. *Narrative of an expedition in H.M.S. 'Terror,' undertaken with
  a view to geographical discovery on the Arctic shores, in the years
  1836–37.* London: John Murray
Barr, W. 1986. The last known letter of Joseph-René Bellot. *Polar Record*
  23(142):61–4
– 1987. Francis Leopold McClintock (1819–1907). *Arctic,* 40(4):352–3
Barrow, J. 1854. Letter to Mme de Bray, 16 November, 1854. SPRI, MS 887
Beattie, O., and J. Geiger. 1987 *Frozen in time: The fate of the Franklin
  expedition.* London: Bloomsbury
Beaujeu-Garnier, J. 1990. La Sociéte de Géographie de Paris et

l'exploration arctique: Gustave Lambert, pionnier de la conquête du pole, in S. Devers, ed., *Pour Jean Malaurie. 102 témoignages en hommage à quarante ans d'études arctiques*. Paris: Plon, pp. 129–38

Beechey, F.W. 1831. *Narrative of a voyage to the Pacific and Bering's Straits, to co-operate with the polar expeditions; performed in His Majesty's Ship 'Blossom' etc.* London: Henry Colburn and Richard Bentley

– 1843. *A voyage of discovery towards the North Pole performed in His Majesty's Ships 'Dorothea' and 'Trent' under the command of Captain David Buchan, R.N. 1818*. London: Richard Bentley

Belcher, E. 1854a. Letter to Emile de Bray, 1 June 1854. SPRI, MS. 887

– 1854b. Letter to the Secretary of the Admiralty, 30 September 1854. SPRI, MS 887

– 1855a. *The last of the arctic voyages; being a narrative of the expedition in H.M.S. 'Assistance' under the command of Captain Sir Edward Belcher, C.B., in search of Sir John Franklin, during the years 1852–53–54*. London: Lovell Reeve, 2 vols.

– 1855b. Copy of confidential letter to Captain Kellett, in *Further papers relative to the recent arctic expeditions in search of Sir John Franklin and the crews of H.M.S. 'Erebus' and 'Terror'* (Great Britain. House of Commons. Sessional Papers, Accounts and Papers, 1854–5, vol. 35, no. 1898). London: Eyre and Spottiswoode, pp. 47–8

Bellot, J.-R. 1855. *Memoirs of Lieutenant Joseph-René Bellot, with his journal of a voyage in the polar seas in search of Sir John Franklin*. London: Hurst and Blackett

Bernier, J.E. 1910. *Report on the Dominion of Canada Government Expedition to the Arctic Islands and Hudson Strait on board the D.G.S. 'Arctic.'* Ottawa: Government Printing Bureau

Blake, E.V. 1874. *Arctic experiences: Containing Capt. George E. Tyson's wonderful drift on the ice-floe, etc.* New York: Harper & Bros

Bockstoce, J., ed. 1988. *The journal of Rochfort Maguire 1852–1854; two years at Point Barrow, Alaska, aboard H.M.S. Plover in the search for Sir John Franklin*. London: Hakluyt Society, 2 vols.

Buddington, J.M. 1858. Letter to Messrs Perkins and Smith, n.d., in *Correspondence respecting H.M.S. 'Resolute,' and the arctic expedition. Presented to the House of Commons by command of Her Majesty, in pursuance of their address dated May 21, 1858* (Great Britain. House of Commons. Sessional Papers, Accounts and Papers, 1857–8, vol. 60, no. 2416). London: Harrison and Sons, p. 8

Burant, J. 1985. George Frederick Mecham, in *Dictionary of Canadian Biography, vol. 8*. Toronto: University of Toronto Press, pp. 623–5.

Callender, G.A.R. 1927. Sir Richard Vesey Hamilton, in *Dictionary of National Biography, 1912–1921*. London: Oxford University Press, pp. 237–8

Clarendon, Earl of. 1858a. Letter to Mr. Dallas, 16 December 1856, in

*Correspondence respecting H.M.S. Resolute,' and the arctic expedition.
Presented to the House of Commons by command of Her Majesty, in
pursuance of their address dated May 21, 1858* (Great Britain. House of
Commons. Sessional Papers, Accounts and Papers, 1857–8, vol. 60,
no. 2416). London: Harrison and Sons, pp. 32–3

– 1858b. Letter to Mr. Dallas, 20 January, 1857, in *Correspondence
respecting H.M.S. 'Resolute,' and the arctic expedition. Presented to the
House of Commons by command of Her Majesty in pursuance of their
address dated May 21, 1858* (Great Britain. House of Commons.
Sessional Papers, Accounts and Papers, 1857–8, vol. 60, no. 2416).
London: Harrison and Sons, pp. 33–4

Collinson, R. 1889. *Journal of H.M.S. Enterprise, on the expedition in
search of Sir John Franklin's ships by Behring Strait, 1850–5.* London:
Sampson, Low, Marston, Searle & Rivington

Conseil de santé, Brest. 1870. Certificat de santé, Lieutenant-de-vaisseau
Emile de Bray, 29 April 1870. SHM CC7 324, no. 23

Conseil de santé, Cherbourg. 1867. Certificat de santé, Lieutenant-de-
vaisseau Emile de Bray, 12 April 1867. SHM CC7 324, no. 19

– 1878. Certificat de santé, Lieutenant-de-vaisseau Emile de Bray, 17 May,
1878. SHM CC7 324, no. 28

Crampton, J.F. 1858a. Letter to the Earl of Clarendon, 31 December 1855,
in *Correspondence respecting H.M.S. 'Resolute,' and the arctic expedition. Presented to the House of Commons by command of Her Majsty,
in pursuance of their address dated May 21, 1858* (Great Britain.
House of Commons. Sessional Papers, Accounts and Papers, 1857–8,
vol. 60, no. 2416). London: Harrison & Sons, pp. 1–5

– 1858b. Letter to Consul Grattan, 26 December 1855, in *Correspondence
respecting H.M.S. 'Resolute,' and the arctic expedition. Presented to the
House of Commons by command of Her Majesty, in pursuance of their
address dated May 21, 1858* (Great Britain. House of Commons.
Sessional Papers, Accounts and Papers, 1857–8, vol. 60, no. 2416).
London: Harrison and Sons, p.1

– 1858c. Letter to Perkins and Smith, 12 February 1856, in *Correspondence
respecting H.M.S. 'Resolute,' and the arctic expedition. Presented to the
House of Commons by command of Her Majesty, in pursuance of their
address, dated May 21, 1858* (Great Britain. House of Commons.
Sessional Papers, Accounts and Papers, 1857–587, vol. 60, no. 2416).
London: Harrison and Sons, p. 10

Crouse, N.M. 1928. *In quest of the Western Ocean.* New York: William
Morrow and Co

Cyriax, R. 1939. *Sir John Franklin's last arctic expedition; a chapter in the
history of the Royal Navy.* London: Methuen

– 1944. Captain Hall and the so-called survivors of the Franklin expedition. *Polar Record* 4(28):170–85

– and A.G.E. Jones. 1954. The papers in the possession of Harry Peglar,

Captain of the Foretop, H.M.S. *Terror*, 1845. *Mariner's Mirror* 40(3): 186–95

Dallas, G.M. 1858. Letter to the Earl of Clarendon, 13 December 1856, in *Correspondence respecting H.M.S. 'Resolute' and the arctic expedition. Presented to the House of Commons by command of Her Majesty in pursuance of their address dated May 21, 1858* (Great Britain. House of Commons. Sessional Papers, Accounts and Papers, 1857–8, vol. 60, no. 2416). London: Harrison and Sons, p. 31

Dawson, L.S. 1885. *Memoirs of hydrography*. Eastbourne: Henry W. Keay (Reprint edition, London: Cornmarket Press 1969)

Deacon, M., and A. Savours, 1976. Sir George Strong Nares (1831–1915), *Polar Record* 18(113):127–41

de Bray, E.F. 1851. Letter to Minister of the Marine and Colonies, 20 December 1851. SPRI, MS 887

– 1854. Letter to Minister of the Marine and Colonies, 12 October 1854. SHM CC7 324, no. 9

– 1855a. Journal of proceedings from the 22nd September to the 8th October 1852, of H.M. Sledge 'Marie,' in *Further papers relative to the recent arctic expeditions in search of Sir John Franklin and the crews of H.M.S.'Erebus' and 'Terror.' Presented to both Houses of Parliament by command of Her Majesty* (Great Britain. House of Commons. Sessional Papers, Accounts and Papers, 1854–5, vol. 35, no. 1898). London: Eyre and Spottiswoode, pp. 660–4

– 1855b. Journal of proceedings from the 4th April to the 18th May 1853, of H.M. Sledge 'Hero,' in *Further papers relative to the recent arctic expeditions in search of Sir John Franklin and the crews of H.M.S. 'Erebus' and 'Terror.' Presented to both Houses of Parliament by command of Her Majesty* (Great Britain. House of Commons. Sessional Papers, Accounts and Papers, 1854–5, vol. 35, no. 1898). London: Eyre and Spottiswoode, pp. 478–89

– 1855c. Letter to Commander Pullen, Her Majesty's Ship 'North Star,' in *Further papers relative to the recent arctic expeditions in search of Sir John Franklin and the crews of H.M.S. 'Erebus' and 'Terror.' Presented to both Houses by command of Her Majesty* (Great Britain. House of Commons. Sessional Papers, Accounts and Papers, 1854–5, vol. 35, no. 1898). London: Eyre and Spottiswoode, pp. 421–2

– 1856. Letter to Minister of the Marine and Colonies, received 15 April 1856. SHM CC7 324, no. 14

– 1861. Letter to Major–General of the Navy at Brest. SHM CC7 324, no. 16 bis

– 1865. Letter to Major-General of the Navy at Brest. SHM CC7 324, no. 17 bis

– 1871. Letter to Major-General of Marine, Brest, 31 May 1871. SHM CC7 324, no. 24

– 1878. Letter to Major-General of Marine, Brest, 25 September 1878. SHM CC7 324, no. 30

de Bray, G. n.d. *Emile de Bray* (typescript). SPRI, MS 864/3,

– 1926. *Notice sur la participation de l'enseigne de vaisseau de Bray a l'expédition britannique de 1852–1854 envoyée à la recherche des navires de Sir John Fanklin perdus dans les mers polaires* (typescript). SPRI, MS 864/2

de Bray, J. 1854a. Letter to Minister of the Marine, received 7 August 1854. SHM CC7 324, no. 8

– 1854b. Letter to His Majesty Napoleon III, Emperor of the French. SHM CC7 324, no. 12

de Veer, G. 1876. *The three voyages of William Barents to the Arctic Regions (1594, 1595 and 1596)*. London: Hakluyt Society

Dobbs, A. 1744. *An account of the countries adjoining to Hudson's Bay in the North-West part of America*. London (Reprint. New York: Johnson Reprint Corporation 1967)

Dodge, E.S. 1973. *The polar Rosses: John and James Clark Ross and their expeditions*. London: Faber and Faber

Domville, W.T. 1855. Report of a sledge journey from Dealy Island to Mercy Bay, May–June, 1853, in *Further papers relative to the recent arctic expeditions in search of Sir John Franklin and the crews of H.M.S. 'Erebus' and 'Terror.' Presented to both Houses of Parliament by command of Her Majesty* (Great Britain. House of Commons. Sessional Papers, Accounts and Papers, 1854–5, vol. 35, no. 1898). London: Eyre and Spottiswoode, pp. 672–7

Ducos, T. 1854. Letter to Emile de Bray, 13 October, 1854. SPRI, MS 887

Dunbar, M. 1961. H.M.S. *Resolute*. The Beaver 292(3):11–17

Dupouy, ?. 1867. Letter to the Minister of the Marine, 25 May 1867. SHM CC7 324, no. 20

Fisher, A. 1821. *A journal of a voyage of discovery to the Arctic Regions in His Majesty's Ships Hecla and Griper in the years 1819 & 1820*. London: Longman, Hurst, Rees, Orme & Brown

Fisher, R.H. 1977. *Bering's voyages: Whither and why?* London: C. Hurst & Co

Franklin, Jane. 1858. Letter to Sir C. Wood, 4 April 1857, in *Correspondence respecting H.M.S. 'Resolute,' and the arctic expedition. Presented to the House of Commons by command of Her Majesty, in pursuance of their address dated May 21, 1858* (Great Britain. House of Commons. Sessional Papers, Accounts and Papers, 1857–8, vol. 60, no. 2416). London: Harrison and Sons, pp. 34–6

Franklin, J. 1823. *Narrative of a journey to the shores of the Polar Ocean, in the years 1819, 20, 21 and 22*. London: John Murray

– 1828. *Narrative of a second expedition to the shores of the Polar Sea in the years 1825, 1826 and 1827 ...* London: John Murray

Gilder, W.H. 1881. *Schwatka's search: Sledging in the Arctic in quest of the Franklin records*. New York: Charles Scribner's Sons

Gilpin, J.D. 1850. Outline of the voyage of H.M.S. *Enterprise* and *Investiga-*

tor to Barrow Strait in search of Sir John Franklin, *Nautical Magazine* 19(1):8–9; 19(2):89–90; 19(3):160–70; 19(4):230

Glenister, B.F., and R. Thorsteinsson. 1963. Herschel Bay and Rigley Bay, in Y.O. Fortier, et al., *Geology of the north-central part of the Arctic Archipelago, Northwest Territories (Operation Franklin)* (Geological Survey of Canada Memoir, 320). Ottawa: Department of Mines and Technical Surveys, pp. 195–201

Godfrey, W.C. 1857. *Godfrey's narrative of the last Grinnell Arctic exploring expedition in search of Sir John Franklin, 1853–4–5.* Philadelphia: J.T. Lloyd and Co

Golder, F.A. 1922. *Bering's Voyages.* 2 vols. New York: American Geographical Society

Goldring, P. 1986. The last voyage of the McLellan. *The Beaver* 66(1): 39–44

Gough, B.M., ed. 1973. *To the Pacific and Arctic with Beechey.* Cambridge: Cambridge University Press (Hakluyt Society)

Graah, W.A. 1837. *Narrative of an expedition to the east coast of Greenland, sent by order of the King of Denmark, in search of the lost colonies, under the command of Captain W.A. Graah of the Danish Royal Navy.* London: John W. Parker

Granville, Earl (G. Leveson-Gower). 1852a. Letter to Count Walewski (A.-F.-J. Colonna), 20 January 1852. SPRI, MS 887

– 1852b. Letter to Count Walewski (A.-F.-J. Colonna), 23 February 1852. SPRI, MS 887

Great Britain. Parliament 1851. *Return to an address of the Honourable the House of Commons dated 7 February 1851 etc.* (House of Commons. Sessional Papers, Accounts and Papers, 1851, vol. 33, no. 97)

Great Britain. 1858. *Correspondence respecting H.M.S. 'Resolute' and the arctic expedition. Presented to the House of Commons by command of Her Majesty, in pursuance of their address dated May 21, 1858* (Great Britain. House of Commons. Sessional Papers, Accounts and Papers, 1857–8, vol. 60, no. 2416). London: Harrison and Sons, pp. 1–24

Greiner, H.R. 1963. Vicinity of Beechey Island to Radstock Bay, in Y.O. Fortier, et al. *Geology of the north-central part of the Arctic Archipelago, Northwest Territories (Operation Franklin).* (Geological Survey of Canada Memoir, 320). Ottawa: Department of Mines and Technical Surveys, pp. 210–17

Grinnell, H. 1858. Letter to Mr Crampton, 1 March 1856, in *Correspondence respecting H.M.S. 'Resolute,' and the arctic expedition. Presented to the House of Commons by command of Her Majesty, in pursuance of their address dated May 21, 1858* (Great Britain. House of Commons. Sessional Papers, Accounts and Papers, 1857–8, vol. 60, no. 2416). London: Harrison and Sons, pp. 13–14

Hall, C.F. 1864. *Life with the Esquimaux: The narrative of Captain*

Charles Francis Hall, of the whaling barque 'George Henry,' from the 29th May, 1860, to the 13th September, 1862 ... London: Sampson Low, Sons and Marston

Hamilton, R.V. 1855. Journal of a sledge journey from Dealy Island to Hecla and Griper Bay and around Sabine Peninsula, April–June, 1853, in *Further papers relative to the recent arctic expeditions in search of Sir John Franklin and the crews of 'Erebus' and 'Terror.' Presented to both Houses of Parliament by command of Her Majesty* (Great Britain. House of Commons. Sessional Papers, Accounts and Papers, 1854–5, vol. 35, no. 1898). London: Eyre and Spottiswoode, pp. 624–41

Hamilton, W.A.B. 1854. Letter to Emile de Bray, 30 September 1854. SHM CC7 324, no 5

– 1855. Letter to Alexander Barclay, Esq., 27 October, 1854, in *Further papers relative to the recent arctic expeditions in search of Sir John Franklin and the crews of H.M.S. 'Erebus' and 'Terror.' Presented to both Houses of Parliament by command of Her Majesty* (Great Britain. House of Commons. Sessional Papers, Accounts and Papers, 1854–5, vol. 35, no. 1898). London: Eyre and Spottiswoode, pp. 846–7

Hayes, I.I. 1860. *An Arctic boat journey in the autumn of 1854.* Boston: Brown and Taggard

Hearne, S. 1795. *A journey from Prince of Wales's Fort, in Hudson's Bay, to the northern ocean ... in the years 1769, 1770, 1771, & 1772.* London: A. Strahan & D. Cadell

Henrat, P. 1982. Une campagne dans les régions arctiques: journal de l'Enseigne de vaisseau Emile Frederic de Bray a bord de la frégate H.M.S. *Resolute* (1852–4). Master's thesis, Université de Brest.

Hodgson, M. 1974. Bellot and Kennedy. A contrast in personalities. *The Beaver* 305(1):55–8

Holland, C. 1970. William Penny, 1809–92: arctic whaling master, *Polar Record* 15(94):25–43

– 1972. Sherard Osborn, in *Dictionary of Canadian Biography*, vol. 10, Toronto: University of Toronto Press, pp. 561–3

– 1985a. Joseph–René Bellot, in *Dictionary of Canadian Biography*, vol. 8. Toronto: University of Toronto Press, pp. 79–81

– 1985b. Kallihirua, in *Dictionary of Canadian Biography*, vol. 8. Toronto: University of Toronto Press, pp. 447–8

– and F.F. Hill. 1972. Sir William Edward Parry's barrel organ. *Polar Record*, 16(102):413–14

Hooper, W.H. 1853. *Ten months among the tents of the Tuski, with incidents of an arctic boat expedition in search of Sir John Franklin, as far as the Mackenzie River and Cape Bathurst.* London: John Murray

Houston, C.S., ed. 1974. *To the Arctic by canoe, 1819–1821: The journal and paintings of Robert Hood, midshipman with Franklin.* Montreal and London: Arctic Institute of North America and McGill-Queen's University Press

– ed. 1984. *Arctic Ordeal: The journal of John Richardson, surgeon-naturalist with Franklin, 1820–1822*. Kingston and Montreal: McGill-Queen's University Press

Inglefield, E. A. 1853. *A summer search for Sir John Franklin with a peep into the Polar Basin*. London: Thomas Harrison

– 1854a. Captain Inglefield's report, 4 October 1853, in *Papers relative to the recent arctic expeditions in search of Sir John Franklin and the crews of H.M.S. 'Erebus' and 'Terror.' Presented to both Houses of Parliament by command of Her Majesty* (Great Britain. House of Commons. Sessional Papers, Accounts and Papers, 1854, vol. 42, no. 1725). London: Eyre and Spottiswoode, pp. 11–18

– 1854b. Reporting the death of Lieutenant Bellot, of the French Imperial Navy, in Great Britain. *Papers relative to the recent arctic expeditions in search of Sir John Franklin and the crews of H.M.S. 'Erebus' and 'Terror.' Presented to both Houses of Parliament by command of Her Majesty* (Great Britain. House of Commons. Sessional Papers, Accounts and Papers, 1854, vol. 42, no. 1725). London: Eyre and Spottiswoode, pp. 19–20

– 1855. Letter from Captain Inglefield reporting his proceedings and arrival at Cork, in *Further papers relative to the recent arctic expeditions in search of Sir John Franklin and the crews of H.M.S. 'Erebus' and 'Terror.' Presented to both Houses of Parliament by command of Her Majesty* (Great Britain. House of Commons. Sessional Papers, Accounts and Papers, 1854–55, vol. 5, no. 1898). London: Eyre and Spottiswoode, pp. 8–11

Ingstad, H. 1959. *Land under the Pole Star*. London: Jonathan Cape

– 1969. *Westward to Vinland. The discovery of Pre-Columbian Norse house-sites in North America*. London: Jonathan Cape

Janes, R.R. 1982. The preservation and ethnohistory of a frozen historic site in the Canadian Arctic. *Arctic* 35(3):358–85

Jones, A.G.E. 1969. Captain Robert Martin: A Peterhead whaling master in the 19th century. *Scottish Geographical Magazine* 85(3):196–202

Jones, G. 1964. *The Norse Atlantic Saga*. London: Oxford University Press

Kane, E. K. 1854. *The U.S. Grinnell expedition in search of Sir John Franklin: A personal narrative*. London: Sampson, Low, Sons & Co

– 1856. *Arctic exploration: The Second Grinnell Expedition in search of Sir John Franklin, 1853, '54, '55*. Philadelphia: Childs and Peterson

Kellett, H. 1854. Letter to Emile de Bray, 28 September 1854. SPRI, MS 887

– 1855a. Proceedings of Captain Kellett, C.B., H.M. Discovery Ship 'Resolute,' in *Further papers relative to the recent arctic expeditions in search of Sir John Franklin and the crews of H.M.S. 'Erebus' and 'Terror.' Presented to both Houses of Parliament by command of Her Majesty* (Great Britain. House of Commons. Sessional Papers, Accounts and Papers, 1854–5, vol. 35, no. 1898). London: Eyre and Spottiswoode, pp. 69–106

– 1855b. Letter to the Secretary of the Admiralty, 14 November 1854, in

Further papers relative to the recent arctic expeditions in search of Sir John Franklin and the crews of H.M.S. 'Erebus' and 'Terror.' Presented to both Houses of Parliament by command of Her Majesty (Great Britain. House of Commons. Sessional Papers, Accounts and Papers, 1854–5, vol. 35, no. 1898). London: Eyre and Spottiswoode, p. 105

Kennedy, W. 1853. *A short narrative of the second voyage of the Prince Albert in search of Sir John Franklin.* London: W.H. Dalton

Klutschak, H.W. 1987. *Overland to Starvation Cove: With the Inuit in search of Franklin, 1878–1880*, trans. and ed. W. Barr, Toronto: University of Toronto Press

Kol, E. and S. Eurola. 1974. Red snow algae from Spitsbergen. *Astarte. Journal of Arctic Biology* 7(2):61–6

Krabbé, F.J. 1855. Journal of the proceedings of Her Majesty's Sledge 'Newton,' detached from Her Majesty's Ship 'Resolute' between 3d April and 13th June 1854, under the command of Mr F.J. Krabbé, Master, in *Further papers relative to the recent arctic expeditions in search of Sir John Franklin and the crews of H.M.S. 'Erebus' and 'Terror.' Presented to both Houses of Parliament by command of Her Majesty* (Great Britain. House of Commons. Sessional Papers, Accounts and Papers, 1854–5, vol. 35, no. 1898). London: Eyre and Spottiswoode, pp. 708–21

Lallour, ?. 1867. Letter, 27 March 1867. SHM CC7 324, no.18

Lamb, W.K. 1970. *The journals and letters of Sir Alexander Mackenzie.* Toronto: Macmillan of Canada for Hakluyt Society

Lambert, G. 1866. *Projet de voyage au Pôle Nord.* Paris: Société de Géographie

– 1868. *L'expédition au Pôle Nord.* Paris: Société de Geographie

Larousse, P. 1873. Gustave Lambert, in *Le Grand Dictionnaire Universel du XIXe Siècle.* Paris: Administration du Grand Dictionnaire Universel, vol. 10, Pt.1:109

Laughton, J.K. 1892. Sir Henry Kellett, in *Dictionary of National Biography*, vol. 30. London: Smith, Elder & Co., p. 342

– 1895. Sherard Osborn, in *Dictionary of National Biography*, vol. 42. London: Smith, Elder & Co., pp. 282–4

Loomis, C.C. 1972. *Weird and tragic shores: The story of Charles Francis Hall, explorer.* New York: Alfred Knopf

Lumley, J.S. 1858. Letter to the Earl of Clarendon, 16 June, 1856, in *Correspondence respecting H.M.S. 'Resolute,' and the arctic expedition. Presented to the House of Commons by command of Her Majesty, in pursuance of their address dated May 21, 1858* (Great Britain. House of Commons. Sessional Papers, Accounts and Papers, 1857–8, vol. 60, no. 2416). London: Harrison and Sons, p. 21

Lyon, G.F. 1824. *The private journal of Captain G.F. Lyon, of H.M.S. Hecla, during the recent voyage of discovery under Captain Parry.* London: John Murray

Mackenzie, A. 1801. *Voyages from Montreal, on the River St. Lawrence, through the continent of North America, to the Frozen and Pacific oceans, in the years 1789 and 1793.* London: T. Cadell, Jr

MacInnis, J. 1982. *The Breadalbane adventure.* Montreal/Toronto: Optimum Publishing International

McClintock, F.L. 1852. Journal of proceedings from the 15th April to the 4th of July, 1851, whilst searching for the missing Expedition under the command of Captain Sir John Franklin, in *Additional papers relative to the Arctic expedition under the orders of Captain Austin and Mr William Penny. Presented to both Houses of Parliament by command of Her Majesty* (Great Britain. House of Commons. Sessional Papers, Accounts and Papers, 1852, vol. 50, no. 1436). London: Eyre and Spottiswoode, pp. 143–92

– 1852–4. The private journal of F.L. McClintock, Commander, H.M. Steamer Intrepid, 1852–4. SPRI MS 1

– 1855a. Journal of the first journey overland from winter quarters to the north shore of Melville Island, with carts, in *Further papers relative to the recent arctic expeditions in search of Sir John Franklin and the crews of H.M.S. 'Erebus' and 'Terror.' Presented to both Houses of Parliament by command of Her Majesty* (Great Britain. House of Commons. Sessional Papers, Accounts and Papers, 1854–5, vol. 35, no. 1898). London: Eyre and Spottiswoode, pp. 468–78

– 1855b. Journal of a sledge journey from Dealy Island to Eglinton and Prince Patrick islands, April–July, 1853, in *Further papers relative to the recent arctic expeditions in search of Sir John Franklin and the crews of H.M.S. 'Erebus' and 'Terror.' Presented to both Houses of Parliament by command of Her Majesty* (Great Britain. House of Commons. Sessional Papers, Accounts and Papers, 1854–5, vol. 35, no. 1898). London: Eyre and Spottiswoode, pp. 540–87

– 1859. *The voyage of the 'Fox' in the arctic seas: A narrative of the discovery of the fate of Sir John Franklin and his companions.* London: John Murray

McCormick, R. 1884. *Voyages of discovery in the Arctic and Antarctic seas and round the world, etc.* 2 vols. London: Sampson, Low, Marston, Searle & Rivington

McDougall, G.F. 1857. *The eventful voyage of H.M. Discovery Ship 'Resolute' to the arctic regions in search of Sir John Franklin and the missing crews of H.M. Discovery Ships 'Erebus' and 'Terror,' 1852, 1853, 1854 etc.* London: Longman, Brown, Green, Longmans and Roberts

Markham, C.R. 1875. *The Arctic Navy List; or, A century of Arctic and Antarctic officers 1773–1873.* London: Griffin & Co

– 1909. *Life of Admiral Sir Leopold McClintock.* London: John Murray

Mary-Rousseliere, G. 1980. *Qitdlarssuaq. L'histoire d'une migration polaire.* Montréal: Les Presses de l'Université de Montréal

Mecham, G.F. 1855a. Journal of a sledge journey from Dealy Island to Eglinton and Prince Patrick islands, April–July, 1853, in *Further papers*

*relative to the recent arctic expeditions in search of Sir John Franklin
and the crews of H.M.S. 'Erebus' and 'Terror.' Presented to both
Houses of Parliament by command of Her Majesty* (Great Britain.
House of Commons. Sessional Papers, Accounts and Papers, 1854–5,
vol. 35, no. 1898). London: Eyre and Spottiswoode, pp. 498–505

– 1855b. Journal of H.M. Sledge 'Discovery' between 3d. April and 12th
June 1854, in *Further papers relative to the recent arctic expeditions in
search of Sir John Franklin and the crews of H.M.S. 'Erebus' and
'Terror.' Presented to both Houses of Parliament by command of Her
Majesty* (Great Britain. House of Commons. Sessional Papers, Accounts
and Papers, 1854–5, vol. 35, no. 1898). London: Eyre and Spottiswoode,
pp. 690–706

Ministre de la Marine, 1869. Telegram to M. le Préfet Maritime à Toulon,
28 May 1869. SHM CC7 324, no. 21

Mumford, W.T. 1852–4. Private journal of an expedition to the arctic
regions to ascertain the fate of Sir John Franklin and his crews, under
the command of Sir Edward Belcher, Kt. C.B., consisting of Her
Majesty's Ships Assistance, Resolute, Pioneer, Intrepid and North Star
in the years 1852, 3, 4. NAC, MG24, H80

Nares, G.S. 1852. Letter to W.H. Nares, 15 April 1852. SPRI MS 876 1/6

– 1855. Journal of a sledge journey from Dealy Island to Eglinton Island,
April–May, 1853, in *Further papers relative to the recent arctic
expeditions in search of Sir John Franklin and the crews of H.M.S.
'Erebus' and 'Terror.' Presented to both Houses of Parliament by
command of Her Majesty* (Great Britain. House of Commons, Sessional Papers, Accounts and Papers, 1854–5, vol. 35, no. 1898). London:
Eyre and Spottiswoode, pp. 601–10

National Intelligencer. 1858. The British ship 'Resolute.' *National
Intelligencer*, 27 June 1856, in *Correspondence respecting H.M.S.
'Resolute,' and the arctic expedition. Presented to the House of Com-
mons by command of Her Majesty, in pursuance of their address dated
May 21, 1858* (Great Britain. House of Commons. Sessional Papers,
Accounts and Papers, 1857–8, vol. 60, no. 2416). London: Harrison and
Sons, pp. 26–9

Neatby, L. H., ed. and trans. 1967. *Frozen ships: The arctic diary of Johann
Miertsching.* Toronto: Macmillan of Canada

– 1973. *Discovery in Russian and Siberian Waters.* Athens: Ohio University Press

– 1982. Bedford Trevelyan Clapperton Pim, in *Dictionary of Canadian
Biography*, vol. 11. Toronto: University of Toronto Press, pp. 691–2

Nelson, J.H. 1850–4 Voyage of H.M.S. Investigator in search of Sir J.
Franklin and resulting in the discovery of the Northwest Passage. SPRI,
MS. 748 1/2

Newton, A.P.W. 1982. Red-coloured snow in Svalbard: Some environmen-
tal factors determining the distribution of *Chlamydomonas nivalis*

(Chlorophyta volvocaeles), *Polar Biology* 1(3):167–72

Nourse, J.E., ed. 1879. *Narrative of the second arctic expedition made by Charles F. Hall: His voyage to Repulse Bay, sledge journeys to the straits of Fury and Hecla and to King William's Land, and residence among the Eskimos during the years 1864–'69.* Washington: Government Printing Office

O'Byrne, W. 1860. *O'Byrne's naval biography: A new and enlarged edition etc.* London: O'Byrne Brothers

Ommanney, E. 1851. Note left at Cape Riley, 23 August 1850, in *Arctic expeditions. Return to an address of the Honourable the House of Commons dated 7 February 1851 etc.* (Great Britain. House of Commons. Sessional Papers, Accounts and Papers, 1851, vol. 33, no. 97). London, p. 70

Osborn, S. 1852. *Stray leaves from an Arctic journal: or, eighteen months in the polar regions, in search of Sir John Franklin's expedition, in the years 1850–51.* London: Longman, Brown, Green & Longman

– 1857. *The discovery of the North-West Passage by H.M.S. 'Investigator,' Capt. R. M'Clure, 1850, 1851, 1852, 1853, 1854.* London: Longman, Brown, Green, Longmans & Roberts

Parry, W. E. 1821. *Journal of a voyage for the discovery of a North-West Passage from the Atlantic to the Pacific; performed in the years 1819–1820, in His Majesty's Ships 'Hecla' and 'Griper'.* London: John Murray

– 1824. *Journal of a second voyage for the discovery of a North-West Passage from the Atlantic to the Pacific; performed in the years 1821–22–23, in His Majesty's Ships 'Fury' and 'Hecla' ...* London: John Murray

– 1826. *Journal of a third voyage for the discovery of a North-West Passage from the Atlantic to the Pacific: performed in the years 1824–25 in His Majesty's Ships 'Hecla' and 'Fury' ...* London: John Murray

– 1828. *Narrative of an attempt to reach the North Pole, in boats fitted for the purpose, and attached to His Majesty's Ship 'Hecla,' in the year MDCCCXXVIIetc ...* London: John Murray

Perkins and Smith. 1858a. Letter to Mr Crampton, 25 February 1856, in *Correspondence respecting H.M.S. 'Resolute,' and the arctic expedition. Presented to the House of Commons by command of Her Majesty, in pursuance of their address dated May 21, 1858* (Great Britain House of Commons. Sessional Papers, Accounts and Papers, 1857–8, vol. 60, no. 2416). London: Harrison and Sons, p. 13

Pim, B.C.T. 1855. Report of a sledge journey from Dealy Island to Mercy Bay, March–April, 1853, in *Further papers relative to the recent arctic expeditions in search of Sir John Franklin and the crews of H.M.S. 'Erebus' and 'Terror.' Presented to both Houses of Parliament by command of Her Majesty* (Great Britain. House of Commons. Sessional Papers, Accounts and Papers, 1854–5, vol. 35, no. 1898). London: Eyre and Spottiswoode, pp. 646–60

Pullen, H.F., ed. 1979. *The Pullen expedition in search of Sir John Franklin.* Toronto: Arctic History Press

- 1982. William John Samuel Pullen, in *Dictionary of Canadian Biography*, vol. 11, Toronto: University of Toronto Press, pp. 718–9

Pullen, T.C. 1853–54. Journal, vol. II, H.M.S. 'North Star,' 29th April 1853 to 29th August 1854, in: *The Pullen Records*. SPRI, MS 274

Pullen, W.S. 1855a. Report of the stranding and recovery of H.M.S. 'North Star' at Beechey Island, September–October, 1852, in *Further papers relative to the recent arctic expeditions in search of Sir John Franklin and the crews of H.M.S. 'Erebus' and 'Terror.' Presented to both Houses of Parliament by command of Her Majesty* (Great Britain. House of Commons. Sessional Papers, Accounts and Papers, 1854–5, vol. 35, no. 1898). London: Eyre and Spottiswoode, pp. 814–29

- 1855b. Continuation of Commander Pullen's journal, Her Majesty's Discovery Ship 'North Star.' From March to December 1853, in *Further papers relative to the recent arctic expeditions in search of Sir John Franklin and the crews of H.M.S. 'Erebus' and 'Terror.' Presented to both Houses of Parliament by command of Her Majesty* (Great Britain. House of Commons. Sessional Papers, Accounts and Papers, 1854–5, vol. 35, no. 1898). London: Eyre and Spottiswoode, pp. 745–95

Rae, J. 1855. Letter to John Barrow, Secretary to the Admiralty, 25 July 1854, Repulse Bay, in *Further papers relative to the recent arctic expeditions in search of Sir John Franklin and the crews of H.M.S. 'Erebus' and 'Terror.' Presented to both Houses of Parliament by command of Her Majesty* (Great Britain. House of Commons. Sessional Papers, Accounts and Papers, 1854–5, vol. 35, no. 1898). London: Eyre and Spottiswoode, pp. 831–3

Rich, E.E. and A.M. Johnson. 1953. *John Rae's correspondence with the Hudson's Bay Company on arctic exploration, 1844–1855.* London: The Hudson's Bay Record Society

Richards, G.H. 1855a. Journal of a sledge journey from 'Assistance' in Northumberland Sound to 'Resolute' at Dealy Island, April–July 1853, in *Further papers relative to the recent arctic expeditions in search of Sir John Franklin and the crews of H.M.S. 'Erebus' and 'Terror.' Presented to both Houses of Parliament by command of Her Majesty* (Great Britain. House of Commons. Sessional Papers, Accounts and Papers, 1854–5, vol. 35, no. 1898). London: Eyre and Spottiswoode, pp. 314–40

- 1855b. A journal of the proceedings of the western division of sledges from Her Majesty's ship 'Assistance', in her winter quarters in the Wellington Channel, towards Melville Island to communicate with Captain Kellett's ships, and to establish depots of provisions etc. From the 22nd of February to the 3rd May, 1854, in *Further papers relative to the recent arctic expeditions in search of Sir John Franklin and the crews of H.M.S. 'Erebus' and 'Terror.' Presented to both Houses of Parliament by command of Her Majesty* (Great Britain. House of Commons. Sessional Papers, Accounts and Papers, 1854–5, vol. 35, no. 1898). London: Eyre and Spottiswoode, pp. 375–85

Richardson, J. 1851. *Arctic searching expedition: A journal of a boat-voyage through Rupert's Land and the Arctic Sea, in search of the discovery ships under command of Sir John Franklin.* 2 vols. London: Longman, Brown, Green and Longmans

Roche, R. 1855. Journal of a sledge journey from Dealy Island to Beechey Island and return, June 1853, in *Further papers relative to the recent arctic expeditions in search of Sir John Franklin and the crews of H.M.S. 'Erebus' and 'Terror.' Presented to both Houses of Parliament by command of Her Majesty* (Great Britain. House of Commons. Sessional Papers, Accounts and Papers, 1854–5, vol. 35, no. 1898). London: Eyre and Spottiswoode, pp. 688–9

Ross, J. 1819. *A voyage of discovery, made under the orders of the Admiralty, in His Majesty's Ships 'Isabella' and 'Alexander' for the purpose of exploring Baffin's Bay, and inquiring into the probability of a North-west Passage.* London: John Murray

– 1835. *Narrative of a second voyage in search of a North-west Passage and of a residence in the Arctic regions during the years 1829, 1830, 1831, 1832, 1833.* London: A. W. Webster

Ross, J.C. 1847. *A voyage of discovery and research in the Southern and Antarctic regions during the years 1839–43.* London: John Murray.

Ross, W.G. 1985. *Arctic whalers, icy seas: Narratives of the Davis Strait whale fishery.* Toronto: Irwin Publishing Co.

Rouch, J. 1938. Emile de Bray, *La Géographie* 59(5–6):257–63

– 1944. Le journal inédit d'Emile de Bray, explorateur polaire français, *Bulletin de la Section de Géographie du Comité des Travaux Historiques et Scientifiques (Paris),* 59(1–9):5–10

– 1945. Deux officiers de marine français, Joseph Bellot et Emile de Bray à bord de navires de S.M. Britannique dans les mers polaires (1852–1854), *France-Grande Bretagne* 194:1–12

Saunders, J. 1851. Narrative of the proceedings of Her Majesty's Ship 'North Star,' Mr James Saunders, Master, Commanding, on an expedition to Barrow Straits, with stores and provisions, in 1849 and 1850, in *Arctic expeditions. Return to an address of the Honourable the House of Commons dated 7 February 1851* etc. (Great Britain. House of Commons. Sessional Papers, Accounts and Papers, 1851, vol. 31, no. 97), pp. 56–64

Scott, R.C. 1852–4. Private journal, H.M.S. Intrepid. SPRI, MS 79

Seemann, B. 1853. *Narrative of the voyage of H.M.S. 'Herald' during the years 1845–51 under the command of Captain Henry Kellett, R.N., C.B., being a circumnavigation of the globe and three cruizes to the Arctic regions in search of Sir John Franklin.* 2 vols. London: Reeve & Co

Seymour, G.F. 1858. Extract of letter to R. Osborne, Secretary to the Admiralty, 30 December, 1856, in *Correspondence respecting H.M.S. 'Resolute,' and the arctic expedition. Presented to the House of Commons by command of Her Majesty in pursuance of their address dated May 21, 1858* (Great Britain. House of Commons. Sessional Papers, Accounts and Papers, 1857–8, vol. 60, no. 2416). London: Harrison and Sons, p. 33

Shaw, E.C. 1982. William Kennedy, in *Dictionary of Canadian Biography*, vol. 11. Toronto: University of Toronto Press, pp. 470–1

Simpson, T. 1843. *Narrative of the discoveries on the north coast of America; effected by the officers of the Hudson's Bay Company during the years 1836–39.* London: Richard Bentley

Snow, W.P. 1851. *Voyage of the 'Prince Albert' in search of Sir John Franklin: A narrative of every-day life in the arctic seas.* London: Longmans, Brown, Green and Longmans

Stackpole, E.A., ed. 1965. *The long arctic search: The narrative of Lieutenant Frederick Schwatka, U.S.A., 1878–1880, seeking the records of the lost Franklin expedition.* Mystic, CN: Marine Historical Association

Stewart, J. 1857. Letter to Count Walewski, 25 July. SPRI, MS 887

Stuart-Stubbs, B. 1972. Sir Edward Belcher, in *Dictionary of Canadian Biography*, vol. 10. Toronto: University of Toronto Press, pp. 42–3

Sutherland, P.C. 1852. *Journal of a voyage in Baffin's Bay and Barrow Straits, in the years 1850–51, performed by H.M. Ships 'Lady Franklin' and 'Sophia' under the command of Mr. William Penny, in search of the missing crews of H.M. Ships 'Erebus' and 'Terror.'* London: Longmans, Brown, Green and Longmans

The Times. 1854a. The late arctic expedition. 18 October, p. 8

– 1854b. The arctic voyagers. 20 October, p. 10

Verne, J. 1866a. *Les Anglais au pôle Nord: les aventures du capitaine Hatteras.* Paris: J. Hetzel

– 1866b. *Le désert de glace; les aventures de capitaine Hatteras.* Paris: J. Hetzel

Vice-Amiral, Préfet Maritime de Brest, 1872. Letter to Minister of Marine and the Colonies, 13 October. SHM CC7 324, no. 25

– 1877. Letter to Minister of the Marine and the Colonies, 6 January. SHM CC7 324, no. 27

Wilson, M. 1973. Sir John Ross's last expedition, in search of Sir John Franklin. *The Musk-Ox* 13:3–11

Woodward, F.J. 1950. Joseph René Bellot. *Polar Record* 5(39):398–407

Index